INSIDE
JAPANESE
BUSINESS

Nanzan University Academic Publication Series

The authors gratefully acknowledge financial support provided by a Pache
Research Grant from Nanzan University.

INSIDE JAPANESE BUSINESS

A Narrative History, 1960–2000

MAKOTO OHTSU

WITH TOMIO IMANARI

Foreword by Solomon B. Levine

AN EAST GATE BOOK

M.E. Sharpe

Armonk, New York
London, England

An East Gate Book

Serialized in *The Japanese Economy: Translations and Studies,* vol. 27, nos. 2–6.

Copyright © 2002 by M. E. Sharpe, Inc.

Library of Congress Cataloging-in-Publication Data

Inside Japanese business : a narrative history : 1960–2000 / Makoto Ohtsu with Tomio
Imanari.
    p. cm.
Includes bibliographical references.
ISBN 0-7656-0781-6 (alk. paper); 0-7656-0782-4 (pbk)
    1. Industrial management—Japan—History. 2. Corporate culture—Japan—History. 3.
Businesspeople—Japan—Interviews. I. Ohtsu, Makoto, 1939– II. Imanari, Tomio, 1938–

HD70.J3 I556 2001
302.3′0952—dc21   2001049149

Printed in the United States of America

The paper used in this publication meets the minimum requirements of
American National Standard for Information Sciences
Permanence of Paper for Printed Library Materials,
ANSI Z 39.48-1984.

BM (c) 10   9   8   7   6   5   4   3   2   1
BM (p) 10   9   8   7   6   5   4   3   2   1

Contents

Part I. Conceptual Framework

Part II. Period of High Economic Growth (1962–1973)

Part III. Period between Two Oil Crises: A Period of Change (1974–1980)

Part IV. Period of Stable Economic Growth to the Bubble Economy (1981–1990)

Part V. Post Bubble Period (1991–2000)

Part VI. Contemporary Views on Japanese Society and Management

List of Figures and Tables

Figures

Tables

Foreword

The study this book represents is unique in the English language, and, perhaps, in Japanese as well. Only Makoto Ohtsu and his coauthor, Tomio Imanari, could have produced it. Both Professor Ohtsu and Mr. Imanari were members of the class at Keio Gijuku University, which provided the sample for the research. As an undergraduate, Ohtsu joined the English Speaking Society at Keio. Later, he earned a Ph.D. in labor and industrial relations at the University of Illinois at Urbana-Champaign and lived in the United States and Canada for many years before assuming his professorial post at Nanzan University in Nagoya, Japan. Imanari, a registered professional consultant, spent his career as an executive in the Kirin Brewery Company and is well known in professional circles as a writer on management analysis. Together they have known virtually all thirty-six of the sampled individuals on a personal basis for much of their lives. The study is a model for both sampling method and factual reliability.

What is especially unique about the study is that, while it relies heavily on a questionnaire administered at a single point in time, through in-depth interviews and long acquaintance, it captures the experiences of the sampled subjects over time in a longitudinal manner. Hence, it probes, in particular, for the changes that have occurred in these persons' careers, and, as a result, avoids the stereotypes so commonly found in horizontal research. The findings reveal the dynamism of the lives and careers of educated business elites in postwar Japan and destroys such outmoded generalizations used to describe Japanese business and society as "lifetime employment," seniority-based salaries, conformity, male dominance, and the like. As seen in the experiences of the sampled individuals, modern Japan, especially in the past forty to fifty years, thus displays everchanging patterns of business organizations, social relationships, and human value systems. How refreshing!

It is my personal joy, most of all, to have known some of the subjects from the time they were undergraduates at Keio University. As a visiting

Fulbright professor at Keio in the spring of 1959, I not only had contact with the Keio English Speaking Society (KESS) but also had some of them in an English language seminar that I taught with the late Professor Hisashi Kawada of the Keio Economics Faculty. My wife, Betty, in fact served as a judge in some of the English language speech competitions held by the KESS. Indeed, this experience had led to a lifetime contact with Keio and some of the members of the class of 1962, including Professor Ohtsu and his family. In the spring of 1959, Keio established its Center for Labor and Management Research (*Sangyo Kenkyujo*, in Japanese), to which I was assigned as a Fulbrighter, and which, much to my gratitude, conferred lifetime honorary membership upon me. I have visited the Center numerous times since.

Also, beginning in the early 1960s, the Keio Center and the Institute of Labor and Industrial Relations of the University of Illinois at Urbana-Champaign, in which I then held an academic appointment, undertook, with the financial assistance of the Ford Foundation, a joint exchange and research program in the field of labor-management relations. Over the course of a decade during which this program continued, some forty individual scholars and graduate students from Japan and the United States participated for up to several years each. Three of the subjects of the Ohtsu-Imanari sample were among the participants of the Keio-Illinois program. It was my great pleasure to have taught, advised, and collaborated with these individuals. Each has played an important role in the development of Japanese business and society in the postwar era.

Yukichi Fukuzawa, the founder of Keio University more than 140 years ago, is well remembered for his famous saying, "Independence and self-reliance." Just as the spirit of these words inspired many of those who were leaders of Japan's emergence as a great power in the latter half of the nineteenth century, the same spirit is also reflected in the character of many of those surveyed by Professor Ohtsu and Mr. Imanari in Japan's postwar recovery and reemergence as a major economy once again in the latter half of the twentieth century. The dynamism of the members of the class of 1962 is representative of many others who were leaders in Japan's modern resurgence.

Solomon B. Levine
Professor Emeritus
University of Wisconsin-Madison
Madison, Wisconsin
November 2000

Acknowledgments

As its subtitle suggests, the main body of this book is a narrative history of a group of thirty-six men and women who entered Keio University in Tokyo, Japan, and who nearly all graduated together four years later. During their university days they were members of a student club, the Keio English Speaking Society (KESS), together with several hundred other students; the number of members was reduced to less than one hundred by the time of their graduation. The bond among the fifty or so core members was so strong that since graduation they have continued to meet twice a year for nearly forty years to maintain their friendship.

At the semiannual meeting in July 1996, one of the coauthors (Ohtsu) suggested to the group that it might be interesting to a foreign business audience, both practitioners and graduate students, if the careers of the group members were documented and published in book form, since virtually all of the male members had worked for representative Japanese corporations in various managerial capacities at home and abroad. It was also suggested that the participation of female members would be valuable because works on Japanese business and management rarely touch on the career histories of university-educated women.

His suggestion was well received by the group and the other coauthor (Imanari) agreed to cooperate. By the next meeting in February 1997, a formal proposal for research and publication had been prepared by the two coauthors, and the group decided to endorse the endeavor as a group publication project.

At the urging of the coauthors, several members volunteered to engage in the research project, despite their busy work schedules. Most of them had survey and research experience and had written articles and book chapters on specific aspects of business and management that were within their expertise. Together, they formed a research team, with the two coauthors acting as leaders, whose names are provided separately. In this way, the project was a unique attempt to blend an academic approach with the firsthand experiences and perspectives of business practitioners. Team membership was not fixed; several original members had to leave the team due to heavy job demands, while several others joined at various stages.

Between April 1977 and June 2000, the team met a total of thirty times. The members engaged in the formulation of an interview guide, the actual interviewing of thirty-six participants (including the team members themselves), the collection of secondary source information, the writing of rough drafts in either Japanese or English, and the translation of Japanese drafts into English. At the meetings members exchanged views on various topics covered by the study. Thus, this book is a result of the joint efforts of team members, although the two coauthors bear the responsibility for the final draft as well as the views expressed in the conclusions.

We owe a great deal to a number of people. We are particularly indebted to Dr. Solomon B. Levine, Professor Emeritus of the University of Wisconsin-Madison. His favorable appraisal of the academic merit of our project was a great encouragement to us. We are grateful for his insightful comments at various stages of the project. Professor Marc Bremer of Nanzan University, a colleague of one of the coauthors, provided advice and assistance of various kinds throughout the project. Professor Yoko Sano of Tokyo International University, Professor Shozo Inouye of St. Paul's University, and Professor Mitsuru Wakabayashi of Nagoya University were kind enough to spend many hours reading an earlier version of the manuscript and provided a number of useful comments, which we have incorporated in this final version as much as possible.

Edmund R. Skrzypczak, a professional editor formerly with Nanzan University and now in residence in Australia, went through the entire manuscript at least twice, straightening out our somewhat broken English. He took the trouble to complete the editing of our manuscript from Australia. Without his highly professional and very prompt efforts, the publication of this book would have been much delayed.

Kazue Kojima, Yoshiko Mizuno, and Tomiko Nezaki have spent a great deal of time over the past two years in word-processing a number of drafts of a more than 400-page manuscript. Their dedication to the work, their patience, and their kindness are very much appreciated.

Finally, we would like to express our gratitude to Nanzan University for providing research grants through the Pache Research Grant Program and through its Center for Management Studies. Also, the Nanzan Academic Society has chosen this work to be included in the Nanzan University Academic Publication Series and has provided a substantial grant for publication. We are grateful for the Society's generosity.

Makoto Ohtsu
Nagoya, Japan
and Tomio Imanari
Tokyo, Japan
January 2001

Members of the Research Team
(as of June 2000)

Ohtsu, Makoto, Professor of Management, Nanzan University (coauthor)

Imanari, Tomio, Registered Professional Consultant (coauthor)

Adachi, Shigeya, Former President, Gambro Teijin Medical Co., Ltd.

Hijikata, Takeshi, President, Van Leer Japan, Ltd.

Kasai, Masafumi, Chairman, Treschic Executive Services, Inc.

Matsunaga, Takuhiko, Senior Managing Director, Parco Co., Ltd.

Mitsunaga, Yukihiro, Former Auditor, Japan Bankers Trust Co., Ltd.

Mizuno, Yoshihiro, General Manager, Human Resources,
Thomson Corporation K.K.

Nagano, Atsuko, President, Joyful Language Plaza

Prologue

Since the collapse of the bubble economy nine years ago, the once-acclaimed Japanese-style management has been under serious criticism both inside and outside Japan. But this is not a new phenomenon. In fact, when we look back over the past fifty years or so, evaluation of Japan and Japanese management has fluctuated widely between extreme affirmation and extreme negation.

Immediately after World War II Japanese management was considered backward, a reflection of the "semifeudal" nature of Japanese society. In the 1960s this view changed to a new one in which Japanese management was characterized as different, or unique, but not necessarily backward. When Japan successfully dealt with the two oil crises in the 1970s and emerged in the early 1980s as an economic superpower, the unique points in Japanese management were considered the source of the country's competitive advantage. It was during this period that the so-called Three Sacred Treasures—permanent employment, length-of-service wage system, and enterprise unionism—were discovered. However, in the 1990s this very positive evaluation was again replaced by a totally negative view. If we assume that the underlying principles of Japanese management have remained more or less stable during the postwar period, this wide fluctuation in the evaluation of one and the same management style is disturbing.

One of the shortcomings of most studies is that the data used are cross-sectional, obtained at one point in time or for a relatively short period of time. As a result, conclusions based upon findings in one time period cannot be justified in another period, because environments have changed over time. One solution is to use longitudinal data to conduct a longitudinal analysis. However, longitudinal data are hard to come by. Still, it cannot be denied that a comprehensive study using longitudinal data is called for.

This book attempts to analyze the development of Japanese business and society since 1960 on the basis of career histories, spanning nearly forty years, of three dozen people (thirty males and six females) who attended the same university in the late 1950s through the early 1960s. We chose 1960 as the starting year of the forty-year period for two reasons. First, Japan's basic directions in terms of international, political, and economic policies to date were formulated in that year. Second, the forty-year period since then roughly corresponds to almost the entire careers of our subjects.

Japan in 1960

In retrospect, 1960 was the turning point of Japan's post–World War II history. The fifteen years between the end of World War II and 1960 were a period of political and social turmoil due to ideological battles between capitalist democracy and "progressive" socialism, which was a reflection of the cold war between the free-world nations and the Communist-bloc nations. In Japan the battles culminated in 1960 and resulted in the victory of capitalist democracy. With this, Japan's political stability was achieved and her economic progress was under way.

In the first five weeks of that year, three important but seemingly unrelated events took place. First, on January 20, the Japan–U.S. Treaty of Mutual Cooperation and Security was signed in Washington (*Japan Times*, January 21, 1960); this replaced the old treaty, which had been signed in 1951 when Japan was still under Allied Occupation. The new pact treated the two countries as nearly equal partners, allowing the United States to deploy its troops in Japan and to use facilities and roads in Japan in return for the obligation to defend Japan from possible external aggression.

Second, only three days later, on January 23, the Mitsui Mining Company proclaimed a lockout at its Miike colliery in Kyushu against workers who had been fighting against the dismissal of some 1,400 members, including 300 union activists (*Japan Times*, January 24, 1960). The retrenchment plan of the company was in response to a coal surplus created by an increasing supply of inexpensive petroleum. In retaliation for management's lockout, the Miike Coal Mine Workers Union went on strike for an indefinite period.

Third, a week later, on February 1, another important event took place; unlike the first two, however, it went largely unnoticed. On that day, both the director general of the Economic Planning Agency and the finance minister said in their policy statements at a plenary session of the House of Representatives that the government had started drafting a long-range economic plan aimed at doubling the country's national income within the next ten years (*Japan Times*, February 2, 1960). They said that the Japanese economy had maintained, and would maintain, high levels of individual spending, equip-

ment investment, and government payments; as a result, through modernization of the nation's industries by developing scientific techniques and improving industrial infrastructure (including ports and roads), high economic
growth without price increases would be achieved. It was not until the inauguration of the Ikeda cabinet six months later that this program attracted the
serious attention of the Japanese people.

When the National Diet resumed its session on January 30, the ratification of the security treaty was not considered a serious challenge to the government, since the ruling Liberal Democratic Party enjoyed a substantial
majority in the House of Representatives, while the opposition Socialists were
divided among themselves. A group of right-wing Socialists, who had split off
from the Japan Socialist Party in October 1959, formed the Democratic Socialist Party on January 24 (*Japan Times*, January 25, 1960). Within the Japan Socialist Party internal strife continued over the election of a chairman.
Although the party voiced its determination to block ratification of the treaty
in the House of Representatives, arguing that the treaty was fraught with the
danger of Japan's involvement in a war, their opposition was considered
doomed.

In the meantime, the Miike strike was into its tenth week when, on March
17, about 3,000 of the 12,000 striking miners broke with the union and formed
a splinter union (or a second union), criticizing the first union's extremist leaders for prolonging the strike unnecessarily (*Japan Times*, March 18, 1960). It
was widely believed that leftist indoctrination by Professor Itsuro Sakisaka
at Kyushu University greatly influenced the official policy of the striking
union. Since a second union is permissible under the Japanese labor law, the
company quickly recognized the second union and signed an agreement to
resume mining operations. After that a series of minor clashes between the two
rival unions took place when members of the second union tried to break
through the picket line. The situation deteriorated when a member of the first
union was stabbed to death by a local thug allegedly connected with the
company.

In order to seek an early solution, the Japan Coal Mine Workers Union,
with which the Miike Coal Mine Workers Union was affiliated, applied to
the Central Labor Relations Commission for mediation, although it went
against the desire of the striking union, which wanted to fight to the bitter
end. A mediation plan of the Central Labor Relations Commission, chaired
by Dr. Keizo Fujibayashi of Keio University, was issued on March 31, with
another issued on April 6, but neither was able to settle the dispute (*Japan
Times*, April 1 and 7, 1960).

Violent confrontation between the first and the second unions continued
through April into May. On May 4, the District Court issued an injunction

banning striking members of the first union from entering the premises of Mikawa Colliery. On May 12, when bailiffs from the District Court attempted to construct a barricade to keep the picketing union members away from the hopper, a final showdown began between 2,500 unionists and 1,000 policemen guarding the bailiffs (*Japan Times*, May 13, 1960). In a series of club-swinging and stone-throwing scuffles, about sixty policemen and an equal number of unionists were injured, some seriously.

After the battle, however, the first union's unyielding policy lost the support of the general public, the mass media, and its own rank-and-file members. An increasing number of members deserted the first union to join the second union. Eventually, the company resumed operations with the help of members of the second union, and the strike gradually fizzled out.

At the National Diet the deliberations on the ratification of the security treaty went nowhere because of seemingly endless interpolations by the Socialists. Finally, on May 19, the chairman of the Lower House Special Committee on the Security Treaty took a vote on a motion to wind up all debate. Shortly after the approval of the vote, a plenary session was held in which the Liberal Democratic Party Diet members unanimously approved the treaty while Opposition members were not present (*Japan Times*, May 20, 1960). The House was able to convene only after the police were called in to break up the sit-down tactics of the Socialists, who had attempted to physically prevent the Speaker from entering the plenary session hall to declare the opening of a session.

After this the Socialists, together with the General Council of Japan Trade Unions (*Sohyo*) and the National Federation of Students' Self-Government Associations (*Zengakuren*), organized a series of demonstrations around the Diet building, demanding the resignation of Prime Minister Kishi and effectively blocking ratification of the treaty in the Upper House.

Of all the various opposition groups, *Zengakuren* was the most militant. They had already made their position clear by organizing a mass demonstration that stormed the Diet building on November 27, 1959, and a few weeks later they ransacked the Haneda Airport terminal building in an attempt to stop a government delegation from leaving for the United States to sign the treaty.

On June 4, a total of 5.6 million students and workers participated in massive protest rallies and demonstrations throughout Japan, the biggest ever staged in Japan. The Prime Minister, however, was adamant and decided to stick to his plan of just waiting for thirty days to elapse, when the decision of the Lower House would become the decision of the Diet.

Zengakuren student demonstrations became increasingly violent, and, on June 15, about 12,000 fanatical students stormed the Diet grounds and engaged in a bloody, club-swinging, stone-throwing battle with the police (*Ja-

pan Times, June 16, 1960). In the battle one female student was killed and a total of 600 students and police were injured, many seriously.

The death of a student turned public opinion against Prime Minister Kishi for his high-handed handling of the security treaty ratification. The following day he had to withdraw, for security reasons, his invitation to U.S. President Eisenhower to visit Japan, a visit that had been scheduled for June 19–20. On June 19, the new security treaty gained automatic Diet approval without the Upper House taking a vote on it. Shortly thereafter, Prime Minister Kishi, taking responsibility for the "mishandling" of the security treaty issue, announced his resignation. The Ikeda cabinet was sworn in on July 19 (*Japan Times*, July 20, 1960).

Prime Minister Ikeda's basic policy was to heal the wounds of social unrest caused by his predecessor's head-on collision with leftist/progressive forces. In line with this policy, he adopted a "low profile" posture on political issues and concentrated on an economic policy. In his inaugural speech he announced his intention to pursue the high-economic-growth policy that had been mentioned at a plenary session of the Diet at the beginning of the year but that had been forgotten since then. He quickly reactivated the plan by approving at the cabinet level the "National Income Doubling Plan." According to this plan, the government would take all measures necessary to maintain the current level of economic growth (approximately 9 percent) so that by 1970 national income would increase by 2.4 times and wages 1.9 times the levels of 1960 (*Japan Times*, September 6, 1960). In retrospect, it can be said that the gross national product (GNP) almost quadrupled, while the increase in real wages was limited to 1.6 times, with a 4.5 times increase in corporate profits (Jiyu Kokuminsha 1992: 44).

Having prepared the groundwork, Prime Minister Ikeda dissolved the Diet in November. He was returned to power with a comfortable margin over the opposition parties combined, an indication of the public's support for the alliance with the United States and for economic growth, as against nonalliance (or neutrality) and economic welfare.

Indeed, by 1960, the Japanese economy, which had already recovered from the wartime destruction, started to expand at a rapid rate. For example, between 1955 and 1960 basic steel production more than doubled, from 9.4 million tons to 22.1 million tons—a figure that represented 6.5 percent of total world production (MITI 1961: 199, 201). More or less the same trends were seen in the other manufacturing industries, including the textile, chemical, electrical machines and appliances, and machine tool industries.

High economic growth favorably affected the labor market. According to the *White Paper on Labor*, the year 1960 was characterized by a high rate of employment growth (11.4 percent) over the previous year (Ministry of Labor 1961: 17). This employment growth was particularly conspicuous in large-scale enterprises in the steel, electrical appliances, and transport equipment industries, where new school graduates were recruited on a massive scale. Although there was an isolated case of mass layoffs in the coal mining industry, as we saw above, the labor market as a whole was very favorable to those seeking work. In 1960 the size of the labor force was about 45 million, an approximately 10 percent increase since 1955, while the unemployment rate was a mere 1.7 percent of the paid labor force, a substantial decrease from 2.5 percent in 1955 (Japan Productivity Center 1983: 30, 42).

Political and social unrest in the first half of 1960 and the healthy economic progress that became apparent in the second half of the year greatly affected university campuses throughout Japan, especially those located in Tokyo. In the first semester (April through July), classes were cancelled on those days when demonstrations against the security treaty were scheduled, as professors yielded to pressure from representatives of the local chapters of the militant *Zengakuren*. The Mita campus of Keio Gijuku University (usually called Keio University) was no exception, but the *Zengakuren* agitators were less successful in mobilizing students there because of the university's long liberal tradition. On the contrary, starting around 1960, this university supplied more and more of its graduates to major corporations.

This book addresses the forty years of development of Japanese business and society since 1960 as seen through the eyes of three dozen alumni of this university. They represented the cream of the 400-strong members of the Keio English Speaking Society (KESS) who entered the university in the spring of 1958. A brief description of Keio University will be in order at this point.

Keio University and KESS

Keio Gijuku, the name of the renowned school corporation in Japan, traces its origin to the small Dutch language school that Fukuzawa Yukichi opened in his own quarters within the estate of the Nakatsu clan in Tsukiji, Yedo (today's Tokyo) (Ogawa 1991: 138). The year was 1858. Originally a retainer of Lord Okudaira of Nakatsu clan, Fukuzawa Yukichi became a great leader in the new thinking that reshaped Japan in the Meiji era; he was one of those who contributed most to the development of Japan's new culture.

The school commenced the work of applying Fukuzawa's theories to the real world with vitality, advocating the acquisition of new knowledge among the populace in order to replace feudal ideas with a new spirit of human rights and freedom.

At first the school had no name. Keio Gijuku, taken from the name of the era (Keio), was decided upon in 1868 when the area around Fukuzawa's school, Tsukiji Teppozu, was made a foreign concession and the school was moved to a new location in Shiba Shinsenza. A new dormitory, large enough for one hundred students, was built. Such a scale for a private school was something extraordinary in those days, and it was more amazing that Keio willingly accepted students from outside the Nakatsu clan.

Fukuzawa announced that the school was not to be his private enterprise but that it was to be maintained by the joint efforts of the people who came together for the common purpose of learning. Keio Gijuku thus became the first school in the country that could be called a higher educational institution in the modern sense of the word. A university division was opened in 1890, the first private university in Japan, with faculties of literature, economics, and law.

The fact that Fukuzawa continued to teach on May 15, 1868, the very day that the Battle of Ueno took place and the booming of guns was heard and the smoke of the battlefield was clearly visible, has become a Keio Gijuku legend, a legend that is repeated on every occasion even to this day (Ogawa 1991: 126).

As we shall see in detail in Chapter 3, what was unique about Fukuzawa was that, while other intellectuals in the early Meiji era were primarily interested in such tangible products of modern civilization as guns, gunboats, steel products, railways, and the like, his interest covered the much wider areas of social institutions: parliamentary systems, taxation systems, government bonds, paper money, military systems, schools, newspapers, hospitals, and the like, as well as the underlying social values. He was particularly articulate in identifying the spirit of self-help as the foundation of the modern business corporation and the cornerstone of modern nation-building.

After the political turmoil of 1881, his influence in government declined and Fukuzawa concentrated his energies on enlightening the public through writings and speeches and on promoting higher education at Keio Gijuku. During his lifetime he supplied a large number of entrepreneurs and business leaders to major corporations, including the Mitsui and Mitsubishi companies. This tradition has continued to the present day, and Keio graduates are the recruits most sought after by business corporations. This is in sharp contrast to University of Tokyo graduates, who prefer to work for government agencies.

A key feature of Keio and other Japanese universities is the prevalence of student clubs for extracurricular activities. They fall into two categories— clubs for sports such as baseball, football, judo, and kendo, and clubs for cultural activities such as choral singing, painting, the tea ceremony, and Noh. The KESS is one of the latter type of clubs. In a sense, student clubs are somewhat like fraternities on university campuses in the United States in that students spend long hours with their own club members and share common goals, objectives, and value orientations.

The KESS has a long history; its predecessor, the Keio English Club, was created in 1893 with the objective of deepening understanding of the United States and European countries through English (not through translation). Its activities were suspended during World War II. But after the war, given the influx of U.S. culture in the form of music, movies, and the like, as well as the presence of a large number of U.S. soldiers and their families, there was a burst of interest in American culture and language among Japanese people in general and students in particular. Keio University was no exception, and KESS was perhaps one of the most popular clubs in those early postwar years. In 1958, for example, more than 400 first-year students joined the club.

The KESS members' immediate objective was to improve their oral English skills so that they could directly communicate with native English speakers, mostly Americans. Their long-term goal was to cultivate an international mind through association with foreign people. Many male members had the more utilitarian goal of becoming an "international businessman" who would be directly involved in dealings with foreign companies and customers in foreign lands. In terms of the members' value orientation, all of them had a strong interest in, or rather respect for, the United States, the American people, and the values that they represent—such as individualism, liberalism, democracy, and a free market economy—the very value premises on which Fukuzawa founded Keio Gijuku. Their attitude was in sharp contrast to that of students in most other universities, especially the national universities, where Marxist intellectual influence was dominant.

To the above ends, KESS members used various means to improve their oral English. Every day during the noon recess there were "free talking" activities in which a group of several students exchanged ideas on current topics. Once a week in the evening, members met on a regional basis (this was called a "home meeting"). At these gatherings discussions took place on a subject that had been announced beforehand. Sometimes more formal debates were conducted. Needless to say, during these activities the use of Japanese was forbidden. On a regular basis, intracampus speech and debate contests were conducted, with visiting professors and scholars usually acting as judges. In addition, there were intercollegiate speech, debate, and drama contests, in which the KESS representatives always did very well, winning a number of trophies.

At the same time, however, KESS activities involved a lot of competition. Those who were not happy with their rate of progress dropped out during the four-year interval, and, by 1962, when those who entered in 1958 graduated, the total membership had declined to less than one hundred. The bond formed among the (fifty or so) core members was so strong that since 1962 the group has met to renew their friendship twice a year without a break.

Study Design

Out of this group of fifty or so alumni, thirty males and six females have participated in this study. Of these three dozen participants a research team consisting of six members was created, with the present two coauthors acting as the team's leaders. Except for one of the coauthors, who is an academic, all are business/management practitioners who have survey and research experience and have written articles and book chapters on specific aspects of business and management that are within their expertise.

After a series of initial discussions, the following key questions were formulated and developed into interview guidelines:
- To what extent is Japanese management unique?
- To what extent do attitudinal attributes alleged to be unique to Japanese, such as harmony, hierarchy acceptance, benevolence, loyalty, and love for learning, affect Japanese management?
- To what extent have Japanese companies overseas practiced Japanese management?
- In what ways is the social life of employees and their families living abroad different from that at home?
- What are the strengths and weaknesses of Japanese management? Or, under what conditions was Japanese management a success (failure)?
- Is Japanese management immutable? Or has it changed over the years?
- In what ways have Japanese women participated in economic activities over the past thirty-five years?
- To what extent has sex-based role differentiation changed over the past thirty-five years?

Interview guidelines were developed in the spring and summer of 1997 on the basis of the above key questions and research frameworks to be discussed in chapters 1 through 3. Intensive interviews of all participants were conducted from the fall of 1997 through the spring of 1998, and these were followed by a number of probing interviews. At the same time, the research team collected secondary source information on the key environmental factors. During this time there was some turnover in team membership. Beginning in the spring of 1998 all members of the team began to write drafts of chapters either in English or Japanese, with the final drafts written by the two coauthors. The following is a list of the positions held by the thirty-six people taking part in this study as of March 1998.

Males

1. President, Gambro Teijin Medical Co., Ltd.; formerly with Teijin, Ltd. (collaborator).

2. General manager, Airport Safety and Maintenance Service Center; formerly with Japan Airlines Co., Ltd.

3. Managing director, Emori and Co., Ltd.; formerly with Mitsui and Co., Ltd.

4. Managing director, Toray Industries, Inc.

5. Managing director, Mitsubishi Chemical Engineering Co., Ltd.; formerly with Mitsubishi Petrochemicals Co., Ltd.

6. President, Komatsu Trading International, Inc.; formerly with Komatsu Ltd.

7. Director, Hitachi Plant Engineering and Construction Co., Ltd.; formerly with Hitachi, Ltd. (collaborator).

8. President, Nippon-Van Leer; formerly with Mitsui Toatsu Chemicals, Inc. (collaborator).

9. Strategic Management Consultant (self-employed); formerly with Noritake Co., Ltd.

10. Registered professional consultant and deputy general manager of marketing, Kirin Brewery Co., Ltd. (coauthor).

11. Senior managing director, Marumasu Plywood Trading Co., Ltd.

12. General manager of marketing, Maruha Corporation.

13. Chairman, Treschic Executive Services, Inc. (in the Philippines); formerly with Japan Airlines Co., Ltd. (collaborator).

14. Senior managing director, Airport Ground Service Co., Ltd.; formerly with Japan Airlines Co., Ltd.

15. Auditor and director, Mitsukoshi, Ltd.

16. Senior manager of general affairs, Fair Trade Center; formerly with Mitsui and Co., Ltd. (collaborator).

17. General manager of public affairs, Esso Sekiyu K.K. (an affiliate of EXXON Corporation).

18. Senior managing director, Parco Co., Ltd.; formerly with the Bank of Tokyo, Ltd. (collaborator).

19. Adviser, Japan Bankers Trust Co., Ltd.; formerly with the Sumitomo Trust and Banking Co., Ltd. (collaborator).

20. Senior consultant, Pasona Bright Career, Inc.; formerly with Tokyo Regional Office of the International Labor Organization (collaborator).

21. General manager of administration, Nomura Housing Management Co., Ltd.; formerly with Mitsui and Co., Ltd.

22. General manager of operations, Japan Emerson Electric Industries, Ltd.; formerly with Toshiba Corporation.

23. Management consultant with National Development Planning Agency, Republic of Indonesia; formerly with Mitsubishi Petrochemical Co., Ltd.

24. Executive counselor, Japan Federation of Economic Organizations.

25. General manager, Publication Department, Union of Machinery Insurers of Japan; formerly with Mitsui Marine and Fire Insurance Co., Ltd.

26. President, JMR (self-employed); formerly with Kawasaki Steel Corp.

27. Director, T and K Toka Co., Ltd.; formerly with Fuji Electric Co., Ltd.

28. Director, Naigai Travel Service Co., Ltd.; formerly with C. Itoh and Co., Ltd.

29. Retired; formerly president, Sumitomo Fine Goods Corporation.

30. Professor of management, Nanzan University; formerly professor at University of Saskatchewan (Canada) (principal/coauthor)

Females

1. Married to president of Nihon Kodo K.K. (Japan Incense Co.).

2. Married to a professor of medicine, Keio University.

3. President, Joyful Language Plaza; married to a general manager of the Industrial Bank of Japan (deceased) (collaborator).

4. Married to an art dealer.

5. Language teacher with Tokyo Julius Academy; married to a director of Kawaguchi Chemical Co., Ltd. (deceased).

6. Assistant to the Chief Representative of Japan, the British Council.

Plan of the Book

Finally, a few words are in order on the plan of the book. It is composed of six parts, each consisting of a few chapters, and a section entitled "Conclusions" at the end. Part I provides the conceptual frameworks of the book. Chapter 1 attempts to put our work in an appropriate theoretical perspective of comparative management, namely, the convergence hypothesis. The central question, therefore, is whether Japanese management practices have been converging toward a common pattern or remain different and unique. Chapter 2 delineates the scope of our study and identifies three specific aspects of Japanese management to be examined: human resource management, managerial decision making, and international operations. More or less universal frameworks are introduced for the description and analysis of the above three aspects. Chapter 3 addresses Japanese national culture with Confucianism as its central focus with a view to assessing in later chapters the extent of the national culture's influence on Japanese management.

Parts II through V are organized in chronological order. Part II covers the period from 1962 to 1973, characterized by a high rate of economic growth that ended with the first oil crisis of 1973. Part III covers the period from 1974 to 1980, characterized by successful industrial adjustment after the two oil crises. Part IV covers the period from 1981 to 1990, during which Japan emerged as an economic superpower, culminating in the burst of the bubble economy. Part V covers the period from 1991 to 2000, characterized by post-bubble stagnation and major structural change.

For each part there is a chapter on the general environment, covering international, political, economic, labor, and social aspects, as well as a chapter on a dozen specific industries where our subjects were working. These two chapters are followed by other chapters covering topics that correspond to the three specific aspects identified in Chapter 2. At the end of each of Parts II through V is a summary that assesses environmental factors and managerial practices in each period. Part VI is a collection of the views of the interviewees on Japanese society and management. Finally, "Conclusions" attempts to answer the key questions mentioned before and to support (or reject) the convergence hypothesis.

References

Japan Productivity Center [Nihon Seisansei Honbu]. 1983. *Katsuyo rodo tokei* [Practical Statistics on Labor]. Tokyo.

Japan Times. January 1–September 30, 1960. Tokyo.

Jiyu Kokumin-sha. 1992. *Gendai yogo-no kiso-chishiki: Bessatsu furoku* [Basic Knowledge About Contemporary Terms: Appendix]. Tokyo: Jiyu Kokumin-sha.

Ogawa, Mitsuru, ed. 1991. "Fukuzawa Yukichi: Kojin-no dokuritsu kokka-no dokuritsu" [Yukichi Fukuzawa: Independence of Individuals and Independence of Nations]. *Rekishi Kaido, Jugatsu-go* [Highways with Histories, October Issue]. Kyoto: PHP Kenkyujo.

Ministry of Labor [Rodosho]. 1961. *Rodo hakusho, 1960* [White Paper on Labor, 1960]. Tokyo: Rodo Horei Kyokai.

MITI (Ministry of International Trade and Industry) [Tsusho Sangyosho]. 1961. *Tekkogyo sanko shiryo, 1960* [Statistical Data on the Iron and Steel Industry, 1960]. Tokyo: Nihon Tekko Renmei [Japan Iron and Steel Industry Association].

Part I

Conceptual Framework

1

The Convergence-Divergence Debate and Japanese Management

This book deals solely with Japanese business and management. This does not mean, however, that it attempts to deal with Japanese business and management in isolation and to "demystify" esoteric Japanese business practices and managerial behavior. Rather, its objective is to relate Japanese experiences to mainline management theory dominated by the American experience, observed and analyzed by American researchers. The foreign experiences that do appear in typical English-language management textbooks are sporadic and anecdotal (Baird, Post, and Mahon 1990; Bartol and Martin 1994; Mosley, Pietri, and Megginson 1996). In this book, we will attempt to examine the extent to which American management theory—which is assumed, if implicitly, to be universally applicable—is indeed useful in analyzing Japanese management.

At the same time, with the current drive toward globalization of business, a field of study called "international management" has gained importance within the management discipline. The main tone of international management literature is to emphasize differences in managerial practices across national borders and explain such differences in terms of national culture—an approach that is the opposite of the universalism of mainline management theories (Adler 1997; Deresky 1997). We, too, will address the issue of national culture and its impact on Japanese management practices.

That Japanese corporations have developed institutions and practices different from those of Western countries, particularly of the United States, has been generally accepted. However, there has been continuous debate as to whether these differences are persistent or disappearing. This is a type of convergence-divergence debate applied to Japanese management practices. The convergence-divergence debate, however, is not limited to Japan or management practices. The purpose of this chapter, therefore, is to review the development of the convergence-divergence debate in general and its application to Japanese management in particular.

We can trace the origin of the convergence-divergence debate to the dialectical materialism of historical development by Marx and Engels (Avineri 1971; Barbalet 1983; Schmidt 1982), and Max Weber's rejection of it and insistence on religion in explaining the origin of modern capitalism (Andreski 1983; Weber 1958). Historical materialism by Marx and Engels is based upon two premises. First, the political, social, and cultural characteristics of societies are determined by their economic structure and process. Second, history moves forward through a series of "class struggles" or struggles between classes of people whose economic interests conflict. Thus, feudal societies were destroyed due to the rise and eventual victory of the bourgeoisie class over the landed aristocrat class. Likewise, capitalist societies will create an innate contradiction—stagnant wages for workers and a progressive enlargement of industrial capacity, resulting in a series of depressions. An increasingly self-conscious and assertive proletariat class will revolt against and overthrow the capitalist class. Once the dictatorship of the proletariat is achieved, a classless society, or a society without any innate contradiction, will be created. Production will be driven forward without any depression to the point of true Communism, where everyone will have a share in cooperative wealth according to his needs. Thus stated, historical materialism represents the convergence hypothesis at the highest level of social aggregation.

On the other hand, Weber argues that there is no law of history (Andreski 1983). Addressing the origin of modern capitalism in Europe, he does not subscribe to either economic determinism or deterministic idealism. Instead, he says that a historically specific conjunction of events led to the emergence of capitalism in the West. He refers to such socioeconomic factors as the separation of the productive enterprise from the household, the development of the Western city, the tradition of Roman law, and the development of the nation-state. However, Weber's central concern is with religion, particularly the Protestant ethic, as a crucial factor in the formation of the spirit of modern capitalism.

In analyzing the source of the spirit of capitalism, Weber starts with Luther's concept of the "calling," or a task set by God. This concept is based upon the central dogma of all Protestant denominations that the only way of living acceptable to God is to fulfill the obligations imposed upon the individual by his position in the world (Weber 1958: 79–92). Related to this Calvinist concept is the doctrine of predestination under Calvinism that only a part of humanity is saved (eternal salvation), while the rest are damned. Thus, in Calvinism success in a calling was considered a duty to attain certainty of one's eternal salvation. Success in a calling, in turn, supplied the individual with the moral energy needed for the accumulation of wealth within a sober and industrious career, leading to the creation of the capitalist entrepreneur (Weber 1958: 98–128). At the same time, the ascetic self-control advocated in other Puritan sects led to the formation of a moral outlook that promoted labor discipline among the lower levels of people in the capitalistic economic system.

Weber also studied other world religions to analyze why modern capitalism did not originate in other parts of the world (Andreski 1983: 59–108). In Hinduism Weber saw certain similarities with Protestantism in that the former has the doctrine of reincarnation and compensation (karma) and that the conduct of an individual in any one incarnation determines that person's fate in the person's next life. Also, in Hinduism there is an important emphasis upon asceticism. The only difference is that, unlike in Calvinism, asceticism in Hinduism is directed toward other-worldly activity, thus inhibiting any economic development comparable to modern European capitalism (Weber 1958: 5–6).

Confucianism, according to Weber, is a this-worldly religion but without the strong ascetic values or activism found in Calvinism. The central virtue under Confucianism is harmonious adjustment of the individual to the established order of things. This passive nature of Confucianism did not generate a moral dynamism in economic activity (Weber 1958: 6). Thus, Weber apparently considered religion as the principal force either for stimulating (as in the case of Protestantism) or retarding (as in the cases of Catholicism, Hinduism, or Confucianism) economic activity. At the same time, however, he qualifies his argument, stating in effect that the Protestant ethic was not the only cause of the development of modern capitalism and referring to other factors mentioned before, and stating that his analysis was limited to the origin of modern capitalism, not its imitation by other nations. Perhaps this latter fact explains why he did not touch on Japan, which was experiencing rapid economic development at the time of his writing (shortly after the turn of the century) yet did not possess anything like a Protestant ethic. In summary, then, Weber's approach is the opposite of economic determinism, emphasizing the significance of cultural divergences among different societies for socioeconomic development.

After Weber, however, the case of Japan with its strong Confucian cultural background remained an anomaly, as no other non-Western nation had successfully started economic modernization. Writing as early as 1915,

Thorstein Veblen addressed this anomaly (Veblen 1964: 248–66). He acknowledged that, with exceptional facility, the Japanese have been taking over and assimilating the industrial ways and means offered by the technological knowledge and material sciences of Western peoples. At the same time, he observes that the institutional fabric, the ethical values, and the conventional principles of conduct remain feudalistic and medieval (which he calls the "Spirit of Old Japan"). According to Veblen, this is in sharp contrast to the English, who took the lead in Europe's industrial advance and brought about institutional conventions consistent with modern industrial arts (Veblen 1964: 251–52).

Veblen holds a strong conviction that the modern industrial society characterized by modern technology, business enterprise, and market competition is, in the long run, incompatible with the prepossessions of medievalism. A radical change in the material ways and means by which people live must change people's scheme of life, because "ideas, ethical values, principles (habits of thought) induced by the conditions of life in the past must presently give place to a different range of ideals, values, and principles . . . to which they owe their force" (Veblen 1964: 256). Thus, we see an element of materialism in Veblen, as in Marx. While for Marx the class struggle is the dynamic force of history, for Veblen technology is the central force.

According to Veblen, technology may be borrowed and assimilated, and it is through this nature of technology that native traits or national culture play a role in social change. He observes certain similarities in intellectual perspective between the Japanese people and those of Western nations. Both "fall into the same ways of thinking and reasoning so that they readily assimilate the same manner of theoretical constructions in science and technology, that the same scheme of conceptual values and logical sequence carries conviction," an intellectual perspective not shared by other peoples such as "the Negro, Polynesian, or East Indian" (Veblen 1964: 257). Their similarities are not limited to the domain of material knowledge. There is apparently a close resemblance in emotional complexion—ideals and ethical values— partly a result of the fact that both Japan and Western Europe experienced the feudal system.

The "Spirit of Old Japan" is a matter of acquired habits of thought, tradition, and training, rather than a matter of a native endowment peculiar to the Japanese. As such, it is necessarily of a transitory nature. For these reasons, Veblen predicts that as soon as the Japanese people have digested the Western state of science and technology and have assimilated its spiritual contents, the "Spirit of Old Japan" will inevitably be dissipated and replaced by materialistic, commercial, and spendthrift concepts (Veblen 1964: 254).

Veblen's perspective may be called a qualified convergence hypothesis in that if people of a nation have the intellectual capacity to borrow and assimilate modern technology, they will go along the road of industrial dominion and individual self-help on which the Western peoples, led by the English, have gone before. In this way, Veblen broadened Weber's perspective, which was limited to the origin of modern capitalism and its relation to the Protestant ethic, to address the industrialization process in general and the intellectual ability to borrow and assimilate modern technology as the central force of industrialization.

Although the Marxist perspective of historical materialism was challenged by Max Weber, as we have already seen, it nevertheless survived and was supported by many for a long time thereafter. The emergence of the Soviet Union as a victorious industrial power after World War II and the subsequent intensification of the cold war begged a new theory of social change that would place capitalism and socialism/communism in the "right" historical context. One such attempt is the study published in 1960 by W.W. Rostow on the stages of economic growth. As its subtitle, "A Non-Communist Manifesto," indicates, he attempted to offer an alternative to Marx's theory based on what he calls a "dynamic theory of production" (Rostow 1960: 1–3).

According to Rostow, a dynamic theory of production requires a flexible and desegregated approach to economic development. Theoretical equilibrium positions need to be determined not only for total output, investment, and consumption, but also for each sector of the economy. He says that sectoral optimum positions are determined by the level of income and population and by the character of tastes on the demand side, and by the state of technology and the quality of entrepreneurship on the supply side. As a result of the interaction of these variables, a set of sectoral paths, or a sequence of optimum patterns of investment, will emerge. He further says that actual historical patterns of investment deviate from the optimum patterns because of such factors as the policies of government, the impact of wars, and the welfare choice of societies (Rostow 1960: 12–16).

With these points in mind, Rostow proposes a five-stage growth model consisting of the traditional society, the preconditions for take-off, the take-off, the drive to maturity, and the age of high mass-consumption. A traditional society is one whose structure is developed within limited production capabilities based on pre-modern science, technology, and attitudes toward the physical world. The preconditions for take-off are the second stage that societies undergo in the process of transition. This arises not endogenously but from some external intrusion, literal or figurative, by more advanced societies (Rostow 1960: 4–7).

The take-off is the third stage, when the resistances to steady growth are finally overcome and the forces making for economic progress expand and come to dominate the society. Growth becomes its normal condition. The take-off stage is followed by a long interval of sustained progress toward maturity. At this stage the use of modern technology is extended over the whole front of its economic activity. Finally, the stage of high mass-consumption is the stage at which the leading sectors shift toward durable consumer goods and services. The emergence of the welfare state is another manifestation of this stage (Rostow 1960: 7–11).

Rostow says that, although he approaches the sequence of social change from an economic perspective, he does not subscribe to Marxist economic determinism. Rather, he views societies as interacting organisms, so that as economic change has political and social consequences, so political and social change have economic consequences, and that most profound economic changes are a consequence of noneconomic human motives and aspirations. He also says that his concern is not only with the uniformities in the sequence of modernization, but also with the uniqueness of each nation's experience, shaped by, among other things, a succession of strategic decisions (Rostow 1960: 2).

Of particular importance in Rostow's theory are the preconditions for take-off and the role of modern Communism in the evolution process. Included in the preconditions are such economic factors as the development of agriculture and extractive industries and the formation of social overhead capital, as well as certain noneconomic factors. Referring to the role of a new leadership in building a modern industrial society, he says, "while the Protestant ethic by no means represents a set of values uniquely suitable for modernization, it is essential that the members of this new elite regard modernization as a possible task, serving some end they judge to be ethically good or otherwise advantageous" (Rostow 1960: 26). This new elite must replace the old land-based elite and divert extra income to the modern sector, and people must become prepared for a life of change and specialized function.

In addition to changes in attitudes, values, social structure, and expectations, he emphasizes the role of political process and political motive in the transition. In particular, nationalism reacting against intrusion from more advanced nations has been a most important and powerful motive force in the transition to modern societies. People holding effective authority or influence uproot traditional societies to protect them from humiliation by foreigners. According to Rostow, then, Japan is a typical example in this sense (Rostow 1960: 26–28). Although he does not explicitly criticize Weber's perspective on the role of the Protestant ethic, it is apparent that Rostow considers a leader's determination to modernize the nation in the face of foreign aggression to be a more important cause of modernization than people's religious desires for eternal salvation.

According to Rostow, modern Communism is an invention of Lenin's to seize political power without support of the industrial working class. As such, it is contrary to Marx's historical materialism. Rostow views modern Communism as a "disease" of the transition at the stage of preconditions for take-off. It is at this stage that conflicts arise not only between the residual traditional elements and those who would favor modernization, but also among the latter groups of people. It is in such a setting of political and social confusion that the seizure of power by a Communist conspiracy is easiest. Once in power, Communist leaders launch a take-off under a centralized dictatorship (Rostow 1960: 162–64). Although Rostow did not elaborate on the fate of modern Communism, his following remark is insightful: "While power can be held with economy of force, nationalism in Eastern Europe cannot be defeated; and, within Russia, Stalin's tactical evocation of nationalism in the 1930s and 1940s, steadily gathering force, has set up important cross-strains" (Rostow 1960: 162).

In the same year (1960) another major study was published by a group of four leading U.S. labor economists. In *Industrialism and Industrial Man*, Kerr, Dunlop, Harbison, and Myers addressed essentially the same issue as that studied by Rostow: which of the two worlds, the West or the East, would come to dominate the industrializing world? To answer this question, in 1954, they formed a research group consisting of a total of seventy-eight persons of eleven different nationalities and conducted research in fifty-five countries during a five-year period (Kerr et al. 1960: 299). Their main conclusion was against the prediction of Marx: worker protest in a capitalist society (or what Marx called the "class struggle") would not result in a Communist revolution; instead, capitalist societies would be more stable than Communist societies throughout the industrialization process.

The key concepts in the approach of the four authors of this book are "industrialism" and "industrialization." According to them, industrialism is the state of the fully industrialized society that the industrialization process inherently tends to create. And industrialization refers to the actual course of transition from the traditional society toward industrialism (Kerr et al. 1960: 33). Their theory is that the development of the new industrial process depends on "a concept of the logic of industrialism, of the strategies of the elites who . . . guide the process . . . in history, and of the crucial cultural and environmental conditions" (Kerr et al. 1960: 2). Hence they reject Marxist economic determinism.

They propose that the dynamic force behind industrialization is the aspiration of the peoples of the world for higher living standards and that they are everywhere on a march toward industrialism. Higher living standards are achieved by, among other things, the application of modern technology far in advance of that of earlier societies (Kerr et al. 1960: 34).

Historically, Great Britain is the first case of industrialization. In the years before World War I, the industrialization process spread widely through the Western World and into Japan. In the interwar years the Soviet Union embarked on its radical industrialization program, and, after World War II, many nations in Asia, Africa, and the Middle East joined the march to industrialization. However, according to the authors, no country (including the United States) was yet fully industrialized as of 1960 (Kerr et al. 1960: 17–18).

In the 1850s (at the time of Marx's writing), there was only one model of successful industrialization. A century later, the four authors witnessed such a variety of methods of achieving the industrial society that the Marxist dichotomy of capitalism vs. socialism/communism was insufficient for a comparative study of the industrialization process. Also, in place of the "class struggle," the four authors assign to the "industrializing elite" the central role in shaping the course of the industrialization process. The industrializing elite refers to a group of leaders, including "the political leaders, industrial organization leaders, top military officers, associated intellectuals, and sometimes leaders of labor organizations" (Kerr et al. 1960: 8).

Depending on the type of elites, they identify five ideal types of industrialization: (1) the dynastic elite, (2) the middle class, (3) the revolutionary intellectuals, (4) the colonial administrators, and (5) the nationalist leaders (Kerr et al. 1960: 50). These elite groups are differentiated primarily in terms of the cultural and economic environment that existed in the pre-industrial society. Thus, the dynastic elites are drawn from the landed or commercial aristocracy, or, less often, from the military/administrative caste. The middle-class elites are drawn from commercial or artisan groups sensitive to the gains from the new means of production, in opposition to the old elites. Revolutionary intellectuals are self-identified for the task of leadership by their acceptance and espousal of the dialectic theory of history. The colonial administrators are doubly "alien" in that they represent not only a new system of production but also an external society. Finally, the nationalist leaders revolt against colonialism. They are the symbols of the new independence (Kerr et al. 1960: 52–70). The main elements of the five ideal types of industrialism are summarized in Table 1.1.

Of particular importance for our purpose is the evolution of the managers of enterprises—part of every industrializing elite—because they are crucial

Table 1.1

Five Types of Industrialization

Main elements of industrialization	Dynastic	Middle class	Revolutionary intellectuals	Colonial administrators	Nationalist leaders
Strategy of the elite	Maintenance of traditional security	Individual self-advancement	Forced industrialization	Servicing the home country	National independence
Characteristics of the society	Paternal community	Open market	Centralized state	Alien control	State-led development
Access to management	Family connections	Initiative and competence	Political affiliations	Home country nationals	Various
Managerial style	Paternalistic	Constitutional or democratic	Dictatorial and authoritarian	Dictatorial or paternalistic	Various
Examples	Germany, Japan	United Kingdom, United States	Soviet Union, China (PRC)	India, Algeria	Egypt, Indonesia

Source: Adapted from Clark Kerr, John T. Dunlop, Frederick H. Harbison, and Charles A. Myers, *Industrialism and Industrial Man* (Cambridge: Harvard University Press, 1960), charts 2 and 6.

to the success of any industrialization effort. Under the leadership of a dynastic elite, family connections tend to control access to the managerial class. Patrimonial management is most likely to be paternalistic in its relationship with the workers. The middle class tends to favor access to the ranks of management on the basis of individual initiative and competence. Management will move toward a constitutional approach to the governing of workers. The revolutionary intellectuals try in the beginning to promote political management by making party loyalty and service the gateway to the managerial hierarchy. Their style of management is dictatorial and authoritarian. The colonial administrators reserve for themselves the controlling positions in management with local nationals assigned to perform lesser jobs in management. Management is likely to be either dictatorial or paternalistic in its relations with the workers. Finally, the nationalist leaders develop political or professional management (Kerr et al. 1960: 160–64).

As industrialization proceeds, an increasingly larger number of trained engineers, technologists, and administrators are required for scientific discovery, technological innovation, and administration of complex enterprise organizations. As a result, patrimonial and political managers tend to be replaced by careerist and professional managers. The advanced industrializing economy will have a fully developed system of general education, and a functionally oriented education will replace arbitrary noneducational barriers to entry into the managerial hierarchy. Also, as industrial societies advance, management becomes less authoritarian in its attitude and policy toward workers, because the government and labor organizations tend to limit the unilateral authority of management.

The industrialization process shapes the evolutionary pattern not only of managers but also of the industrializing elites and society. The colonial system is the most transient of the several ideal types of elites. Segmented colonialism gives way to nationalism, and settler colonialism ceases to be colonialism by becoming the system of the country itself (Kerr et al. 1960: 276–77). Successful industrialization will erode the economic and social foundations of the landed dynastic elite. New members will have to be recruited from the lower strata of society through the mechanisms of higher education. The society is moving more toward the middle-class ideal type, in which tradition and status mean less, and competition and contracts mean more (Kerr et al. 1960: 272–73).

The revolutionary intellectuals and nationalist leaders follow essentially the same pattern of evaluation as that of the dynastic elite. Both communist revolution and national independence require leaders with political and military skills; however, once a revolution or independence has been achieved, such skills will become of less importance than those required for successful industrialization. In a communist society, as more enterprises are involved in the production and distribution of an increasing variety of consumer goods and services, central control becomes less possible and localized decisions and markets will take its place. The new generations of leaders will become more professionally oriented than ideologically oriented. In a nationalist society, state-owned industries will gradually be taken over by private enterprises, and state control will be replaced by markets (Kerr et al. 1960: 274–77). Thus, both communism and nationalism will tend to adopt a modified version of the middle-class approach, with heavier emphasis on the state.

The middle-class system is the most stable of the five types. Unlike other types of elites, as industrialization proceeds successfully, the middle class from which elites are recruited grows in size, thereby supplying an increasing number of leaders to all sectors of industrial society. The open market system may lose some of its influence to the government, the labor movement, or other large organizations; nevertheless, the markets will remain major instruments for making economic decisions. Worker protest will not result in an overthrow of the middle-class system; rather, it will be controlled, organized, and channeled into the institution of collective bargaining (Kerr et al. 1960: 273–74).

Although the four authors conclude that the industrialization process will converge toward "pluralistic industrialism," characterized by professional managers, effectiveness of industrial organizations, and checks and balances in decision making, it is apparent that pluralistic industrialism models after the middle class system (Kerr et al. 1960: 297). This way, the four authors reversed the Marxist proposition that capitalism will evolve into socialism and communism.

They did not specifically mention what would happen to Japanese society and management. But from their prediction that a dynastic society, Japan being a typical example, will evolve into a middle-class society, we can draw certain inferences: social values will shift from the maintenance of traditions to individual self-advancement; managerial style will become less paternalistic and more constitutional or democratic; workers will become less dependent on their employers and more independent.

In 1958, two years prior to the publication of *Industrialism and Industrial Man*, two pioneering studies on Japanese management centering on the employment system were published. One was *Industrial Relations in Postwar Japan* by Solomon Levine, and the other, *The Japanese Factory* by James Abegglen. Levine's study is a comprehensive coverage of the Japanese industrial relations system, with one chapter devoted to the management system, the main subject of our interest here (Levine 1958: 31–58).

Levine says that the outstanding feature of Japanese management practices in its early industrialization process was the incorporation, within the modern enterprise, of traditional behavior patterns characterized by "personal loyalty, subservience of subordinate to superior, and close interdependence of individuals within tightly knit social units" (Levine 1958: 32). Thus, according to Levine, Japanese management practices were basically paternalistic in that basic relationships between workers and management were vertical, and subordinates preferred to rely upon management's beneficence to better their lot. This made a sharp contrast to the early Western system of horizontalism, where the parties were on equal terms and bargained collectively (Levine 1958: 40).

Levine distinguishes between two types of paternalism: "despotic" and "patriarchal." Within the large enterprise sector despotic paternalism was predominant in the prewar era, while after World War II, when labor unions obtained legal status, despotic tendencies were largely dispelled and replaced by managerial paternalism of the patriarchal type with an emphasis on increased welfare benefits and employment security measures. He believes that managerial paternalism, although supported by employees in general, is not as effective in increasing productive efficiency as "advanced" personnel practices like job classification and evaluation, incentive systems tied to production, and training-within-industry programs identified with managerial efficiency in American industry (Levine 1958: 55).

Levine predicts, therefore, that the need to increase Japanese industrial productivity would necessitate the spread of horizontal relations throughout its society; otherwise, despotism could quickly reemerge. Thus, he takes the same position as that of the four authors mentioned before: the Japanese approach to management will converge toward the Western model, although the development will be slow.

Indeed, drawing heavily on the studies by Levine and by James Abegglen (to be discussed shortly), Frederick Harbison, one of the four authors, observed that the pressure of external competition and the examples set by progressive enterprises in other countries have led the Japanese to recognize that individual initiative and some atypical behavior other than respect for age and reliance on group decision making might be indispensable for the healthy development of modern managerial organizations. Thus, he predicts, "unless basic rather than trivial or technical changes in the broad philosophy of organization building are forthcoming, Japan is destined to fall behind in the ranks of modern industrial nations" (Harbison and Myers 1959: 254).

James Abegglen's *The Japanese Factory,* published in 1958, is another classic on Japanese employment practices. On the basis of observations and interviews conducted at nineteen large factories in 1955 and 1956, he identified the following six elements as the key features of the Japanese organization: (1) permanent employment, (2) employee selection on the basis of education and general background rather than specific job skills, (3) employee status largely determined by education at the time of hiring, (4) pay based on age, education, and length of service rather than job difficulty, (5) decision making by groups of people and responsibility not assigned to individuals, and (6) management involvement in employees' nonbusiness activities (Abegglen 1958: 128–29).

According to Abegglen, the above list represents the elements of social organization and social relations of preindustrial Japan, and it contrasts sharply with the Western model with its emphasis on individuality, the workplace as a purely economic grouping, and subordination of noneconomic values and interests in business activity. The introduction of industry into Japan, which did not share these Western values and had a markedly different social system, made necessary the fitting of the industrial mechanism to the earlier social system (Abegglen 1958: 129–30).

He makes reference to the convergence theory, using the dichotomy between "particularism" and "universalism," or a value emphasis on loyalty and intragroup harmony and a value emphasis on efficiency and performance. He does not view Japan at some midpoint in the development from particularism toward universalism; instead, the Japanese factory system appears to him to be self-consistent and stable. He acknowledges that a pre-industrial system of organization and Western technology has created problems for Japanese industry, and predicts that their solution would not lie "in the direction of greater change toward the Western business model" (Abegglen 1958: 140). Thus, he clearly rejected the convergence view.

In 1966, ten years after his original study, Abegglen re-examined some of the conclusions of the original study. On the basis of information collected from twenty-five large companies, he found little change in the patterns of hiring, compensation and benefits, and worker turnover from his original study. The proportion of employees recruited directly from school out of total new recruits increased; the level of starting salary continued to be a function of educational background and base salary continued to increase in direct relation to length of service; and exits from the workforce as percentage of total workforce remained very low (3 to 5 percent) except for female employees (Abegglen 1973: 175–92). Thus he concludes, "This study of the 1956–1966 period indicates again the durability of Japan's approach to industrial organization. There has been a general tendency to assume that Japanese companies are changing in their methods of organization. This data does not encourage that view" (Abegglen 1973: 191–92).

After Levine and Abegglen the convergence-divergence debate has continued to the present date. Instead of following the historical development of the debate, we will identify, in the next chapter, those elements of Japanese management that are alleged to be unique, and we shall provide theories or approaches useful for the analysis of those elements. These theories or approaches will guide our entire study.

2

Characteristics of Japanese Business and Management

Ever since the late 1950s, when pioneering foreign scholars began serious academic inquiries into Japanese business and management (Abegglen 1958; Levine 1958; Karsh and Cole 1968; Cole 1971), a long list of practices have been identified as uniquely Japanese (Okochi, Karsh, and Levine 1974; Patrick and Rosovsky 1976; Ouchi 1981; Shirai 1983; Koike 1988; Fruin 1992; Aoki and Dore 1994). While some were discovered early (e.g., permanent employment), others were added to the list more recently (e.g., corporate governance).

Depending on when they were discovered, individual practices may be categorized into the following six groups or aspects: (1) human resource management and industrial relations, including employer paternalism, permanent employment, length-of-service-based promotion and wages, emphasis on on-the-job training (OJT), enterprise unionism, and cooperative labor-management relations; (2) interorganizational relations, including the subcontracting system, corporate grouping through mutual holding of stocks and the "main bank" system, manufacturers' control of distribution channels, and cooperative business-government relations; (3) management decision making and implementation, including consensus decision making, group decision making, bottom-up decision making, informal consultation, and slow decision making but quick implementation; (4) production management, including quality control (QC) activities, total quality control (TQC) movements, the just-in-time system, multiskilling, and group work; (5) international operations, including export-based international strategy, a multilocal investment strategy, ethnocentrism, long-term orientation, and emphasis on the market share; and, most recently; (6) corporate governance, including self-perpetuation of top management, weak commitment to the disclosure of financial information, the role of the board of directors, and problems with business ethics and social responsibility.

A considerable amount of time has been spent on debating such problems as which of the above practices are genuinely Japanese, to what extent each practice is actually used, to what extent each practice is immutable, to what extent each practice was a success (or failure), and similar questions (Iida 1998). We, too, will attempt to answer all of these questions. In order to do so, however, we will first accurately describe what took place and then analyze why, using the framework that will be presented later. We will defer the overall evaluation of Japanese management until the last chapter, after all descriptive information has been provided.

Here it will be useful to delineate the scope of our study. Of the six main areas mentioned above, this book will emphasize item no. 1, human resource management, item no. 3, management decision making, and item no. 5, international operations, although some reference will be made to interorganizational relations and corporate governance. Given the nature of our sample, that is, managers with academic background in social sciences and business, there will be little reference to production management.

Thus, this book does not deal with such popular topics as total quality management (TQM) or just-in-time (JIT) delivery, and semiautonomous work groups. In a sense, this is a shortcoming of the book. However, a great deal has already been written about these topics, and what takes place at the shop-floor level is quite well known. What is not so well known are management practices at offices both at home and abroad, at corporate headquarters, and especially in the boardroom. The emphasis of this book, therefore, is on the activities of white-collar workers and managers at all levels of corporate hierarchy.

The General Framework

This chapter and the next chapter will be on the descriptive/analytical frameworks of the behaviors of corporate managers and the corporate environments within which such behaviors take place. We will make a conscious effort not to fall into a common trap. That is, many studies assume, even if only implicitly, that Japanese management is unique and that in order to analyze unique Japanese practices, a unique framework has to be developed. But this is methodologically wrong. A framework has to be applied to all cases, not just one case (Japan). The latter approach leads to an "ad hoc" explanation rather than a framework for descriptive and/or analytical purposes (Ohtsu 1991: 49–55).

Therefore, this study uses a universal framework as well as specific tools for the description and analysis of management behaviors. One such framework is the contingency approach, or the assumption that different conditions and situations require the application of different management techniques. Closely related to the contingency approach is the open system view, which states that an organization needs to adapt to its environment by changing its internal structure and processes as the need arises.

It is generally believed that an organizational environment is composed of the external and internal environments, with the external environment further divided into the general environment and the operating environment. In this work we will concentrate on the external environment, because specific components of the internal environment such as a communication network, organization structure, organization policies, procedures, and rules, labor relations, turnover and absenteeism, and market segmentation are things over which the organization has a large degree of control and therefore they are almost indistinguishable from the management practices that we attempt to explain in terms of environmental factors.

The components of the general environment that apply to all industries and to which we will pay special attention are the following five: international, political, economic, labor, and social factors. We assume that the first four factors change over time, and that they therefore need to be treated separately for each of the four subperiods. The first subperiod (1962–73) was a period of high economic growth that ended with the first oil crisis of 1973. The second subperiod (1974–80) was a period of successful industrial readjustment. The third subperiod (1981–90) was a period of Japan's emergence as an economic superpower followed by a bubble economy culminating in 1990. The fourth subperiod (1991–present) has been a period of post-bubble stagnation.

With respect to the social factors, which are generally considered to include demographic forces and society's values, we will concentrate on the latter. Furthermore, we assume that society's values are deeply rooted in national culture and that the latter remains more or less stable over the years. Therefore, there will be a single treatment of Japanese culture and values in the next chapter.

The components of the operating environment that affect individual industries and that we will therefore study include suppliers, substitutes, buyers, and competitors (drawing upon Michael Porter's [1985] model of competitive industry structure). Again, because of the nature of our sample, we have chosen the following industries: textile, chemical, steel, construction machinery, electrical machinery, retailing, general trading, wholesaling of construction materials, banking, and air transport. Although this list does not include automobiles, the single most extensively and intensively analyzed industry, it still represents a reasonable array of industries for our purposes.

We will now turn to the discussion of meaningful ways to describe our key "dependent variables," that is, human resource management, management decision making, and international operations. As mentioned before, we will not subscribe to the assumption that any Japanese practice is unique in its own right because it is Japanese. Instead, we will adopt those classification schemes that have been well tested and widely accepted in literature, even though they may not be the most current.

Human Resource Management

Although literature is replete with detailed descriptions of the allegedly unique methods by which Japanese corporations manage their employees, not much systematic treatment has been given to showing how Japanese managers and would-be managers make career decisions of their own. The general assumption is that the Japanese manager makes only one career decision, that is, the decision as to which company to work for upon school graduation. He continues to work for the initial employer until mandatory retirement, usually at the age of sixty. This is the practice of permanent employment that is alleged to be mutually endorsed by the employer and the employee. But do all managers as employees subscribe to this practice? To what extent do managers in our sample follow this practice?

A useful framework for answering these questions is the concept of "career anchors" originally developed by Edgar Schein (1978). According to Schein, a career anchor is an occupational self-concept that the employee develops after a certain period of time during which he gradually gains self-knowledge about his talents and abilities, motives and needs, and attitudes and values. Some of the key features of the concept of career anchors are as follows. First, it is not possible to predict career anchors from such things as preemployment tests. Second, career anchors can be discovered only over a number of years. Third, the concept identifies a growing area of stability within the person.

After developing the concept, Schein identifies five types of career anchors. They are technical/functional anchors, managerial anchors, security/stability anchors, creativity anchors, and autonomy/independence anchors. People with a technical/functional career anchor make career choices based on the functional content of the work, such as engineering or financial analysis. People who have a strong managerial anchor want to rise to higher levels of management. The career anchor of creativity represents a need to build something that is entirely one's own product and is typically found in the career of the entrepreneur. Autonomy and independence as career anchors mean a person's need to be on his own, free from the dependence that arises when one works in a large organization. Consultants, university professors, and freelance writers are examples of careers with autonomy and independence as anchors. Finally, a security/stability career anchor means long-term career stability and job security. There are two types of security: geographical security and organizational security. While the former refers to maintaining a stable career in familiar surroundings, the latter means tying one's career to a certain organization.

Out of these five career anchors, the Japanese-style employment system seems to emphasize managerial and security anchors, which may mirror the dominant attitudes and values of Japanese society. Simply put, all male graduates from prestigious universities opt to work for government ministries or large corporations where they pursue the general management career; technical/functional careers are less preferred and are usually pursued by graduates from less prestigious universities or by high school graduates. At the same time, male employees of all kinds rarely change jobs, highly valuing what Schein calls organizational security; therefore, their need for creativity or autonomy and independence is low. This is a stereotypical view of the Japanese-style employment system put within Schein's framework of career anchors.

With respect to human resource management practices by the employer, including permanent employment, length-of-service-based promotion and wages, emphasis on OJT, as well as employer paternalism, two schools of thought have been developed in an attempt to explain allegedly unique practices. They are (1) the culturalist school (Abegglen 1958) and (2) the economic rationalist school (Taira 1962). The argument of the culturalist school will be elaborated in the next chapter in the light of the development of Japanese culture and work values. At this point, only the views of the economic rationalist school will be addressed.

Economic rationalists appear to have based their argument on the earlier work of Doeringer and Piore (1971), who stated that large-scale modern firms tend to develop an internal labor market within which there evolve well-established organizational hierarchies and stable employment relationships of mutual benefit to managers and workers. The job security and opportunities for career advancement that are so important to workers are also of value to management as ways of retaining a workforce that has accumulated enterprise-specific skills and informal on-the-job training. Firms that invest in company-specific training tend to reduce turnover cost by paying high wages, granting job security, and providing career advancement. The net result is a harmonious employee-employer relationship. As Doeringer and Piore suggest, the internal labor market does not emerge automatically. Certain conditions have to prevail; these include the existence of technological specificity and skill specificity that necessitate company-specific OJT. The fact that typical large-scale Japanese firms consciously develop internal labor markets may thus be seen more as a rational economic response to prevailing environmental conditions. The internal labor market model, thus advanced, is largely intended to justify seemingly paternalistic practices for blue-collar workers. Whether it can equally apply to white-collar workers and managers requires empirical investigation.

Harmonious labor-management relations have often been identified as another unique feature deeply rooted in Japanese culture. Alternatively, Richard Walton and Robert McKersie (1965) offer a specific framework to categorize labor-management relations under the heading of "attitudinal structuring." It means the pattern of relationships between the parties that is defined by the attitudes of each party toward the other. They suggest five patterns of relationship: conflict, containment-aggression, accommodation, cooperation, and collusion. They represent the stages of development or maturity of labor-management relations, although the last type (collusion) represents a situation in which "cooperation" between union leaders and the employer goes too far.

Walton and McKersie seem to view "cooperation" as representing the most mature relationship. However, it is important to note that, for there to be genuine cooperation, there has to be more or less even distribution of power between labor and management. If the power balance is very favorable to management and if management carries out paternalistic personnel practices, as American big businesses did in the 1920s, labor-management relations look, at least superficially, nonadversarial or cooperative. This is what Walter Galenson pointed out more than two decades ago (Patrick and Rosovsky 1976: 669–71).

Management Decision Making

In his well-known book, *Theory Z* (1981), William Ouchi says that a participative approach to decision making is a distinctive feature of Japanese organizations. He describes the process as follows:

> When a major decision is to be made, a written proposal lays out one "best" alternative for consideration. The task of writing the proposal goes to the youngest and newest member of the department involved. . . . He talks to everyone, soliciting their opinions. . . . In so doing he is seeking a common ground. . . . Ultimately, a formal proposal is written and then circulated from the bottom of the organization to the top. At each stage, the manager in question signifies his agreement by affixing his seal to the document. At the end of this *ringi* process, the proposal is literally covered with the stamps of approval of sixty to eighty people. (Ouchi 1981: 44–45)

Ouchi argues that although the *ringi* decision making takes a long time, once a decision is reached, everyone affected by it will be likely to support it. What is important is not the content of the decision but rather how committed and informed people are.

More recently, Noboru Yoshimura and Philip Anderson (1997) argue that decision making is not bottom-up. Although they agree that a *ringi-sho*, or a consensus-building formal document, starts from the lowest-level employee affected by the proposal and works its way upward, the suggested courses of action actually originate with a division manager. Knowing what his boss wants, a lower-level employee formally writes up the *ringi-sho* and begins circulating it from the bottom up. Often, such employees prepare several alternatives from which their superiors can choose. Yoshimura and Anderson conclude, therefore, that the *ringi* method of decision making is an illusion that Japanese corporations create in order to motivate employees. It assures employees that they will be informed when the decision is made, and it commits them to supporting it, but it is not bottom-up decision making.

Thus, both Ouchi and Yoshimura and Anderson agree that *ringi* is the major process of decision making in Japanese corporations, but they disagree as to where the locus of decision-making power lies. While Ouchi believes in genuine participation by all employees concerned, Yoshimura and Anderson argue that *ringi* is a form of "window-dressing" and that real decisions are made by division managers. Neither discusses, however, forms of decision making other than *ringi*. Therefore, a much broader framework is called for.

A useful frame of reference in analyzing the nature of Japanese-style decision making is the decision tree theory, first proposed by Victor Vroom and Philip Yetton (1973). Although they create decision tree models in both individual and group problem situations, our direct concern is with the latter. In this model, they identify five types of decision-making styles, depending largely on the degree of participation by subordinates: (1) the manager makes the decision himself, using information available at the time; (2) the manager obtains the necessary information from subordinates, then makes the decision himself; (3) the manager shares the problem with subordinates individually, getting their ideas and suggestions, and then makes the decision himself; (4) the manager shares the problem with subordinates as a group, obtaining their collective ideas and suggestions, and then makes the decision himself; and (5) the manager shares the problem with subordinates as a group, and serves in the role of a chairman engaging the group in reaching a consensus on a decision, which decision he is willing to accept (Miner 1980: 357).

Among the above five styles, (1) and (2) may be called autocratic, (3) and (4) consultative, and (5) group consensus decision-making styles. Certainly, the Vroom-Yetton approach provides a much more comprehensive framework for the analysis of decision making than the *ringi* approach, which tends to neglect other methods of decision making in Japanese organizations.

International Operations

Since one of the objectives of this study is to identify main features in the process of globalization of Japanese businesses over the past forty years or so, a dynamic frame of reference is called for. For most manufacturing companies the usual evolution of global operations is considered to consist of six stages: (1) intermittent exports, (2) commitment to continuing exports, (3) direct sales through an overseas sales office or marketing subsidiary, (4) the licensing of a foreign firm to produce locally, (5) local production and sales, and (6) total global strategy.

The product life cycle theory provides a basis for the above pattern of evolution (Taoka and Beeman 1991). According to this theory a new product goes through five stages: introduction, rapid growth, competitive turbulence, maturity, and decline. During the introduction stage the product is designed to meet the needs of the home market, and there are usually no international activities, or, at most, minimal exports (intermittent exports). During the rapid growth and competitive turbulence stages, exports to other developed nations expand rapidly (commitment to continuing exports), because increased domestic competition brings down market prices and foreign markets begin to look attractive. Exports usually occur in three steps: first to similar markets, next to other industrialized nations, and finally to less developed nations (through overseas sales offices or marketing subsidiaries).

During the competitive turbulence stage foreign production begins usually in industrialized nations and later spreads to less developed nations. Early in the mature stage the replacement of imports with local production is accelerated by import barriers, which lead to licensing agreements or direct investments. As the home country market continues to mature, the price competition becomes keener, with the result that increased investments are made in low-wage-rate developing nations. Imports begin to enter the home country and exports begin to disappear.

During the decline stage, producers in the home country can no longer meet the competition provided by imports. Home country production begins to disappear. To retain their global and domestic market share, home country manufacturers set up plants in low-labor-cost areas. Finally, multinational companies will develop a globalization strategy whereby the company views the world as consisting of a single (global) market and locates each individual activity, such as research and development, design, manufacturing, marketing, and selling, in a few countries (or even a single country) most appropriate for that activity (Yip 1995).

Although the above framework is useful in describing and analyzing the development of international operations in our sample companies, more specific frameworks are needed to study specific functions. One such framework concerns managerial staffing abroad (Deresky 1997). Alternate philosophies are known as the ethnocentric, polycentric, geocentric, and regiocentric approaches. Firms using an ethnocentric approach fill key managerial positions abroad with parent-country nationals (PCNs) from headquarters. The advantages of this approach include PCNs' familiarity with how to get things accomplished through headquarters and their loyalty to the company rather than to the host country. Disadvantages include the lack of opportunities for local managers, thereby decreasing their motivation and loyalty to the company, as well as preventing the company from taking advantage of its worldwide pool of management skill.

The polycentric approach means that host-country nationals (HCNs) are hired to fill key positions in their own country. This approach is most suitable when the company adopts a multilocal strategy that attempts to cater to the local needs as much as possible. Another advantage is that it is less expensive to hire a local manager than to transfer one from headquarters.

With the geocentric approach, the most qualified managers are recruited from either within or outside the company, regardless of nationality. This is the staffing approach under the total global strategy mentioned before. This policy provides the greatest pool of qualified and motivated applicants from which to choose. Often the geocentric approach results in placing third-country nationals (TCNs) in key positions in subsidiaries. They usually bring more cultural flexibility and adaptability than PCNs.

Finally, in a regiocentric approach, the staffing of key positions is done on a regional basis. Thus, most of the key features of the geocentric approach are applicable on a regional scale.

Among the four approaches mentioned above, Japanese firms are known for their ethnocentric practices. Studies suggest that Japanese multinational companies tend to use PCNs more extensively in the top and middle management positions in their foreign subsidiaries than do U.S. or European counterparts (Tung 1984). For this reason, they review more carefully employees' qualifications before selecting the candidates for overseas assignments, provide more pre-assignment training, and provide a more comprehensive support system for the PCNs once they are overseas. As a result, the "failure rates," or the incidences in which PCNs have to be recalled to headquarters prematurely due to their inability to perform effectively in a foreign country, were found to be much lower in Japanese firms. However, according to a more recent study, the failure rates were found to be much higher among Japanese subsidiaries in East Asia.

At the same time, however, Japanese firms make less effort to prepare local nationals for advancement than do U.S. or European firms. As a result, recent studies suggest that Japanese firms experience some personnel problems among local national staff, such as difficulty in attracting high-caliber local nationals, a high turnover, friction and poor communication with PCNs, and complaints about the lack of opportunities for advancement.

Corporate Governance

Since the collapse of the bubble economy in 1991, a number of leading Japanese companies have been involved in lawsuits both at home and abroad, and an increasing number of top managers or former top managers have been found guilty of wrongdoing. A recent change in the Commercial Code has made it much easier for a stockholder to take an individual member (or members) of the board of directors to court. Thus, corporate governance or lack of it has been identified as another unique (negative) feature of Japanese management.

Corporate governance addresses the question of who governs the corporation. The answer, of course, is stockholders. A related, yet different, question is, for whom is the corporation responsible? Here, the standard answer is stakeholders. While the latter question, which comes under corporate social responsibility or business ethics, is widely discussed in the United States and Europe, in Japan our interest is the relationship between corporate managers and stockholders.

As early as 1933, Berle and Means argued that the management of the corporation was shifted to paid managers rather than kept in the hands of the owners (stockholders). According to them, "separation of ownership and management" is caused by the indifference of stockholders, the use of the proxy, and management self-perpetuation.

As owners of the corporation, stockholders have certain legal rights, including a share in profits when dividends are declared, inspection of corporate records, and the right to vote for members of the board of directors. However, most stockholders look upon their shares strictly as an investment, and as long as regular dividends are paid or the stock appreciates in value, they usually are satisfied and are indifferent about the details of management. If they are dissatisfied, the usual reaction is to sell their stock rather than to change management.

Moreover, for most stockholders, attendance at the annual general meeting is a burden; therefore, they vote by proxy if they want to exercise their right. The proxy is a legal form to transfer stockholders' voting rights to someone else, usually a director or officer of the corporation, a member of the management group. In this way, management is empowered to vote large blocks of stock through proxies.

Legally, the stockholders elect a board of directors that guides the affairs of the corporation and protects stockholder interests. Boards typically elect a chairperson who is responsible for overseeing board business. Boards also select the officers of the company. In reality, however, the management, or a team of top executive officers, selects the directors through the use of proxies mentioned above (Galbraith 1967).

The above description of the process of separation of ownership and management seems to apply equally to Japanese corporations. What is different in Japan is that, generally speaking, the degree of management self-perpetuation is so strong that virtually all members of the board are corporate officers appointed by the president. The chairman of the board often becomes a nominal position that is usually filled by the retired former president. Board members usually carry functional responsibilities such as general manager of a division, department, or branch office. Thus, the board of directors becomes a de facto executive body that is under the control of the president instead of a body to protect stockholder interest. Naturally, advocates of corporate governance argue that the role of the board has to be changed as stipulated in the Commercial Code. The degree of management self-perpetuation is an important variable when examining the internal environment of the Japanese corporation.

3
Japanese National Values and Confucianism

One of the major works that traced the role of national culture in organizational behavior is the study by Geet Hofstede (1983). On the basis of the data from 116,000 employees working for a large multinational corporation located in forty countries, he was able to identify four dimensions of culture: (1) individualism versus collectivism, (2) high versus low power distance, (3) strong versus weak uncertainty avoidance, and (4) masculinity versus femininity.

The first dimension, "individualism versus collectivism," refers to the relationship between an individual and his/her fellow individuals. In the individualist society, the ties between individuals are very loose. Such a society leaves individuals a large amount of freedom, and everybody is supposed to look after their own self-interest. On the other hand, in the collectivist society, the ties between individuals are very tight. People are born into collectivities or in-groups where everybody is supposed to share the opinions and beliefs of the in-group.

The second dimension, "power distance," concerns how society deals with the fact that people are unequal. The high power distance society accepts more readily the unequal distribution of power than the low power distance society. Therefore, in the workplace boss-subordinate relationships are more hierarchical, resulting in more centralized decision making and autocratic leadership style in the high society as compared to the low society.

The third dimension, "uncertainty avoidance," involves how society deals with future uncertainty. Societies with weak uncertainty avoidance more readily accept uncertainty and people take risks more easily. On the other hand, in societies with strong uncertainty avoidance people have a high level of anxiety about the essentially unpredictable nature of the future. Such societies tend to develop institutions that foster security and avoid risk.

The fourth dimension, "masculinity versus femininity," relates to the division of roles between the sexes in society. Masculine societies make a sharp division between what men should do and what women should do, while feminine societies allow both men and women to take many different roles with a relatively minor social sex-role division.

Japan was one of the forty countries included in the Hofstede study, and, as such, Japanese culture was measured by each of the four dimensions. In terms of the individualism index, Japan leans slightly toward collectivism, though it is much more collectivist compared to the United States, which is the most individualistic of all the nations. In terms of the power distance index, Japan is slightly toward the high end of the scale, while the United States is slightly toward the low end. In terms of the uncertainty avoidance scale, Japan is very much toward the strong end of the scale—second only to Germany—while the United States is more toward the weak end. Finally, in terms of the masculinity index, Japan is the most masculine of all nations surveyed, while the United States tends slightly toward masculinity.

Thus, among the forty nations surveyed, Japan stands out as dominant in uncertainty avoidance and masculinity. While it is not so dominant in individualism and power distance, Japan is more collectivist and higher in power distance than the United States. Hofstede's findings about Japanese culture seem to be supported by more recent studies in which collectivism has been identified as the most important feature of Japanese culture.

Hofstede himself has not offered any explanation as to why Japanese culture exhibits the characteristics he has discovered. Helen Deresky attempts this in her recent book (1997). According to her, much of Japanese culture can be explained by the principles of *wa* (peace and harmony) and *amae* (indulgent love). The principle of *wa*, in turn, is considered to have originated in the Shinto religion, which focuses on spiritual and physical harmony. The concept of *amae*, which was first identified by Dr. Doi as the principal element in the psychological makeup of the Japanese people, results in *shin'yo*, which, according to Deresky, refers to mutual confidence, faith, and honor.

It is reasonable to argue, as Deresky does, that the principle of *wa* carries forth into the work group, resulting in participative management, consensus problem solving, and decision making with a patient, long-term perspective. Simply said, it may be argued that *wa* is the foundation of collectivism. However, its link with the Shinto religion is less certain. One could argue with equal plausibility that *wa* derives from Buddhism. After all, one of the teachings of Prince Shotoku, who was instrumental in importing and popularizing Buddhism in the seventh century, was the importance of *wa*.

Furthermore, neither *wa* nor *amae* can adequately explain the other attributes: power distance, uncertainty avoidance, and masculinity. Certainly, a different explanation is called for. In the following section we will argue that Confucianism has shaped the basic value system of the Japanese people (Kaizuka 1966) and that Confucianism has been consciously and actively promoted by political and business leaders as well as educators to achieve certain political and business goals over the past four centuries, although their efforts seem less successful since World War II.

Confucianism

Although Confucius (551–479 B.C.), an educator and scholar, taught on a wide variety of topics including poetry, literature, rites, music, and history, what is usually called "Confucianism" consists of his ethical and political teachings recorded by his disciples in the Analects. Confucius lived in a period when the ancient feudalistic Chou dynasty (1110–249 B.C.) was in the process of disintegrating into a number of feudal states and social order was in great chaos.

To Confucius, the actions of these feudal lords were morally wrong because they were undermining the political status of the royal court of Chou and the traditional Chou civilization. He strongly felt that only by restoring the order of ancient Chou would peace and harmony be achieved; he did not propose to create an entirely new social order. Herein lies the basic traditionalist or conservative orientation of his teachings.

According to Confucius, ethical behavior on the part of the ruler and his ministers is the key to the restoration of social order. But his teachings were largely ignored by the rulers. So he turned to education with a view to producing princely or superior men. He expected some of his disciples would then be employed by the rulers as their advisors and ministers, and they, in turn, would put his teachings into practice. For Confucius, politics was just an extension of his moral education. This does not mean, however, that his interest was limited to promoting ethical behavior among rulers and ministers. He taught ethical behavior in general. Indeed, his school was open to all, noble and non-noble alike.

Confucianism, then, may be called a "normative philosophy," as its objective was to achieve social harmony through the ethical behavior of individuals. Simply put, if all members of a family behave in an ethical manner, the family will be harmonious. Likewise, if all members of a state, both those of the ruling class and the commoners, behave in an ethical manner, then social harmony will result. Thus, the study of ethical actions or virtues becomes the central focus of Confucianism.

Of all the Confucian virtues, what is called *jen* is the most important. *Jen* roughly means love or kindness, but it is different from the Western concept of love in several senses. First, *jen* has a strong hierarchical connotation in that it exists between a superior and an inferior, for example a father and his son, a ruler and his subjects, and so forth, although Confucius does not deny the existence of *jen* between social equals such as friends. Thus, *jen* takes different forms depending upon social relationships. For example, a father's *jen* for his son takes the form of "benevolence," while the son's *jen* takes the form of "filial devotion." Second, *jen* is expected to be reciprocal and to be initiated by the superior in a given relationship. Therefore, by practicing *jen* a ruler can expect his ministers to be "loyal" to him and his subjects to show him "respect" (Chang 1980: 16, 73–79).

Besides *jen* there is a long list of virtues mentioned in the Analects. They include righteousness, courage, trustworthiness, empathy, public spirit, straightforwardness, sincerity, calmness, firmness, thrift, modesty, and willingness to yield (Chang 1980: 15). Because these virtues are of secondary importance, no attempt is made here to interpret them or analyze the relationships among them. Indeed, interpretations and analyses of these virtues, including *jen*, have become an important task of Confucian scholars since Confucius, and, as a result, there are innumerable theories.

Finally, Confucianism is not a religion, because although Confucius accepts the existence of God, which he calls *t'ien* (or heaven), Confucianism does not depend on a supernatural God for its legitimacy. Also, his teachings are concerned strictly with life here on earth, not life after death.

We can summarize the essence of Confucian values as follows. First, harmony is emphasized as the ultimate goal of society. Second, social hierarchy is accepted as natural and right. Third, benevolence by the superior and devotion by the inferior are emphasized as fundamental virtues governing interpersonal relations. Fourth, learning is regarded as essential in gaining virtues, and government by "learned men" is considered ideal.

Confucianism quickly spread after Confucius's death, and during the Han dynasty (202 B.C. to A.D. 220), it became the official teaching at the National University and thousands of local schools run by the government. Successive dynasties promoted Confucianism to varying degrees.

Confucianism in Tokugawa Japan

Although Confucianism was introduced into Japan in A.D. 285, it was not until the Tokugawa era (1600–1868) that serious attention was given to it by political leaders and intellectuals. The Tokugawa era was preceded by the Warring Period of more than a century characterized by a series of wars and power politics among the regional warlords and by the complete collapse of political authority and social norms. The biggest problem for the founder of the Tokugawa military government, Ieyasu (1542–1616), therefore, was how to maintain the national unity and peace that he had achieved with his military power. Aware of the role of Confucianism during the Han dynasty, Ieyasu quickly turned to Confucianism as a means of legitimizing his regime and as a set of principles for governing the nation (Hwang 1982: 316, 325).

For it to become a practical political ideology, however, certain modifications were needed to "fit" Chinese Confucianism to Japan's realities at the time. Hayashi Razan (1583–1657), a follower of the Neo-Confucianism of Cheng-Chu, undertook the task of the "Japanization" of Confucianism and created the Japanese version of Neo-Confucianism. Thereafter, the Hayashi family became the official Confucian advisors to the military government.

Under Razan the basic Confucian values mentioned earlier were reinterpreted or modified. First, "harmony," the basic Confucian social goal, was reinterpreted to mean the maintenance of national unity and peace under Tokugawa rule. Second, the concept of social hierarchy was quite relevant to Tokugawa Japan, whose political/economic structure resembled that of the ancient feudalistic Chou dynasty that gave rise to Confucianism. However, the social hierarchy of Tokugawa Japan was much more rigid than that of China. The hierarchy consisted of four classes, with the samurai warrior class at the top followed by farmers and peasants, craftsmen, and merchants in that order. In addition, mobility among these four classes was forbidden. Finally, these four classes were ascriptive, meaning that one was born into a certain class. Therefore, Chinese Confucianism was modified to justify such a caste system of stratification (Hwang 1982: 327).

Third, both benevolence by the superior and devotion by the inferior were recognized as the fundamental virtues. Devotion by the inferior was especially emphasized. Thus, loyalty to the lord and filial piety to parents were stressed as the absolute duties of a person. The mere fact that one exists was considered to be a result of benevolence on the part of the lord and one's parents. Finally, the importance of learning was emphasized, especially among samurai. Under the peace and harmony achieved by the Tokugawa regime, there was no need for the warrior skills of samurai. The samurai constituting the ruling class sought legitimacy for their status and power by becoming, through education, princely or superior men who would govern the commoners on the basis of moral superiority (Yui 1977: 179–81).

Thus, under state patronage Confucianism became the doctrine that was principally to be studied. While in the early Tokugawa period the teaching of Confucianism was largely limited to the samurai class, gradually the teaching of it spread to commoners as well. Of particular importance, in view of Japan's economic modernization, was the spread of Confucianism to the merchant class.

Perhaps the most instrumental in this respect was Ishida Baigan (1685–1744). Himself an employed merchant clerk in his younger days, he started the Shingaku (Knowing Mind) school for the purpose of teaching merchants how to lead their lives so as to cultivate happiness of mind. Strictly speaking, he was not a Confucianist because he did not receive a systematic Confucian education. He mixed elements of Buddhism, Taoism, and Shintoism with Confucianism in his teachings, but the teachings themselves can be described as essentially Confucian (Hwang 1982: 423–24).

Baigan challenged the view that merchants were ethically the lowest of the four classes and argued that the merchant's work was as noble as that of any other class, including the samurai class. According to Baigan, it is the obligation of all classes to help the princely or superior men administer the world by devotion to their respective occupations. In this respect all classes are considered equal in their functional worth. For the merchant class, the highest spiritual attainments could be reached by diligence in buying and selling, frugality in managing their livelihood, and honesty in earning profits (Hwang 1982: 429).

After Baigan's death the Shingaku movement grew even more popular among merchants by providing them with a sense of self-identity and self-respect. At the same time, hierarchical relationships within the merchant class came to be emphasized, and loyalty, obedience, and unrestricted service to the merchant House were demanded. In this way, the focus shifted from the ethical behavior of independent merchants to that of employed merchant clerks. Naturally, the Shingaku movement was entirely consistent with the feudal policy of the military government (Hirschmeier and Yui 1981: 54).

Baigan and his followers were not the only ones who popularized Confucianism among commoners. There were many others. It is safe to say that, by the late eighteenth century, Confucianism, as an integral part or perhaps even the core of Japanese culture, was shared by people of all classes. It is apparent that, under these circumstances, the emergence of entrepreneurship was impossible: while entrepreneurship requires a progressive, individualistic, and utilitarian mentality, that of Tokugawa merchants was exactly the opposite: conservative, collectivist, and doctrinal (Hirschmeier and Yui 1981: 54).

The momentum for social change came from entirely different intellectual currents: the Rangaku (Dutch Studies) school and the Kokugaku (National Studies) school. Under the national seclusion policy of the Tokugawa regime, Holland was the only Western nation with which Japan maintained diplomatic and trade relations. As a result, Western knowledge was brought into Japan only through Holland. The interest in Dutch Studies increased after the beginning of the nineteenth century, and the military government itself opened an office to translate Dutch books into Japanese. Later many private schools were established. Originally, interest was in practical subjects such as medicine and astronomy, but gradually natural sciences like physics and chemistry came to be studied. Needless to say, the study of the Dutch language itself was very much emphasized (Imazu 1977: 150).

In the 1850s the scope of interest expanded to shipping, shipbuilding, electricity, gunnery, and social science subjects such as political science and economics. Also, language studies no longer were limited to Dutch. All major European languages, including English, German, French, and Russian, came to be studied. Thus, Dutch Studies now became Western Studies with a view to the importation of the whole corpus of knowledge of Western civilization (Imazu 1977: 157–58). After 1860 the military government as well as major fiefs (territotial units each administered by its own feudal lord) began to send students to European countries for further study of Western science, technology, and social institutions. It is estimated that a total of 153 students were sent abroad by the year 1868, when the military government collapsed (Imazu 1977: 164).

It is important to note that during this period Confucian scholars did not object to the importation of Western knowledge. In fact, many students of Dutch Studies had received Confucian education in their younger days. This lack of animosity is usually attributed to the fact that Japanese Neo-Confucianism emphasized the principle of *li*, which respects objective knowledge and rational thinking (Hwang 1982: 414).

A Kokugaku school was started by Motoori Norinaga (1730–1801) toward the end of the eighteenth century. He advocated a return to the study of ancient Japanese literature, poetry, and folk culture in general. His thought also contained nationalistic sentiments, such as a belief in the supremacy of the imperial institution and Shinto (the Way of the Gods) (Hwang 1982: 414).

In the 1850s and 1860s the Kokugaku school became increasingly critical of the legitimacy of the military government and supportive of the cause of the Imperial Family. Certainly, the nationalistic ideology of this school contributed to the *Sonno-tobaku* (Revere the Emperor, Overthrow the Bakufu) movement that ended in the Meiji Restoration of 1868 (Hirschmeier and Yui 1981: 71).

No attempt is made here to analyze the processes that brought about the Meiji Restoration. Suffice it to note the following. First, on the intellectual level, an unintended coalition of Western Studies utilitarianism and Kokugaku radicalism overcame conservative Confucian orthodoxy to bring about the downfall of the Tokugawa feudal regime. Second, the Meiji Restoration was a political coup d'état; economic modernization was yet to come.

Meiji Economic Modernization

In 1868 the manifesto of the new government was proclaimed by the Emperor in the form of the Charter Oath of the Five Articles, which stated:

1. Deliberative assemblies shall be widely established and all matters decided by public discussion.

2. All classes, high and low, shall unite in vigorously carrying out the administration of affairs of state.

3. The common people, no less than the civil and military officials, shall all be allowed to pursue their own callings so that there may be no discontent.

4. Evil customs of the past shall be broken off and everything based upon the just laws of Nature.

5. Knowledge shall be sought throughout the world so as to strengthen the foundations of imperial rule (Hirschmeier and Yui 1981: 73–75).

These articles reflect the commitment of the new government to the ideology of progress and the total rejection of Confucian conservatism.

The government lost no time in creating the socioeconomic framework conducive to the rise of modern capitalism in Japan. The feudal class system was abolished and the freedom of occupation and mobility was guaranteed. The merchant guild system was abolished and the freedom of business was ensured. Various "infrastructures" were created. It was expected that the old merchant class, freed from feudal rules and regulations, would take the initiative in business modernization. The merchant class, however, especially the large merchant Houses, were unwilling to invest in new industries or engage in foreign trade (Hirschmeier and Yui 1981: 86). Unable to adjust to the new environment, most merchant houses eventually went bankrupt. In view of our earlier discussion of the influence of Confucianism upon the values of the Tokugawa merchant class, such conservative behavior is not surprising.

Modern entrepreneurship came from different sources. One was the government itself. In 1870 a Ministry of Industry was established under the leadership of Okuma Shigenobu (1838–1922), a brilliant economic administrator, and government pilot enterprises were built with a view to serving as a model for private enterprises (Hirschmeier and Yui 1981: 87).

Some high-ranking government officials even resigned from the government as they felt that the creation of modern business was much more important. Shibusawa Eiichi and Godai Tomoatsu were the most successful examples. Shibusawa was especially instrumental in introducing the corporate form of business in Japan. Under his leadership a large number of corporate enterprises were created—banking, cotton spinning, paper manufacturing, chemical fertilizers, and so forth (Hirschmeier and Yui 1981: 100–101; more on Shibusawa and his values later.)

The second source was entrepreneurs in the true sense of the term. Fujita Denzaburo, Okura Kihachiro, Furukawa Ichibei, Yasuda Zenjiro, Asano Soichiro, and Kasawaki Shozo were among the most successful. They were born to propertied rural families who had been involved in trade and/or traditional manufacturing, typically "sake" brewing; none was of samurai origin. All were self-made men in that they left home in their youth for either Tokyo or Osaka, where each of them started his business from scratch and eventually created a business empire (Kobayashi 1987).

The case of Iwasaki Yataro was slightly different. He was of a lower-class samurai origin from the Tosa fiefdom that played an important role in the Meiji Restoration. His first appointment, at the fief's Nagasaki office, involved trading with foreign merchants. He quickly rose to the position of general manager, and when Tosa was dissolved after the Meiji Restoration, he inherited the fief's business and founded Mitsubishi Shokai. Thus, he was doubly advantaged compared with self-made men. First, because he was of samurai origin, he started his career as an administrator of the fief's trade business, which he eventually inherited. Second, because he was from the rather influential Tosa fief, he had personal connections with some of the key individuals in the central government (Hirschmeier and Yui 1981: 138–42).

Finally, some merchant Houses from the Tokugawa period survived the period of turmoil even as many others failed to do so. Mitsui and Sumitomo, in particular, were able not only to survive but also to thrive. The success of these two Houses is largely attributed to the superior abilities of their general managers, who were sensitive to the changing environment and who made special efforts to keep their businesses in line with the progressive economic policy of the government (Kobayashi 1987). It is well known that Mitsui, Mitsubishi, and Sumitomo became government protégés and later developed into huge *zaibatsu* combines.

Although the above-mentioned entrepreneurs were shrewd businessmen and were instrumental in pioneering modern enterprises, they were not capable of articulating or advocating modern business ideology and breaking down traditional prejudices against business. That task was undertaken almost single-handedly by the great educator and thinker Fukuzawa Yukichi (1835–1901).

Like other youths from a samurai family, Fukuzawa was exposed to Confucian classics as a young boy. However, Confucianism never interested or impressed him, and he especially despised the feudalistic social hierarchy. Before long he came to reject Confucianism outright and turned to Dutch Studies. In 1858 he founded his own private school (later to become Keio Gijuku College), where he taught Western Studies using primarily British and American materials. His interest was in social sciences rather than medicine, technology, or natural science.

After the Meiji Restoration he began to write many popular books in an attempt to enlighten the general public. He was quite successful at it; for example, his most popular book, *Gakumon no susume* (An Encouragement of Learning) is estimated to have sold 3.5 million copies between 1872 and 1876 (Hirschmeier and Yui 1981: 100). His ultimate concern was how to maintain national independence against the threat of Western powers, a concern he shared with other leaders of the time. He felt that the key would be the creation of independent-minded, not submissive, citizens. Thus he advocated Western individualism, liberalism, and utilitarianism (Hirschmeier and Yui 1981: 121).

More specifically, he regarded the role of businessmen to be crucial to economic progress, which, in turn, would be the basis of national independence. Therefore, at Keio Gijuku he came to concentrate on the teaching of business and economics from a rational and utilitarian point of view. He strongly advocated the importance of self-reliance and the profit motive, psychological factors that underpin the modern business mentality. He urged his students to pursue a career in business rather than government. As a result, many graduates from Keio Gijuku became notable business leaders either as entrepreneurs or as senior managers in modern business (especially in Mitsui and Mitsubishi), thereby demonstrating the effectiveness of Fukuzawa's teachings (Hirschmeier and Yui 1981: 100).

In addition, Fukuzawa's views considerably influenced government policy, especially in the areas of the economy and education, through progressive leaders such as Okuma Shigenobu. Still, liberalism was not shared by all government leaders. Leaders became increasingly impressed with Bismarck's Germany, which had adopted a more conservative approach. Finally, in 1881 Okuma and other liberal leaders were expelled from the government oligarchy. As a result, Fukuzawa's liberalism ceased to influence government policy, and thereafter he concentrated on education at Keio Gijuku (Kobayashi 1987: 300–3).

Revival of Confucianism

With the downfall of Okuma and Fukuzawa, the supremacy of the Western Studies school in general came to be challenged by the traditionalists, that is, Confucianists and Shintoists. The Imperial Constitution of 1889 and the Imperial Rescript on Education of 1890 are clear evidence of the revival of Confucianism in Japan. The Imperial Rescript on Education was issued as the basic guideline for moral education at public schools. It was the joint product of a national Shintoist bureaucrat, Inoue Tsuyoshi, and a Confucian scholar, Motoda Eifu. It stressed loyalty to the emperor, filial piety to parents, and some other Confucian virtues. Although a simple document, it served until 1945 as the most potent tool for indoctrinating Japanese school children (Hirschmeier and Yui 1981: 214).

Why was there a revival of Confucianism at this time? The Meiji "Restoration" was really a coup by which young, lower-class samurai came to occupy a position of power in the name of the emperor. They vigorously imported and successfully transplanted Western institutions to make Japan rich and strong. What would they need next? Political and social stability.

It is not difficult to imagine that, just as Confucianism was useful to Ieyasu, the founder of the Tokugawa military government, as a means to legitimize that government's rule, so it was attractive to Meiji leaders as a means to achieve political and social stability. While the Tokugawa regime more or less limited the teaching of Confucianism to the ruling class, the Meiji government maneuvered, with considerable success, to indoctrinate the entire population through public education.

The Confucian influence was not limited to the government and education. It came to influence the business sector as well. Shibusawa Eiichi, whose role as successful "transplanter" of Western business institutions has already been discussed, was a champion in "Confucianizing" the business sector. Shibusawa shared with Fukuzawa a belief in the need to upgrade the social status of businessmen. They differed in that, while Fukuzawa attempted to do so on the basis of Western liberal, individualistic, and utilitarian values, Shibusawa's approach was to cultivate business ethics on the basis of Confucian virtues (Kobayashi 1987: 244).

One of the virtues he stressed most was social responsibility. According to Shibusawa, the social status of any group should be determined by the degree it contributes to the nation's goals, and therefore there is no inherent reason why the status of businessmen should be lower than that of government officials. By serving the needs of the nation, businessmen could fulfill their obligations and gain social respect. At the ideological level, then, we could say that Shibusawa played a role very similar to that of Ishida Baigan in the Tokugawa period, who popularized Confucianism, until then a samurai ideology, among the merchant class. Indeed, Shibusawa advocated that businessmen should behave according to the former samurai code of ethics, Bushido (Hirschmeier and Yui 1981: 101).

Baigan's teachings were later incorporated into the rules of large-city merchant Houses, and they regulated, among other things, the relationship between the owner and his employees. We note exactly the same development in Meiji Japan. In 1891 Shibusawa himself wrote a House Rule emphasizing the duty of the family members to be loyal to the emperor and to work unceasingly for the prosperity of the merchant House (Hirschmeier and Yui 1981:

222). Following Shibusawa, many business leaders came to write "House constitutions" for their companies. According to those constitutions, top executives of a family company were expected to be loyal servants of the owner-families, and, by setting an example, these executives could in turn expect loyalty and dedication from middle management and every employee. In this way, companies were made replicas of a family; this was later referred to as *keiei kazokushugi* (management familism) (Hirschmeier and Yui 1981: 216). Confucian values became directly relevant to the internal administration of the company.

Under management familism, the employer-employee relationship is essentially regarded as modeled on the parent-child relationship and thus based on benevolence and loyalty. According to Confucianism, benevolence and loyalty are reciprocal, and, of the two, benevolence should be initiated first. Thus, in order to make management familism operational, Japanese employers began to show benevolence in a tangible form. The first attempt was the creation of a group insurance scheme by the Japan National Railway Corporation in 1907 (Sumiya 1966: 80–81). Many large companies followed suit. By the mid-1920s, "Japanese-style personnel management" was created through the introduction of such well-known features as permanent employment, internal training, wages and promotion on the basis of length of service, and various welfare schemes—all as evidence of employer benevolence. Needless to say, in return for employer benevolence, employee loyalty was demanded. It is safe to say that the Japanese-style personnel management thus created has continued to the present day.

Implications of Confucianism for Business Performance

No attempt is made here to analyze the strengths and weaknesses of Japanese-style personnel management, because a large number of studies have already been conducted and published. The only point to be made is that, if Confucian values positively affect business performance, it is through the actions of a "princely" or "superior" employee who has the following attributes:

1. Harmony: he is a "harmonious" employee. He functions well as a member of the group. He does not disrupt the group order. He puts the group's interest before his own interest. He does not believe that his relations with his superior are essentially adversarial.

2. Hierarchy: he accepts organizational "hierarchy." He believes that organizational hierarchy is natural and necessary. He readily accepts managerial authority. He does not challenge his superior. He does not regard his subordinate as his potential rival.

3. Benevolence: he tries to be "benevolent" to any subordinate. He is kind

and understanding. Rather than authoritarian, he is paternalistic. He is willing to teach and help his subordinate.

4. Loyalty: he is a "loyal" employee. He is loyal both to his supervisor and to his company as a whole. He is dedicated to his job. He is grateful for the benevolence shown by his superior. He does not believe that he has any right to make demands of his superior. He feels strong emotional attachment to his superior. He identifies himself with the company.

5. Learning: he loves to "learn" about his job. He is eager to obtain and increase job knowledge. He is eager to acquire and improve job skills. He is willing to undergo training for different jobs. He is motivated to develop himself into a "superior" employee.

Confucian values may be taught at schools or in a family, but it is the direct responsibility of the company to create a Confucian employee. Thus, the personnel a dministration function of business may be positively affected by Confucianism. In other areas of business Confucianism does not help entrepreneurs, because entrepreneurship requires, among other things, individualism, the profit motive, and a risk-taking mentality—things that run counter to Confucianism.

Conclusion

We will now turn to the relations between the Japanese version of Confucianism and Japanese national values as measured by Hofstede's four dimensions of culture.

First, the moderately strong collectivism may be primarily explained by the Confucian value of harmony. Japanese employees, both managers and workers, prefer to work as members of the group. They are expected to put the group's interest before the individual's interest. Benevolence and loyalty also strengthen collectivism through the strong emotional relationship between the superior and the subordinate. In exchange for the benevolence shown by the superior, the subordinate becomes loyal to both his superior and the company as a whole. With all these Confucian values we would expect a much higher level of collectivism among Japanese employees. Some additional explanation is called for.

Second, the slightly high power distance may be largely explained by the Confucian values of respect for hierarchy. Japanese employees believe that organizational hierarchy is natural. They readily accept managerial authority. However, because of the emphasis on learning, the hierarchical boss-subordinate relationship does not lead to centralized decision making or to autocratic leadership. Japanese employees are expected to learn not only about their own tasks but also about anything that will contribute to improving the overall performance of the company. The benevolent superior encourages his subordinates, thus enlightened, to participate in decision making. This represents a paternalistic and participative leadership style that, in turn, may reflect slightly high power distance.

Third, the very strong uncertainty avoidance may be caused, if partially, by the respect for hierarchy. A key feature of the hierarchical organization is that every member's position within the organization is clearly known and that subordinates expect to obtain clear-cut directions from their superior. In other words, the hierarchical organization is an institution that minimizes role uncertainties among employees. It could be that employee loyalty to the company presumes a high degree of job security that minimizes future uncertainty.

Fourth, the very high degree of masculinity may be a result of respect for hierarchy not within the organization but between the sexes. Indeed, since the Tokugawa era there have been a number of popularized teachings of Confucianism that emphasize gender-based role differentiation between men and women. However, such a notion once existed in cultures that exhibit low masculinity scores today, for example, England in the Victorian era. Therefore, it is rather difficult to argue that this value is uniquely Confucian.

With respect to the possible influence of national cultures on the nations' economic performance, Hofstede found that there was a strong positive correlation between the degree of individualism and national wealth measured by GNP per capita in 1970. From the discussion of Japanese Confucianism in the preceding sections we will posit the following two propositions:

1. Confucianism hinders major political/economic changes such as the Meiji Restoration or change after World War II because of its conservative values. Therefore, to achieve major political/economic change, Confucian values have to be discarded or temporarily suspended.

2. Once major change in political/economic systems is achieved, Confucian values can positively affect business performance through the creation of a "superior" workforce.

Part II

Period of High Economic Growth (1962-1973)

4
General Environment, 1962–73

The international environment surrounding Japan was volatile during the period of high economic growth (1962–73). In July 1962, a border conflict between Communist China and India broke out (Ministry of Foreign Affairs [MOFA] 1963: 10). The Soviet Union's support of India angered Communist China and sowed the seeds of conflict between China and the USSR. In October of that year, the Cuban Missile crisis occurred, which might have turned the cold war into a hot war between the United States and the Soviet Union (MOFA 1963: 1). Although the crisis was narrowly averted when the Soviet Union backed down from its attempt to bring nuclear warheads into Cuba, the incident reminded the world's people of the fragility of peace between the two superpowers.

Communist China openly criticized the Soviet Union's action as "defeatist," while Russia called the Chinese position "adventurous" (MOFA 1963: 4). Relations between the two countries quickly deteriorated. China, meanwhile, pursuing a policy of hegemony, conducted its first nuclear test in October 1964 (MOFA 1965: 22), and, seven months later, became the fifth nuclear power. Internally, the Cultural Revolution broke out, with the Red Guards denouncing all "revisionists" (MOFA 1968: 7). This meant Communist China was isolated internationally and in great turmoil domestically throughout the rest of the 1960s.

The Soviet Union under the new leadership of Brezhnev started the SALT arms control talks with the United States for "peaceful coexistence," but at the same time it assisted various pro-Soviet nations fighting proxy wars, the largest of which was the Vietnam War. In August 1964, the United States started military intervention in Vietnam in an attempt to protect South Vietnam from communist takeover (MOFA 1965: 11). The war escalated when

North Vietnam was bombed the following year. It would not be until 1973 that the United States would finally give up its effort to save South Vietnam—partly as a result of the antiwar movement that raged within the United States.

The Russo-Chinese split deteriorated further toward the end of the 1960s, resulting in a series of military clashes on the two countries' borders (MOFA 1970: 5). This prompted both governments to improve their relations with the United States. China invited President Nixon to Beijing in February 1972 to normalize diplomatic relations between the two nations. Three months later President Nixon visited Moscow to sign the SALT agreement. This was reciprocated by Brezhnev's visit to Washington the following year for the SALT II negotiations.

Throughout the 1960s the United States was plagued by trade deficits resulting from the increased competitive power of European countries and Japan in the world markets. U.S. trade deficits put downward pressure on the U.S. dollar, the value of which, vis-à-vis all other currencies, was fixed under the Bretton Woods system. After the Smithsonian Agreement in December 1971, the dollar was officially devalued against the Japanese yen by 17.07 percent and against the German mark by 13.57 percent (Economic Planning Agency 1974: 209–14). The British pound and the French franc retained their values relative to the U.S. dollar. However, these measures were insufficient to remedy the deficit problem of the United States and the value of the dollar. As a result, in February 1973 the major currencies of the world (including the Japanese yen) were permitted to float, ending the fixed rate system. In less than two years the value of the yen increased from ¥360 per dollar to ¥260 per dollar. It was feared that such a large increase in the value of the yen would lead to Japan's loss of its overseas markets.

Another blow to the Japanese economy was the oil crisis (Economic Planning Agency 1975: 1, 2). In October 1973 the fourth Middle East War broke out. The OPEC international cartel, which had become increasingly active, adopted a resolution to restrict supplying crude oil to anti-Arab nations and to increase the crude oil price substantially. As a result, the price of crude oil became 3.5 times higher by January of the following year. The wholesale price index increased by 29 percent between December 1972 and December 1973. This first oil crisis put an end to the high growth period of the Japanese economy.

Unlike the volatile international environment, the domestic political environment during this period was stable under successive governments of the conservative Liberal Democratic Party (LDP) led by Hayato Ikeda (1962–64), Eisaku Sato (1964–72), and Kakuei Tanaka (1972–74), despite a series of radical student movements (Tomita et al. 1983: 212–18). Prime Minister

Ikeda continued with his low-profile policy vis-à-vis the opposition socialist and communist parties and concentrated on policies for high economic growth. Sato, who succeeded Ikeda after the latter's sudden illness, made public two political goals: the return of Okinawa (then occupied by the United States) and the normalization of relations with South Korea.

An attempt to normalize relations with South Korea had begun in 1962 under the Ikeda Cabinet; progress, however, was slow, partly as a result of the strong anti-Japanese feelings of the Korean people. By 1965, under the strong leadership of a military government, South Korea decided to conclude a peace treaty with Japan (MOFA 1966: 106–13). The Treaty on Basic Relations between Japan and the Republic of Korea and several related agreements were signed in June 1965 and ratified in November despite opposition by both the Japan Socialist Party and the Japan Communist Party. The ratified documents were exchanged in Seoul in December 1965.

The return of Okinawa took much longer. In January 1965, just two months after forming a cabinet, Prime Minister Sato visited the United States and met with President Johnson. At the meeting Sato raised the issue of Okinawa for the first time, but apparently no progress was made (MOFA 1965: 110). In August he visited Okinawa as the first Japanese prime minister to do so there since World War II. He declared, "The war is not over for Japan until the return of Okinawa to its motherland is achieved." He was greeted by a mass demonstration requesting the return of Okinawa to Japan.

It was another four years before the governments of Japan and the United States agreed on the return of Okinawa. In November 1969 Prime Minister Sato visited Washington, where he and President Nixon agreed to the return of Okinawa on two conditions: that the United States would continue to use the military bases on the island, and that both countries would automatically extend the Security Treaty, whose renewal was due in 1970 (MOFA 1970: 124–27). It was also suspected that Prime Minister Sato agreed to a voluntary restriction of textile exports to the United States as part of the package deal. Okinawa was formally returned in May 1972, to become the forty-eighth prefecture of Japan less than two months before the resignation of Sato.

For Kakuei Tanaka, who succeeded Sato in July 1972, normalization of diplomatic relations with Communist China was on his immediate political agenda. The official position of the Japanese Government had been to recognize the Republic of China (Taiwan) as the sole legitimate government of mainland China as well as Taiwan, with total disregard of the People's Republic of China (Communist China). As mentioned before, the United States had already broken the ice for the normalization of relations with Communist China in February; Prime Minister Tanaka wasted no time, flying to Beijing in September to sign a joint declaration that ended the war and that

Table 4.1

Number of Seats in General Elections by Party

Party	November 1963	January 1967	December 1969	December 1972
Liberal Democratic (LDP)	283	277	288	271
Japan Socialist (JSP)	144	140	90	118
Democratic Socialist (DSP)	23	30	31	19
Japan Communist (JCP)	5	5	14	38
Komeito	NA	25	47	29
[Nonaffiliated]	[12]	[9]	[16]	[11]
Total	467	486	486	486

Source: Nobuo Tomita et al., *Nihon seiji-no hensen: shiryo-to kiso-chishiki* [Changes in Japanese Politics: Data and Basic Knowledge] (Tokyo: Gakubun-sha, 1983), p. 235.

normalized diplomatic relations between the two nations (MOFA 1973: 126–29). The Republic of China (Taiwan) immediately severed diplomatic relations with Japan.

Throughout this period the opposition socialist and communist parties made no headway. Their attempts to "neutralize" Japan by abolishing the Japan-U.S. Security Treaty did not win much public support, and their opposition to the extension of the Treaty in June 1970 was easily handled by the Sato Cabinet. Table 4.1 summarizes the results of the House of Representatives elections during this period. As can be seen from the table, the conservative LDP continued to hold a comfortable majority, while the combined seats of the leftist Japan Socialist Party and Japan Communist Party were around half those of the LDP. The middle-of-the-road Democratic Socialist Party and the Buddhist Komeito remained minor groups.

It seems that the LDP's continued victories were helped to a great extent by the rapid growth of the Japanese economy. When Prime Minister Ikeda announced his Income Doubling Plan in 1960, many people were skeptical. However, during this period people not only witnessed the rapid growth of the economy but also enjoyed the fruits of this growth. Table 4.2 summarizes a few key economic indicators.

With the exception of 1962, real gross national product (GNP) growth rates exceeded 10 percent all the way up to 1970. Although economic growth slowed somewhat beginning in 1970, expansion of the Japanese economy

Table 4.2

GNP Growth Rate, Consumer Price Index, Trade Balance, and Foreign Reserves

Year	Increase in GNP (real, %)	Increase in CPI (%)	Trade balance (nominal, million USD)	Foreign reserves (nominal, million USD)
1962	7.0	6.7	401	1,841
1963	10.5	7.7	−166	1,878
1964	13.1	3.8	377	1,999
1965	—	6.6	1,901	2,107
1966	10.6	5.2	2,275	2,074
1967	10.8	3.8	1,160	2,005
1968	12.7	5.4	2,529	2,891
1969	12.3	5.4	3,699	3,496
1970	9.9	7.6	3,963	4,399
1971	4.7	6.1	7,787	15,235
1972	9.0	4.5	8,971	18,365
1973	8.8	11.7	3,688	12,246

Source: Economic Planning Agency, *Keizai yoran* [Summary Statistics on the Economy] (Tokyo: Okurasho insatsu-kyoku [Ministry of Finance, Printing Bureau], 1962–73).

during this period was phenomenal. By 1968 the Japanese GNP was ranked number two in the free world, second only to that of the United States. The Japanese trade balance, which had fluctuated between surplus and deficit positions until 1964, started continuously registering a surplus after 1965, reflecting the increased competitive power of Japanese industries. As a result, gold and foreign exchange reserves quickly increased toward the end of the 1960s and into the 1970s, although the 1973 oil crisis halted this trend temporarily. The rate of price increases was generally high by today's standards, but this often accompanies rapid economic growth. One consequence was that the labor movement aggressively fought for high wage increases through annual *Shunto* spring wage negotiations.

Japan's economic success was internationally recognized as early as 1964, when the country was admitted to the Organization for Economic Cooperation and Development (OECD), an organization created in 1961 by the industrialized nations of the world (Ministry of Foreign Affairs 1965: 240–53). Also in 1964, Japan's status in the International Monetary Fund (IMF) changed from an Article 11 nation to an Article 8 nation, meaning that Japan could no longer resort to foreign exchange controls to balance international payments.

In the same year, the Tokaido "bullet train" started operations between To-kyo and Osaka, just ten days prior to the opening of the Tokyo Olympic Games, the first games ever held in an Asian city. Prime Minister Ikeda, who had laid the foundation for Japan's later emergence as an economic super-power, died shortly after the conclusion of the Olympic Games.

After a brief period of readjustment in 1965, the Japanese economy re-turned to its high growth trend in a burst that lasted from October 1965 to July 1970 (referred to in Japan as the "Izanagi Boom"). The boom was led by strong private consumption and corporate investment. The three Cs—color television sets, "coolers" (air conditioners), and cars—became the second-generation "three sacred treasures" of ordinary households (the first-generation three sacred treasures had been black-and-white television sets, refrigerators, and washing machines in the late 1950s). The boom ended in 1970 when the government switched to a tight money policy to fight the inflation that had plagued the Japanese economy throughout the 1960s. To make up for the decline in domestic demand, Japanese industries stepped up their efforts to export. Their export drive was further accelerated by two "shocks" to the Japanese economy—the successive revaluation of the yen after December 1971 and the first oil crisis in October 1973.

The rapid expansion in the size of the Japanese economy during this pe-riod brought about noticeable changes in the labor market (Table 4.3).

As shown in the table, the labor force steadily increased, while the unem-ployment rate remained at a very low level, ranging between 1.1 percent and 1.4 percent. On the other hand, the ratio of job openings to applicants showed a rising trend that reached its peak of 1.76 in 1973. This clearly shows an increasing labor shortage that corresponded to an increasing rate of wage increases (in the manufacturing industry).

Besides the level of employment, the composition of employment also changed during the period. While employment in agriculture substantially decreased, the number of wage earners in the nonagricultural sectors of the economy increased by approximately 1 million, from 2.5 million in 1962 to 3.5 million in 1973 (Japan Productivity Center 1974: 26). The increase was most noticeable in large-scale enterprises in such industries as steel, nonfer-rous metals, electrical appliances, transport equipment, construction, whole-sale and retail trade, finance and insurance, and services. In order to meet their increasing manpower requirements, large enterprises continued to re-cruit a large number of new graduates as well as mid-career workers (Minis-try of Labor 1967: 40–52).

New graduates were in particular demand, so that, typically, several job offers were made for each graduate at all levels of education. Middle school graduates who were looking for a job became especially scarce, so much so

Table 4.3

Labor Market Trends

Year	Labor force (thousands)	Unemployment rate (%)	Active job opening rate (%)	Real wage increase (%)
1962	4,614	1.3	0.65	3.0
1963	4,652	1.3	0.72	1.9
1964	4,710	1.1	0.80	6.4
1965	4,787	1.2	0.64	2.2
1966	4,891	1.3	0.74	5.9
1967	4,983	1.3	1.00	9.0
1968	5,061	1.2	1.12	8.7
1969	5,098	1.1	1.30	10.4
1970	5,153	1.2	1.41	9.6
1971	5,186	1.2	1.12	7.6
1972	5,200	1.4	1.16	10.2
1973	5,326	1.3	1.76	10.5

Source: Ministry of Labor, *Rodo tokei yoran* [Summary Statistics on Labor] (Tokyo: 1962–73).

that they were called "golden eggs." More and more workers moved from small to large enterprises, thereby improving their wage and working conditions. Also, an increasing number of temporary or contract workers switched their status to "regular" workers, thus coming under the protection of "permanent employment" status.

The expansion of the size of the economy was accompanied by technological innovation introduced into plants in the high-growth sectors. This led to a serious shortage of technicians and skilled workers. At the same time, the expansion of the tertiary sector caused a serious labor shortage in wholesale and retail trade, services, and the finance and insurance industries. This resulted in an increased demand for female workers on both a full-time and a part-time basis.

Since virtually all Japanese labor unions are organized on an enterprise basis, usually with the protection of a "union shop," and since unions are more organized in large than in small enterprises, an increase in employment in the large enterprises during this period meant an automatic increase in the overall rate of unionization. This rate noticeably increased from the previous period and stayed at a high level (35 percent or so) during this period, resulting in increased bargaining power for the labor movement (Japan Productivity Center 1974: 146). Unlike the situation in the period up to 1960, labor-management relations became more peaceful at the enterprise level; enterprise unions concentrated their energy on annual *Shunto* spring wage negotiations under the leadership of their peak federation, Sohyo (General Council of Japan Trade Unions), although Sohyo was occasionally involved in political activities (such as a one-day strike in October 1996 to protest against the Vietnam War).

Japanese society, which had already entered into what Rostow calls the "stage of high mass-consumption" in the late 1950s, accelerated its rate of consumption during this period. The boom in sales of the "three sacred treasures" in the late 1960s has already been mentioned. Other key features of this period included urbanization of the population and motorization. There was a mass migration of youth from rural to urban areas. Every year hundreds of thousands of new middle school and high school graduates from rural areas obtained jobs in urban industrial areas. As a result, the populations of large cities swelled. Tokyo's population exceeded 10 million as early as 1962.

Motorization was another key feature. To illustrate this, the number of automobiles registered in Tokyo exceeded 1 million in 1964. In the same year, the Meishin Expressway was opened between Nagoya and Kobe, followed shortly afterward by the opening of the Tomei (Tokyo–Nagoya) Expressway. Along with motorization came an increase in the consumption of petroleum, which accounted for 55.7 percent of total energy consumption in 1964.

People's demand for leisure and recreation also increased. The hosting of the Tokyo Olympic Games in 1964 was followed by a relaxation of controls on overseas tourism in the same year (the most popular destination was Hawaii). Held in 1970, the Osaka Expo attracted 64 million people during the six months it was open. This figure was equivalent to two-thirds of the total population of Japan, which reached 100 million that same year. In 1972, the Winter Olympic Games in Sapporo attracted more than 1,200 athletes from thirty-five countries. Thus, during this period Japan reentered the world community in a major way, not only in trade but also in sports and recreation.

The rapid industrialization, however, created certain undesirable side effects. Environmental pollution was one such side effect, along with its attendant diseases. Some of the diseases had begun appearing prior to this period, but it was in this period that the causes were established through the process of lawsuits. Among the various lawsuits, the Minamata case, the *itai-itai* case, the Yokkaichi pollution case, and the Niigata Minamata case were called the "four major pollution cases." It was established that the Minamata disease was caused by eating fish contaminated by mercury contained in the waste effluent from a nearby factory. The *itai-itai* disease, which is characterized by extreme brittleness of bones, was found to be caused by cadmium poisoning. The Yokkaichi asthma was caused by sulfur dioxide included in smoke from Yokkaichi City's industrial complex. People suffering these diseases sued the companies involved between 1967 and 1969, and the plaintiffs won their cases in the district courts between 1971 and 1973.

Alarmed by the rapid deterioration of the environment and an increasing number of lawsuits, in 1967 the government enacted the Basic Pollution Measures Act. The Act stipulated the definition of environmental pollution to be covered by the Act, the responsibilities of the parties involved in regard to prevention of environmental pollution, basic guidelines for the methods of pollution control, and so forth The first *White Paper on Pollution* (later to be renamed *White Paper on Environment*) was issued in 1968, and the Environment Agency was created in 1972 (Environment Agency 1972: 284).

As a result of various preventive and control measures, air pollution caused by dust, carbon monoxide, and sulfur dioxide decreased after 1968. Also, water contamination caused by mercury and cadmium discharges decreased after 1967. However, new pollutants were discovered in this period (Ministry of Welfare 1971: 19 and 20). Among them were: photochemical smog caused by auto exhausts; polychlorinated biphenyl (PCB), a petrochemical product; certain pesticides; and sludge, particularly paper sludge from paper mills. Air and water pollution caused by these substances worsened over the years.

If we turn to the status of women during this period, we find that the total number of working women (the female labor force) increased by approximately 1.5 million, from 18.5 million in 1962 to 20 million in 1973 (Japan Productivity Center 1974: 26). During the same time, the female population ages fifteen years and above increased by approximately 7 million, from 35 million to 42 million. As a result, the female labor force participation rate (or the proportion of labor force to the total population of those fifteen years of age and above) declined substantially, approximately 8 percentage points, from 55 percent in 1962 to 47 percent in 1973.

This decline may be explained partly by the fact that an increasing number of female middle school graduates went on to high schools instead of working. But the major reason was the combination of mass migration of young people from rural to urban areas and the change in the life patterns of the married women who migrated to cities. While women in rural areas continued to work in agriculture as family workers even after marriage, those who migrated to cities worked for a few years before marriage, but upon marriage they stopped working and became full-time housewives. Put differently, as high economic growth caused a mass migration of the youth population, males typically became salaried workers and females became full-time housewives after a few years of work experience.

This tendency is shown in the number of female wage earners as a proportion of female population ages fifteen and above by age group. The ratios in nonagricultural sectors in 1973 were 59 percent for ages twenty to twenty-four, 28 percent for ages twenty-five to twenty-nine, and 22 percent for ages thirty to thirty-four (Japan Productivity Center 1974: 115). Assuming that virtually all women were married by age thirty in 1973, the above figure of 22 percent suggests that only about one out of every five married women was working as a wage earner.

Whether a majority of married women became full-time housewives voluntarily or not is a controversial question. There were two broadly publicized cases addressing this very question during this period. In March 1964, a female employee of a cement manufacturing company in Tokyo received a dismissal notice on the day she reported to work after a honeymoon trip (Maruoka 1982: 139, 140). The company based this decision on a company rule established in 1958, which stated, in effect, that a female employee shall retire when she gets married or when she reaches the age of thirty-five, whichever comes first. The labor union of which she was a member brought the case to court, arguing that the company's decision was unconstitutional, citing among other things Article 14 of the Constitution, which says, "All of the people are equal under the law and there shall be no discrimination in political, economic, or social relations because of race, creed, sex, social status, or family origin." The court ruled in favor of the plaintiff in 1966. Although the company appealed to the higher court, the case was settled out of court two years later in favor of the plaintiff. The employee was reinstated and the disputed company rule abolished.

The second case involved a female employee of a broadcasting company located in Nagoya (Ito 1990: 308–19). In January 1969, three months before she became thirty, the company informed her that her employment would be terminated under the company rule stating that the mandatory retirement age is fifty-five for men and thirty for women. She, too, took the matter to the labor union, which appealed to the court. On her birthday she was given a termination notice and severance pay, which she refused to accept. In 1972 the court decided in favor of the plaintiff, nullifying both the company rule and the dismissal decision. Although the company appealed the decision to a higher court, the latter upheld the lower court decision in 1974 and the employee was reinstated shortly thereafter.

It is not certain to what extent or in what numbers married women then wanted to stay on their jobs. But these two court decisions as well as many similar ones suggest that during this period the Japanese legal system began to take major steps forward in removing certain discriminatory practices against women.

5
Industry-Specific Environment, 1962–73

The Iron and Steel Industry

During the period of high economic growth, expansion of domestic demand brought about remarkable growth in automobiles, industrial machinery, electric machines, and shipbuilding, as well as in construction (building and engineering works), which had long been a purchaser of steel.

All the steel makers, keeping pace with these developments, implemented a Second (1956 through 1960) and a Third (1961 and thereafter) Rationalization Plan. They built new steel plants and introduced large-scale blast furnaces and LD converters, the latter of which subsequently became mainstream in the steel-making process. They greatly expanded hot and cold strip mills in the area of rolling. This enabled them to achieve mass production of steel plates/sheets and better quality products.

In order to secure basic materials, namely, iron ores and coals, they proceeded to import from abroad, including from China, and to develop resources overseas. By opting for large iron ore carriers and coal carriers, they availed themselves of the benefit of having steel plants located on the coasts.

As a result of the above management initiatives, crude-steel production jumped conspicuously, from 27 million metric tons in 1962 to 119 million metric tons in 1973, when production reached its peak (see Table 5.1). In 1970, Yahata Steel and Fuji Steel, into which Nippon Steel Corp. had been divided soon after the end of World War II, were reunited. This merger created the world's largest steel maker, Nippon Steel Corporation.

President Nixon's dollar defense policy in 1971, the Smithsonian Agreement, and the consequent revaluation of the yen led to stagnant domestic demand, mainly as a result of declines in private engineering works and plant investments, and a decrease in exports by steel purchasing industries. The strong yen and a U.S. import surcharge reduced steel exports. Crude-steel production in 1971 sank below the previous year's level for the first time during the period of high economic growth. The difficult situation in the steel industry, however, was overcome with only relatively light damage, thanks to countermeasures taken by both the public and private sectors.

Exports of steel increased rapidly, recording 5,638 thousand metric tons (tmt) in 1963, 9,909 tmt in 1965, 17,981 tmt in 1970, and 25,562 tmt in 1973 (see Table 5.2). In 1970 Japan had 25.9 percent of the world's steel trade market (European Coal and Steel Community [ECSC] intra-trades excluded) and was the world's largest exporter of steel, surpassing even the ECSC. Beginning in 1960, the export of steel amounted to from 10 percent to 15 percent of Japan's total exports, the largest share of all export items.

It was in this period that Japan's increasing steel exports resulted in trade disputes with the United States and Europe. Japan's exports of steel to the United States, which had been constantly increasing substantially ever since 1962, jumped to 6,916 tmt in 1968, more than ten times what had been exported in 1961, and the bulk of Japan's total steel exports (52.6 percent) was concentrated in the United States. With worsening U.S. balance-of-payment figures and rising protectionism, Japan was urged to exercise voluntary control in steel exports. It did so in 1969 for the first time, and then again in 1972. Furthermore, in 1972, it also exercised voluntary control of steel exports to Europe. Thereafter, Japan shifted its priorities in steel export from quantity to quality.

After the mid-1960s, the overseas operations of Japan's steel industry became substantial. Initially they centered on resource developments with a view to acquisition of raw materials, and then expanded to active investment in the marketing of products. Integrated steel plants such as those at Usiminas (in Brazil), Malayawata (in Malaysia), and Illigan (in the Philippines) went into operation through financial aid and technical assistance from Japan. Overseas businesses in galvanized steel plates/sheets, tinplates, wire rod processed products, and electric resistance welded pipes or bars, were expanded, mainly in Southeast Asia. The pace of such expansion reached its maximum in 1970 or earlier.

Table 5.1

Basic Statistical Data on the Iron and Steel Industry

Year	Shipment amount (billion yen)			Number of employees (thousand)			Crude-steel production (thousand metric tons)		
	Iron and steel (A)	All industries (B)	(A)/(B) (%)	Iron and steel (C)	All industries (D)	(C)/(D) (%)	Production capacity	Output	World market share (%)
1960	1,651	15,294	10.8	422	7,602	5.5	28,194	22,138	6.5
1961	2,122	18,734	11.3	476	8,188	5.8	30,765	28,268	8.0
1962	1,912	20,561	9.3	468	8,445	5.5	36,072	27,546	7.6
1963	2,110	22,354	9.4	473	8,093	5.9	41,731	31,501	8.1
1964	2,629	26,039	10.1	485	8,258	5.9	47,479	39,799	9.1
1965	2,669	27,801	9.6	468	8,322	5.6	53,256	41,161	8.9
1966	3,028	32,177	9.4	474	8,582	5.5	56,110	47,784	10.0
1967	3,910	38,818	10.1	487	8,826	5.5	78,476	62,154	12.6
1968	4,222	45,561	9.3	506	9,109	5.6	87,228	66,893	12.6
1969	5,229	54,705	9.6	525	9,520	5.5	103,200	82,166	14.3
1970	6,565	69,035	9.5	552	11,680	4.7	114,635	93,322	15.6
1971	6,247	72,895	8.6	535	11,464	4.7	119,196	88,557	15.1
1972	6,691	80,962	8.3	529	11,783	4.5	123,301	96,900	15.3
1973	9,220	103,362	8.9	528	11,961	4.4	139,042	119,322	17.1

Sources: Adapted from Ministry of International Trade and Industry (MITI) *Kogyo tokei-hyo* [Census of Manufacturers] (annual); and Japan Iron and Steel Federation, *Handbook for Iron and Steel Statistics* (annual).

Table 5.2

Exports and Imports of Iron and Steel

Exports of all iron and steel products
(thousand metric tons)

Year	Total exports	To the United States	To the EC	To Asia (including China)	To China	Total imports (thousand metric tons)
1961	2,513	624	13	1,252	41	201
1962	4,132	1,163	250	1,555	57	49
1963	5,638	1,796	462	1,895	47	38
1964	6,921	2,587	296	2,233	165	22
1965	9,909	4,349	161	2,609	220	16
1966	9,895	4,696	269	2,990	646	15
1967	9,135	4,349	182	2,986	610	99
1968	13,153	6,916	208	3,661	1,005	11
1969	16,006	5,651	967	4,763	1,258	21
1970	17,981	5,922	953	5,353	1,569	28
1971	24,178	6,268	1,647	7,280	1,948	14
1972	21,978	6,258	1,516	7,101	1,716	31
1973	25,562	5,287	1,278	9,790	2,661	78

Source: Japan Iron and Steel Federation, *Handbook for Iron and Steel Statistics* (annual).

Synthetic Fiber Manufacturers

The production of synthetic fibers started in the 1950s. Interest in synthetic fibers had grown primarily among chemical fiber companies: Asahi Chemical and three other manufacturers got started at an early stage in the production of acrylic, thought of in Japan as a replacement for wool; Toray was a pioneer in nylon production, followed by Nippon Rayon (currently Unitika). Only Toray enjoyed profitability, thanks to its large production scale. The big winner in synthetic fibers was polyester (see Table 5.3).

Whether a textile manufacturer entered into the polyester market or not decided that manufacturer's fate. Toray entered the polyester market after it had succeeded in nylon. Teijin, whose earnings had been sluggish because of rayon's decline, also succeeded in this area by co-introducing, with Toray, techniques from ICI in the United Kingdom. This success enabled Teijin to

Table 5.3

Yarn Production (billion metric tons)

	1960	(%)	1970	(%)
Natural fibers	8.12	(61)	8.61	(40)
Rayon and acetate	3.58	(27)	3.99	(18)
Synthetic fibers	1.54	(12)	8.98	(42)
of which:				
Polyester	—	—	3.32	(15)
Polyamide	—	—	2.97	(14)
Polyacrylic	—	—	1.52	(7)
Vinylon	—	—	0.80	(4)
Others	—	—	0.37	(2)
Total	13.24	(100)	21.58	(100)

Source: Ministry of International Trade and Industry (MITI), *Kogyo tokei-hyo* [Census of Manufacturers] (1960, 1970).

rebuild its foundations for future expansion. Polyester's superiority to other fibers lies in its chemical properties; it can be adapted not only to garments but also to a wide range of purposes, such as industrial materials or plastics. Making use of these properties, Toray and Teijin created one technical innovation after another.

The two companies also brought in new ideas in production and distribution. Toray formed production teams, each team consisting of companies from five areas of the textile industry (spinning, weaving, dyeing, sewing, and distributing), and in this way built up its market. Teijin followed suit. For any given company in each area, the key to expansion lay in belonging to a production team and handling polyester.

The two companies also launched a new type of marketing. In addition to newspapers, their traditional medium, they made active use of television, a new medium, to encourage demand. The functional qualities of products were stressed in advertising. As a result, blouses, skirts, slacks, shirts, and the like, manufactured by their production teams were preferred by consumers to the brand-name products of famous department stores. The result of their new approach was that they gained the initiative in distribution.

This marketing approach, with its freshness, impressed people accustomed to the conventional types of marketing. Applied to one new consumer product placed on the market after another, it led to huge outlays for advertising, which, in turn, supported the rise of the mass media, and Japan's economy rapidly changed into an advanced type of economy in which consumers play a major role. The manufacturers of synthetic fibers contributed in large measure to this change.

Their expansion policy was also evident in ready-made clothes. Abundance in supply and in the variety of sizes encouraged consumers to purchase, and encouraged distributors (normally afraid to stock merchandise that would go unsold) to carry such clothing. After great success in advertising short-sleeved shirts, the manufacturers enjoyed greater shares of the market in ready-made blouses, skirts, long-sleeved shirts, and even men's suits, where made-to-order suits had long had the major share. One effect was a decline in the need for the services of tailors.

Toray and Teijin adopted a common trade name, "Tetoron," for their polyester, then launched a series of advertising campaigns. The successful advertising campaigns forced department stores to deal in Tetoron products without sticking solely to their own brand names. Garment companies such as Renown and Onward, which were later to establish their own brand names, grew in proportion to the sale of ready-made articles.

The fast-growing synthetic fiber industry was attractive to trading companies. Most of the textile wholesalers had been the big trading companies, which were financially strong enough to survive the fluctuating cotton market. The "Big 5" in cotton wholesalers, Tomen, Nichimen, Gosho, Marubeni, and C. Itoh, were compelled to rebuild their textile businesses because their shares in the overall textile market had dropped when the cotton spinning industry went into decline. Obtaining a substitute for cotton through belonging to some of the production teams mentioned above, they demonstrated their trading skills by expanding business overseas as well as in the domestic market.

In the area of distribution, "supermarkets" that had been introduced from the United States and had a sales approach different from the face-to-face sales normally practiced in the Japanese department store, brought about a change in consumer behavior. The synthetic fiber manufacturers initially feared supermarkets would have control over prices, but later they adopted a positive, quantity-oriented policy for mass distributors, driven by a growing number of new entries into the market.

Under the circumstances textile manufacturers without synthetic fiber plants were quick to invest in such plants, while the early pioneers increased their lines of synthetic fibers. Thus, for example, Asahi Chemical, Teijin, Kanebo, and Kurehabo added nylon, while Toyobo, Kuraray, and Nichiray added polyester. All these plants were completed more or less around the same time, in 1964 and 1965, just when the economy slowed down. The outlook for the synthetic fiber industry was uncertain.

The manufacturers, in cooperating with the Ministry of International Trade and Industry (MITI), took active steps to counteract the slump through such things as inventory control to revive the market, and relief measures for factory-located areas damaged by the sluggish business. MITI had a law passed for this specific purpose and effective for a limited period, and it expressed its determination not to repeat the same mistakes it had made in the case of the cotton spinning or chemical fiber industries. The law was put into force in 1964 and restricted the industry's production facilities by adopting a "scrapping and building" (of production facilities) approach.

Even after synthetic fiber had replaced cotton as the main product of the textile industry, the manufacturers were still turning for outlets to foreign countries, especially to the United States. This led to a political "trade friction" with the U.S. textile industry. In 1971 an export curb was imposed on textile goods after three years of Japan-U.S. textile talks.

Since this was a political issue between Japan and the United States, the Japanese government, in return for accepting the U.S. demand, directed ¥15 billion in fiscal expenditure and ¥60 billion in long-term loans at low interest rates toward the damage-stricken textile industry. From the 1972 budget, ¥128 billion was allotted for relief funds, and ¥38 billion for purchasing excess facilities. Moreover, severance pay was set aside for displaced workers. In 1972, the existing "Provisional Law for Restructuring Specific Areas of the Textile Industry" was revised; the revision provided for a framework in which the government took the initiative in restructuring and the relevant manufacturers reduced production. Toray played a leading role; it determined to reduce its workforce by 4,000, not to hire 1,900 new graduates from junior or senior high schools, and to defer capital investments. The Fair Trade Commission (FTC) judged that the series of countermeasures by manufacturers were concerted actions based on a mutual agreement to curtail production, and recommended that they repeal the agreement.

Textile manufacturers diversified their range of products and operations. Some examples follow.

Toray: (1) synthetic resin, petrochemical products (polypropylene, acrylonitrile butadiene-styrene-ABS); (2) housing, realty; (3) the antipollution industry; and (4) labor-saving facilities (robots, workerless plants).

Asahi Chemical: (1) petrochemical products (resin, synthetic rubber); (2) housing; (3) foods; and (4) pharmaceuticals—a technical link-up with Toyo Brewery Co.

Teijin: (1) petrochemical products (paraxylene, polystyrene, ABS); (2) housing, realty; and (3) foods, titanium.

Table 5.4

Amounts Shipped in Chemical Industry, by Area (firms with four or more employees)

Year	Total amount of shipment (billion yen)	Fertilizers (%)	Petro- chemicals (%)	Pharma- ceuticals[a] (%)	Inorganic chemicals (%)	Oils and fats (%)	Others (%)
1960	924	17.8	5.2	20.0	13.4	7.5	27.8
1965	1,723	12.8	14.7	24.0	11.5	6.5	22.8
1970	4,518	6.7	25.0	20.0	11.5	5.2	23.7

Source: Ministry of International Trade and Industry (MITI) *Kogyo tokei-hyo* [Census of Manufacturers] (1960, 1965, 1970).

[a]In this period it was frequently appropriate to refer to pharmaceuticals as an industry independent of the chemical industry.

The common aim of the synthetic fiber manufacturers was to cover a product range tracing back from fibers to their raw materials, petrochemical products.

The Petrochemical Industry

After Japan's economy switched from postwar recovery to high growth, the chemical industry enlarged its scale of activities. The amount of goods shipped almost doubled in five years, from 924 billion yen in 1960 to 1,723 billion yen in 1965, then went on to reach 4,518 billion yen in 1970, for a fivefold increase in ten years (Table 5.4).

Within the various areas of the chemical industry, it was the petrochemical area that, promoted by the government, grew to colossal size, with one *zaibatsu* (industry group) enterprise after another entering the field. The value of its total production exceeded ¥1 trillion in 1964, surpassing that of chemical fertilizers. This meant that the lead in the chemical industry as a whole had shifted from chemical fertilizers to petrochemical products. The impressive thing about this is that it took place within just twenty years after the end of the war.

The petrochemical industry, with its wide range of interindustry relations, was one of the principal factors in the postwar industrial restructuring that made Japan's high economic growth possible. Interindustry relations are seen, for example, in the benzine or carbolic acid used as material for nylon, in the ethylene glycol used for polyester, and in synthetic resins such as vinyl chloride, polyethylene, or polypropylene, which are used as materials for many parts of electric appliances and automobiles.

Rapidly expanding petrochemical makers built petrochemical complexes across the country that were connected with oil refineries by pipelines. As ethylene, demand for which was greater than any other petrochemical, was mass produced, it replaced carbide as material for the vinyl chloride monomer. Ammonia, methanol, sulfuric acid, and phosphoric acid likewise were produced by the complexes.

In 1967, the government set a production standard per ethylene plant of 300,000 metric tons per year and pressured the industry to strengthen its international competitiveness through the formation of an oligopoly. The results, however, did not come up to the government's expectations. With the exception of Mitsui Chemical and Toyo Koatsu, which merged in 1968, the manufacturers did not resort to mergers but expanded their own plants under a rapidly growing need to meet the higher production standard set by the government. In 1972, twelve manufacturers had ethylene plants that satisfied the production standard. Meantime, the growth in demand for petrochemicals slowed down after 1970. Cartels were formed for some products, yet the industry as a whole was not restructured. As regards manufacturers of petrochemicals other than ethylene or ethylene-related products, the government also expected the formation of an oligopoly by merger. The merger took place only in 1971, but no competitive manufacturer emerged.

Ethylene factories were operating at more than 100 percent capacity in 1973. Excessive operations led to frequent plant accidents. More capacity was required. Further competition was the result.

Environmental issues arose after the rapid expansion. Companies were forced to invest a large amount of money in antipollution measures beginning in the first half of the 1970s.

Naphtha, the basic material for petrochemicals in Japan and Europe (ethane was the basic material in the United States and Canada, and in Middle Eastern countries), was less lucrative than other petroleum products like gasoline, heavy oil, or light oil. There were always disputes over quantities and prices between ethylene manufacturers and oil refiners, the suppliers of naphtha.

The first ethylene cartel was authorized in April 1971. Thus, the petrochemical industry had reached the first stage of maturity before the oil crisis arose. The industry was referred to as a child of administrative advice because of the way it formed cartels very frequently after April 1971.

The Industrial Machinery Industry

The importance of raising Japan's industrial structure to that of a more advanced economy, or of basing export industries more on the heavy or chemical industries, had already been widely understood by 1964. Consequently, new industries such as petrochemicals, synthetic fibers, automobiles, or electrical appliances emerged. Even the iron and steel industry, a conventional one, invested heavily in the enlargement of blast furnaces and automation of the rolling process. These developments spurred on plant investments for technological innovation, and this, in turn, allowed the industrial machinery industry to enter an era of expansion. The industry, however, was not on a par with its counterparts in advanced Western countries, nor had it reached a technological level that was able to satisfy even domestic customers. Many manufacturers in this industry, therefore, competed in bringing in overseas technologies.

The rate of Japan's economic growth in 1968 exceeded 10 percent per year, and the gross national product rose to second place in the free world, surpassing that of West Germany. The amount of industrial machinery produced by Japan also ranked second in the world.

Machine Tools

When it came to performance, imported machine tools had always been better than domestic products. The introduction of numerically controlled (NC) machine tools, however, put the domestic machine tool industry into gear. Japan learned of NC-type machine tools from the United States and took the lead in their mass production. Confidence in their ability to do well in producing practical appliances enabled Japan's machine tool makers to try to compete against leading manufacturers in the United States and Europe. NC-type machine tools brought to Japanese industry the benefits of automated factories and a mechatronic industry. The proportion of NC-type machine tools in total machine tool production was 7.8 percent in 1970, but this rose to 17.3 percent in 1975. Meanwhile, penetration of the U.S. market commenced (Takamura and Koyama 1994 [vol. 3]: 93).

Construction Machines

The postwar growth in the construction machine industry started from dismantling and learning everything about machines disposed of by the U.S. Occupation Forces. Technical cooperation was a frequent occurrence, too. With the building of dams to produce electrical power, one of the priorities in the early postwar period, the performances and power of Japanese construction machinery began to rise. For large-scale dams such as Sakuma or Kuroyon, bulldozers, dump trucks, and power shovels were introduced. Human-powered works, common in prewar days, disappeared, and engineering works rapidly became mechanized. This mechanization initially depended overwhelmingly on imported machines, which were superior in quality to domestic machines. But then Japanese construction machinery improved remarkably in quality through technical cooperation deals, and, in a short time, they equaled imported ones in quality. This made it possible to undertake large engineering and construction projects, which, in turn, supported rapid economic growth. The following are some examples of such big projects:

• an expressway between Nagoya and Kobe, completed in 1963, the first asphaltic pavement in Japan;
• the building of Housing Corporation apartment houses all over the country;
• facilities for the Tokyo Olympics;
• the construction of the Tokaido Shinkansen (bullet trains);
• the construction of subway networks established in big cities;
• Kasumigaseki Building, the first skyscraper in Japan.

In each of these projects innovation occurred in construction machine production, from which new architectural technology was learned and accumulated in Japan (JSIMM, 1998:71).

The Electric Machine Industry

Heavy Electric Equipment

During the period of high economic growth triggered by the income doubling plan of the Ikeda government, the heavy and the chemical industries grew considerably in importance in the economy. This trend encouraged a demand for electric power, with the result that there was a sharp rise in demand for heavy electric equipment.

The development of power resources during this period was characterized by a switch in the major power source from water (hydroelectric power generation) to heat (thermal power generation). The demand for power during the latter half of the 1960s grew at an average annual rate of 13 percent, and a succession of thermal power plants with 30 MW unit capacities was built. The first supercritical pressure was achieved in Japan in 1968.

As power resources developed, demand for super-high-tension transmission facilities increased rapidly, and there was a remarkable increase in the production of related equipment. The biggest change in the heavy electric industry in Japan during this period was the establishment of nuclear power generation. Following in the footsteps of the Japan Atomic Power Co., which was run in line with national policy and commenced commercial power supply at its Tokai Power Plant in 1965, two private companies, Kansai Electric Power Co. and Tokyo Electric Power Co., started to build nuclear power plants.

If we look at other industrial uses, we find that production of rolling mills for the steel industry increased, as did production of electrolyzing equipment and refining facilities for the nonferrous metal industry, and of motors and control devices for petrochemical plants (*Nihon kogyo nenkan*: 659; Takamura and Koyama 1994 [vol. 3]: 67–70).

Electrical Appliances

Electrical appliances came into widespread use for a variety of reasons, among them being a rise in per capita national income, a change in lifestyles or modes of thought, and the flow of population from rural areas to cities. It was a time when the Western lifestyle was thought to be a most desirable goal.

In 1964, however, falls in retail prices aggravated business conditions for manufacturers and retailers. It was color televisions that saved the industry from this slump. Once color telecasts could be picked up all over Japan in 1966, color televisions rapidly became popular. The number of color television sets surpassed that of black-and-white televisions in 1973, and, for some time, a color television, an automobile, and an air conditioner constituted "the three Cs" (see chapter 4).

Rapid economic growth raised the level of affluence in society, while, at the same time, it caused imbalances in the economy, such as pollution. The two-tier pricing system of color televisions was a symbol of the imbalance. The system received so much harsh criticism that it developed into a boycott of Matsushita Electric products. The issue was settled when manufacturers yielded. The price control of electrical appliances by the manufacturers was resisted not only by consumers but also by supermarkets. Such a development led to large-scale retail stores increasing their power over manufacturers.

Increasing trade disputes were another issue. Japan's electrical appliance manufacturers, which had become export-competitive in terms both of quality and of price in the 1960s, rapidly increased exports to the United States and Europe. In 1970 the U.S. Treasury Department decided that the export prices of color televisions were violating the Anti-Dumping Act, and in European countries the inclination to wield official control over import quantity became conspicuous. In order to avoid trade disputes, manufacturers of electrical appliances expanded overseas production at an increasing pace, including production bases built in Asian NIEs and in Southeast Asia. Overseas operations were further accelerated after the upward valuation of the yen as a result of the dollar defense policy launched by President Nixon in 1971. Thus, manufacturers of electrical appliances expanded their production networks across the world, becoming the spearhead of globalizing Japanese enterprises (Takamura and Koyama [vol. 2] 1994: 68).

General Trading Companies

Restructuring of the trading industry went on in the midst of Japan's economic growth during the fifteen years from 1954, when Mitsubishi Corporation finished reunifying the many small trading companies into which the prewar Mitsubishi Corp. had been divided after the end of the war, to 1968, when Nissho Trading Company and Iwai Sangyo merged into Nissho-Iwai Co., Ltd. The restructuring created ten Sogo Shosha (general trading companies, hereafter referred to as "GTCs") through mergers and acquisitions, in contrast to the mere two that had existed in the prewar days: Mitsubishi Corp. and Mitsui and Co. The ten were Mitsubishi, Mitsui, C. Itoh, Marubeni, Sumitomo Corp., Nissho-Iwai, Tomen, Kanematsu, Nichimen, and Ataka, which was merged into C. Itoh in 1977 (Asuka 1998: 33–34, and Shimada 1991: 151).

The factor that played the key role in the restructuring (mergers and acquisitions) process was the iron and steel business: mergers were made for better business relationships with the iron and steel manufacturers. Trading companies having business relations with iron and steel makers were pivotal in the restructuring. The iron and steel industry was one of the most important key industries, and its products were regarded by trading houses as strategic merchandise at a time when Japan's economy was expected to be based increasingly on the heavy and chemical industries. The merger of Nissho and Iwai was referred to as a "marriage between iron and iron" (Shimada 1991: 154). The later growth of GTCs turned out to be determined by how strong a company was in the iron and steel business (Shimada 1991: 115–24, 153–59).

Transition to an open economy occurred concurrently with the restructuring. The government was positive toward the liberalization of trade and exchange. Trade was liberalized, from 40 percent in 1960 up to 93 percent in 1965 (with the liberalization of passenger cars in October), when the issue was settled for the time being. A year earlier Japan had become a member of the Organization for Economic Cooperation and Development (OECD) and reclassified as an International Monetary Fund (IMF) Article 8 nation (chapter 4; Shimada 1991: 132–33).

The driving forces behind the high economic growth were technological innovation (and consequent investments in facilities) and mass consumption. Exports, backed by a changing industrial structure in which the heavy and chemical industries were becoming key industries, increased remarkably and contributed substantially to growth. During the postwar recovery period, Japan's economic growth was restricted by trade balance deficits, so that promotion of exports had been one of the most important economic policies of the government. After 1965 the trade balance continuously registered a surplus (chapter 4; Miwa 1993: 190–93; Shimada 1991: 133–34).

Under these circumstances, GTCs contributed to economic growth by making good use of their business functions, such as the development of overseas export markets and the mass importing of raw materials, and they expanded their businesses remarkably. At the beginning of the period in question, the opinion was voiced that GTCs were a declining or useless industry because manufacturers themselves would gradually engage in the export and import business. GTCs made strenuous efforts to cope with their seemingly unfavorable business environment; these included strengthening information-related activities, developing new markets (e.g., bowling), expanding their financial function, and investing in future businesses. The earlier opinion was proved wrong (Kawahara and Hayashikawa 1999: 47–48; Shimada 1991: 144–50).

Through this experience GTCs acquired an excellent coordinating ability, brought about by consolidating their variety of functions. This ability enabled GTCs to take a leading role in the entry of industrial groups (like Mitsubishi or Mitsui) into new industries such as petrochemicals or a nuclear-energy-related industry. Take the industrialization of petrochemicals, for instance. In the preparatory stage, a GTC worked for the introduction of overseas technology and the acquisition of a plant. Once the plant commenced operations, the same GTC endeavored to develop export markets and also sold the products on the domestic market (Shimada 1991: 159–63).

Their function as coordinators opened up new fields of business activities for GTCs, namely, the development of overseas resources and large-scale plant exports, areas in which they were fully involved from the early 1970s on (Table 5.5). During the period of high economic growth, the rapid increase in the amount of raw materials consumed resulted in big jumps in imports of them. It became important to secure feedstocks.

It was becoming increasingly difficult to secure raw materials, however, first, because resource protectionism was growing stronger in resource-rich countries, and second, because feedstock markets were seller's markets because of the industrialized nations' rush for raw materials. Here the *development-and-import formula* was devised to benefit resource-rich countries while securing for Japan a long-term supply of raw materials. A joint venture was usually formed to carry out some resource development project in which a GTC participated as a coordinator. A few examples of successful projects in which GTCs participated are the following: Liquefied Natural Gas (LNG), Brunei/Indonesia— Mitsubishi Corporation; iron ore deposits, Mt. Newman/Australia—Mitsui and Co. and C. Itoh; and copper ore deposits, Bougainville/Papua New Guinea— Mitsui and Co. and Mitsubishi Corporation (Shimada 1991: 163, 175–82).

Table 5.5

Amounts of Major Imported Raw Materials

Raw materials	1965 (A)	1970 (B)	(B)/(A)	Degree of dependence on imports 1970
Petroleum	84,143 thousand kiloliters	197,108	2.3 times	99.7
Coal	17,080 thousand metric tons	50,173	2.9	78.5
Iron ore	39,018 thousand metric tons	102,091	2.6	87.9
Nonferrous metal ores	5,421 thousand metric tons	15,585	2.9	N/A
copper				75.6
lead				54.6
zinc				54.5
nickel				100.0
aluminum				100.0

Source: Katsumi Shimada, *Shosha—Sangyo no showa shakai-shi* [Trading Companies—Social History of the Showa Era's Industry] (Tokyo: Nihon keizai hyoronsha, 1991), p. 176.

The 1970s saw the emergence of many environmental pollution issues, one after another. A tide of criticism of big businesses spread across the nation. In 1971 and 1972 excess liquidity resulted from Tokyo Gnomes' sales of dollars after Nixon's announcement of his dollar defense policy, a substantial surplus in the balance of payments, and monetary relaxation. In July 1972, Kakuei Tanaka formed a cabinet whose policy was to remodel the Japanese archipelago. Large enterprises used surplus funds for land speculation. Thus, rising consumer prices and land speculation reigned over Japan from 1972 to 1973. It was the GTCs that bore the brunt of all the criticism as being the causes of all the evils society experienced (Shimada 1991: 195–99).

The Banking Industry

The following are the three characteristics of postwar Japan's financial market and financial system (Enkyo 1995: 85–94; Kaizuka and Ueda 1994: 34–44):

(1) bank loans were by far the main source of financing (the financial market and the capital market). Under such a financing system, enterprises

with insufficient capital accumulation depended too much on borrowing (the overborrowing phenomenon);

(2) banks (especially city banks) were always in a position of overlending;

(3) the government's financial policy was aimed at low interest rates and money allocation.

This system, applied to reconstruction of the postwar economy, was similar to the system that had been used during the war in order to concentrate money on the munitions industry (Enkyo 1995: 83–84). In a situation in which the entire postwar economy suffered from a shortage of funds, the most important economic issue was to supply money in a stable fashion to those industrial sectors that were deemed indispensable to economic reconstruction.

Specifically, the following policies were carried out:

1. Financial institutions were classified into different categories, with each category specializing in a specific function (Enkyo 1995: 87).

First, government financial institutions were founded, including the Japan Development Bank (in 1951) and the Export-Import Bank of Japan (in 1951). The Long-Term Credit Bank Law took effect in 1952; it strengthened the function of long-term credit banks such as the Industrial Bank of Japan. They, and trust banks, for example, Mitsui Trust, Mitsubishi Trust, and Sumitomo Trust, were classified as long-term financial institutions. This ensured a stable supply of long-term funds to industry.

Second, for international businesses, a Foreign Exchange Bank Law became effective in 1954; it categorized the Bank of Tokyo and other authorized foreign exchange banks as financial institutions specializing in foreign exchange business.

Third, working funds were to be supplied by financial institutions other than those mentioned above, with major commercial banks (city banks) being the key players.

Fourth, four key industries (electric power, coal mining, iron and steel, and shipbuilding) and export-related enterprises were prioritized in money allocations.

2. The Overlending Policy.

The demand for funds for key industries or exporting enterprises centered on city banks. They did not have sufficient deposits or capital of their own to meet the demand, so the deficit was financed first by borrowing surplus funds from other financial institutions like regional banks, and ultimately by borrowing from the Bank of Japan (the overlending phenomenon). For funds for foreign trade, various types of trade financing backed by the government were available, as, for example, the Bank of Japan's rediscounting of trade bills.

Overlending, which was quite an extraordinary financial condition, was possible because the government and financial institutions formed a harmonious whole in running the financial system.

3. The Low Interest Policy.

As seen above, the financial system stressed the supply side of money. What was noteworthy at the same time was that funds were supplied at comparatively low interest rates. In other words, financial institutions were in a managerial environment such that a profit was guaranteed even if they loaned to others at low interest (Enkyo 1995: 89).

Specifically: First, the system was devised to restrict competition among financial institutions. Financial functions were diversified into different categories and each institution was restricted to one category. Every expansion of a branch network or new entry into the financial industry was regulated. The domestic and international financial markets were separated from each other. Second, the Ministry of Finance and the Bank of Japan assigned a credit limit to each bank through their "window guidance" and thus controlled the total amount of credit given by all the banks. Third, there was a ceiling on interest rates. Banks' lending rates were linked to and moved together with the Bank of Japan's official discount rate. Fourth, each financial institution was under the strict control of the Ministry of Finance concerning financial reports. The Ministry gave recommendations or directions on financial ratios and accounting (Enkyo 1995: 92–93).

4. Finally, the "convoy system" was adopted. This system aimed at preventing banks from collapsing and also at preventing the occurrence of credit uncertainty (Enkyo 1995: 93).

In Japan's postwar economy, where capital or wealth was in short supply, such a financial system was an effective tool for economic reconstruction and the high economic growth that followed.

Besides the key industries, new industrial sectors that enthusiastically introduced overseas technologies gained power as mass-producers. These were the manufacturers of durable consumer goods, exemplified by electric appliances such as television sets, refrigerators, and washing machines, and by automobiles. Synthetic fiber manufacturing was one of these industries. Banks were as willing to loan money to these manufacturers as they were to loan to the key industries. Banks likewise supplied money to the subcontractors (suppliers of parts) of these manufacturers in the form of bill discounting (trade bills included). An indirect loan route, in which trading companies lent to such subcontractors money they had borrowed from banks, was also available. Only a financial system such as this, peculiar to Japan, could have met such a rapidly growing demand for money.

In the midst of the shift in Japan to an open economy (seen in the fact that Japan was admitted to the OECD in 1964 and that its status in the IMF changed to an Article 8 nation in the same year), the Ministry of Finance was beginning to consider financial liberalization. It launched a series of measures relaxing restrictions on banks such as the restrictions on dividends to be paid or on real estate acquired. Banks, for their part, were beginning to think of scaling up or improving efficiency. Such developments resulted in mergers between Daiichi Bank and Nippon Kangyo Bank in 1971 (creating Daiichi Kangyo Bank), and between Kobe Bank and Taiyo Bank in 1973 (creating Taiyo Kobe Bank).

The Air Transport Industry

At the beginning of the high economic growth period the major carriers in Japan were still overseas airlines such as PAA, Northwest, BOAC, and Air France. Japan Air Lines (JAL), Japan's national flag carrier, was still a minor carrier and was experiencing hard times, since passengers preferred overseas airlines to JAL.

As the economy continued to grow rapidly, diversification and luxury came to be expected from means of traffic, and demand for air transportation increased rapidly. JAL adapted itself positively to this changing demand. Between 1961 and 1970 it inaugurated one international route after another and established a network linking the world's major cities. In 1967 it fulfilled its dream of establishing around-the-world air routes. In 1970 it introduced Boeing 747 jumbo jets after five years of preparations, during which time Japanese flight crews were trained. The jumbo jet flights raised people's opinion of JAL's safety and comfort standards.

On the domestic scene, Okinawa was returned in 1964, and the flights to and from Okinawa, previously international flights, became domestic ones. There was a rapid increase in the number of passengers using this new domestic line. The Tokyo Olympics, held in 1964, encouraged people to replace conventional and old things with new and modern things. By 1969 JAL had advanced to the ranking of sixth place among the world's private airlines, from thirteenth place in 1961. It successfully carried out its mission as the national flag carrier, flying special planes for VIPs such as the Emperor and Empress when they visited Europe in 1971, the Crown Prince and Princess, prime ministers, and the Pope (Japan Airlines 1985: 29).

The government set the following basic policy for air transportation in 1970 and 1972: (1) the promotion of a switch from propeller-driven airplanes to jet planes, and the upsizing of planes; and (2) the sharing of air transportation by three airlines: JAL—domestic trunk-line flights and international flights; international air cargoes; All Nippon Airways—domestic trunk-line and local-line flights; chartered international flights for short distances; Toa Domestic Airlines (formed by the merger of Japan Domestic Airlines and Toa Airlines in 1971)—domestic local-line flights. This policy lasted until 1987.

The economies of industrialized countries fell into recession in the 1970s. The dollar defense policy launched by U.S. President Nixon in summer 1971 threw the world economy into a state of instability. The demand for air transport slackened. In 1972 an oversupply in air transport surfaced on a global scale. IATA was enforcing its airfare tariff scheme, while the chartered flights of non-IATA carriers took a 32 percent share of the total international air transport market by offering lower prices. This expanded the supply-demand gap. There was no end to airfare competition: various types of discounted fares were offered, and the profits of airline companies deteriorated (Japan Airlines 1985: 114).

The Beer Industry: Distribution

The demand for beer grew constantly in this period. In 1959 beer consumption surpassed that of "sake," which had long held the largest share of the alcoholic beverage market. The margin widened thereafter. In 1962 beer held 50 percent of the market of all alcoholic beverages. Beer had definitely taken root as a popular beverage. Kirin Brewery Company expanded its share in the beer market, topping 50 percent in 1966. It frequently assigned its agencies the quantities to be sold. Sapporo Breweries and Asahi Breweries competed fiercely with each other in sales to restaurants or other places in which beer can be consumed (hereafter the "service-industry-related market").

A brewer's marketing strategy was to expand its share through maintenance of its own distribution channel. A brewer benefited very much from an increase in share; besides the general competitive edge that it gave over rivals, it also improved profits by lowering the break-even point and enabled the brewer to build another brewery. (Building a brewery was the best sales ploy as far as the area where the brewery was to be built was concerned.) And breweries scattered all over the country meant a lower distribution cost.

Kirin began in 1966 to tackle the rationalization of physical distribution between breweries and agencies. It took advantage of its expanding share and successfully completed rationalization before the oil crisis. In its rationalization Kirin palletized beer from the breweries to the agencies by heavy-duty trucks. To cope with this mass transportation, it urged its agencies to introduce forklift trucks and to move to the outskirts of cities in order to have more working space. The recommendations were accepted by most agencies. The distribution from agencies to retail shops, however, is still labor-intensive and remains to be rationalized (Kirin 1969: 277).

The main products were still bottled beer and draft beer (served in restaurants). Canned beer was sold only in train stations, sightseeing spots, and the like.

Sales activities stressed the maintenance of affiliated distribution channels through agencies. The brewers organized their sales divisions by districts. A sales staff's job was to request affiliated agencies to promote sales. Sales people themselves often visited retail shops for sales promotion in big cities or in branch-located cities, but they did little more than say hello. Restaurants, bars, department stores, hotels, railway-related places/shops, and so forth (the service-industry-related market) were clients that required separate sales activities.

Food and beverage markets during this period were more or less a seller's market. Still, keen competition commenced among food manufacturers to develop the service industry related market. This was also true of the brewers. Distribution channels, meanwhile, remained in the firm grip of the gigantic brewers, while some agencies, ranging from large ones with nationwide networks to major local ones, made remarkable increases in sales and established strong business foundations (Miyashita 1997: 100).

Department Stores

Department stores, which were quick to recover after the war, enjoyed a rapid growth in sales. Their sales rose 2.42 times during the five years from 1969 to 1973, or approximately 19.3 percent average growth per year; this was larger than the 15.7 percent average growth for all retailers' sales during the same period. Their share of sales in the total retail industry set a record of 9.1 percent in 1973, the largest ever in postwar times, and a record that still remains to be broken. In this period. department stores had larger sales than supermarkets and dominated over other types of retail business on both the business area level and the store level (Table 5.6).

Supermarkets, which started growing in the 1960s, adopted a low-pricing policy based on self-service and opened chain stores aggressively. Their average rate of growth in sales was approximately 30.8 percent per year, higher than that of department stores. In 1972 Daiei, the largest chain operator, outstripped Mitsukoshi, the largest department store, in sales; in 1973, when the rapid economic growth came to an end, the margin in market share between supermarkets and department stores had narrowed to 0.9 percent. The next year the chain stores surpassed the department stores in sales. In the period of high economic growth department stores were at the top of the retail industry, yet toward the end of the period that position was in jeopardy (Koyama 1997: 63).

Table 5.6

Growth of Sales by Style of Business

Year	Growth of sales (%)			Consumption elasticity		Share of nationwide retail market (%)	
	Dept. stores	Super-markets	Retailers overall	Dept. stores	Super-markets	Dept. stores	Super-markets
1968 (base)	100.0	100.0	100.0	—	—	7.8	4.4
1969	117.9	121.0	116.0	1.02	1.04	7.9	4.6
1970	142.1	164.3	131.9	1.06	1.19	8.4	5.5
1971	165.2	214.7	151.6	1.01	1.14	8.5	6.3
1972	196.8	280.0	171.4	1.05	1.15	8.9	7.3
1973	242.1	383.6	207.8	1.01	1.13	9.1	8.2
Average annual growth	19.3	30.8	15.7	—	—	—	—

Sources: Adapted from Japan Department Stores Association, *Sales Statistics* (annual); Japan Chain Stores Association, *Sales Statistics* (annual); and Ministry of International Trade and Industry (MITI) *Census of Commerce* (annual).

While old department stores recovered quickly to keep pace with the post-war economic reconstruction, new department stores were opened by railway companies in their train terminals. Shopping in department stores was a status symbol to consumers, who in line with the rise in their income, tried to copy American affluence. In response to customer expectations, department stores, adopting the traditional idea that "the customer is always right," stressed "customer satisfaction" in daily business and surpassed other categories of retailers in both face-to-face sales in stores and in direct sales (to big-order customers), with seasonal gifts as their stock in trade. With convenient locations and merchandise lines ahead of the times, such as prêt-à-porter, department stores led the retail industry in both quantity (sales) and quality (merchandise) in this period.

Department stores continued their prewar business practice in regard to payments for ordered merchandise. Payment was not made on a delivery basis, but on a sales (to customers) basis. Fashionable goods, such as garments, were regarded as "purchased" when they were sold to customers. Department stores paid their suppliers only for goods thus sold. Goods left unsold were returned to suppliers. Goods with frequent turnover, such as foods, were sold in the department stores by the suppliers' own salespeople. Department stores charged a rent that was a certain portion of sales. Both in the case of fashionable goods and in the case of frequent-turnover goods, the burden of inventory fell on the suppliers.

The advantage in this system lay in the department store being free from the risk of goods left unsold, while making it easier for the department store to have an abundance of goods in the store and to vary the goods in keeping with the season. This gave the impression that the store was right up to date and on the move all the time. The disadvantage was low profitability on the department store side, because suppliers, who had the power to decide prices, added to the delivery price the related costs of returned goods. The transfer of inventory risk to the suppliers also impeded the merchandising function of the department store. Moreover, the FTC had frequent need to investigate unfair trading practices connected with traditional business practices and often warned department stores to correct their ways. Such old practices have, however, basically survived until the present day, so that FTC warnings and Japan Department Stores Association agreements to exercise self-regulation are a regular occurrence (Koyama 1997: 144).

Building Materials: Distribution

A good supply of housing was an urgent requirement in Japan when it was in the process of recovery from wartime devastation. The housing shortage was still in existence in the period of high economic growth, and this created strong demand. As shown in Table 5.7, housing starts recorded an average growth of 11.3 percent per year during the period. This growth rate is higher than those of later periods; 1.9 million houses in 1973 is a record for annual housing starts that still stands.

Houses are made of wood and other building materials. Plywood is the most widely used building material; it is used for ceilings, partitions, preparatory work, prefabricated houses, and the like. For this reason, the country imported timber and processed it into plywood.

Until the mid-1960s Japan largely depended on the Philippines for timber, or "South Sea logs," which were mostly lauan. Of the imported South Sea logs, 93.3 percent came from the Philippines in 1950, about the time a movement for conservation of resources started growing there. Gradually the Philippine share of imported South Sea logs fell, reaching only 60.5 percent in 1965, but still far ahead of other sources.

Beginning in 1965, the South Sea timber-related businesses gave up on the Philippines as their main supplier and sought to diversify sources. Indo-

Table 5.7

Housing Starts

Year	Number of houses	Year-on-year change (%)
1962 (base year)	586,122	100.0
1963	688,743	117.5
1964	751,429	109.1
1965	842,596	112.1
1966	856,579	101.7
1967	991,158	115.7
1968	1,201,675	121.2
1969	1,346,612	112.1
1970	1,484,556	110.2
1971	1,463,760	98.6
1972	1,807,581	123.5
1973	1,905,112	105.4
Average year-on-year change		111.3

Source: Ministry of Construction, *Housing Statistics* (annual).

Table 5. 8

Share of Imported South Sea Logs (as percent)

Year	Philip-pines	Indo-nesia	Malaysia Subtotal	Sabah	Sara-wak	West Malaysia	Others	Total
1950	93.3	0.0	6.7	6.7	0.0	0.0	0.0	100.00
1955	91.2	0.9	7.9	7.9	0.0	0.0	0.0	100.00
1960	74.2	0.4	24.5	21.9	2.1	0.4	0.9	100.00
1965	60.5	1.1	37.3	30.2	6.9	0.2	1.1	100.00
1970	37.1	30.1	29.7	19.6	9.3	0.9	2.9	100.00
1971	28.1	40.4	28.4	20.4	7.3	0.7	3.1	100.00
1972	23.6	41.3	31.6	24.9	6.3	0.4	3.4	100.00
1973	22.0	41.9	32.3	27.3	4.7	0.4	3.8	100.00

Source: Japan South Sea Timber Council, *Chronological Data on Imported Logs* (annual).

nesia surfaced as a major source. Japan had imported logs from Indonesia in prewar days, but then stayed clear of it for many years, primarily because of its long-standing conflict with the Netherlands after gaining independence. In 1970, imports from Indonesia grew substantially. As shown in Table 5.8, Indonesia became the top supplier in 1971 with 40.4 percent. The Philippine share steadily declined.

In this way, postwar housing starts rose continuously, symbolizing the high economic growth. As part of one of the housing-related industries, the distributors of building materials, plywood in particular, were blessed with an enormous amount of business that was within their capacity to handle, and they enjoyed large profits.

6

Career Entry

In accordance with Edgar Schein's (1978) concept of "stages of career cycle," the career histories of our thirty-six alumni may be divided into three stages: early, middle, and late. The early career stage consists of exploration and trial substages. The mid-career stage consists of stabilization and mid-career crisis substages. The late career stage consists of maintenance and decline substages. These three stages roughly correspond to the four distinct periods in the development of the Japanese economy. As shown in Table 6.1, the mid-career stage covers two subperiods, 1974–80 and 1981–90.

As stated in Chapter 2, one of Schein's propositions is that career anchors are created over a period of ten to twelve years after graduation, or by the end of the early career stage shown in Table 6.1. This chapter will examine the process of career entry of the thirty-six study participants. Chapter 7, which follows, will examine how career anchors were created during the first subperiod (1962–73).

All six female students and twenty-eight of the thirty male students graduated from the university in 1962. Two male students went to the United States in their senior year to study at Stanford University as exchange students for one year, after which they returned to Japan and completed their undergraduate study in 1963. Two female students studied at the same university for three summer months as exchange students. The lifestyle of the American students and the people in general was so different from that of Japanese people that it left a lasting impact on the four twenty-year-old students. One female student recalls, "The lifestyle of women in the United States thirty-five years ago was positive and flexible. Their attitude of accepting people for who they are and the Christian concept that it is more blessed to give than to receive are still the basis of my attitude toward life."

Table 6.1

Career Stages and Stages of Economic Development

Career stage	Period	Key features in Japanese economy
Early	1962–73	High economic growth
Middle	1974–80	Successful adjustment to oil crises
	1981–90	Prosperity leading to a bubble economy
Late	1991–99	Post-bubble stagnation

Of the twenty-eight male students who graduated in 1962, one stayed with the university to do graduate study with a view to becoming an academic, while all others obtained a job and started to work. All but one entered large corporations whose stocks were traded on the Tokyo Stock Exchange, the single exception being someone who joined a small family business that had been founded by his uncle. Of the two male students who graduated in 1963 after one year's study in the United States, one joined a large manufacturing company, while the other stayed with the university to do graduate study.

Of the six female students, four obtained a job. The two students who spent three summer months in the United States were included in this category. In fact, one had started working while still at school and continued to work for the same employer after graduation. The other took a job with a foreign firm as an assistant secretary. The third female student was employed by a major electric appliance company, while the fourth worked as a part-time reporter for a major newspaper. Of the remaining two, one went to the United States to study at the University of Washington for a year. Upon her return to Japan in 1963 she began working for her father, who owned a lumber import company. The sixth student married before graduation and after graduation remained a full-time housewife. Table 6.2 summarizes the patterns of initial career decisions of the thirty-six participants as of April 1962.

In the table, "manufacturing" covers a variety of industries, including the textile, chemical, petroleum/petrochemical, steel, construction machinery, electrical machinery, and foodstuff industries. "Trading" includes general trading companies, a department store, and a wholesaler of construction-related materials. The "finance/insurance" category includes two banks and a marine insurance company. "Transportation" represents a major airline company.

As mentioned in the Prologue, the labor market was quickly changing

Table 6.2

Initial Career Decisions of Thirty-six Participants (1962)

Career decision	Number of participants
Males, total	30
Employment with corporations	27
manufacturing	14
trading	8
finance/insurance	3
transportation	2
Graduate work	1
Study abroad	2
Females, total	6
Employment with corporations	4
full-time	3
part-time	1
Study abroad	1
Marriage	1
Total	36

from a buyer's to a seller's market due to the rapid growth of the Japanese economy. And our alumni had a relatively easy time finding a job of their choice. In those days, large companies followed the traditional Japanese practice of hiring only newly graduated students who would begin employment beginning on April 1 every year. Recruitment and screening of university students took place in the spring through summer of the previous year. Some companies sent representatives to the campuses of major universities to advertise their job openings, although campus recruitment as such was not conducted. More aggressive companies approached professors to recommend their seminar students. On the whole, though, it was students who took the initiative and approached companies.

Generally speaking, the methods of screening job applicants differed between banks and general trading companies, on the one hand, and manufacturing companies, on the other. In the former case, applicants were first screened in terms of the prestige of the universities they were attending. Major corporations had a list of "designated schools" that consisted of half a dozen or so national and private universities, including Keio University. Students from universities not on the list were simply turned down unless a student had a "connection" or someone who would recommend him to the prospective employer. Second, an applicant's GPA up to the third year was examined. Banks had the highest cut-off level, followed by general trading companies. Finally, an interview or two would be conducted by personnel managers and/or senior executives, sometimes including the president.

In the case of manufacturing companies, different methods were used for science/engineering majors and for business/social science majors. The hiring of science/engineering majors was conducted on the basis of recommendations of graduating students known by seminar professors with whom the company enjoyed close relationships. The "designated school" system was not closely adhered to, so that students were hired from a number of universities throughout Japan.

For business/social science majors, too, the general practice was to make opportunities available to all students regardless of the university they were attending. In the case of very prestigious and therefore popular companies, the "connection" was used as a screening device to reduce the number of potential applicants to a manageable figure. The GPA was not given serious consideration because the applicants came from a number of different universities, thus creating the problem of comparability. Instead, a written test was given, usually consisting of one part on the applicant's area of study (e.g., business, economics, political science, or law) and one part on English. Finally, an interview or two would be conducted.

With respect to the recruitment and screening processes one alumnus recalls, "In fact, this company [the trust bank] was my number three choice, after a brewing company and a general trading company. In the meantime, my seminar professor had been asked to recommend a student to this company, and the professor chose me." An interview, which was more or less a matter of formality, was conducted by the general manager of the bank's Tokyo branch. The student was given a job offer before the summer break. He accepted the offer because the companies that were his first and second choices were not ready to start screening.

Another member started visiting companies in May with his friends from the Keio English Speaking Society. At the first company he visited (an electric machine manufacturer), an offer was made on the spot. As he was interested in exploring other opportunities, he did not take it. He continues:

> One day I visited a building that housed the headquarters of several companies that belonged to one of the former *zaibatsu* groups. At one of the companies [a general trading company] the personnel officer I talked to happened to be a person I used to know from my high school days. As he

strongly urged me to apply for the company, I agreed to do so. The following day I was interviewed by the general manager of the Personnel Office, and shortly thereafter by the president. Right after the interviews, I was told that an offer would be made provided I was ready to accept it. As I was no longer interested in continuing with company visits, I decided to accept it.

The other two dozen or so male alumni had more or less similar experiences. All of them landed the jobs (or the companies) they had hoped to land. In fact, several of them spent an agonizing summer torn between equally attractive job offers. The successful job hunts on the part of our alumni were due to a combination of several factors: the prestige of the university, above-average GPA results, and English proficiency, in addition to the favorable labor market conditions.

All together, twenty-two companies hired our twenty-seven male alumni in 1962. The number of university graduates who were hired by these companies through "regular hiring" to begin from April 1 ranged between one (the wholesaler of construction-related materials) to approximately 300 (electric machine manufacturers). Generally speaking, manufacturing companies hired more engineers and scientists than business and social science majors, while financial institutions and general trading companies hired very few scientists and engineers, if any. If we look only at business and social science majors, we find that general trading companies hired, on average, the largest number (200–250), followed by manufacturing companies, which hired between 40 and 120, depending on the size of the company. The financial institutions hired the smallest numbers (between 20 and 40).

Two of the twenty-two companies hired not only for themselves but also for their subsidiaries (one in the petrochemical and the other in the electronics industries), because these industries were largely unknown and not popular, so that the subsidiaries themselves were unable to attract a sufficient number of superior university graduates. In two other cases, special divisions did the recruiting and screening, besides centralized hiring by the headquarters. One company (an electric machinery manufacturer) needed people with special skills and motivation for its rapidly expanding overseas business division, while the other company (a general trading company) needed, for political reasons, to recruit separately for one of its divisions (legally a separate entity) engaged in doing business with the Soviet-bloc nations. Unlike these Japanese counterparts, a U.S.-owned petroleum company hired a large number of people with prior job experience, and only a relatively small number of newly graduated university students.

These favorable market conditions did not exist for female students. Virtually all Japanese companies, large and small, openly practiced gender-based job segregation, in that only male university students were hired into the management track. Females were largely hired to perform unskilled clerical jobs requiring high school or at most junior college education. University-educated female students were simply "overeducated" for those positions.

In exceptional cases, female students with specific qualifications or tangible skills were hired to perform specific duties. For example, female students with English skills were hired for jobs involving interpreting and translation. In addition, some foreign companies hired newly graduated female students with English skills to act as secretaries for foreign managers whose command of Japanese was usually low. Female job openings were advertised in daily newspapers. In some cases, recruitment was conducted through "connections."

As mentioned before, four of our six alumnae obtained a job—three full-time and one part-time. The experience of one alumna provides a typical example of the recruitment and screening of female students. She obtained a job as an assistant secretary in a foreign firm. This company advertised the opening in the *Japan Times* (an English-language daily newspaper), and she applied for it. She was first asked to write an essay in English. After successfully passing this screening, she was interviewed by the branch manager, who was British, and after this she was offered the job.

Such job segregation is clearly in violation of the equal employment legislation of today. In retrospect, however, gender-based role differentiation was widely endorsed even by women, and nobody seriously questioned the different practices in hiring women, although there was a grandmother clause in the Japanese Constitution prohibiting discrimination of all kinds, including one on the basis of gender. The year 1962 preceded by two years the enactment of the Civil Rights Act in the United States prohibiting, among other things, employment discrimination against women. In Japan, it was not until 1985 that similar legislation was put into effect.

The twenty-seven alumni who started to work for large corporations gave a variety of reasons for joining those corporations. Some of the typical explanations were as follows:

> I majored in international economics; therefore, I was interested in international trade. I chose this particular company because it was not too large and so there was a lot of freedom. (general trading company)

> For the simple reason that I wanted to work overseas as a member of a general trading company. (general trading company)

> Because the steel industry was rapidly growing, and this company was the leader in technological innovation. Good pay (¥23,000 per month) was another reason. (steel company)

As I thought that manufacturing was the foundation of an economy, I wanted to work for a manufacturing company. I chose this company on the recommendation of my seminar professor, who had been approached by the company to recommend some students. (electrical machine manufacturer)

Because my major was international trade, I was interested in working for a company involved in international business. The reason for choosing this particular company was that my uncle was a senior executive in it. (insurance company)

My hope then was to go to the United States in some capacity. One way was to obtain a scholarship to do graduate work at a U.S. university. I was told that working at the headquarters of a large manufacturing company would not be very demanding time-wise, so that there would be sufficient time to prepare for graduate work in the United States. (petrochemical company)

During my university days there were occasional lectures by business executives. I was most interested in the talk by a well-known president of a major chemical company. I chose the petrochemical industry as it was new and rapidly growing. I chose this particular company because it belonged to the same group of companies (in a former *zaibatsu*) as the one for which my father was working. (petrochemical company)

I was interested in working overseas, so I made a list of companies with a heavy emphasis on overseas operations. From among the companies on the list I chose the one that was stable and at the same time had high growth potential. (electrical machine manufacturer)

Because it was the company my father was working for. (general trading company)

No particular reason, except that high growth was expected in the new business this bank was starting. (trust bank)

Because this bank was specializing in overseas operations, which I thought would be a future growth area. (bank)

I thought that air transportation would be essential for the development of the Japanese economy. (airline company)

I just wanted to go abroad, and also I was interested in overseas transactions. (general trading company)

My father owned and managed a warehousing company specializing in marine products. I thought that working for the largest company in the industry would provide me with good experience for when I succeeded to my father's business. (fishing company)

A review of these answers reveals a common tendency among the alumni: a genuine interest in English, foreign countries (especially the United States), and international business activity. However, their career goals were still somewhat vague. This can be seen from their answers to the question, "What was your aspiration when you joined the company?" Here are some of the answers.

> I felt relieved that I landed a job after a period of searching. I did not have any aspiration. I had no idea about my future. (textile company)

> I wanted to become an international business person through my job in the airline industry. Besides, I wanted to have many friends and acquaintances abroad, so that I could contribute to cultural exchange between Japan and foreign countries. (airline company)

> I had an interest in exporting, an overseas assignment, and living in foreign countries. (textile company)

> I wanted to contribute to the development of the Japanese economy. (petrochemical company)

> I wanted to contribute to Japan's economic prosperity through exporting. (machine manufacturing company, ceramics manufacturing company, electrical machine manufacturing company)

> To become an indispensable figure within the company. I intended to stay with the company until mandatory retirement. (brewing company)

> I intended to succeed to my father's business eventually. (fishing company)

> I wanted to go abroad. As a result, I was exploring opportunities for an overseas assignment. (general trading company)

> To contribute to the growth of the company so that it would become a global airline. (airline company)

> To become competent in the job. (bank)

> To devote all my energies and abilities to the work. (trust bank)

> To become a global business person. (general trading company)

> To experience living abroad. (electrical machine manufacturing company)

> To become a senior officer of the company. (petrochemical company)

> I did not intend to stay with the company for a long time. Instead, I wanted to do some kind of work that has a big social impact. (petrochemical company)

> To contribute to the growth of the company and to become a senior executive through hard work. (petrochemical company)

To learn everything I could about my work, marry after I was twenty-eight years old, and become a family-oriented person while becoming a successful global business person. (general trading company)

I simply had a great yearning for foreign countries. (general trading company)

At this stage, only two of the thirty alumni had reasonably clear career goals. The alumnus who joined his uncle's business (a wholesaler of construction-related materials) had as his goal joining the top management of the company. To the question, "Why did you choose to join your uncle's company?" he answered:

Ever since I started to think about my career during my university days, I always felt that I was more or less destined to work for my uncle, helping him make the company bigger and stronger. I have never thought of starting my career as a junior employee in a large organization.

The goal of one of the two graduates who went on to graduate study was to become an academic. Asked why he decided to do graduate work, he answered:

In my junior year (1960) there was a major strike involving coal miners. A U.S. sociologist, who was a visiting professor at my university, organized a research team with my seminar professor and some other researchers to study the coal miners' strike. I joined the project as a research assistant. After that, I became very interested in sociological field study, and I decided to enroll in the graduate program to study further about sociological research.

Asked what his career aspiration was, he answered, "I wanted to pursue an academic goal."

Another graduate who enrolled in a graduate program after one year's study in the United States did not as yet have a clear-cut career goal, as can be seen from his remarks. He said that his experience at the U.S. university prompted him to do graduate work. Asked about his career aspirations, he answered, "I wanted to put myself in a position where I could guide the future direction of the Japanese economy. Also, I doubted that my personality was suited to working for a profit-seeking private corporation."

As for the six alumnae, none had a clear career goal as such when they left school in 1962. As mentioned before, one was already married and was a full-time housewife. According to her, "Marriage was arranged and forced upon me by my parents. I could not willingly accept it and I felt rather uncomfortable." Another alumna went to the United States for further study. She says, "Although I had a vague idea of getting a job that would take advantage of the English skills I acquired while in the United States, I was not confident enough to work as an English teacher. The remaining four alumnae got jobs, but none had a strong intention to make careers out of their jobs. One alumna said, "All I wanted was to obtain some real world experience through the job. Therefore, I intended to quit the job when I got married."

From the above descriptions, it is safe to say that our alumni and alumnae exhibited more or less the stereotypical Japanese pattern of career entry—high expectations for their initial employers on the part of male alumni and acceptance of gender-based role differentiation on the part of female alumnae.

7
Career Formulation

Education for the Newly Hired

In Japan, getting a job did not mean getting hired to perform a specific service. It meant, rather, being hired by a company as a lifetime employee. Though students were thought to have potential, they were not perceived to have strong job skills. For this reason, training the new employees was believed necessary. Normal practice was for the Company Entrance Ceremony to be held on April 1, during which the company president would instruct new employees on internal and external financial conditions, the state of affairs of the industry, and the mental attitude they would need as new members of the company. Newspapers ran articles (complete with photographs) on the admonitory address given by presidents of the most prestigious companies.

The Entrance Ceremony was followed by group education that lasted from several weeks to several months. The curriculum was often quite general, with company officials and division heads explaining the company's history and outlining its most important points. Through group education, the spirit of loving the company would be repeatedly brought up, pounding the concept into the fledgling employees' minds. Also, an "awareness of being a member of a group of recruits in the same year" grew and was continually and firmly maintained. Furthermore, while manufacturers would often conduct factory training, trading firms did not. After completing intensive training, the new employees assumed their assigned posts, at which time they were given on-the-job training (OJT) for the first time. In the case of manufacturers, this was often accompanied by factory training.

I spent two months getting training at the main company in Kobe, the Fukiai Plant (open-hearth furnace), and the Nishinomiya Plant (slitter line). During that time, I learned about purchasing materials, process supervision, and so on. (steel company)

For group education I underwent training at the Komatsu plant. My awareness of myself as being part of a particular group of contemporaneously hired employees grew. You do not see such a thing in other countries. (machine manufacturer)

We had two months of group education. On April 1, we went from Ueno to Hitachi on an especially reserved train. It felt like a collective work force. seven-hundred and eighty new employees assembled at the Shohei Kaikan in the city of Hitachi. We had one month of group education, and one month of plant training. I learned a lot about what happened in a plant. We all stayed in a dormitory and our seniors taught us relentlessly about the company spirit. (electrical machine manufacturer)

It lasted for three months all together; one month of general training and two months of plant training. For plant training, we were trained on the refrigerator assembly line for one and a half months and on the industrial motors assembly line for less than a month. (electrical machine manufacturer)

Group education lasted two months, during which time we got hands-on training by working on production lines at the main plant. We learned, for example, about such things as the manufacturing of transformers. As a clerical employee I found it a little annoying that all of our instructors preached "technology first" during group education. (electrical machine manufacturer)

We had one month of plant training and one month of business training. It was experiential education, and at the plant we worked on a three-shift rotation, while business training was conducted at a synthetic fabric production center (Hokuriku). Since there were not enough business staff, the company's intention at that time was apparently to quickly educate us and assign us to our official posts. (textile company)

I went through eight weeks of live-in group education. There were overall explanations of the company, required diary submissions, and so on. The last six weeks were for plant training. I got first-hand experience in working on rotating shifts at the Ehime plant. At night we went drinking in Matsuyama. It was a lot of fun. (textile company)

We went through four weeks of training at a dormitory in Yokohama. In the morning, the line managers explained the main points of the job, and in the afternoon we attended talks by external consultants. At night we drank and played mahjong in the dormitory. (petrochemical company)

First we had two weeks of group education conducted by training consult-ants at the main company. We experienced working on rotating shifts for three months in the plant. (petrochemical company)

But even among manufacturers, there were cases where plant training was not always conducted.

There were two weeks of group education instructed by company officials. I found the company explanations and tour visits to plants of other compa-nies very beneficial. (chemical company)

I had one month of intensive orientation. (oil company)

There was one month of training. It consisted of sessions on company his-tory and plant tours. (ceramics company)

I went through one week of group education at a company facility in the city. The program consisted of a company outline, visits to related facili-ties, and so forth. (fisheries company)

Three weeks of group education. We mainly covered a summary of the main features of the company and had explanations by line managers. There were also plant visits. (brewing company)

In the case of general trading companies, new employees assumed their assigned posts immediately after completing short-term intensive training.

We had about two weeks of group education. The department heads all turned out to give lectures. At the time, since the company was new, the department managers were all professionals collected from Sumitomo-af-filiated industries. The accounting person was from Sumitomo Bank, the transportation person was from Osaka Merchant Shipping, and so on, so we were able to learn a lot of different things. A trading firm is comprised of business, management, and support departments. I chose the business department. I visited the operations department, and, for the most part, got a taste of the atmosphere. (general trading company)

We spent four weeks in group education in the company's large confer-ence room. We heard talks on issues from the dismantling of former *zaibatsu* trading companies after the war to the difficulties encountered during their rebirth. Among other things, we also underwent training in using an aba-cus. (general trading company)

We had a very simple orientation that included an overall explanation of the company, accounting knowledge, and practice with the abacus. (gen-eral trading company)

> We had a one-week intensive lecture at the head office that mainly covered an outline of the company. (general trading company)

In other industries training varied.

> Our group education lasted about a month. We were given an explanation of the past, present, and future of the company, company organization, and company regulations. We were also lectured on group-specific services and rules of conduct as company employees and full-fledged members of society. (airline company)

> Training was done in a live-in style program over the course of a few days. The labor union, which was very powerful, provided a similar program of education. I don't remember what we did, but from the point of view of communication, I think the interaction with my contemporaries in the evenings was very beneficial. (bank)

> Our group training was held at the head office in Osaka over a three-week period. There was an explanation of the outline of the company and its main operations, as well as training in the abacus and counting bundles of paper money. (trust bank)

> In our two-week group education program, the instructors were mainly managers of department-head level and the content was mostly related to an introduction and explanation of duties. (casualty insurance company)

> I entered a small-scale family owned enterprise, which did not provide education alone; rather, I took part in a program of new employee education conducted by an association of fifteen strong companies in the Tokyo area [Veneer Wholesaler's Association] for companies in the same line of business. In this system, more experienced company employees acted as instructors during the week-long live-in program. (family-owned enterprise)

On-the-Job Training

Though college graduates were considered candidates for future executive positions, new employees were busy trying fervently to keep up with the work assigned to them and they had no chance to take part in managerial decision making in the system of seniority inherent to lifetime employment. Under such circumstances, the patterns of OJT varied widely between manufacturers and general trading companies. Manufacturers were somewhat systematical and methodical, and one could sense their objectives in fostering their employees. It was clear that an enterprising spirit and a sense of the unexpected were also taught owing to having greater latitude in terms of time. In the case of general trading companies, on the other hand, one was expected early on to deal with matters requiring sharp job skills.

In comparison to what I do now, the amount of work was not as great at that time. My superiors would take great care to give me detailed explanations of the work I had to do. They also taught me technical things. (electrical machine manufacturer)

After assuming my assigned post, the subsection chief taught me what to do. There was no off-the-job training. (electrical machine manufacturer)

There was no systematized OJT in particular. I learned by doing the job firsthand. (electrical machine manufacturer)

In the Planning Division, even though we received no particular training in English, one day my superior told me to try translating something in one hour. After completing the task, I was praised for my ability in English. In the General Affairs Division, the subsection chief corrected the drafts of proposals I wrote. (petrochemical company)

After starting my new duties, I learned business law and trading practices on my job. At first my duties had to do with exporting, and since I had to deal with international time differences, I had a lot of free time during the day so I spent a lot of time reading English contracts. After that, as a result of job rotation, I became the liaison for consulting lawyers. Though I was responsible for matters related to technology and legal affairs, I found that studying up on contracts had been extremely beneficial. (machine manufacturer)

I worked overtime every night until 12 o'clock, checking for errors in the figures that female clerks had calculated on the abacus and typed up. Other divisions sometimes would offer support, fostering a sense of camaraderie. (machine manufacturer)

I prepared sales forecasts using what I was taught about marketing (estimating supply and demand). To check how the database I had developed was being used, I attended of my own volition the sales meetings held in a certain sales (line) department once a week. (textile company)

I underwent OJT in the following areas: knowledge of textiles, plant management methods and supervising operations, product inspection, methods of negotiation with buyers, and so on. In addition to this, I would accompany my superior or technicians to inspect products at the dyeing plant in Hokuriku. This, too, was another kind of OJT. (textile company)

When the assistant to the section chief was too busy, I would pick up all his work. Overseas business trips were also frequent. (petrochemical company)

Those who held positions lower than section manager provided the OJT.

For off-the-job training, I frequently attended external seminars. I wrote reports on their contents that were used by everyone in the department. (chemical company)

I learned about company policy and tradition. Without much warning I was immediately made responsible for sales, and since there were many receptions for sales agents, I also learned drinking manners from the receptions. (fisheries company)

After I assumed my post, I had OJT for three days from the group head. I learned about the calculation system of the accounting department. After that, I learned on the job. (brewing company)

I got my OJT from the senior employee who sat next to me. There was no off-the-job training in particular. Even when I was to start my work in Okinawa, there was no orientation to speak of. (ceramics company)

OJT in customer services (attitude, speaking and enunciation, how to make announcements, and so on for dealing with Japanese and foreign customers). We also learned how to issue airplane tickets, how to make weight and balance, and how to process baggage complaints. (airline company)

OJT, and also through lectures we learned about the International Freight Agreement, the Warsaw Pact, the Customs Act, and so on. (airline company)

Although the situation in general trading companies seemed somewhat harsh to new employees who were expected to quickly develop strong job skills, a tendency to treat all employees equally was evident. Financial firms, on the other hand, had a tradition of nurturing their employees with the utmost care.

We had almost no training. At that time, you were expected to learn in the process of executing your duties. That was the tendency of the era. (general trading company)

All of it was OJT, even learning how to operate the calculator. (general trading company)

We were not given any training. I had to develop my skills by stealing bits and pieces of knowledge from the subsection chief. I also sat through 'lectures' on the train when we brought buyers from India and the Philippines to tour our plant. (general trading company)

Things were different then; there was practically no systematic education for new employees. After assuming our assigned posts we tried like mad to absorb knowledge and practical skills from senior employees through intuition and by following their examples. (general trading company)

OJT after assuming our posts was the fundamental system of education. (general trading company)

We had OJT right off the bat. As for off-the-job training, since I was responsible for trade with Russia and Eastern Europe, I took Russian language classes. (general trading company)

For the first three years after I entered the company, I had OJT in physical distribution, accounting, foreign exchange, and so on, in the transportation department, which was a second line unit. For career formation, it had been decided that the course would be decided within that period of time. (general trading company)

Our company did not provide any OJT. You could say we trained ourselves by quickly mastering a current job, and by making preparations for dealing with international interests. (family-owned enterprise)

Although there was no off-the-job training, we did have OJT. My first direct superior (whose highest degree was a high school diploma) was an expert in work procedures and very kindly taught me. My next superior also taught me a lot. I think it is probably true that the character of the superior teaching you has a lot to do with the effectiveness of the teaching. (casualty insurance company)

I had copious and detailed OJT in all the areas that I was in charge of. For off-the-job training there were in-house education and study groups on issues related to tax law, new ventures (annuity trusts), and so on. (trust bank)

In general, it was normal to be educated through OJT in matters dealing with trade operations. Employees holding a position of subsection chief or higher would be assigned as instructors. (bank)

Job Rotation and Career Formation

After about three years, an employee was assumed to have become sufficiently familiar with the duties of his first post, and then job rotation would be ordered so that the employee could gain experience in a wider range of duties. After only three years of employment, young employees were still far from being considered for managerial posts, so it was easy to make changes in duties. An employee's career developed gradually but steadily under the system of seniority through job rotation in the early years, and experience was accumulated to determine one's future area of responsibilities and career. The main form of job rotation was, first and foremost, simply a change in an employee's duties (for example, rotating an employee from account settlement to receipts and disbursements, but still within the framework of accounting operations). Other forms were: transfer to a different department in the same office, transfer to a different office, or dispatch to a post in a foreign country. Dispatchment overseas was often assigned to someone from among those employees who continually expressed a desire to be considered for such a move. In the summary statements that follow, the names of departments an alumnus was assigned to during this period are identified, with the type of work performed enclosed within parentheses.

One unique trait of manufacturers was the nurturing of new employees as generalists while attempting at the same time to develop the areas in which individual employees showed promise and skill.

> Production management of hot rolling processing → rationalization of the entire process from receipt of order to shipment, systemization using computers in order to supervise online real time information regarding the process from start to finish. (steel company, resigned in 1969)

> Foreign Technology Department (blueprint translation, price-setting, exporting) → Foreign Market Research Office (making contracts between foreign agents) → Liaison Office in Sydney (sales promotion). (machine manufacturer)

> Export Department (exportation of hydroelectric power plants) → Seoul Office (liaison) → Foreign Business Head Office, Thermal Power Department (exportation of thermoelectric power plants). (electrical machine manufacturer)

> Trading Department (market research) → First Export Department (exportation of lighting products) → First International Enterprise Department (exportation to Southeast Asia and Australia) → Sydney Office and Melbourne Office (sales of electrical appliances). (electrical machine company)

> Business Management Department (market research, demand estimation) → Synthetic Fiber Sales Second Division (sale of nylon fabric) → Export Department (exportation of tetoron fabric). (textile company)

> Export Department (exportation of nylon fabric) → New York Office (liaison and sales promotion) → Trading Department (fabric exportation). (textile company)

> Plastics First Division (domestic sales of plastics) → Overseas Business Department (exportation of plastics) → Plastics Sales Department (domestic sales of plastics). (petrochemical company)

Products Department, Yokkaichi Plant (product shipment, later introduction of computer for production, stocktaking, and shipment) → Sales Department, Head Office (sales of petrochemical products) → New Plant Construction Project (development of computerized total physical distribution system). (petrochemical company)

Research Department (market research) → Liaison Office (establishment of a joint venture with a U.S. company) → New York Office (research and public relations) → Overseas Department (granting of licenses to Asian companies). (chemical company)

Sales Planning Section (prediction of sales for all domestic enterprises) → Sales Division (management guidance for customer oil-filling stations) → overseas study for MBA → Business Research Department (financial evaluation of investment projects, market research including brand image) → Tokyo Second Service Stations Relations Office (management guidance to SS managers). (oil company)

Sales Second Division (sales of canned products, wholesaler relations) → Research Section, President's Office (market and 'special' research) → Secretarial Section, President's Office (Secretary to the President). (fisheries company)

Accounting Section, Hiroshima Branch Office (account settlement, receipts and disbursements) → Labor Union Headquarters Officer → General Affairs Section, Hiroshima Branch Office → Sales Section, Hiroshima Branch Office (sales) → temporary assignment to sales subsidiary (manager). (brewing company)

Trading Department (preparation of proposals for strategies for implementation by sales agencies in Southeast Asia) → Okinawa Office (sales to U.S. forces) → wholly owned subsidiary in Thailand (president) → Trading Department (exporting for all areas excluding North America). (ceramics company)

Computer Room, Mie Plant (preparation of statistical data) → Planning Section, Head Office (retailer relations). (electric machine manufacturer, resigned in 1966)

Purchasing Department (buying material wood and synthetic planking from Southeast Asia). (family-owned enterprise)

Planning Department (technological importation, cost accounting) → General Affairs Department (preparation of applications in compliance with foreign capital law and foreign exchange law). (petrochemical company, resigned in 1966)

Study abroad for M.A. → completion of Ph.D. course work through alma mater university → lecturer at a domestic university → international institution, Tokyo branch office (research). (scholar, research officer)

Passenger Transportation Section (Osaka → Fukuoka → Rome Airport Offices) → Passenger Transportation Planning Section, Head Office (planning of passenger services) → Judicial Insurance Section, Head Office (settlements of casualties caused by airplane accidents). (airline company)

International Cargo Section, Haneda Airport (handling of export and import cargo) → San Francisco Airport Office (the first trainee under the newly established Overseas Dispatch Trainee System) → International Cargo Division (program planning, handling of damaged cargo claims) → New York Airport Office (liaison of construction of cargo terminal). (airline company)

In general trading companies, the aim was to nurture specialists in various fields, and so the area for which an employee would be responsible for the rest of his life with the company was decided almost from the time that employee entered the company. The only job rotation would be between different offices, including those overseas. In such instances, too, the employee would be under the direct supervision of the division he belongs to at the Head Office, rather than under the supervision of the head of the local branch office. Orders regarding work would come directly from the Head Office.

Commodities Division, Headquarters (importing and exporting of cement, glass paneling, etc.) → Johannesburg office (in charge of commodities). (general trading company)

Export Machinery Department (exportation of chemical plants) → Melbourne Office (importing of machinery from Japan). (general trading company)

Accounting Department (accounting work for employees assigned overseas) → Accounting Department, Machinery Division (accounting work for electrical machinery exporting → Melbourne Office (accounting, finance and administration). (general trading company)

Russia and Eastern Europe Department (trading in steel and nonferrous metals) → Moscow Office (importing of steel, nonferrous metals, and textiles from Japan) → Steel General Affairs Department (research and planning) → Steel Export Department (exporting of steel plates to the United States and Europe). (general trading company)

Transportation Department (importing of sugar) → Synthetic Resin Department (exporting, importing, and domestic sale of synthetic resin. (general trading company)

Textiles Department (import, export, and domestic sales of textile materials and products for industrial use). (general trading company, resigned in 1970)

In financial firms, there were extremely frequent transfers within the country. Later, an overseas assignment may be decided, taking into account the employee's capabilities and intentions. Such an experience and their achievements prepare employees to take charge of international matters in the future.

Marine Department (marine insurance) → Overseas Department (liaison with representatives in residence abroad and with foreign insurance companies). (insurance company)

Branch offices (five branches; selling of trust certificates, corporate lending) → temporary transfer to a semigovernmental agency (lending to coal mining companies) → Research Department → Inspection Department. (trust bank)

Branch offices (four branches; trade financing) → London Office (corporate lending). (bank, international affairs)

After Five

In this section, we will summarize the activities engaged in by our alumni after five, whether inside or outside their companies, or for personal development. These activities reflect the characteristics of the eras in which our alumni lived and their respective life stages. Furthermore, it is evident that all alumni have adapted to the changes in personal environments, enjoying themselves as they lived their lives with forward-looking optimistic attitudes.

This was the period directly following entry into a new company, a time when employees could pursue various activities with relative freedom, and when they would often be invited by senior colleagues to participate in company activities. It was a time when company activities flourished. However, in general trading companies it was often the case that work took so much of their time directly after they were hired that there was little opportunity to take part in any company activity other than work.

There was a call for essays in commemoration of the tenth anniversary of the bank's first foreign exchange banking services after World War II. The theme was 'Moving International Capital,' and I was very happy to have been awarded the second prize for the paper I submitted. (bank)

One of my most memorable experiences was when I led new employees in organizing and performing a highly acclaimed drama depicting the history of the company during our company's culture festival. Although the colleagues I entered the company with were of all sorts, I acted as secretary for the party we held for people who were hired at the same time. I also joined the kendo club. (insurance company)

The pay wasn't very good, but work would be over by 16:45, and having a lot of energy to expend, I could do three different things every evening. It was like being in heaven. I entertained myself with such sports as skiing, rugby, and sailing. I also started practicing aikido then, which I still do now. In the Reading Society, we read such authors as Joseph A. Schumpeter and Masao Maruyama. It was all really enlightening. In the interim I studied for the Fulbright examination and subsequently went on to study at the University of Illinois Graduate School. (petrochemical company)

I started a skiing club and a tennis club as I had level-one certification in skiing. (airline company)

Work got so busy that I had very little free time. My only pastime was the company chorus. I was the director of about fifty people. We made a newspaper and performed in Osaka Festival Hall. Through those activities, I also joined and was active in a noncompany-related male chorus. (textile company)

During this period, an employee often became an officer in the labor union. All of the labor unions were enterprise unions. In the same way that they would engage in general company activities, the young employees would each take a turn at holding an officer's position in the union. It was the golden age of the labor offensive, and activities were quite spirited even in enterprise unions. An employee would often be recognized for the work done as an officer in the local chapter, and might subsequently be elected to become a head-office official. However, during the oil crisis, since many alumni had been promoted to positions of section managers as part of career development, they could no longer be members of the unions and stopped participating in union activities altogether.

I was elected an officer of the labor union and was quite enthusiastic in taking part in education and information activities. I organized my colleagues and I worked toward getting the union bulletins written in more easily understood language. (oil company)

As vice president and director of education and information activities of the local chapter, I opposed a young men and women's movement organized by the Communist Party, thus making possible the normalization of the union. I was successful in getting improvements made in the labor conditions of female employees and ridding the union of the influence of the Communist Party. I also worked hard as head of the Culture Club and the Athletics Club to provide ways for employees to release their discontent. (textile company)

I became interested in the activities of the labor union. Including the year I served as a member of the central executive committee of the employee labor union, I spent a total of three to four years taking part in union activities. (trust bank)

I was an officer in our labor union local. I was later elected to the position of full-time labor official at union headquarters. (brewing company)

Some alumni, though, suffered when they found themselves caught between the union and the labor policies of their companies.

While I was head of the executive committee, a storm of dissension raged within the ranks of the union, and a second union was formed. I did my best during the year I acted as head of the executive committee of the first union, but it was really difficult being subjected to various kinds of persecution. (airline company)

The ways of thinking of different people show more variety than their company activities. A positive attitude runs through all their opinions. One can also sense a youthfulness and energy in the lifestyles of those who adapted to their overseas environments during the era of overseas dispatch. Alumni were open and unabashed in their comments about leisure activities and hobbies.

I played mahjong, but never with company colleagues. I also enjoyed music; I listened to tango music, and played Hawaiian music. (general trading company)

I like music and enjoyed genres such as jazz piano. (insurance company)

I spent my time traveling domestically and taking care of the plants in my garden. (general trading company)

I devoted all my energies to the pastimes of drinking—I like to call it drink communication—and playing golf. I didn't play mahjong. (petrochemical company)

After work I would often spend time with my contemporaries and senior colleagues in the beer hall on the first floor of our office building. (brewing company)

My room in the bachelors' dormitory would be transformed into a mahjong parlor after work. (steel company)

But it has to be admitted that not all alumni were able to enjoy leisure activities, especially not those in general trading companies.

When I was still a freshman employee, I was so bogged down with work that it was all I could do to get in a game of mahjong. (general trading company)

Pastimes during overseas assignments were also quite diverse.

When I was in Seoul, I spent time with my associates, took trips, and studied about history. Reading became a habit. I bought at a night bazaar, and eventually read, a complete collection of literary works. (electrical machine manufacturer)

While I was working on my MBA as a student at the University of Pennsylvania's Wharton School of Business, I dropped in on international student meetings and quite enthusiastically told people about Japanese culture. For example, I hosted "A Night in Japan." I also took part in group trips. (oil company)

I had nothing to do when I was stationed in Moscow, so I would go to the Bolshoi Opera and go skating in the winter. (general trading company)

I spent all my time drinking while I was stationed in Okinawa. (ceramics company)

I studied at the University of Illinois Graduate School, where I swam and played tennis. I enjoyed going to football games, but the tickets were $5 each, which was expensive for me. Concerts and movies were $1.50. (scholar, turned officer with international organization)

In New York I played golf and went for drives. I got the impression that in those days America was much better off economically and socially than Japan. (textile company)

I was dispatched to New York, where I spent my free time playing golf. I also went to musicals and art museums, and often visited Greenwich Village. (chemical company)

Taking an interest in sports was a characteristic unique to this era. One can see that a great deal of energy has been expended in the pursuit of leisure activities. In this area, we see a division between company and personal activities.

Since orders were passed down prohibiting overtime work, I had a lot of excess time and energy, all of which I channeled into my pursuit of sports. I frequently played tennis, baseball, and especially soccer. After I started working for myself, I stopped playing sports altogether. (electrical machine manufacturer)

I went to the sea in the summer and skiing in the winter with other people from my year-of-entry group (electrical machine manufacturer)

I joined the baseball club; we played on Saturdays and Sundays. I also played soccer. (brewing company)

From Saturday afternoon to Sunday, the time was my own and I joined a club where I enjoyed playing tennis. (fisheries company, machine manufacturer—two alumni)

While I was in Sydney and Melbourne, I enjoyed surfing—the ocean was right outside my house—and playing golf. (electrical machine manufacturer)

Personal Development

Everyone was still young. They had experienced very little and there was much they had to do. It was a good time, one in which the concepts "play hard" and "study hard" were truly practiced. Whether they were at home or at work, they engaged in wide-ranging activities grounded in concrete objectives. In the arena of language study, they worked at brushing up and improving the language skills they had acquired as students.

My interest in English continued, and, desiring some kind of contact with the language, I joined the Japan-British Society, eventually becoming one of its trustees. (insurance company)

I studied English once a week as part of OJT. I also learned how to speak the kind of English that would be easily understood in actual social situations. I worked hard at reading books and magazines, not for the purpose of learning 'how to,' but in order to broaden my education. When I worked as a secretary, I went to school to take lessons in improving my hearing skills. I also studied letter-writing skills, not for writing business letters, but for writing thank-you letters for business trips, and so on. (fisheries company)

I sometimes read books for practicing English conversation, but I came to believe that language (English) ability improves only when you are faced with a need for it. The English I learned at KESS (Keio English Speaking Society) was still not enough. (general trading company)

I even studied English conversation (instructed by Edith Hanson). I was really surprised at the low level of the other students. (textile company)

I studied English conversation with my associates once a week. My KESS friends and I sometimes held study sessions together. (petrochemical company)

A study-abroad program was started in my company, so I studied English in order to qualify for it. (oil company)

I took the Eiken (STEP) test many times. (I finally passed level 1 at my last sitting.) (petrochemical company)

Some members made attempts to learn other languages in addition to English. Through their jobs they learned that there are many countries in which English is not as easily understood as the native language (Spanish, for example).

I studied a little Spanish. (airline company)

I studied books on topics related to the Spanish language. (general trading company)

I studied Spanish with my colleagues. (electrical machine manufacturer)

Not a single day did I let pass without studying English because my goal was to go to America or somewhere in Oceania. At first I was interested in going to Europe but I decided against it because of the language problem. (electrical machine manufacturer)

I started studying German (in preparation for the inevitable advent of restructuring of the financial industry and internationalization). With the support of my company, I studied with a German instructor for about one year. (trust bank)

Before I went to Moscow, I went to school to study Russian and was able to learn enough to at least communicate. It turned out to be very helpful during the time I later spent in Eastern Europe for business. (general trading company)

In dealing with company duties, everyone channeled their efforts into personal development. Let us take a look at some of the more unique cases.

I had specialists from in-house and from outside the company (those from outside were mostly specialists in commerce) teach me about issues related to working with fabrics, dyeing, exchange, claims, and so on. (textile company)

In order to start a business in importing, I studied on my own. In that connection, I studied Business English and practiced typewriting (I bought the typewriter at my own expense). (family-owned enterprise)

I did some studying in the expectation that computers would eventually downsize and be introduced for utilization in office environments. At the time, computers were just evolving from punch cards to tape. (electrical machine manufacturer)

During my time as a union officer, I studied about qualification-based salary scales and salary scales based on ability assessment. (trust bank)

On the recommendation of my company, I studied for certification as a small- and medium-sized enterprise consultant. I also read books on labor issues. (textile company)

I read books on management and history. I also studied calligraphy. I also studied by attending external lectures on M&A. (chemical company)

I studied about the bill clearing system. During my union days, I researched the three major labor laws. (brewing company)

During breaks from work, some also took time to consider issues related to themselves or to culture.

I became interested in life theory, and read any book I could find on related topics. (trust bank)

Although I have no particularly religious background, on my days off I visited shrines and Buddhist temples. (bank)

Nonmanagerial Careers and Early Job Changes

As mentioned in Chapter 6, two of the thirty alumni decided not to seek general management careers when they undertook graduate work. This was because Japanese corporations rarely hire someone with M.A. or Ph.D. degrees in social sciences, as they are "overeducated." Instead, corporations hire bachelor degree holders as candidates for general management and train them internally. This tendency was even stronger thirty-five years ago than it is today.

Thus, one of the two alumni who began graduate work in 1963 obtained an M.A. degree in economics in 1965. Upon graduation he joined one of the four national-level employers' associations. Since then he has stayed with the job. Throughout his career his primary responsibility has been to conduct research on topics of major concern to the Japanese business community. They include economic assistance to developing nations, Japan–United States trade relations, administrative reform, Japan–United Kingdom economic relations, General Agreement on Tariffs and Trade (GATT) trade negotiations, and, most recently, environmental protection. His career also includes overseas assignments: three years in Washington DC and two years in London, during which periods his duties included not only conducting research and writing reports but also giving lecturers and seminars on the Japanese economy and business.

From the above description it is fairly clear that his career anchor is what Schein calls technical/functional competence (in research). Also, it is reasonable to assume that his career anchor was created at a relatively early stage (before 1973). Although he held down various positions of managerial responsibility within the organization, it was apparent from interviewing him that management per se was not his primary interest; research has been his main concern throughout his career.

Another alumnus who began graduate work in 1962 had the reasonably clear career goal of becoming an academic as early as the summer of 1963, when an opportunity arose for him to pursue his studies at University of Illinois. He seized on the opportunity and went to the United States, enrolling in a graduate program on industrial relations. Upon obtaining an M.A. degree, he came back to Japan in 1967 and enrolled in the doctorate program of his alma mater. At the same time, he obtained a full-time position with a private university, first as a researcher, and then, in his second year there, as a lecturer.

After three years, though, he quit the university job because he discovered that an academic career was not as exciting as he had expected. As a result, in 1970 he obtained a position with the Tokyo branch of an international organization specializing in labor problems. His primary responsibility was to conduct research. He stayed with this organization for seven years before moving on to a consulting company specializing in human resource management. In terms of Schein's career anchors, then, he was making a conscious effort to anchor himself in autonomy and independence by seeking an academic career. After a trial period of three years, however, he found himself anchored in technical/functional competence in human resource management.

Of the remaining twenty-eight alumni, four changed their jobs at the early stage. One who intended to do graduate work in the United States on a scholarship did indeed obtain the scholarship and quit his company in 1966. He studied at the University of Illinois and obtained M.A. and Ph.D. degrees. In 1971 he started an academic career in Canada, which he has continued to date. In his case, it is doubtful if he was serious about pursuing a management career. Rather, the four-year period during which he was employed by the company was a sort of preparation period for a different career goal. Here again, his career anchor, that is, autonomy, was formed toward the end of the early stage.

During this period (1962–73), two other alumni quit their jobs for a similar reason (i.e., to succeed to a family business). One of them left the electrical machine manufacturing company in 1966 and joined his father's company, which was involved in the importation and domestic sale of chemical components used for lubrication.

Another reason for his resignation was his dissatisfaction with the company. Prior to his resignation, he had been assigned to that section of the Marketing Department that handled home electrical appliances that were sold to consumers through sole agent stores. Since the performance of some stores was judged to be inefficient, it became the company's policy to terminate sales contracts with them. It was his job to talk with the owners of those stores and tell them that the company no longer needed them, although the owners wanted to maintain the long-established relations. To his way of thinking, this was nothing but the egotism of a large corporation seeking only its own profits at the expense of small family businesses.

Another alumnus quit his first job with a steel company in 1969, also to succeed to the business related to construction materials that his father had just begun, but he could not continue because of illness. He, too, was not totally happy with the company's or industry's business practices. That is, although the steel industry, a typical oligopoly consisting of a handful of large companies, was growing at a healthy rate, it was plagued by excessive investment. Therefore, when business was slow, the industry had to resort to the "production adjustment" or production control agreement sanctioned by the Ministry of International Trade and Industry, whereby the participating companies reduced production to an agreed-upon level.

However, the mutual distrust of the companies was so strong that each company would send a surveillance team to other companies to make sure that no cheating would take place. His displeasure with the practice of mutual surveillance as well as the underlying mutual distrust among the companies was another reason for his leaving the company.

The fourth alumnus who changed his job during this period had started his career working for a major general trading company with the hope of obtaining an overseas assignment. His work day was very long; every day there were a few hours of overtime and this left no time for his personal life. As he was assigned to the department dealing with the exporting of textiles, he was uncomfortable with the hierarchical relationships with major spinning companies and small textile companies. Moreover, an overseas assignment was nowhere in sight. Therefore, after eight years of service, he quit the company and joined a major airline company, again with the hope of working abroad.

He continued to work for the company for twenty years or so, took an early retirement, and set up his own company in the Philippines. It is difficult to pinpoint his career anchor, because he worked for two large organizations in various managerial capacities, and this would imply managerial competency as being his career anchor. However, the fact that he finally founded his own company in a foreign country suggests that throughout his career he was anchored in autonomy and independence.

Thus, by the end of the first subperiod (1973), six of the thirty alumni deviated from the typical career pattern based on permanent employment, in that they either had not joined or had left a large corporation.

Female Careers

As expected, female participants followed different career paths from their male counterparts. Here are the stories of the six alumnae.

> After graduating from college, I worked as a secretary of a representative of a Japanese flower arrangement school until one year after I married. My duties included translation and correspondence. I continued to help my husband with his correspondence and entertaining foreign visitors for another three years. For the next fifteen years, I concentrated on my family life and raising children.
>
> At a major electric appliance company that I had joined after graduation, my job was located in the science museum and promotion center. I was assigned as a guide for foreign and domestic visitors. When my husband was transferred to another city, I resigned from the company. For the next ten years, I devoted my life to my family life and raising children.
>
> I married before I had a chance to start working and devoted myself to family life and raising children. I taught English and cooking within the constraints of my family life, but this work did not give me satisfaction. Gradually, engraving, which was my hobby, became my vocation. I did everything from production to sales all by myself. I was satisfied mentally, but it took a toll on me physically. I became critically ill.
>
> After graduation, I worked as a part-time reporter for a major newspaper. I was in charge of the home section of the Art and Science Department. I

also worked part-time for a major broadcasting company in charge of producing superimposed images for TV dramas. I became ill from the stress of the jobs. I also experienced jealousy from my female colleagues. Because of our long engagement, I came to have a good understanding of my husband's unusual work. After our marriage, I resigned from my jobs and became a secretary and advisor for my husband. I still work in this capacity.

After graduation I worked for a foreign firm as an assistant secretary. I was in charge of translating documents and entertaining foreign visitors. When I married, I resigned from my job. Since then, I devoted myself to family life and raising children. I also taught English at home a few days a week.

After returning from studying abroad for a year, I worked as a secretary for three and a half years for my father, who owned an import agency. After that, I applied for a job I found in the newspaper and was employed at a foreign educational commission. I was in charge of audiovisual materials for two years, and then as a secretary for staff in charge of English education for ten years.

Of the five alumnae who held a job after graduation, four resigned from their jobs when they married or soon after. One alumna held a job and stayed single. As for the reasons why they resigned from a job three alumnae provided the same answer: "because I concentrated on my family life and raising the children." In fact, this was the answer given by an alumna who married before graduation, when she was asked why she did not seek a job. One alumna answered she preferred helping her husband to holding down a hard and stressful job. It was apparent that, in those years, concentration on family life and raising children was a norm rather than an option for a married woman with children, even if she was college educated. Of course, women had the option of having a career and not getting married, as in the case of one of our six alumnae.

8

Overseas Assignments, 1962–73

As we saw in Chapter 2, the usual evolution of the globalization of businesses consists of six stages: (1) intermittent exports, (2) commitment to continuing exports, (3) direct sales through an overseas sales office or marketing subsidiary, (4) the licensing of a foreign firm to produce locally, (5) local production and sales, and (6) total global strategy. During the period 1962–73, most Japanese firms were at either stage two or three, and only a few were at stage four.

At stages one and two, exporting is done not by manufacturers but by intermediaries. In Japan the intermediaries are the giant general trading companies. During this period, traditional industries such as textiles, shipbuilding, and steel were at stage two and were largely dependent on the general trading companies for the export of their products. On the other hand, new industries such as electric appliances (e.g., Sony) and motorcycles and automobiles (e.g., Honda and Toyota) started direct sales through their own overseas sales offices without involving the general trading companies.

Owing to a large technological gap with the United States and with European countries in the wake of World War II, most Japanese companies were licensees of technological know-how in the 1960s, chemical fertilizer manufacturers being some of the few exceptions. Typically, the electric appliance industry and the petrochemical industry were major recipients of Western technology. It was not until the 1980s that Japanese companies became exporters of production techniques as licensors. Thus, during this period, exporting was the main form of international operation of most Japanese firms, whether conducted through general trading companies or by themselves.

Out of the thirty alumni, a total of fifteen were sent overseas by their employers in one form or another, with a couple of them even being sent

Table 8.1

Overseas Assignments

Case	Industry	Duration	Place	Purpose
1	Airline	(1) 1965–66	San Francisco	Job training
		(2) 1969–73	New York	Terminal construction
2	Airline	1967–68	Rome	Job training
3	Construction machinery	(1) 1968	Boston/San Jose	Job training
		(2) 1970–76	Sydney	Sales promotion
4	Petroleum	1966–68	Philadelphia	Graduate study (MBA)
5	Trust bank	1973–74	Frankfurt	Language and job training
6	Textile	1967–72	New York	Research and sales promotion
7	Chemical	1965–67	New York	Liaison and research
8	Electric machinery	1967–71	Seoul	Liaison
9	General trading	1967	Moscow	Trading
10	General trading	1967–73	Melbourne	Trading
11	General trading	1972–77	Johannesburg	Trading
12	Electric machinery	1967–72	Sydney/ Melbourne	Marketing and sales
13	Ceramics	1968–71	Bangkok	Marketing and sales
14	Banking	1970–77	London	Lending
15	General trading	1969–74	Melbourne	General administration

overseas twice during this period (Table 8.1). Generally speaking, they can be grouped into two categories in terms of objectives: study abroad/training and work assignments. Of the fifteen alumni, five were sent overseas for study or training purposes. Two alumni who were employed by the airline company were sent to the company's branch offices in San Francisco (Case 1-1) and Rome (Case 2), respectively, to receive training for one year.

This company had created an overseas training program in 1965, and the alumnus who was sent to San Francisco was among the first group of trainees in this program. Of the objectives of this program he says: "As I understand it, the objective is to give opportunities to employees to experience a broad range of jobs abroad while they are young, for the sake of their future career progress." Indeed, he was assigned to the company's New York office a year and a half after he had completed training in San Francisco and come back to Tokyo. The second alumnus simply says that the objective of the overseas training is "to develop future senior managers."

The third alumnus to be sent overseas for training, who was employed by the overseas business division of a construction machine manufacturer (Case 3-1), was sent in 1968 to a U.S. company with which his employer had a business alliance. He received training at two of the company's sales offices for six months. He feels that his superior English ability and his job knowledge were the reasons for his selection as a trainee. Two years after his return to Japan, he was sent to Sydney as the general manager of the liaison office there (Case 3-2).

The fourth alumnus, who was employed by the foreign-owned petroleum company (Case 4), was sent to Wharton Graduate School at the University of Pennsylvania in 1966 under the company's program to send employees to overseas graduate schools. The program was created in 1966 as a part of the human resource development strategy of the foreign parent company, and our alumnus was among the first group of employees to be selected under the program. He studied at the Wharton School for two years and earned an MBA in 1968. Later (in 1973) he was assigned to the parent company's headquarters in New York to receive on-the-job training (OJT) for a year and a half.

The fifth alumnus, whose primary responsibility was corporate lending as a loan officer with the trust bank (Case 5), was sent to Germany in 1973 for a year. He studied German at the Goethe Institute and at the same time received OJT at a bank with which his employer had a business alliance. While in Japan, he had anticipated that Germany's importance would increase in line with the internationalization of finance, and so he had started studying German, first on his own and later with support from the company. Asked his view about the reason why he was chosen as a trainee, he responded that senior managers shared his views about the increasing importance of Germany and that they were favorably impressed by his work on credit assessment as well as by his efforts to study German, and also by his proven English ability. Shortly after his return to Japan, he was sent back to Germany to open and operate a new office in Frankfurt, as we shall see in Chapter 12. Thus, all five of these alumni were selected for overseas education or training on the basis of formal screening or close personal assessment. After the completion of their training, which was followed by work assignments in Japan (of varying lengths), all were sent back to overseas assignments.

A total of twelve alumni were sent overseas for work assignments. This figure includes the two alumni who were sent overseas twice (Cases 1 and

3), the first time being for training purposes. The breakdown of the twelve by the place of assignment is as follows: New York (3), Sydney/Melbourne (4), London (1), Johannesburg (1), Moscow (1), Seoul (1), and Bangkok (1). The breakdown by industry is as follows: manufacturing (6), general trading (4), airline (1), and banking (1).

The twelve alumni may be grouped into three categories in terms of job content: research, liaison, and sales promotion (4); marketing and sales (6); and administration (2). The four alumni whose jobs were research, liaison, and sales promotion were all working for manufacturing companies—in the textile, heavy electric machinery, chemical, and construction machinery industries. These companies depended on general trading companies for overseas sales, so our alumni were not directly involved in sales activities, which means that these three industries were still at stage two of the evolution of business globalization.

Brief reference was already made to the alumnus employed by the construction machinery manufacturer who received OJT in the United States for several months. Shortly after his return to Japan, he was sent to Australia in 1970 as the general manager of the Sydney liaison office for six years (Case 3-2).

His superior English ability coupled with a few months of OJT in the United States made him the perfect candidate for the position. He says, "I was the second general manager of the Sydney office. Out of 150 colleagues who joined the company in the same year (1962), I was the only one whose command of English was good enough to conduct business in English." He was responsible for establishing and managing local agents who sold construction machinery to mining and forestry companies as well as providing services to customers in Australia, New Zealand, Fiji, Papua New Guinea, and the rest of the South Pacific region. Actual export shipment from Japan to Australia and trade financing were undertaken by a general trading company. As for the reasons, he recollects, "the company in those days was making heavy investment every year in the expansion of its manufacturing facilities to meet growing sales and was not in a position to appropriate its limited funds to trading activities such as local distributor inventory finance."

Work assignments for the alumnus working for the textile company (Case 6), who spent five years (1967–72) in New York, included the collection of information on textiles in general (including the progress of Japan–U. S. textile negotiations), as well as sales promotion conducted by accompanying the sales representatives of general trading companies on visits to customers. For example, he gave technical support and advice on advertising and made an effort to sell new products. He says that the reasons he was chosen for overseas assignments were "because of my one-year study at Stanford University before joining the company, my English ability, as well as my knowledge of commodities that the company exports to the United States."

The alumnus working for the chemical company (Case 7) was also sent to New York for three years beginning in 1965. He had passed an examination for the company-supported study-abroad program; this, he feels, was taken into consideration when he obtained the New York assignment. His main duties included market research as well as liaison work with major U.S. chemical companies. He was also busy attending to the needs of company executives who were on business trips to New York. He was fortunate to have opportunities to meet VIPs from his company as well as from his customers' companies. This, according to him, became very helpful in his later work.

The alumnus who worked for the electric machinery manufacturer (Case 8) was sent to Seoul for four years (1967–71). With the normalization of diplomatic relations between Japan and the Republic of Korea in 1965, economic relations between the two nations resumed. One outcome was the export by his company of three power generators to Korea. His work was to oversee the installation and operation of the power generators to ensure they were done as stipulated in the contract. As a liaison officer between his company and the client—the government-owned power company—he spent much of his energy on closing the gap between the two. As for the reasons for assignment to Korea, he says that he was hired by the overseas division of the company, and overseas assignments were considered a part of the division's job rotation.

The breakdown by industry of the six alumni who were sent abroad for line duties, primarily marketing and sales, were as follows: general trading companies (3), manufacturers (2), and a bank (1). One of the three alumni working for general trading companies (Case 9) was assigned to Moscow in 1967 because he was employed by a division of the company dealing with the Soviet Union and East European nations. In Moscow he was in charge of selling steel, nonferrous metals, and textile products. His assignment in Moscow was prematurely terminated after ten months, however, when, for political reasons, the Soviet government reduced the number of visas for Japanese staff stationed there from eight to four.

The second alumnus, working for another general trading company (Case 10), was assigned to the Melbourne office in 1967 for six years. The assignment was part of a regular rotation of personnel within the company's machinery export division. His main job was to sell machinery to the iron ore mining company in which his company had an investment. However, tariffs on machinery were prohibitively high, and it was difficult to sell machines that were made in Japan. Although Japanese machine manufacturers insisted on selling 100-percent-made-in-Japan machines, he persuaded them to let local manufacturers make some parts according to the specifications of the Japanese manufacturers, while exporting other parts from Japan, thereby reducing tariffs and closing deals successfully.

The third alumnus, working for yet another general trading company (Case 11), was assigned to the Johannesburg branch in 1972 for five years. His transfer was also due to the regular rotation of personnel within the company's commodities division. At that time, he was very much involved in the exportation of cement to China, so he was not happy with the personnel department's sudden decision to transfer him to Johannesburg. According to him, the company's Johannesburg office was short-staffed as the result of an increasing volume of business, such as the importation of uranium and ferrochrome. He feels that his broad experience and job knowledge, rather than his English abilities, were the reason for his selection, as his colleagues were equally capable of conducting business in English.

One of the most successful job experiences for this alumnus was the importation to Japan of high-quality wood chips used for paper production. Foreseeing the appreciation of the yen, he successfully negotiated a long-term contract involving a local agricultural cooperative and a Japanese paper manufacturer. As the yen appreciated, especially after the oil crisis of 1973, he invested in the chip production plant, and this made it possible to export wood chips in large quantities. As sales and profits increased steadily throughout his stay in Johannesburg for more than five years, the members of the co-op appreciated his efforts and treated him like a VIP. He says, "I felt my efforts were worthwhile."

The two alumni who were working for manufacturers and who were sent abroad for marketing and sales during this period followed more or less similar career paths. Both were assigned to international trade divisions upon employment, obtained job knowledge through OJT, and were sent overseas at a relatively young age.

The first alumnus, employed by the electric machinery manufacturer (Case 12), was also sent to Australia, first as the sole sales representative in Sydney (1967–69) and then as the first chief representative in Melbourne (1969–72). The company was gradually switching its exporting strategy from reliance on general trading companies to direct sales by its own employees.

As he was eager to work overseas and worked very hard to obtain an overseas assignment, he was extremely happy when he obtained one. He feels that his efforts at gaining technical knowledge about home electric appliances as well as job knowledge about exporting were acknowledged by his superiors, and this resulted in his selection for the position in Sydney. His job in Australia was to sell home electric appliances directly to customers and also through sales agents. To that end, developing good sales agents was also an important part of his job.

The second alumnus, employed by the ceramics company (Case 13), was involved from the very beginning in the exporting of chinaware to Southeast Asian countries. His first assignment was the sale of chinaware to families of U.S. soldiers stationed in Okinawa, which was still under U.S. occupation. At that time the company was exporting through local agents in various countries. Not all sales agents did well. Thailand was one of the places where sales through local agents were not very successful. The decision was made, consequently, to switch to direct sales by creating a wholly owned sales company. Since our alumnus was very much involved in the creation of the sales company in Thailand, he was appointed its first president (1968–71). The Bangkok office was responsible not only for the Thai market but also for the Vietnam and Singapore markets. It was his job to reorganize the marketing channels by controlling sales agents in various locations and by creating and operating the sales outlet directly owned by the company. The business was profitable and stable because the biggest customer was the American military force stationed in Thailand. The work assignments of the above two alumni suggest that the home electric appliance and the ceramics industries were at stage three of business globalization.

One alumnus, working for a major bank with a strong tradition in international operations (Case 14), was transferred to the London branch in 1970. There he was engaged in the international investment business that had been revitalized after the Nixon shock and the implementation of a floating exchange rate system. He says, "The relaxation of foreign exchange controls quickly accelerated, and the bank I was working for was now able to make use of its expertise to increase its profits." Starting with simple trade financing, he proceeded to financing for the construction of factories by local subsidiaries of Japanese corporations. Later he was engaged in "project financing" in the field of energy development.

During this period two alumni were sent overseas to fill staff positions. One alumnus, working for the airline company (Case 1-2), was transferred to the New York office in 1969, less than three years after his return to Japan from his fruitful training in San Francisco (mentioned before). According to him, his training in San Francisco as well as his job knowledge about air cargo were the main reasons for his transfer. In New York he was assigned to a special project to build a freight terminal with automatic cargo handling and information processing functions within the J.F. Kennedy Airport. It was his job to entrust the construction to a contractor and oversee the progress of the construction.

The other alumnus, working for a general trading company (Case 15), was transferred to Melbourne in 1969 for five years. Up to that point he had been working in the company's accounting department and was well versed in all aspects of accounting work. His overseas assignment was a part of regular job rotation within the company's administrative (or staff) sector. In Melbourne his duties included not only accounting but also finance and general administration.

Above, brief descriptions of the overseas assignments of fifteen alumni have been provided in terms of selection criteria and work content. Selection criteria were found to be different in the case of those who were sent abroad for study/training purposes and in the case of those sent overseas for work assignments. In the former case, either formal screening mechanisms existed (airline company, foreign-owned petroleum company), or, in their absence, the candidates' language ability was emphasized (construction machine manufacturer, bank). In the latter case, the individuals' knowledge of the job and product as well as their enthusiasm for overseas assignments played the most important role. Language ability, although important, was not, on the whole, a crucial factor.

Another distinctive difference between the two cases is the length of stay. In the former case, the length ranged from six months of OJT to two years of study for an MBA, with an average of 1.1 years. In the latter case, the length of the overseas assignments ranged from ten months to six and a half years, with an average of 4.5 years. It should be noted that the overseas assignment of ten months was that of the alumnus who worked in the Moscow office and who had to leave the country when the number of Japanese staff stationed there was reduced by the Russian government; therefore, it does not represent a "failure" in overseas assignments. No other alumnus returned home prematurely as a result of maladjustment to overseas conditions.

In Chapter 2, it was reported that the "failure rates" of parent-country nationals (PCNs) were much lower in Japanese than in U.S. firms, at least until the early 1980s (Tung 1984), and three factors were identified to account for the low failure rates: (1) careful review of employees' qualifications in selecting the candidates for overseas assignments, (2) provision of more pre-assignment training, and (3) provision of a more comprehensive support system for the PCN once he is overseas.

The experiences of our twelve alumni confirm that failure rates were indeed low (zero percent) and that careful screening did indeed contribute to the low rates. What about the other two factors? In terms of pre-assignment training and orientation, eight of the twelve did not receive any training, because their work experience prior to overseas assignments was closely related to their work overseas, so that there was no need for special training in regard to job duties. Besides, for some companies the sending of their employees on overseas assignments was a new experience, so that the companies themselves did not have the know-how for pre-assignment training or orientation.

Three alumni received some pre-assignment training. One alumnus who worked for the airline company (Case 1-2) received a two-week training course in accounting because his duties overseas were to include accounting, an area in which he had no experience. The second, who worked for the electric machinery manufacturer (Case 12), received intensive training on the technical aspects of the products that the company intended to introduce into the market (Australia) through the newly created office that he was assigned to head. The third, who worked for a general trading company (Case 9), received three months of intensive training in Russian, because he was to be assigned to Moscow. He was the only alumnus who received language training. All other alumni were sent either to English-speaking countries or to countries where business was conducted in English (Thailand) or in Japanese (South Korea), and all our alumni were proficient in English.

In terms of post-assignment training and assistance, on the whole, our alumni did not receive systematic training as such, although brief orientations were given by predecessors or general managers (or chief representatives) of the assigned offices. Procedures for loans, company-subsidized housing, and educational assistance overseas were already established for the general trading companies, an airline company, and a bank. Those who belonged to small-scale offices or those who were assigned to start a new base had to take care of everything themselves. In order to become accustomed to the new country, one alumnus stayed with an English family as a live-in guest for six months and spent time with the family (they ate breakfast and supper together).

From the above description it does not seem that either pre- or post-assignment training and orientation accounted substantially for the low failure rates of our alumni. At this point, we can point out the aptitudes of our alumni, in terms of job knowledge, language ability, and eagerness to work overseas, as the single most important factor. We will later consider other factors.

In Chapter 2, ethnocentrism was identified as another key feature common to Japanese companies operating abroad. We will first look at the staffing of the overseas offices to which our alumni were assigned. In terms of the number of employees, these offices ranged from 2 (liaison office of a chemical company) to approximately 200 (airport office of an airline company). Generally speaking, manufacturers' liaison offices were the smallest (2, 6, 7, and 18 employees, respectively) followed by manufacturers' sales offices (21 and 22 employees, respectively). General trading companies' offices were medium-sized (11, 20, 27, and 52 employees, respectively). The largest was the airline's office (mentioned above), followed by the bank's branch office with approximately 80 employees.

The number of Japanese PCNs ranged between one (liaison office of chemical company) and twenty (branch offices of airline company and bank). In all but one of twelve offices the top positions (general manager/chief representative) were filled by Japanese PCNs—the liaison office of the chemical company was the exception, with a Japanese American the chief representative. In addition to the top position, all other key positions in all twelve offices were filled by Japanese PCNs. Local employees were hired largely to fill nonmanagerial positions.

As an example, the New York liaison office of the textile company was staffed by a total of eighteen people—eight Japanese and ten American employees. The Japanese PCNs filled the position of chief representative as well as all staff positions in marketing, technology, research, and planning. All ten American employees were females and were performing assistant, secretarial, and receptionist jobs. In another example, the Melbourne branch office of a general trading company employed a total of twenty-seven people—twelve Japanese and fifteen Australian employees. The Japanese PCNs filled the positions of general manager, assistant general manager, and managers in six line sections dealing with wool, machinery, iron and coal, textiles, foodstuff, and chemicals. Of the fifteen Australian employees, eight worked under Japanese managers as line workers, five as secretaries, and one each as telex operator and receptionist. Our alumnus, who was a manager of the machinery section, recalls, "As I was still in my twenties, it was difficult to manage a host-nation's subordinate who was in his forties and who had been working there since before my appointment."

The above description tends to confirm that, at least during this period, the twelve Japanese companies under observation took an ethnocentric approach in managerial staffing abroad. It needs to be added, however, that some offices were too small to hire local staff other than for secretarial positions, while other offices were newly established to carry out important strategies of headquarters, so they needed parent-country nationals who would faithfully carry out those strategies, and local nationals might be considered unfit for that purpose.

Related to the underlying principles of managerial staffing is the question of the extent to which Japanese-style business and management were practiced in the twelve overseas offices. In the three offices of general trading companies, located in Melbourne (Cases 10 and 15) and Johannesburg (Case 11), business transactions were conducted following procedures long established within each company, subject to the laws and regulations of the respective host countries. Local laws and regulations affected, for example, the style of sales and/or purchase contracts between a local company and the headquarters in Japan as well as Japanese customers. Overall, though, these offices of the general trading companies followed the Japanese-style of business transactions partly because general trading companies were uniquely Japanese institutions and, therefore, there was no local model to follow.

In terms of the management of local employees, however, the three offices followed local practices with varying degrees of Japanese touches, ranging from length-of-service-based pay components to hiring and training of fresh graduates from school. The latter practice, however, was soon discontinued because of the high turnover rates among trained employees (Case 15).

Another office of a general trading company was located in Moscow (Case 9). There, the activities of the Japanese PCNs were tightly controlled by the host country's regulations. All local customers were public corporations and personal contacts with their employees were prohibited. Local employees of the office were sent from a government agency to which their wages, unilaterally determined by the agency, were paid in U.S. dollars.

In three offices of manufacturing companies, those located in Sydney (Case 3-2), Melbourne (Case 12), and Bangkok (Case 13), business was conducted on a trial-and-error basis, because all three offices were newly created for direct sales without the involvement of trading companies. The alumnus who headed, as its first president, the Bangkok-based subsidiary of the ceramics company (Case 13) followed the Japanese way of developing marketing channels and controlling agents, as there was no readily available alternative. In the management of local employees, too, he followed the Japanese practice of permanent employment, although laws permitted employers to dismiss employees at will. At the same time, he tried to respect the host country's culture. For example, unlike in Japan, he did not clean his own desk, because cleaning a desk was not considered part of a president's job.

On the other hand, the alumnus assigned to be the first chief representative of the Melbourne office of the electric appliance company (Case 12) said that he followed more or less the local practices in developing distribution channels and selling directly to customers. This was an entirely new experience for the company, which had depended on general training companies for overseas sales. For the management of local employees, too, he followed the host country's practices. For example, to decide the annual pay increase he had to negotiate with individual subordinates, a practice to which he had not been accustomed back in Japan.

Still, the other alumnus, assigned to Australia as the second chief representative in the Sydney office of the construction machine company (Case 3-2), said it was extremely difficult to play a liaison role between headquarters and local sales agents. Naturally, he had to follow the Japanese way in dealing with headquarters, while in dealing with local agents he had to follow the Australian way. In dealing with the local employees of the office, he had to follow the Australian practices. For example, when he tried to introduce the Japanese form of salary payment in which a substantial portion is paid in bonuses, local employees demanded that their salaries should be paid in the form of a monthly salary alone without any bonuses tied to the company's (or office's) performance.

Among the three liaison offices of manufacturing companies, some variation was observed in terms of business style. In the New York offices of the textile company (Case 6) and the chemical company (Case 7), the American style was adopted for different reasons. While the textile company's office was eager to learn the American way, at least in connection with sales promotion, the chemical company's office was headed by a U.S. national of Japanese ancestry. In the former office, management of the local staff also followed the American way; this was characterized, for example, by open recruitment and the payment of a market-rate salary. The second office did not employ any local staff. In Seoul, our alumnus, as a liaison officer between his company (electric machine manufacturer) and the client (government-owned power company), was experiencing the same difficulties as those experienced by the alumnus with the construction machine manufacturer who headed the company's Sydney office.

To summarize the above discussion: in the style of business, there was variation among industries. While general trading companies more or less followed their own (Japanese) ways, manufacturing companies adopted host country practices to a varying degree. In this sense, host country laws and regulations seem to be the strongest constraining factor. In terms of the management of local employees, all offices, with the exception of the one in Bangkok, used essentially host country practices. Attempts to introduce Japanese elements yielded mixed results.

Ethnocentrism is often associated with centralized home country control of overseas operations with a focus on sales targets. Therefore, we will next examine, through the experiences of our alumni, to what extent the overseas offices to which they were assigned were controlled by their headquarters.

In the case of general trading companies, it seems that their organizational structures as well as staffing policies had been well established by the early 1960s, when our alumni started working. These structures and policies have remained essentially unchanged to date. A trading company's organizational structure typically consists of line divisions that carry out business transactions, both international and domestic, and staff divisions in such functional areas as accounting, finance, personnel, and general administration (including legal affairs). Line divisions are further divided into a number of departments, depending on the line of commodities handled, such as steel, textiles, chemicals, and machinery. Over the years, the size of the department changes according to the volume of commodities it handles.

As briefly discussed in Chapter 7, the staffing policy is such that a person who, upon initial employment, is assigned to a department dealing with a certain line of commodities continues to deal with the same line of commodities until retirement. This practice is based on the assumption that, in the case of a line department, knowledge about the commodities one deals with is the fundamental component of an employee's competence, which, in turn, becomes a source of the competitive advantage of the company. Job specialization also applies to employees in staff departments, although the scope of their job duties expands with their career progress.

In such a system an employee's primary affiliation is with the commodity-based department, and the geographical location of an assignment becomes of secondary importance. In the case of an overseas assignment, then, an employee is sent by a particular department to an overseas office to deal with a particular line of commodities that is within the jurisdiction of the department. In a small-scale office, however, an employee handles a line (or lines) of commodities other than his primary line of commodities. Also, an employee in a staff department is assigned to a broader range of duties than his primary job duties in a single functional area.

Since an overseas office is staffed by employees sent from different departments, they report not only to the general manager of the overseas office but also to the general manager of the department back at headquarters from which they are sent. For the general manager of the department back at headquarters, overseas offices are like an extension of his department. He gives directives to overseas staff in accordance with the department's and the company's global strategy.

Such was the institutional arrangement under which our four alumni were stationed overseas: in Moscow trading steel, nonferrous metals, and textiles (Case 9); in Melbourne selling machinery, ships, and manufacturing plants (Case 10); in Johannesburg trading wood chips, chemicals, and textiles (Case 11); and in Melbourne in a staff position covering finance and general administration in addition to accounting (Case 15). They were by no means passive receivers of directives from headquarters. Those in the line departments tried very hard to identify and to seize upon potential business opportunities, making full use of their ingenuity and negotiation skills. In the process they had to "sell" their ideas to headquarters. The importation of wood chips by the alumnus in Johannesburg and the exportation of machine parts by the alumnus in Melbourne were two successful examples of local (overseas) initiatives. Overall, though, it is fair to say that overseas offices of general trading companies were closely controlled by their headquarters through various line departments.

In the case of sales offices of manufacturing companies, these offices were formally under the control of the overseas business division or export division at headquarters. From the experiences of our alumni it seems that these offices enjoyed a considerable degree of autonomy, because direct overseas sales was a new experience for the companies, and, as a result, the headquarters itself did not have much expertise upon which to base any directives. Apparently the companies lacked a total global strategy and adopted a local-market-oriented approach. In this sense, the initiatives of overseas offices were the crucial factor for success in international business. Successful introduction of the companies' products in the host country markets as well as those of neighboring countries, followed by a rapid increase in sales under the leadership of our alumni in Melbourne and in Bangkok, attest to this point.

Two of the three liaison offices of manufacturing companies, both in New York, also enjoyed a relatively high degree of autonomy, because their main function was to gather information, which did not require the need for directives from headquarters. The third liaison office, located in Seoul, was involved in liaison work with a local customer concerning the installation of power generators. Our alumnus was involved in negotiations not only with the customer but also with the factory that made power generators, and that was the company's profit center. This suggests that the office had some degree of autonomy.

In the case of the branch office in New York of the airline company (Case 1-2), where our alumnus was involved in the cargo terminal construction project, there was substantial involvement by headquarters because the project required a large amount of funds. According to the alumnus, "We had to go through the lengthy process of reporting to headquarters, waiting for the decision to be made through the time-consuming *ringi* system [to be discussed in detail in Chapters 16 and 21] and conveyed to us, and negotiating with the contractor. Local people ridiculed this as a slow approval cycle." In a sense, the substantial involvement of headquarters is understandable because building a cargo terminal is a strategic decision with company-wide implications.

At the London branch of the bank our alumnus (Case 14) was engaged in lending to corporate customers (mostly Japanese). The decision to approve a loan was made in one of the following three ways depending on the case: (1) by submission of *ringi* to headquarters; (2) by a decision at the London branch; or (3) by a decision of the department itself. If the loan was within a certain range, he was given full power to make decisions; in other cases he wrote up proposals upon which his superiors decided. It is fair to say that this branch had some degree of autonomy.

The above discussion suggests that since virtually all overseas establishments were branch offices with limited functions, they were under the control of their headquarters. The degree of control, however, differed among different offices. On the whole, general trading companies seem more centrally controlled than manufacturing and other companies, because the latter companies are dependent on the initiative of overseas offices for the successful internationalization of their businesses. Furthermore, when a major investment is involved, headquarters exercises tighter control.

To return to the question of the failure rates of PCNs: it was noted in Chapter 2 that some studies reported relatively high failure rates among overseas Japanese establishments as a result of maladjustment of PCNs and/or their family members to host country cultures (Fukuda and Chu 1994). In the next few pages, therefore, we will examine how our alumni and their families adjusted to the host country cultures.

At the time of their overseas transfers, ten out of twelve alumni were married. In four cases their families accompanied our alumni, while in six cases their families joined (or were to join) a few months to a year later. This latter practice was based on the companies' assumption that it would take this much time for their employees to settle in and get used to their jobs and to host country cultures; therefore, for the families to settle in smoothly, it would be better for them to join later. However, such a practice was considered strange in host countries such as the United States and Australia, and some alumni felt that one year of separation was too long.

Generally speaking, those alumni and their families who were sent to the United States (3 cases) and Australia (4 cases) were favorably impressed with the host country cultures—open-mindedness and material wealth in the United States, and friendliness and closeness to nature in Australia. Although there were negative aspects, such as racial tension in the United States and anti-Japanese feeling among the older generation in Australia, overall they felt comfortable in the U.S. and Australian cultures.

Wives were happy because, unlike in Japan, their husbands paid more attention to their family lives and spent more time with their families. They also developed friendships with the local people through the children's schools, sporting clubs, and churches, and actively engaged in community activities. As the children were still very young (in fact several were born while abroad), they easily became accustomed to the local way of life. Many alumni reported forming close family friendships during their overseas stay that they have maintained up to the present.

More or less the same can be said for the alumni who were transferred to London and to Johannesburg. In London our alumnus stayed with a local family for the first six months before being joined by his family (wife and two children). During holidays they enjoyed traveling not only in the UK but also in many countries of continental Europe. They particularly enjoyed traveling in Italy, Spain, and France.

In Johannesburg our alumnus was joined by his family (wife and three children) three months after his arrival there. Since the country still had the apartheid policy, racial problems were very complex. Although Japanese were classified as "honorary white," our alumnus and his family did not have very comfortable social lives. This was partly compensated for by the very luxurious way of life: a large house with housemaids. There was a well-organized Japanese community and a Japanese school that the children attended.

Another alumnus and family (wife and a child) also enjoyed a luxurious life in Bangkok: a large house with live-in maids. Thailand was then under military rule and there was occasional political and social turmoil, but there was no immediate danger to the alumnus's business or private life. He sent their child to a British kindergarten. His wife was concerned about social order and sanitary conditions. Since they had to renew their visas every two months, they took advantage of these occasions to enjoy traveling in neighboring countries. Overall, then, our alumnus says that he and his family enjoyed their three years' stay in Bangkok.

Our alumnus who stayed in Moscow was not as happy as others. First of all, he was not allowed to be accompanied by his wife. Nor was he allowed to travel freely or to make friends with local people. There was nothing much in the way of recreation and entertainment. And, although he had to leave the country prematurely for the reason mentioned earlier, he does not regret it.

Another alumnus who experienced difficulties in his private life is the one who stayed in Seoul for four and a half years. When he was transferred to Seoul, he was engaged. A year later they married. However, his wife could not join him in Seoul, because a visa for her was not issued—a reflection of the still cool relations between the two countries. As a result, he had to stay by himself for three and a half years, although during this time his wife visited him several times on a tourist visa.

To summarize, in almost all cases cultural factors worked favorably for our alumni and their families. In two countries—the Soviet Union and South Korea—our alumni experienced difficulties. However, it was not national cultures as such but government policies that caused the difficulties. Both Thailand and South Korea are Asian countries and therefore share more or less similar cultures, but their governments' policies were different. Therefore, when we talk about the "success" or "failure" of PCNs, we should not overemphasize culture and forget government policy. Our alumnus successfully completed his mission in Korea despite the extremely unfavorable conditions. He might be an exception to the general rule. There will be more discussion of the influence of culture in Chapters 12 and 17.

Summary to Part II

The dozen years between 1962 and 1973 show an interesting contrast between the volatile international political environment and stable domestic politics under the LDP government. As mentioned in the Prologue, the foundation of Japan's political stability was achieved in 1960 when the Kishi Cabinet concluded the revised Japan-U.S. Security Treaty whereby Japan firmly positioned itself as a member of the free world nations. The long reign of Prime Minister Sato's government (1964–72) added to the domestic political stability.

Thanks to this political stability the Japanese people were able to concentrate their energies upon the achievement of high economic growth, a goal that had been articulated by Prime Minister Ikeda in 1960. The Japanese GNP nearly quintupled during this period with a result that as early as 1968 Japan's GNP ranked second in the free world, behind only that of the U.S.

High economic growth was achieved by a combination of strong domestic consumption, corporate investments, and exports. The strong domestic consumption was exemplified by the "three sacred treasures" of color TV sets, air conditioners, and automobiles, all of which ordinary householders aspired to acquire. To meet the strong demand of consumers, electrical appliance and automobile manufacturers invested heavily in their plant facilities, and this in turn caused chain reactions in other industries, including the basic steel and petrochemical industries, as we saw in Chapter 5.

The Japanese trade balance, long plagued by deficits, started continuously registering a surplus after 1965, a reflection of the increased competitive power of Japanese industries. The surplus was moderate until 1970, when the government switched to a tight money policy to fight inflation. To make up for the decline in domestic demand, Japanese industries stepped up their efforts to export. "Excessive exports" by a number of industries created trade frictions with foreign countries, especially the U.S. As a result, "voluntary" restraints were exercised in such industries as the basic steel, synthetic fiber, and electric machine industries in the late 1960s and early 1970s.

In light of the above discussion, it is fair to say that the Japanese economy reached the stage of maturity by the late 1960s. The admission of Japan to the OECD and the change in the status of Japan within the IMF to an Article

8 nation (a nation that cannot resort to foreign exchange controls to balance international payments) further confirm such a conclusion.

However, despite international pressure for trade and capital liberalization, Japanese policy makers, who were firm believers in the "infant industry theory" of economic development, did not discard protective economic policies. Industries, on their part, further accelerated their export drives as a result of two "shocks" to the Japanese economy—the successive revaluation of the yen after 1971 and the first oil crisis of 1973.

The psychological impact of these two shocks upon the Japanese people was so strong that increasing productivity became a national goal shared by industry, the government, and even the labor movement. In the process, the importance of domestic consumption, which had served as the engine for unprecedented economic growth in the 1960s, was to be permanently forgotten.

While the economy was undergoing a drastic change, social values were slow to change. The old Confucian values in particular survived the postwar democratic reform and remained instrumental in instilling in "princely" or "superior" employees such attributes as harmony, acceptance of hierarchy, loyalty, and love for learning.

A belief in gender-based role differentiation also persisted. Women were expected to work in "female" jobs only when they were single. For a married woman, and especially one with children, concentration on family life and the raising of children was a norm rather than an option, even if she had a college education.

It was against these economic and social backgrounds that our alumni and alumnae started their careers. While virtually all alumni stared management-track careers with large corporations, all but one alumna opted to concentrate on family life and raising children after a brief stint at "female" jobs.

All alumni, working for large corporations, went through a typical training system consisting of initial group education of several weeks followed by years of OJT and job rotation. The economic environment of the time greatly affected their jobs. A rapid growth in exports in manufacturing industries created a strong need for employees with expertise in export-related jobs, not only in manufacturing but also in other industries including commerce, banking, insurance, and air transportation.

Thus, with a few exceptions most of our alumni ended up, after a series of job rotation, with export-related jobs in Japan and abroad. That exactly one half of the thirty alumni were assigned to overseas posts attests to this point.

Upon closer examination, however, we found that actual sales jobs were conducted by those employed by general trading companies. Among the manufacturing industries in which our alumni were employed, only in electrical appliances and ceramics were our alumni assigned to direct overseas sales jobs. Those alumni assigned to overseas offices in the textile, chemical, construction machinery, and heavy electrical machinery industries were engaged in market research, liaison, and sales promotion.

The "failure rate," or premature termination of an overseas assignment as a result of poor performance, was zero. This was due primarily to our alumni's job knowledge, language ability, and eagerness to work overseas rather than to any pre- or post-assignment training and orientation. Their work experience prior to overseas assignments was closely related to their work overseas; therefore, no specific training was necessary.

Overall, our alumni and their families adjusted well to the host country cultures. This was especially true of those who were sent to English-speaking countries: the U.S., Australia, and the U.K. There were only two cases where our alumni experienced hardships—in the Soviet Union and South Korea. It was not the national cultures of these countries, however, but their government policies that caused the difficulties.

As for the operation of overseas offices, our findings suggest that, although an ethnocentric staffing policy was uniformly practiced, other elements of Japanese-style management were not widely practiced in overseas offices during this period. In regard to the management of local employees in particular, all offices (with the exception of the one in Bangkok) used essentially host country practices.

As mentioned in Chapter 6, 28 alumni started management careers. During this period only four left their original employers. It is fair to say that, overall, our alumni's job commitment, an important element of permanent employment, was considerably high. In terms of Schein's career anchors, a total of six—the four who changed their jobs, as well as the two who did not opt for a management track—formed their career anchors during this period. The remaining 24 alumni continued pursuing their management careers, although it is not clear to what extent they were firmly anchored in them.

Part III

Period between Two Oil Crises:
A Period of Change (1974–1980)

9
General Environment, 1974–80

During this period (1974–80) the basic framework of international politics remained the same as in the previous period. The cold war between the free-world nations and the Communist-bloc nations continued, although it seemed that both the Soviet Union and Communist China attempted to ease tensions with the United States, while the relationship between Russia and China continued to be strained.

A new destabilizing element in international politics was the emergence of Islamic nations equipped with "oil money" and Islamic religious fervor. The declining power of Shah Pahlavi of Iran was the most disturbing development for the United States and its allies, because a pro–United States Iran had been an important pillar of U.S. strategy for the Middle East (Ministry of Foreign Affairs 1979: 153). The political destabilization in the region was particularly disturbing to Japan, which heavily depended on the region for its oil supply.

In order to deal with the oil crisis, in February 1974, the U.S. government took the initiative in holding international meetings of oil-consuming nations, meetings attended by the foreign ministers and finance ministers of thirteen nations: the United States, Canada, Norway, Japan, and nine (EC) member nations (Ministry of Foreign Affairs 1974: 68, 69). At the meetings the United States advocated the creation of an organization of oil-consuming nations that would work as a countervailing force against the OPEC international cartel. It was proposed that this organization would directly negotiate with OPEC on behalf of member nations so that they could consolidate their bargaining powers.

This proposal did not gain acceptance because of a strong objection by

France, which contended that each nation should maintain its own bargaining power to deal with individual OPEC members. The thirteen nations met again in Brussels in July, which led to the creation within the Organization for Economic Cooperation and Development (OECD) of the International Energy Association with the main objective being that in times of emergency member nations would be allowed to borrow from the pooled reserves of oil (Ministry of Foreign Affairs 1975: 201–5).

In the meantime, the United States quickly lost its influence in international politics because of the domestic political scandal that ended with the resignation of President Nixon in August 1974 (Ministry of Foreign Affairs 1975: 130, 131). It was France that took the initiative in holding what has come to be known as the "Group of Seven (G-7) Economic Summit Meetings." The first summit meetings were called by the French president. In November 1975, the top political leaders of the seven advanced industrial nations (the United States, Japan, West Germany, France, the United Kingdom, Italy, and Canada) gathered in Rambouillet Castle in France for three days (Ministry of Foreign Affairs 1976: 36–38).

They discussed broad economic issues such as the current status and future directions of world economy, international trade, currencies, energy, North–South problems, and East–West economic relations. On the final day of the meetings they adopted the Rambouillet Declaration pledging mutual cooperation by the member nations to advance the economic prosperity of the free-world nations.

In the international sphere, the Middle East continued to be the trouble spot. After the exile of Shah Pahlavi, Iran became an Islamic republic and adopted an anti–United States policy, resulting in the termination of diplomatic relations with the United States (Ministry of Foreign Affairs 1980: 114). The weaker U.S. influence in the region created an opportunity for the Soviet Union to make its presence felt. In December 1979, the Soviet Union, under the leadership of Leonid Brezhnev, invaded Afghanistan, reminding the peoples of the world that they were still living under a volatile cold war regime (Ministry of Foreign Affairs 1980: 149, 150). The war between Iran and Iraq that broke out in September 1980 caused further confusion in the Middle East (Ministry of Foreign Affairs 1981: 173, 174).

With regard to bilateral relations with major powers of the world, Japan, as a member of the free-world nations, maintained close and harmonious relations with the United States. Whenever there were cabinet reshuffles in Japan, it was customary for the new Japanese prime minister to meet with the U.S. president and issue joint declarations to reaffirm close political and economic relations and defense collaboration between the two nations. During this relatively short period of seven years, four such joint declarations were issued: the Tanaka–Ford declaration in October 1974, the Miki–Ford declaration in August 1975, the Fukuda–Carter declaration in March 1977, and the Ohira–Carter declaration in May 1979.

There was no progress in relations between Japan and the Soviet Union. Ever since the two nations signed a joint declaration in 1956 to end the war and to restore diplomatic relations between the two nations, negotiations took place from time to time in an attempt to sign a formal peace treaty. The stumbling block was sovereignty over the four islands located off the eastern coast of Hokkaido to the southern part of the Kuriles; these islands have been occupied by the Soviet Union effectively since the end of World War II, but both nations have been adamant in claiming possession of them.

During this period, meetings were held between the foreign ministers of the two nations twice: in 1974 and 1978. However, no progress was achieved (Ministry of Foreign Affairs 1979: 142, 143). The fact of the matter is that, in a cold war framework in which the two nations belonged to opposite camps, it was not realistic to expect that either nation would make any compromise on the issue, and the Japanese government was well aware of this. After the meetings in 1978, all ministerial-level talks to do with a peace treaty were suspended until 1986, when the Soviet Union was under the leadership of Mikhail Gorbachev.

With regard to the relationship with Communist China, shortly after the signing in 1972 of a joint declaration that ended the war and that normalized diplomatic relations between the two nations, negotiations began toward the signing of a formal peace treaty. The negotiations took an unexpectedly long time, largely due to the difference between the two nations in their positions vis-à-vis the Soviet Union. While China demanded the inclusion of a clause denouncing the Soviet Union hegemony, Japan was opposed to it, as its official position was to maintain peaceful and friendly relations with all nations, including the Soviet Union.

After four years of negotiations, a Treaty of Peace and Friendship between Japan and the People's Republic of China was signed in Beijing on August 12, 1978 (Ministry of Foreign Affairs 1979: 16, 17). The treaty was quickly ratified in both nations. Deng Xiaoping, then vice premier, visited Japan in October to exchange the ratified copies of the treaty. His visit was reciprocated by a visit to China by Japan's prime minister, Ohira, a year later, on which occasion he promised to extend a large amount of low-interest loans to China (Ministry of Foreign Affairs 1980: 60–62). After this, political, economic, and cultural exchanges between the two nations progressed in a smooth fashion.

While Japan's relations with Communist China improved rather smoothly, its relations with Southeast Asian countries were volatile. In January 1974

Prime Minister Kakuei Tanaka made an official visit to five Southeast Asian countries (the Philippines, Thailand, Malaysia, Singapore, and Indonesia) to discuss with the government leaders mutual economic cooperation and a high level of official development assistance (ODA) to these countries (Ministry of Foreign Affairs 1974: 20–22).

His visit to the Philippines, the first of the five nations he visited, was well received. In the other four countries, however, he was met with large-scale anti-Japanese demonstrations led by students (Jiyu Kokumin-sha 1992: 78, 79). At Bangkok Airport he was greeted by a 5,000-strong group of student demonstrators chanting "Tanaka go home!" and "Down with Japanese economic imperialism." People started to boycott Japanese products.

In Jakarta more than 10,000 people demonstrated with slogans such as "Down with economic invasion by Japanese imperialism." The demonstration soon turned into a riot in which people indiscriminately destroyed more than 800 Japanese-made automobiles and motorcycles, burned down more than 300 Japanese corporate offices and Japanese restaurants, and pulled down the national flag of the Japanese embassy. Tanaka narrowly escaped from the riot-stricken downtown area by helicopter to the airport. After three days the riot was subdued only when the Indonesian government placed Jakarta under curfew. During this time three people were killed and 300 people were arrested.

Similar anti-Japanese demonstrations took place in Seoul in September of the same year, nine years after the conclusion of a peace treaty. The demonstrators attacked the Japanese embassy and pulled down the national flag.

The anti-Japanese demonstrations throughout Southeast Asia caught the Japanese government by surprise, because Japan, fully acknowledging its responsibility in World War II, had paid these nations large sums of money in reparations. But government officials quickly learned that the anti-Japanese movements were not the result of Japan's past (wartime) activities but of its more recent activities.

As a result of Japan's postwar economic success, by the early 1970s, Japanese products had flooded the markets of Southeast Asia. As a result, these countries registered large trade deficits with Japan. Massive exports from Japan were followed by direct investments from Japan. As an increasing number of Japanese companies started to build factories and began producing locally, they drove local businesses out of the market. Japanese businessmen tended to look down on local employees and did not associate with local people in general. Furthermore, they allegedly made large "political donations" to high government officials of the host nations to win their favors, sometimes against the interest of the people of those countries.

Alarmed by these developments, the Japanese government decided to take a more active role in improving relations with these nations. It not only increased the amount of ODA but also scrutinized their objectives to make sure that the assistance would directly benefit the people of the host nations. Many Japanese companies created "guidelines for responsible behavior abroad" to be observed by all of their employees assigned to Asian countries.

In 1977 Prime Minister Fukuda announced the so-called Fukuda Doctrine to serve as the guidelines for Japan's foreign policy toward Southeast Asian countries (Ministry of Foreign Affairs 1978: 42–44). The guidelines included the promises that Japan would not become a military power, that Japan would build relationships of mutual trust with Southeast Asian countries and become their true friend, and that Japan would contribute to the peace and prosperity of the entire region as an equal partner. In 1980, with the aid of the Japanese government under Prime Minister Suzuki, an Association of Southeast Asian Nations (ASEAN) human resource development center was built in each ASEAN member (Ministry of Foreign Affairs 1981: 22). With these initiatives taken on the part of Japan, anti-Japanese feelings in Southeast Asian countries began to subside.

With regard to domestic politics, domination by the conservative Liberal Democratic Party (LDP) continued during this period, although its margin over the opposition parties narrowed (in terms of the number of seats in the House of Representatives). In addition, successive cabinets after the long reign of Eisaku Sato (1964–72) were short-lived: these were the cabinets of Kakuei Tanaka (1972–1974), Takeo Miki (1974–76), Takeo Fukuda (1976–78), and Masayoshi Ohira (1978–80).

Kakuei Tanaka, once very popular among Japanese people because of his humble origin, fell victim to the oil crisis. Both hyperinflation and negative growth in gross national product (GNP), until then not experienced by the postwar Japanese economy, caused hardships in the people's lives. Tanaka's expansionist economic policy was an easy scapegoat (Jiyu Kokuminsha 1992: 75). Tanaka quickly reversed his policy in an attempt to fight inflation. In January 1974, a special law was enacted to control the consumption of oil and electricity. In March the government implemented a policy that froze the prices of fifty-three items directly related to people's daily lives (Economic Planning Agency 1979: 163). ·

Meanwhile, in February, the Fair Trade Commission (FTC) prosecuted twelve oil companies as well as the Association of the Petroleum Industry for violation of the Anti-Monopoly Law (FTC 1974: 27, 28). It was found that these petroleum companies had conspired to maintain oil retailing prices at a high level, which resulted in general price increases. The House of Representatives lost no time in conducting hearings before the Budget Committee, where representatives of the major petroleum companies and general

trading companies were questioned about their alleged wrongdoings in raising the prices of oil and other commodities (Jiyu Kokuminsha 1992: 76). In
March the government established price guidelines for petroleum products.

The final blow to Tanaka was that a series of money scandals connected
with him were disclosed, thus fueling popular anger at him. Several influential members of his cabinet resigned in protest against his actions. In the end,
Tanaka himself decided to resign in December 1974 (Jiyu Kokuminsha 1992:
76, 77). In less than two years he was arrested and indicted for taking a bribe
from the Lockheed Corporation. After a series of appeals the Supreme Court
found him guilty.

The immediate task of Tanaka's successor, Takeo Miki, on the one hand,
was to clean up the dirty image of the LDP tarnished by Tanaka, and, on the
other hand, to bring inflation under control and steer the Japanese economy
back to a growth course. In order to clean up politics, Miki drafted a proposal banning all political donations from corporations and labor unions; he
had to withdraw his proposal, because of strong objections from within the
LDP (Jiyu Kokuminsha 1992: 80). His only "accomplishment" was to let
Tanaka be arrested.

On the economic front, Miki undertook, in 1975, a series of measures to
prop up the economy, as hyperinflation was followed by a serious recession
(Economic Planning Agency 1976: 54–60). These measures consisted of:
providing small and medium-sized companies with low interest loans (in
February); implementing public works (in March); promoting housing construction (in May); and further promoting public works (in September). These
spending sprees put a heavy burden on the government budget. As a result,
in July of the following year, a special law was enacted to issue government
bonds, representing the first time in many years that bonds were to be issued.

It turned out that, by the end of 1976, when Miki was forced to resign
after a "defeat" in the general election, inflation was under control and the
Japanese economy was growing at a healthy rate.

During the successive two cabinets of Fukuda and Ohira there was no
major domestic political agendum. Government efforts were directed to economic issues that became increasingly affected by international factors. Table
9.1 summarizes a few key economic indicators.

The figures clearly reflect the effects of the first oil crisis in 1973 and
the second oil crisis in 1979–80 (to be discussed later). The immediate
effect of the first oil crisis was a high rate of inflation as shown by the 24.5
percent increase in the consumer price index (CPI) in 1974. A high rate of
inflation as well as a shortage in oil supply created economic chaos and
slowed down economic activities, resulting in the negative GNP growth
rate (–1.2 percent) for the same year. Trade balance, or the difference be-

Table 9.1

GNP Growth Rate, Consumer Price Index (CPI), Trade Balance, Foreign Reserves, and Exchange Rates

Year	Increase in GNP (real, %)	Increase in CPI (%)	Trade balance (nominal, million USD)	Foreign reserves (nominal, million USD)	Exchange rates (yen to USD)
1974	−1.2	24.5	1,436	13,518	300.95
1975	2.4	11.8	5,028	12,815	300.15
1976	5.3	9.3	9,887	16,604	292.80
1977	5.3	8.1	17,311	22,848	240.00
1978	5.1	3.8	24,596	33,019	194.60
1979	5.2	3.6	1,845	20,327	239.70
1980	4.8	8.0	2,125	25,232	203.00

Source: Economic Planning Agency, *Keizai yoran* [Summary Statistics on the Economy] (annual).

tween exports and imports, declined from $3.688 billion in 1973 (see Table 4.2 in Chapter 4) to $1.436 billion in 1974, reflecting a large increase in the import price of crude oil.

However, these figures (CPI, GNP, and trade balance) showed signs of recovery as early as 1975, and, by 1978, it seems that the Japanese economy was fully adjusted to the new economic environment; inflation was under control, with only a 3.8 percent increase in CPI, and the GNP growth rate exceed 5 percent. What had happened?

Shortly after the skyrocketing increases in oil prices, Japanese manufacturing companies embarked on aggressive rationalization measures, investment in less energy-consuming machines and equipment, technological change, and bold restructuring (Jiyu Kokumin-sha 1992: 101). In addition, the "Japanese production system," consisting of such elements as the just-in-time delivery system, zero defect movement, and quality control (QC) activities, was in the process of completion. Although these activities had begun before the oil crisis, it was the shock of the oil crisis that accelerated the pace of reform of the production system.

In addition, a dynamic mechanism of technological innovation was under way. That is, in assembly industries such as the automobile industry, one result of long-term relations between the assemblers and the parts manufacturers was that they were able to share information on technology develop-

Table 9.2

Percentage Increase in Labor Productivity and Wages in Manufacturing in Five Countries (1975–1980)

	Japan	United States	United Kingdom	West Germany	France
Productivity	56	9	6	24	31
Wages	49	51	100	35	89

Sources: Japan Productivity Center [Nihon Seisansei Honbu], *Katsuyo rodo tokei* [Practical Statistics on Labor] (Tokyo: 1983, 1989).

ment at an early stage, for example, at the stage of designing parts. Through the fusion of technologies in related but different industries, new technologies were developed in such industries as electronics, automobiles, industrial machinery, and semiconductors. Thus, toward the end of the 1970s, the industrial structure of Japan shifted from that of an economy led by the energy consuming "heavy-thick-long-large industries," such as basic steel and shipbuilding, to an economy led by the less energy-consuming assembly industries.

In comparison with the other four leading industrialized countries, Japan was the only one in which productivity increases exceeded wage increases between 1975 and 1980 (Table 9.2). In the United States, the United Kingdom, West Germany, and France, productivity increases lagged far behind wage increases. The wage-cost advantage, coupled with substantial improvement in the quality of products, strengthened the competitiveness of Japanese products in international markets. Now Japan's main export items changed from textiles, iron and steel products, and ships to automobiles, electric appliances, and industrial and office machines—a reflection of the change in its industrial structure.

By 1978, Japan's trade balance registered a large surplus, resulting in a big increase in foreign reserves. Consecutive surpluses in trade balance as well as a steady increase in the amount of foreign reserves held by Japan put upward pressure on the value of the yen. The exchange rate of the yen to the U.S. dollar, which had stayed around ¥300 to the dollar until 1976, started to increase rapidly thereafter. Naturally, Japanese exporting industries became alarmed by the development. In November 1977, the Bank of Japan intervened and purchased a large amount of U.S. dollars in an attempt to stop the yen's further rise, but this was to no avail (Jiyu Kokuminsha 1992: 85). In less than a month the rate hit ¥238 to the dollar, an appreciation of 23 percent from a year earlier.

Japan's large trade surplus meant that its major trading partners, namely the United States and the EC nations, registered large trade deficits with it. Naturally, external pressure was applied to it in various forms (Economic Planning Agency 1978: 178). On February 7, 1977, an EC committee judged that Japanese bearing companies had been engaged in dumping. On March 2, the United States sued five Japanese steel makers for dumping. On March 8, Japanese color television makers were forced to exercise self-restraint in exporting to the United States. On June 23, the OECD cabinet committee accused Japan of running up an excessive trade surplus.

In January 1978, ministerial-level negotiations between Japan and the United States took place in Tokyo to address the whole trade issue between the two nations; this resulted in a joint statement in which Japan agreed to increase domestic demand, reduce trade surplus, ease import controls on agricultural products, and double the amount of its ODA in five years (Ministry of Foreign Affairs 1979: 109, 110).

However, the United States showed no sympathy with Japan's plea that concerted actions be taken to stop further increases in the value of the yen. In October 1978 the exchange rate hit the highest level ($1 = ¥175) ever experienced up to that time. At this point, the U.S. administration reversed its position and started taking measures to stop further decline of the value of the dollar.

Later the Japanese government announced international economic policies in which it pledged to increase imports by reducing tariffs. This policy was reaffirmed at the Tokyo round of GATT negotiations in July 1979, where Japan agreed to halve import tariffs on minerals and industrial goods, from 6 percent to 3 percent (Ministry of Foreign Affairs 1980: 189–92).

In the meantime, in December 1978, large-scale demonstrations demanding the resignation of Shah Pahlavi took place throughout Iran; these destabilized the entire Arab world. It was against this background that OPEC decided to increase the crude oil price in 1979 by 5 percent initially and ultimately by 14.5 percent by the end of the year (Jiyu Kokuminsha 1992: 74). The reason for the intended increases was the fall, during the two-year period up to then, in oil revenues for OPEC member nations due to depreciation of the U.S. dollar, coupled with rapid increases in commodities imported from industrialized nations.

This pulled the trigger on what has come to be known as the second oil crisis. As it turned out, the crude oil price was increased six times in 1979, from $14.54 per barrel in March to $23.50 in December, and to $32 in July 1980. In Japan the price of heating oil increased by 70 percent and that of

Table 9.3

Labor Market Trends

Year	Labor force (thousands)	Unemployment rate (%)	Active job opening rate (%)	Real wage increase (%)
1974	5,310	1.4	1.20	2.2
1975	5,323	1.9	0.61	2.7
1976	5,378	2.0	0.64	2.9
1977	5,452	2.0	0.56	0.5
1978	5,532	2.2	0.56	2.5
1979	5,596	2.1	0.71	2.3
1980	5,650	2.0	0.75	−1.6

Source: Ministry of Labor, *Rodo tokei yoran* [Summary Statistics on Labor] (annual).

fuel for industrial use by 60–100 percent between January and December 1979. The crude oil price peaked at $34 in late 1980. Thus, the second oil crisis sent more shockwaves through the world economy.

However, Table 9.1 shows that the Japanese economy absorbed the shock rather well this time. Although the CPI increased from 3.6 percent in 1979 to 8.0 percent in 1980, the GNP growth rate suffered a moderate decline, from 5.2 percent in 1979 to 4.8 percent in 1980. The amount of trade surplus declined substantially, reflecting higher import costs of crude oil. This put downward pressure on the value of the yen.

The impact of the second oil crisis on the Japanese economy was minor, because, by that time, the economy had completed its transformation from an energy-consuming one to an energy-conserving one. Also, it was ironic that the depreciation of the yen, which had been hoped for so much, was achieved at the cost of the second oil crisis.

In June 1979, in the middle of the second oil crisis, Japan hosted the fifth economic summit meetings (Ministry of Foreign Affairs 1980: 183–86). Naturally, the main topic was energy. In order to cope with the OPEC monopoly, the summit leaders agreed to set a limit on the amount of crude oil each of the oil importing nations would import, thereby controlling the excessive demand for crude oil. In addition to energy, they discussed overall economic policies, international trade, currencies, and North-South problems.

We turn next to a review of conditions in the labor market (Table 9.3).

Here, again, we can clearly see the effects of the two oil crises. First of all, the labor force declined from 5,326,000 in 1973 (see Table 4.3 in Chapter 4) to 5,310,000 in 1974, suggesting that some unemployed workers (notably female workers) became so pessimistic about their job opportunities that they stopped looking for jobs, thus dropping out of the labor force, a phenomenon expected under the "discouraged worker hypothesis." However, as the economy was picking up, some workers returned to "participate" in the labor force. As a result, the size of the labor force in 1976 almost equaled that of 1973.

With regard to the increase in real wages, we observe a sudden and drastic reduction in the rate of increase, from 10.5 percent in 1973 to a mere 2.2 percent in 1974. In five of the seven cases, the rate of change exceeded 2 percent, but these figures are no comparison with those of the late 1960s and early 1970s when the rate of increase exceeded or was very close to 10 percent (see Table 4.3 in Chapter 4). It is worth noting that in 1980, when the Japanese economy was hit by the second oil crisis, the rate of wage increase was negative, perhaps a result of the fact that the rate of inflation was so great (8 percent) that a nominal wage increase could not keep up with it. At any rate, we observe that during this period Japanese workers and labor unions restrained their wage demands.

While the impact of the oil crisis on the labor force and wage increases was immediate, we observe a time lag of a year or so in regard to the unemployment rate and the active job opening rate, as we do not find much difference from the previous period. Unemployment jumped from 1.4 percent in 1974 to 1.9 percent in 1975 and stayed around 2 percent for the rest of the period. The active job opening rate halved from 1.20 percent in 1974 to 0.61 percent in 1975, and remained at that level thereafter.

Thus, these two sets of figures (the unemployment rate and the active job opening rate) indicate the same trend in the labor market: the labor market "softened" about a year after the beginning of the first oil crisis in late 1973 and remained soft for the rest of the period; Japan could no longer enjoy a full employment economy.

In advanced industrialized nations organized labor has played an important role in shaping the course of the national economy through collective bargaining and political action. Japan is no exception. We shall look at organized labor and argue that, in the latter half of the 1970s (and throughout most of the 1980s), the labor movement adopted a wage restraint policy that resulted in distorting the "normal" development of the Japanese economy.

When Nikkeiren (the Japan Federation of Employers' Associations) had advocated in 1969 the "productivity principle" of wage increases (which simply states that the rate of wage increases must not exceed that of productivity increases if one wants to achieve economic growth without inflation), it was largely ignored not only by the labor unions but also by individual employers who were capable of granting, and willing to grant, large wage increases. Despite a decline in the real GNP growth rate to single-digit figures after 1973, *Shunto* wage increases continued to register double-digit figures, and in 1973 the increase exceeded 20 percent, the highest figure since *Shunto* campaigns began (Japan Productivity Center 1983 [hereafter JPC]: 45).

The first oil crisis in the fall of 1973 immediately provoked high inflation. To recover the loss caused by inflation and in anticipation of further inflation in the immediate future, the labor movement fought aggressively in the 1974 *Shunto* campaign, which led to the highest number ever recorded of working days lost due to strikes. The result was an average wage rise of 32.9 percent, while the rate of increase in the CPI for 1974 was 24.5 percent (JPC 1983: 45). In the following year, the *Shunto* wage increase was 13.1 percent, while the CPI increase was 11.8 percent. A wage-price spiral had apparently been set in motion (JPC 1983: 45).

It was against this background that the government and leading employer groups, as well as major labor confederations, came to recognize the necessity of stabilizing the economy. Thus emerged a social contract whereby organized labor would restrain their wage demands in exchange for a fair share of economic gains as well as an improvement in social security and welfare measures. From then on, Nikkeiren's wage guidelines based on the productivity principle came to exert a strong influence upon employers' wage offers and final settlements in *Shunto* negotiations.

Thus, during the five-year period between 1976 and 1980 the annual average *Shunto* wage increase declined to 7.2 percent, while the annual productivity increase was 9.3 percent (JPC 1983: 45). Organized labor's wage restraint appeared to hold up successfully at the time of the second oil crisis in late 1979. Inflation was limited to a 8.0 percent CPI increase for 1980 (JPC 1983: 45). As mentioned before, during these five years, Japanese manufacturing successfully transformed itself so as to become less energy-dependent and more efficient with the help of industrial robots, the just-in-time system, quality control circles, and so on. It has to be added, however, that organized labor's wage restraint policy contributed to the Japanese style of export-driven economic development.

Throughout the period, female workers served to cushion effects in the labor market. So when there was reduction in the labor force from 1974 to 1975, the decline was conspicuous among female workers, especially those in their thirties and those aged sixty-five or above. When there was a recovery in the Japanese economy, there was an increase in the female workforce, especially in the tertiary sector, such as wholesale and retail trade, finance and insurance, and service industries.

The year 1975 was named the "United Nations Year of Women," and a treaty to eliminate discrimination against women was signed (Ministry of Foreign Affairs 1976: 281). The objectives of the treaty included: protection of women's fundamental human rights by the elimination of discrimination against women, securing of career opportunities for women in all areas of society, and elimination of gender-based role differentiation. Japan was among the signatory nations of the treaty. Still, no concrete action was taken by Japanese legislators to eliminate discrimination against women.

10
Industry-Specific Environment, 1974–80

The Iron and Steel industry

Japan's steel industry, which recorded the largest-ever crude-steel production of 119 million metric tons in 1973, entered a slow-growth stage after the first oil crisis in October 1973. As a result of lower demand in both the domestic and overseas (export) markets, crude-steel production hovered around 100 million metric tons per year between 1975 and 1978 (Table 10.1). Afterward, production increased slightly, but growth in quantity was no longer expected, as steel was being replaced in production of capital goods by other materials that were becoming lighter, thinner, shorter, and smaller.

Faced with this difficult situation, and aiming at profitability even when operating at 70 percent of capacity, the steel industry endeavored to reduce costs through downsizing and technical enhancements. At the same time, the manufacturers upgraded products or developed new products, adapting themselves to the changing demands for materials, and entered other industrial areas, such as engineering. Mergers also occurred among manufacturers with electric furnaces or among specialty steel makers.

Japan's steel exports, without being interrupted by the oil crisis, continued to expand until 1976, when they reached a record amount of 37 million metric tons (Table 10.2). The expansion was attributed to higher demand in anticipation of steel price rises; increased imports by petroleum-producing

Table 10.1

Basic Statistical Data on the Iron and Steel Industry

Year	Shipment amount (billion yen)			Number of employees (thousands)			Crude-steel production (thousand metric tons)		
	Iron and steel (A)	All industries (B)	(A)/(B) (%)	Iron and steel (C)	All industries (D)	(C)/(D) (%)	Production capacity	Output	World market share (%)
1973	9,220	103,362	8.9	528	11,961	4.4	139,042	119,322	17.1
1974	12,195	127,308	9.6	522	11,487	4.5	150,760	117,131	16.6
1975	11,306	127,521	8.9	506	11,296	4.5	152,010	102,313	15.9
1976	12,512	145,359	8.6	478	11,174	4.3	161,308	107,399	15.9
1977	13,270	156,918	8.5	468	10,875	4.3	167,538	102,405	15.2
1978	13,471	164,810	8.2	449	10,890	4.1	151,819	102,105	14.2
1979	15,759	184,257	8.6	438	10,860	4.0	156,829	111,748	15.0
1980	17,896	214,700	8.3	433	10,932	4.0	158,724	111,395	15.6

Sources: Adapted from Ministry of International Trade and Industry [Tsusan-sho], *Kogyo tokei-hyo* [Census of Manufacturers] (Tokyo: Ministry of Finance, Printing Bureau, annual); and Japan Iron and Steel Federation [Nihon Tekko Renmei], *Tekko tokei yoran* [Statistical Handbook of the Iron and Steel Industry] (Tokyo: annual).

Table 10.2

Exports and Imports of the Iron and Steel Industry

Export of all iron and steel products (thousand metric tons)

Year	Total exports	To the United States	To the EC	To Asia (including China)	To China	Import of steel products (thousand metric tons)
1973	25,562	5,287	1,278	9,790	2,661	78
1974	33,124	6,510	1,090	10,995	2,877	70
1975	29,994	5,724	1,640	8,920	2,836	22
1976	37,035	7,444	1,616	10,865	3,518	30
1977	34,982	7,596	1,286	12,895	4,532	46
1978	31,554	6,053	618	14,268	5,628	215
1979	31,496	6,196	754	13,494	4,467	896
1980	30,327	5,185	634	13,074	3,215	696

Source: Japan Iron and Steel Federation [Nihon Tekko Renmei], *Tekko tokei yoran* [Statistical Handbook of the Iron and Steel Industry] (Tokyo: annual).

Note: These figures are for accounting years (from April to March of the following year).

countries; increased demand for semi-processed products by industrializing steel-producing countries; increased imports by China; and other factors.

Steel exports decreased from 1977 through 1982 as a result of import restrictions imposed in the United States and Europe; competition in overseas markets with industrializing steel-producing countries, which led to reduced orders; hovering imports by Middle Eastern countries; a decrease in China's imports; growing risks in Central and South American countries; and so forth.

The amount of steel exported in 1974 reached 19.4 percent of Japan's total exports in that year. The percentage declined after 1975, while the automobile industry recorded a rapid rise in exports after the oil crisis. In 1977 steel, which had remained at the top of Japan's exports for over fifteen years, was replaced by automobiles.

The U.S. steel industry was in a serious slump and demanded import restrictions. Anti-dumping suits were filed against Japan's steel manufacturers in 1977. The U.S. government launched a package of relief measures, including the Trigger Price Mechanism, which took effect in January 1978. The European Community (EC) also set up a Basic Price Mechanism against imported steel in 1978; it was similar to the U.S. Trigger Price Mechanism.

Industrializing steel-producing countries continued to raise their production capacities. In 1977 the total steel exports of ten such countries (South Korea, Taiwan, India, Australia, Canada, Spain, South Africa, Brazil, Argentina, and Mexico) outnumbered their total imports, and they began competing with Japan in export markets. Japan's steel imports, mainly from these countries, rose sharply after 1979.

Synthetic Fiber Manufacturers

The first oil crisis of 1973 caused a sharp rise in the costs of materials and fuel, but demand, in anticipation of rising textile prices, brought about a substantial increase in profits. From 1974 to 1977, however, there was a sudden decline in demand, sending the textile industry into its most serious depression ever. Kojin, a big rayon manufacturer, went bankrupt in 1975. Synthetic fiber manufacturers and the banks had to prop up major textile trading companies like Chori and Ichimura Industries, which had fallen into crisis. The top seven synthetic fiber manufacturers ended up ¥41.5 billion in the red in 1975. The total number of employees in the textile industry, which had long been on the increase, declined quickly and fell below one million (Table 10.3).

A prolonged period of a strong yen and starts in production by NIEs like Korea or Taiwan made competition more severe in the export market that had constituted 50 percent of Japan's domestic demand (Table 10.4). Major

Table 10.3

Size of Textile Industry

	1970	1975	1980
Total number of establishments	112,754	114,111	101,955
Total number of employees	1,264,000	996,000	813,000

Source: MITI (Ministry of International Trade and Industry) [Tsusan-sho], *Kogyo tokei-hyo* [Census of Manufacturers] (Tokyo: Ministry of Finance, Printing Bureau, annual).

synthetic fiber manufacturers hastened to set up overseas joint ventures to neutralize rising nationalism (Table 10.5). Meanwhile, protectionist trade policies were growing stronger among industrialized countries. Such a development led to the 1974 General Agreement on Tarriffs and Trade (GATT) sanction of orderly marketing, a move that Japan supported. In 1978 the Japan Chemical Fibers Association formed an Anti-Dumping Investigation Committee to deal with rapidly increasing imports from neighboring countries.

Synthetic fiber manufacturers were beginning to build producing centers (mainly for polyester) in Thailand, Indonesia, Malaysia, and so on. They regarded each country/region as both a producing place and a market. Such overseas operations are considered to have set a precedent for Japanese companies that expanded businesses overseas after the revaluation of the yen. In this period one of our alumni took an active part in such an operation. According to the Ministry of International Trade and Industry (MITI), textile manufacturers' overseas investments increased rapidly around 1970 and amounted to $488 million covering 255 investments in the one-year period from 1972 to 1973.

The MITI urged synthetic fiber manufacturers in 1977 to cut operations and sanctioned formation of a depression cartel in April 1978. A special-purpose law effective for a limited period was enacted in May 1978 to serve as a countermeasure against structural recessions. Permissions for production facilities for synthetic fibers were frozen. Thus, the synthetic fiber industry ceased to grow and started shrinking. The Fair Trade Commission approved the 1978 depression cartel. The ten polyester manufacturers reduced their annual production quotas by 25–30 percent, which put their operations back into the black. Meanwhile, the top seven manufacturers of synthetic fibers reduced their workforces by more than 8,000.

After five years of a serious recession following the first oil crisis, synthetic fiber manufacturers adopted the following three policies.

Table 10. 4

Demand and Supply for Textiles and Garments (in terms of yarn: thousand metric tons)

| | Demand | | | | | Supply | | | | | | |
| | Domestic demand (A) | Exports | Exports broken down | | | Domestic production | Imports (B) | Imports broken down | | | Year-end inventory | (B) / (A) × 100 |
Year			Yarns	Fabrics	Garments			Yarns	Fabrics	Garments		
1970	1,448	610	192	262	156	2,040	63	25	22	16	482	4.4
1975	1,309	639	232	283	125	1,776	131	45	36	51	634	10.0
1980	1,706	601	219	267	114	2,050	278	117	62	99	625	16.3

Source: MITI (Ministry of International Trade and Industry) [Tsusan-sho], *Kogyo tokei-hyo* [Census of Manufacturers] [Tokyo: Ministry of Finance, Printing Bureau, annual).

Table 10.5

Textile Manufacturers' Overseas Investments

Period	1968–71	1972–73	1974–77	1978–81	1982–83
Number of investments	166.0	255.0	183.0	251.0	113.0
Amount (million dollars)	163.0	488.4	543.3	442.9	241.0

Source: MITI (Ministry of International Trade and Industry) [Tsusan-sho], *Kogyo tokei-hyo* [Census of Manufacturers] (Tokyo: Ministry of Finance, Printing Bureau, annual).

1. Downsizing: The top seven companies reduced their workforces by 40 percent altogether, scrapped 14 percent of their machines, and repaid long-term debts of ¥210 billion by selling assets worth ¥230 billion.

2. Strengthening textile fields by lining up products of higher quality: The manufacturers made good use of their technological know-how and developed "new synthetic fibers" with high added value; in this way they strengthened their competitiveness and recovered superiority in quality over imported goods.

3. Selecting and intensifying diversified nontextile businesses: Diversification into nontextile fields was brought about by technologies gained in their main business (textiles) and by further development of high-polymer chemistry. Synthetic resin (Toray, Teijin, Toyobo), carbon fibers (Toho Rayon, Toray), optical fibers (Mitsubishi Rayon), pharmaceuticals (Teijin, Toray), materials for artificial organs (Asahi Chemical, Toray, Teijin, Kuraray, Toyobo), and housing (Asahi Chemical) were major examples of nontextile businesses. Nontextile businesses amounted to 27 percent of the total businesses of the nine synthetic fiber manufacturers in 1977. This percentage showed a stable growth and reached 37 percent in 1985.

The only alliances made in the industry involved two joint ventures set up by four manufacturers in order to sell synthetic fibers.

The Petrochemical Industry

The chemical industry, which had grown under government backing and protection, was exposed in this period to various factors that influenced and brought fluctuations to its business.

There was a rise in demand immediately after the first oil crisis, based on the anticipation of petrochemical price rises and on fears of a provisional

Table 10.6

Naphtha: Domestic Production and Imports (million metric kiloliters)

	1970	1975	1976	1977	1978	1979	1980
Domestic production and:							
Imports (A)	2,407	2,288	2,760	2,764	2,852	2,838	2,480
Imports (B)	591	412	718	748	942	953	722
(B) / (A) × 100 (percent)	25	18	26	27	33	34	29

Source: Japan Petrochemical Industry Association (JPCA) [Sekiyu Kagaku Kogyo Kyokai], *Sekiyu kagaku kogyo no genjo* [The Petrochemical Industry as It Is] (Tokyo: 1998).

shortage. The industry maintained a substantial level of production for nearly a year, then production plummeted toward the end of 1974.

The steep rise in crude oil prices caused significant increases in the costs of raw materials, and excess capacity under contracting demand led to increased fixed costs. The 1975 financial results of the twelve ethylene makers were the worst they experienced in the postwar period. Government-led recovery measures were expected. The manufacturers watched for a chance to form a cartel.

MITI, which intended to equalize demand for and supply of ethylene derivatives, set up a production guideline in 1975 for multipurpose plastics such as polyethylene. Despite the government's guidance, low-density polyethylene and polypropylene suffered negative growth until 1977, and a cartel was formed for vinyl chloride. In 1977 crude oil prices declined, demand revived, and the petrochemical industry pulled out of the first oil crisis.

Meanwhile, imports of naphtha were increasing; in 1978, they exceeded 30 percent of the total supply (domestic production plus imports), and were still showing an upward trend (Table 10.6). It was obvious that domestic naphtha lacked international competitiveness.

The government was thinking of a shift in its basic policy, from protection of the chemical industry through sanctioning cartels or guiding production toward strengthening international competitive power. It launched the following policies in 1978 in order to secure low-priced raw materials:

(1) strengthening the negotiating power on naphtha prices by founding a joint enterprise for importing naphtha; and

(2) encouraging efficient utilization of oil resources and diversifying raw materials.

The second oil crisis in 1979 brought about a fictitious demand at first, as in the first oil crisis, and this caused a rapid increase in production. The production of ethylene rose to an all-time high of 4.8 million metric tons per year. However, business eased off rapidly in 1980, and the petrochemical industry slipped into the red, with an excess capacity of 2 million metric tons of ethylene per year.

The Industrial Machinery Industry

Weak domestic demand caused by the first oil crisis led to an export drive. Japan's exports grew at a double-digit rate from 1975 through 1977. The second oil crisis in 1979 resulted in serious damage to the economies of the industrialized nations. The energy-conservation issue came up at the 1979 Tokyo Economic Summit Meetings and continued to be on the agenda—ahead of economic growth—at meetings that followed. The energy-conservation era set in globally. The Japanese government promoted the development of energy-conserving equipment and facilities.

Machine Tools

Although the industrial world was in recession, Japan's NC technology, based on progress in IC technology, met the structural change in a world machinery industry that required energy-conserving techniques and higher productivity. At home, by way of measures to cope with the strong yen after President Nixon's announcement of the dollar defense policy package in 1971, all manufacturing industries took positive steps to make rationalization investments. This increased the demand for NC-type machine tools. The automobile, electric machinery, and electric appliance industries were especially active. They played an important role in spurring machine tool manufacturers to produce energy-conserving, labor-saving equipment, and automated equipment, or to downsize machinery. Meanwhile, in 1972, Japan surpassed the United States in the production of machine tools and became the world's largest producer in this field.

Trade disputes in the textile industry hinted at the possibility that machine tool manufacturers might also become involved in similar issues in the future (Takamura and Koyama 1994 [vol. 3]: 261).

Construction Machines

Investments in construction projects sank after the first oil crisis, declining by 14 percent in 1974. Yet the prices of construction materials rose sharply.

The result was an increase in exports, raising the export ratio from 30 percent to 40 percent. The main competitor on the world market was Caterpillar.

Since large public works were restrained, there was increased production of types of construction machines that were easy to turn around and appropriate for urban uses, especially power shovels, bulldozers, and truck cranes. The total production amount of all construction machines exceeded ¥1 trillion for the first time in 1979 (JSIMM 1998: 7).

The Electric Machine Industry

Heavy Electric Equipment (HEE)

The HEE industry recovered from the first oil crisis earlier than other equipment investment-related industries, because investments grew in electric power, which was to replace petroleum energy, and in energy-conserving investments. As a promising alternative energy source, nuclear power generation came into the spotlight, and it supported the HEE industry in the latter half of the 1970s, when it was suffering from a sluggish business environment.

There was also a rise in demand for energy-saving HEE. As demand for power grew and power plant capacities were upgraded, transmission voltage was raised from 275,000 to 500,000 volts.

The oil-producing countries of the Middle East and the Near East invested the huge amounts of money they received from oil in the creation of infrastructures. These investments created large markets for thermal power plants, transformer substations, seawater desalting plants, chemical plants, and the like. Japan's export of HEE to this region rose sharply and helped the industry move out of the doldrums caused by the first oil crisis (Takamura and Koyama 1994 [vol. 3]: 271–73).

Electrical Appliances (EAs)

The first oil crisis, by causing skyrocketing prices and negative growth, had a serious effect on the electrical appliance industry. Because the ratio of color television ownership had reached approximately 90 percent in 1974, thus leaving little room for growth in this area, the recession prompted a general decline in demand for EAs.

For Japan, a resource-poor country, the conservation of energy and resources was an urgent requirement. EA manufacturers tackled the problem energetically. As a result, the EA industry recovered from the oil crisis faster than other industries. The dedication with which manufacturers rationalized and developed products led to stronger export competitiveness.

The "Walkman," placed on the market in 1979 by Sony, proved to be a big hit among young people. Microcomputers, which were popularized after 1975 when their prices started falling, served to accelerate efforts to make EAs better, more complex, multifunctional, and high-performing.

Videotape recorders (VTRs) became the "breadwinner" of the EA industry in the first half of the 1980s. Their production expanded from 120,000 in 1975 to 4,400,000 in 1980, and leaped to 27,100,000 in 1984. Japan became the world's production base through the Beta System developed by Sony and the Video Home System (VHS) developed by Japan Victor and adopted by all Japanese makers except Sony. The latter system conquered the world market.

A rapid increase in the export of color televisions intensified trade disputes and EA manufacturers were forced to exercise self-restraint in exports. They started up local production in industrialized countries where there was strong demand (Takamura and Koyama 1994 [vol. 3]: 278–84).

General Trading Companies (GTCs)

The skyrocketing inflation renewed broad criticism of general trading companies (GTCs). The government took the following two measures that ostensibly aimed at restricting the domestic activities of GTCs:

1. The Ministry of Finance issued a memorandum on loan restriction to the banks in December 1974. The banks reduced loans to eight of the ten GTCs.

2. A revised Anti-Monopoly Law took effect in 1977, restricting the total stock holdings of big businesses. Nine GTCs held more stocks at the end of 1976 than the revised law was to permit them to hold.

GTC fund-raising was restricted in the domestic market and their corporate grouping by stock holdings was tightened. The result was that they conducted more active fund-raising abroad and increased overseas investments in place of domestic investments. This led GTCs to commence reconsidering their overseas businesses, including export-import activities (Shimada 1991: 202–4; Kawahara and Hayashikawa 1999: 49–50).

The major overseas businesses/activities during this period were the following:

1. Projects of resource development. At the strong request of resource-rich countries, the *development-and-import-formula* was replaced by the *processing-and-import-formula* because it aided such countries in their industrialization to add value to their resources.

2. Petroleum. Through the two oil crises, petroleum-producing countries' direct-deal oil increased in the petroleum market as major international oil companies substantially lost their supply capacity. GTCs imported such direct-deal oil for domestic oil-refining companies that did not have foreign

Table 10.7

Total Amount of Sales and Distribution Ratio in Four Categories

Accounting year (April to March)	Total sales Billion yen (%)	Distribution ratio			
		Domestic yen	Export (%)	Import (%)	Offshore (%)
1973	35,965	55.5	15.5	21.3	7.7
1974	44,778	47.4	20.7	22.7	9.2
1975	44,280	48.4	21.0	21.2	9.4
1976	48,425	48.5	21.4	21.0	9.1
1977	47,009	48.7	22.8	19.9	8.6
1978	46,021	50.8	20.9	19.0	9.3
1979	61,735	45.9	19.1	24.4	10.6
1980	72,583	43.5	20.2	24.3	12.0

Source: Shigetaka Asuka, *Sogo shosha ron* [A Treatise on GTCs] (Tokyo: Chuo Keizai-sha, 1998), p. 210.

capital affiliation. The share of GTCs in Japan's crude oil imports jumped from 17.5 percent in 1975 to 37.8 percent in 1981.

3. Plant export. As the petroleum-producing countries in the Middle East invested huge amounts of oil dollars in industrialization, Japan's plant exports to that area expanded. GTCs participated in the projects as coordinators.

4. Entry into the grain market. Following Mitsui and Co., which obtained a grain elevator in the United States in 1968, GTCs penetrated the U.S. grain market one after another between 1971 and 1982. This business not only served to secure food for Japan but also helped GTCs establish distribution centers overseas.

5. Offshore transactions. Sales through offshore transactions (or transactions that do not involve Japan) increased in importance, as shown in Table 10.7. The major trading merchandise was petroleum, grains, oils and fats, and raw cotton. All were traded internationally and in bulk (Shimada 1991: 184, 207–9, 216–26).

If we compare GTCs with other industries in terms of their recovery of ordinary profits after the damage caused by the first oil crisis, we see that GTCs improved less than the other industries (Shimada 1991: 245).

After the first oil crisis GTCs were thrown into the doldrums, a situation that would continue up to the bubble economy. This was the "GTCs-in-Winter Period." "The basic factor that brought 'winter' to the GTCs was the change in the industrial structure after the oil crisis, whereby the expansion of material industries came to an end" (Shimada 1991: 244–46; JFTC 1998: 51–53).

As GTC businesses expanded globally, risk management emerged as an important managerial issue. Ataka collapsed because of a failure in the petroleum business and was merged into C. Itoh in 1977. Mitsui and Co. was 85 percent of the way toward completion of its petrochemical project in Iran, when the Iran-Iraq War broke out in September 1980. (Mitsui was to abandon the project ultimately.) C. Itoh had difficulties in the management of Toa Oil, an oil-refining subsidiary. Failures in risk management led to huge amounts of bad-debt losses. GTCs were aggressively investing in material industries or their related projects/businesses. Such investments resulted in bad-debt losses and heavy interest payments, a serious burden on the GTCs (Shimada 1991: 228–37, 247–48; JFTC 1998: 57).

The Banking Industry

Revaluation of the yen after the floating of major currencies in February 1973 and a sharp rise in material prices after the first oil crisis in October 1973 caused the high-growth Japanese economy to slow down. As stated in Chapter 9, the government was forced to issue red-ink bonds in 1976 to counter the recession. The capital market had not grown enough to absorb the government bonds, so financial institutions were compelled to purchase them. Because bonds at that time were not allowed to be sold in the market, the banks had to hold onto them. Their money positions thus deteriorated.

Under these circumstances the importance of the capital market was widely understood. In the latter half of the 1970s the capital market was beginning to work properly, mainly because the economy was picking up again, income levels had risen during the high economic growth, and substantial amounts of capital accumulated in the private sector. Government bonds were increasingly absorbed by the capital market, which now had the capacity to take up the industrial bonds of key industries.

In the latter half of the 1970s, although the economy had recovered, the overall demand-supply situation of money eased because demand on the side of business enterprises was slack owing to economic growth in this period that was lower than that in the high economic growth period. Business enterprises' financial activities were meant not only to secure necessary amounts of funds but also to minimize financial costs, while individuals began to pursue higher yields. The government was requested to relax its restrictions on the financial sector (Enkyo 1995: 101), and relaxation eventually took place. Business enterprises were permitted to raise funds in foreign currencies, and they were allowed a wider choice of finances. Negotiable Certificates of Deposit (with unregulated interest rates), which had already become entrenched in U.S. and European markets, were introduced in 1979. Restrictions on interest rates also began to be relaxed.

On the international scene, surprising events occurred in the middle of this period. Franklin National Bank (United States) and Herstadt Bank (West Germany) failed in 1974. They had not coped successfully with the change in the oil dollar situation after the first oil crisis. Their failures sent the Eurodollar market into turmoil. The international activities of Japan's foreign exchange banks were influenced. In 1975, Ataka, one of the ten general trading companies, collapsed when its petroleum business failed. As international transactions rapidly involved larger and larger amounts of money, these events acted as a warning to banks to reconsider risk management.

The Foreign Exchange and Foreign Trade Control Law was totally revised in December 1980. It switched from a principle of prohibition to one of freedom. It reflected the trend of expanding capital transactions (Enkyo 1995: 103).

Meanwhile, Japanese banks activated their international business and increased their presence overseas. They expanded their businesses, ranging from conventional documentary transactions dealing with exports or imports to loans to local overseas subsidiaries of Japanese companies, loans syndicated with major U.S. and European banks that they managed or participated in, and project finances that required a high degree of skill in assessing credit risk. Banks also helped business enterprises manage exchange risks in futures contracts or in loans denominated in the currencies of the countries where those enterprises had their subsidiaries.

The key issue in the international financial market after the first oil crisis was how to recycle the Arab oil surplus profits to poorer developing nations. In 1975, banks in ten advanced countries and the International Monetary Fund (IMF) reached a financial aid accord in which Japanese banks actively participated. This arrangement turned out to be the cause of mounting cumulative debts for developing nations, a situation that would become a burden to banks in the latter half of the 1980s.

The Air Transport Industry

After the first oil crisis in 1973, the world's airline companies suffered from fuel shortages and a sharp rise in the price of fuel, which soared four times higher than fuel prices of a month earlier. Each airline reduced flights. Airfares rose 20 percent in ten months. Japan Airlines (JAL) faced a crisis. It downsized by curtailing its workforce or streamlining the organization. It still fell into the red and suspended dividends (JAL 1985: 159).

In 1972 diplomatic relations between Japan and China were restored, while Japan and Taiwan broke off diplomatic relations. A civil aviation agreement between Japan and China was signed and the Japan–China air route was inaugurated in 1974. The Japan–Taiwan air route was temporarily suspended, but reopened again in 1975 by the founding of Japan Asia Airlines.

The San'yo Shinkansen was extended to Hakata (Fukuoka City in Kyushu) in 1975, and this made competition between the Shinkansen and the airlines even more fierce. The domestic airlines were rather ineffective competitors, but the international airlines could be competitive.

JAL carried out its mission as the national flag carrier again in 1975, when the Emperor and Empress visited the United States. In the same year JAL edged slightly into the black; it resumed granting dividends in 1977. The turmoil caused by the first oil crisis had come to an end by this time. Aircraft fuel prices had stabilized at a high level.

The New Tokyo International Airport at Narita opened in 1978. The volume of air cargo for international transportation handled by JAL took JAL to the top of the International Air Transport Association (IATA) members in this category in 1980. This result was achieved by purchasing large numbers of jumbo jet planes and raising the airline's capacity for carrying cargo as well as passengers. The major competitors in the international air cargo business were Lufthansa and Air France on European routes and Flying Tiger on the Pacific route. Performing Arts Abroad was not in cargo plane operations at the time.

The second oil crisis occurred in 1979. As in the earlier crisis, fuel supplies were restricted and airfares went up (JAL 1985: 410).

The Beer Industry: Distribution

Kirin was affected by the first oil crisis, and it revised its pricing schedules in 1974. It changed its price structure from a two-tier to a three-tier system, consisting of a producer's price, a wholesale price, and a retail price. In doing this, Kirin intended to clear up the misunderstanding that the producer controlled distribution. The significant influence of rising prices lingered until 1980, when beer prices were raised again. The other three brewery companies also introduced the three-tier system (Kirin 1985: 139).

Traditionally, retail stores were classified by type of business/industry, rather than by style of business. Beer makers' clients were "liquor" stores, and, like drugstores or candy stores, they belonged to a specific industry, the liquor industry. Besides liquor stores there were service-industry-related markets like department stores, hotels, or the railway-related market. In the period in question organized retailers emerged. Supermarkets were already established across the country. They attracted a large number of consumers. Few of these stores, however, had obtained liquor licenses, although most were applying for them. On the other hand, many convenience stores under a chain operator like Seven–Eleven used to be liquor stores and so they had liquor licenses. These organized retailers came to be named "new business style" retailers. In either of the two "new business style" retailers, beer was purchased by the headquarter buyers of the chain operator, and business was done in a businesslike manner. Canned beer was the major item sold in this way; refrigerated, it was convenient because consumers could drink it immediately after purchasing it.

Business was done through agencies, except where producers had direct contact with chain operators. In many cases major nationwide or major regional agencies were involved, but in some districts leading local agencies were involved. Delivery differed from store to store. Products of all four brewers were delivered at the same time to some stores, while to other stores each brewer delivered its own products separately. Kirin had long been delivering its products through its own agencies and its agencies had dealt with Kirin products only. As these "new business style" retailers grew, however, Kirin allowed its agencies to deliver competitors' products, or allowed competitors' agencies to deliver Kirin Beer. Thus, beer agencies came to handle the products of two or more brewers, although the number of clients (stores) they delivered to was still limited (Miyashita 1997: 99).

The information network expanded in this period. Brewers began with in-house networks. Then brewers and agencies began, on completion of palletization, to share information concerning physical distribution. The coverage extended to inventory information and then to information on sales to retail shops. Brewers were now in a position to get real-time information on the sales activities of agencies. This information aided the marketing strategies of brewers. Among the organized retailers, chain operators obtained information on each store's inventory and sales. On the basis of such information chain operators directed individual stores to remove articles that did not sell well, and strengthened their negotiation power for buying-in talks.

Department Stores

Weak consumer spending caused by the first oil crisis lasted a long time. The average growth rates of sales at department stores, supermarkets, and retailers overall nationwide were approximately 9.1 percent, 16.1 percent, and

12.9 percent, respectively, on a year-on-year basis during this period (Table 10.8). Placed in order of growth rates, supermarkets ranked at the top, retailers overall were second, and department stores were at the bottom. These figures already showed that department stores' growth was beginning to decline. This trend would remain unchanged in the following periods.

A new style of retail store different from the supermarket also appeared on the scene: the specialty chain store and the discounter. Department stores were thus increasingly subjected to keen competition, and their consumption elasticity fell below 1.00. Their market share slumped by two percentage points between 1973 and 1980. Consequently, their prestigious position in the retail industry declined sharply and they were no longer in a position to lead the industry.

To combat the recession, department stores invested surplus funds in fixed assets, but as before, avoided taking on inventory risk. That is, they maintained the old framework in which merchandise was sold on sales space rented to merchandise suppliers. This led to less growth in know-how, less and less distinctiveness between one department store and another, and a further decline in profitability. The department stores lost competitive power against discounters of electric appliances and cameras. To survive as retailers, they followed the pattern of American department stores in specializing in certain merchandise lines. Compared with chain stores, however, the image of the style of business they were aiming at was fuzzy and unclear. No longer blessed with superior know-how or managerial genius, increasing numbers of major provincial department stores were in trouble and affiliated with large department stores with nationwide networks. No innovative developments were seen in this period; instead, a structural managerial crisis became evident.

Supermarkets were not satisfied with their slow growth in sales, nor with the slow increase in the number of their stores (attributable to the regulations of the Large-Scale Retail Store Law). They went heavily into affiliating with "new business style" stores like convenience stores. Now supporting the supermarkets, these affiliates let the 'bud' of innovation grow successfully within the trend of the times. In contrast, department stores failed to dismiss outmoded practices, making decisions only on the basis of what was happening in the department store arena. Shaken into action by sluggish sales, they could not come up with answers, and their position in the retail industry kept falling (Koyama 1997: 68).

Building Materials: Distribution

Annual housing starts hit the record high of 1.9 million houses in 1973. That autumn the first oil crisis occurred. Affected by the crisis, housing starts

Table 10.8

Growth of Sales by Style of Business

Year	Growth of sales (%)			Consumption elasticity		Share in nationwide retail market (%)	
	Dept. store	Supermarkets	Retailers overall	Dept. stores	Supermarkets	Dept. stores	Supermarkets
1973 (base)	100.0	100.0	100.0	1.01	1.13	9.1	8.2
1974	118.5	129.0	117.5	1.01	1.10	9.1	9.0
1975	130.8	147.5	140.4	0.92	0.96	8.4	8.6
1976	141.8	180.3	163.4	0.93	1.05	7.9	9.1
1977	149.3	209.1	180.4	0.95	1.05	7.5	9.5
1978	157.4	226.5	197.5	0.96	0.99	7.2	9.4
1979	167.9	256.6	214.5	0.98	1.04	7.1	9.8
1980	184.1	284.6	234.3	1.00	1.02	7.1	10.0
Average annual growth (%)	9.1	16.1	12.9				

Sources: Adapted from Japan Department Stores Association, *Sales Statistics* (annual); Japan Chain Stores Association, *Sales Statistics* (annual); and MITI (Ministry of International Trade and Industry), *Census of Commerce* (annual).

Table 10.9

Housing Starts

Year	Number of houses	Year-on-year change (%)
1973 (base year)	1,905,112	105.4
1974	1,316,100	69.1
1975	1,356,286	103.1
1976	1,523,844	112.4
1977	1,508,260	99.0
1978	1,549,362	102.7
1979	1,493,023	96.4
1980	1,268,626	85.0
Average year-on-year change		94.3

Source: Ministry of Construction, *Housing Statistics* (annual).

Table 10.10

Share of Imported South Sea Logs (%)

Year	Philippines	Indonesia	Malaysia	Others	Total
1974	16.1	47.3	33.0	3.7	100.0
1975	16.5	42.1	38.4	3.0	100.0
1976	7.6	43.5	46.2	2.7	100.0
1977	7.2	44.3	46.0	2.6	100.0
1978	7.2	41.2	49.2	2.5	100.0
1979	5.7	44.2	47.4	2.6	100.0
1980	5.7	45.6	45.3	3.5	100.0

Source: Japan South Sea Timber Council, *Chronological Data on Imported Logs* (annual).

dropped sharply in 1974 to 1.3 million, or only 69.1 percent of the previous year's figure. Stimulative measures were then taken in both the public and private sectors, and housing starts recovered slightly. The second oil crisis in 1979, however, struck another blow. Housing starts in 1980 plunged to less than 1.3 million, below the level of 1974. The average year-on-year change fell to 94.3 percent (Table 10.9).

This was the first time that the building materials industry had ever been pushed into a slump by international economic developments. Distributors' sales declined sharply and accumulated profits were almost used up. All distributors could do was to wait for the economy to recover.

There was a significant change in log suppliers (Table 10.10). Indonesia continued to supply more than 40 percent of Japan's imported logs. Malaysia replaced the Philippines as a supplier of logs, and it rapidly increased its share in the imported South Sea logs, until Malaysian and Indonesian logs were imported in nearly equal quantities. Indonesia launched a new policy in regard to forestry and forest products in 1979, and in 1982 it started to promote its own plywood industry, banning the export of logs altogether in 1985.

11
Career Progress

By the end of the previous period (1973) many of our alumni working for private companies had already been promoted to lower management positions. During this period (1974–80) an increasing number of them were promoted to middle management positions. A typical corporate hierarchy involving middle and lower level management positions is shown in Figure 11.1.

The traditional hierarchy consisted of three levels of management: *bucho*, *kacho*, and *kakaricho*. However, with the rapid growth in the size of business organizations in the 1960s and into the early 1970s, in some organizations, the higher position of *honbucho* (general manager of division) was created above that of *bucho*. Also, a number of obscure positions were created in between the three traditional positions. For example, beneath the *bucho* position were such positions as *jicho*, *fukubucho*, or *bucho-dairi* (deputy general manager) and *bucho-hosa* (assistant general manager). Theoretically, the former were line positions with the authority to make decisions, while the last-named was a staff position whose authority was limited to making recommendations to the immediate superior (*bucho*). But, in reality, this distinction was not strictly observed in all organizations. The actual authority and duties of these positions varied from one organization to another.

Beneath *kacho* were *kacho-dairi* (deputy manager), theoretically a line position, and *kacho-hosa* (assistant manager), theoretically a staff position. *Shunin* was also an ambiguous position in that not all organizations had this position as the lowest level of management. When this position did exist, it was usually below *kakaricho*, while in some other cases this title was used in lieu of *kakaricho*.

In both the main office and branch offices, both domestic and overseas,

Figure 11.1. **Typical Middle and Lower Management Hierarchy**

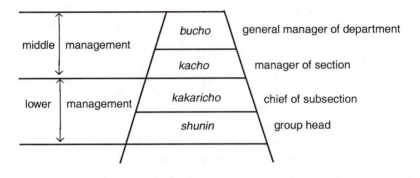

and in factories and other establishments, a similar management hierarchy to that depicted in Figure 11.1 existed. However, the same title (for example, *kacho*) might be used in the main office and in a branch office, but it did not denote the same status within the organization. The titles at a branch office represented a lower status than those at the main office. As a result, a *bucho* at a branch office might be equivalent to a *bucho-dairi* at the main office. Such a difference existed not only between the main office and all branch offices but also between one branch office and another. Therefore, career progress followed spiral routes involving a number of different offices, as we shall see shortly.

Career Advancement

As mentioned in Chapter 7, at the end of 1973, twenty-five of the thirty alumni continued with their original employers, all but one with private companies. (The last-named alumnus would continue to work for an economic association that he joined in 1965 after he completed his graduate study.) At the beginning of 1974, nine out of the twenty-five alumni were in overseas assignments. Five additional alumni were transferred to overseas offices by the end of this period (1980). The overseas experiences of these fourteen alumni will be discussed in Chapter 12. This chapter will focus on the domestic work experiences of our alumni.

The following is a snapshot of a dozen or so alumni who were working in the domestic offices of their original employers in 1974.

One alumnus was working in the Osaka office of a synthetic fiber manufacturer after a five-year assignment in New York. Upon return to Japan in 1972, he was promoted to deputy manager (*kacho-dairi*) of a section exporting textiles through trading companies. He recalls that this was a difficult time for his company because increases in crude oil prices could not be passed on in the company's product prices and because several companies entered into the market, thereby making competition keener. As a result, his company started to diversify its operations by entering into the production of such products as synthetic leather, plastics, films, wrapping materials, carbon fibers, and even man-made kidneys. Our alumnus was in this lowest management position in the organization for which he was working for three years, until 1975, when he was promoted to section manager, "or kacho" (to be discussed later). During this time his work was demanding, requiring two to three hours of overtime every day.

In the petrochemical industry two alumni were employed by the same company. One was a deputy manager (*kacho-dairi*) of a section in charge of sales of synthetic resin for molding and blowing purposes. The other alumnus was already promoted to the position of section manager (*kacho*), and his experience will be discussed in the latter part of this chapter dealing with the functions of the section manager. The first alumnus started his career in the domestic sales of synthetic resin, was transferred to an overseas business department where he was engaged in the exporting of synthetic resins, and was transferred back to the original department in 1972 as a deputy manager. After the first oil crisis, he, too, felt the effects of "excessive" competition that resulted in serious recession, although demand for home electric appliances and for automobiles was increasing. He sold 70 percent of his products directly to corporate customers, while the remaining 30 percent was handled by general trading companies. He recalls that during those days he went home after midnight almost every day, for which be received no overtime pay. Rather, his pay was cut and all bonuses were frozen.

Still another alumnus working for a chemical company was engaged in the creation of international joint ventures and licensing agreements with companies in then developing countries such as Korea. The company was a major producer of fertilizer, particularly ammonium sulfate, and, as such, it had accumulated technological know-how in fertilizer production. Although it had stayed away from the production of petrochemicals, in 1974, it merged with another chemical company belonging to the same former *zaibatsu* group and entered into the petrochemical field. The result was an oversupply of petrochemicals.

Another industry that was seriously affected by the oil crisis was the airline industry. With the introduction of jumbo jet planes in the early 1970s, the supply of air transportation services dramatically increased, and then the oil crisis hit the industry. With exorbitant increases in jet fuel prices, coupled with stagnant demand for the industry's services, most airline companies suffered losses. Our alumnus's company was no exception, and it started various cost-cutting measures. Our alumnus, who had been involved in cargo-related work in both Japan and the United States, was transferred to the company's industrial relations department in 1973. As a deputy section manager, he was engaged in collective bargaining with a labor union representing cabin attendants over such issues as wages, allowances, and working conditions. Since this was a new experience for him, he received education in the areas of pay structures, working conditions, training, and promotion/demotion systems. His work was very demanding, requiring on average three hours of overtime. Sometimes he had to work on holidays as well.

There were industries that were less affected by the oil crisis. The electrical machine industry was one. An alumnus who had stayed in South Korea for four and a half years all by himself, came back to Japan in 1971 when he was assigned to the thermal power plant department within the international sales division. In his absence the company had reorganized its structure by eliminating the sections. As a result, section managers became deputy general managers of departments. As a group head (*shunin*) he was engaged in the exporting of power plants, first to North America and then to Central and South America. Actual exporting work was done by general trading companies that possessed finance and physical distribution functions. His most important duty was to make initial recommendations on export prices on the basis of negotiations with the production people involved. He recalls he would report to work at 8 A.M. to take Spanish lessons before his workday began.

Another alumnus working for an electric machine manufacturer returned from Australia in 1972 and became a head (*shunin*) of the group in charge of exporting household electric appliances to Central and South America. In this company, too, sections had been eliminated by then. The International Household Electric Appliances Sales Division was divided on a regional basis and the Central and South America Group and the North America Group constituted one department (America). He, too, had a hard time with the Spanish language. He says, "I was tutored at my office. Later, when I came to understand the language better, I had amusing experiences, as I could understand the meaning of conversations among the buyers about price negotiations with us."

An alumnus with a brewing company, who had been transferred to the company's soft drink subsidiary in 1969, was still with the subsidiary in 1974. He was the manager of the operations section, where he was engaged in various kinds of sales support activities. Although the total demand for soft drinks was increasing, competition was very keen as new companies (mostly foreign) participated in the industry. Workers' commitment was low, with an annual turnover rate of 100 percent, and it was difficult to achieve sales goals. As a new manager, he received management training, picking up such things as the KJ method (an idea generation technique developed by Dr. Jiro Kawakita). It was not until 1975 that he returned to the original employer (the brewing company).

Another alumnus was working in a different kind of food industry, the marine product industry. After a few years' experience in sales, he was appointed in 1967 to be personal secretary to the president, in which position he remained for eleven years until the death of the president. The company specialized in whaling and other ocean fishery. The fishing industry was a tightly regulated industry that operated on licenses from the government. The total amount of catch was first determined by intergovernmental agreements involving countries such as the United States, Canada, and the Soviet Union. On the basis of those agreements, licenses were issued to individual companies. As the personal secretary to the president (with the title of deputy section manager), our alumnus accompanied the president when he engaged in various negotiations with foreign officials. When resource nationalism arose in the United States, Canada, the Soviet Union, and other major countries in the early 1970s, the company started to experience a difficult time.

The kind of career change experienced by our alumnus in the preceding case did not take place in general trading companies. In 1974 two alumni were working in domestic offices. One alumnus continued to work in the steel division exporting hot-rolled steel sheets to Europe and galvanized steel sheets to the United States. Prior to his transfer to this department in 1971, he was engaged in the exporting of steel and nonferrous metals to the Soviet Union and East European nations (this necessitated a stay of ten months in Moscow), and then in market research of steel products in Eastern Europe. In 1975 he was transferred to Houston to sell flat-rolled steel sheets and galvanized steel sheets to local corporate customers (to be discussed in the next chapter). According to this alumnus, total steel exports reached their peak in 1975 volume-wise and started to decline thereafter, although they were able to maintain the peak level money-wise. Exports grew rapidly in the early 1970s, but general trading companies did not make much money, while the steel producers made huge profits—a reflection of the power balance between the two industries. Our alumnus recalls: "Steel makers refused to do business over the telephone. I had to make a personal visit and then wait until the person in charge was available. That's why I had to do overtime often." According to him, basic prices were determined by the manufacturer and the final export prices were determined by the section manager. Although he was involved in the preliminary assessment of certain junior employees in the same section, his administrative responsibility was small.

Another alumnus belonged to the machinery export division of a general trading company that was different from the preceding one. In 1973 he came back from Melbourne, where he had been selling Japanese machines and plants (steel, power) to Australian customers. Back in Japan he was assigned to the chemical plant export department and was engaged in the exporting of refineries to the Middle East, especially Iran and Iraq, with a view to securing energy sources in the post–oil-crisis period. In 1976 he was to be transferred to the company's subsidiary specializing in the exportation of small plants.

In the casualty insurance industry, one alumnus was assigned to the Foreign Department, where he was engaged in the sale of insurance to Japanese companies operating in North America, Europe, the Middle East, and Africa. With an increasing number of Japanese companies operating overseas, his department's business increased. In the industry as a whole, the relative weight of marine insurance sales declined, while that of automobile insurance sales increased. With respect to overseas insurance, information on local conditions was a key factor in obtaining a contract. Our alumnus says: "In selling fire insurance associated with plant exportation, for example, information on such items as the location of fire stations and hospitals as well as local legislation on casualty compensation was crucial." As a deputy manager of the department, he solicited the opinions of his subordinates and made recommendations to the superior. In 1975 he was transferred to a project team, where he spent less than a year before he was assigned to Teheran (to be discussed in the next chapter).

The alumnus who joined his uncle's plywood wholesaling company spent eleven years primarily in purchasing lumber from Asian countries before being appointed general manager of the Administration Department, which was newly created in 1973. In the following year he was elected to the board of directors, and he created within the department a computer office with the initial objective of credit control. Later, computer-assisted control systems were adopted in sales and other functional areas of the company. The construction materials industry, which had enjoyed rapid growth until the oil crisis in the fall of 1973, started to experience unstable market conditions thereafter. His company was no exception, and this, according to our alumnus, made the introduction of computers inevitable.

A quick review of the above dozen cases reveals certain common tendencies among them, with the exception of the last case involving an alumnus who joined a small family business. First, by 1974, the *kakari* (subsection) had disappeared as the smallest unit of work organization in most large corporations. As a result, the title of *kakaricho* (subsection chief) was no longer in use; it was replaced by either *shunin* (group head) or *kacho-dairi* (deputy manager). It must be added, however, that there is every reason to believe that *kakari*s existed in most factories in that period. In certain large organizations, even *ka* (section) and *kacho* (section manager) had been abolished and replaced by the "group" or other more flexible work units. This suggests that, even before the oil crisis, the traditional three-tier middle and lower management structure of *bu*, *ka*, and *kakari* was considered too rigid to accommodate many changes that had taken place after sustained growth of more than a decade.

Second, within the above-mentioned new structure, virtually all of the dozen alumni had the title of deputy section manager or group head—the lowest management position. Apparently, these positions did not carry many supervisory responsibilities; they were largely limited to initial performance appraisal of subordinates. Although it was not clear from the interviews whether or not our two alumni employed by general trading companies were in these positions, their jobs apparently required the above-mentioned supervisory duties. In terms of career anchors, which were discussed in Chapter 2, at this stage of our alumni's career development, the employers evidently expected from them technical/functional competencies rather than managerial competencies.

Third, the amount of decision-making authority associated with these positions differed from one organization to another, and, perhaps, from one department to another within the same organization. The general tendency seems to be that the newer the job the larger the amount of decision-making power delegated to the lowest level of management; in other words, "bottom-up" decision making was practiced. This was simply because higher-level managers usually did not possess sufficient knowledge to make decisions on their own. Thus, deputy section managers in petrochemical and overseas insurance businesses, for example, enjoyed more power than their counterparts in established businesses such as the exporting of steel.

The Section Manager: The Man in the Middle

During this period, fourteen out of the twenty-five alumni who remained with their original employers were promoted to the position of *kacho* (section manager) either at the main offices or at major branch offices. In addition, a number of alumni were assigned to various managerial positions in domestic subsidiaries or overseas subsidiaries and branch offices. However, in this section we will not deal with the latter group of alumni, because our concern is with the functions of middle managers in large Japanese organizations. Furthermore, of the fourteen alumni, detailed information was not available from three. As a result, our discussion is limited to the eleven individuals whose key features are summarized in Table 11.1. They are listed in the order of their appointment to the section manager position. It must be

Table 11.1

Key Features of Section Managers

Case	Industry	Status of office	Section	Period	Number of subordinates	Report to
1	Petrochemical	Main	Feedstock purchasing	1973–77	4	Dept. general manager
2	Electric appliances	Main	Television exporting	1974–80	N/A	Dept. general manager
3	Textile	Main	Textile exporting	1975–79	10	Dept. general manager
4	Electric machines	Main	Power plant parts exporting	1975–82	7	Dept. general manager
5	General trading	Main	Paper exporting	1977–86	10	Div. general manager
6	Marine products	Main	Sales advertising	1978–85	2	Dept. general manager
7	Textile	Main	Tire cord sales	1978–86	4	Dept. general manager
8	General trading	Branch	Steel exporting	1979–80	3	N/A
9	Ceramics	Main	Foreign trade	1979–80	15	Dept. general manager
10	Petrochemical	Branch	Plastic resin sales	1979–83	7	Branch general manager
11	Brewery	Branch	Sales	1980–84	10	Branch general manager

noted, however, that the dates shown in the table do not necessarily reflect the pace of promotion. The reason is that some companies maintained a qualification system whereby an employee's eligibility for promotion to various management positions was determined by regular appraisals. Under that system, an eligible employee might have to wait for some time until a suitable management position became available. In such a case, the date on which the qualification was obtained would be more meaningful than the date of actual promotion. However, such information was not collected because we were not particularly interested in the relative pace of promotion of our alumni.

We turn now to a review of the duties of the section managers with special attention to decision making and supervision of the subordinates. The first alumnus who was promoted to section manager was the one working for a petrochemical company (Case 1). As mentioned in Chapter 7, prior to his promotion in 1973, he had spent five years in the Physical Distribution Planning Section as a deputy manager; there he was engaged in the development of online real-time computer systems for the distribution of petrochemicals to customers located in various parts of Japan. He was awarded the company's presidential commendation for the successful development and implementation of the pioneer program. Perhaps this achievement was instrumental in his rapid promotion to a crucial position at the company, the manager of the Feedstock Procurement Section, only eleven years after joining the company.

Shortly after his assignment to the position, the oil crisis started and the price of crude oil jumped from $2 per barrel to $10 per barrel. What made his job even more difficult was the policy of the Ministry of International Trade and Industry (MITI) whereby the price of feedstock was maintained at a high level in order to prevent excessive rises in the price of heating oil for household consumers. Furthermore, the importing of much cheaper foreign feedstock was controlled by the Petroleum Industry Act. The petrochemical industry protested against MITI's policy as being unfair, but to no avail. At that time, the conflict between MITI and the industry was called the "Naphtha (feedstock) War."

The alumnus's job was to procure main feedstock naphtha, fuels, and other petroleum products for petrochemicals, as well as other raw materials. He had four subordinates: one deputy manager and three nonmanagerial employees. He says:

> As we were purchasing large quantities primarily from two nearby refineries, we did not need much staff. The most important issue was the decision on the purchase price. It was made through discussion with the general manager of the departments, and also in consideration of the activities of

other companies. The final decision-making authority was with the general manager. Usually, a procurement contract was made quarterly. . . . After the oil crisis the supply from domestic companies became short. So we had to import indirectly from Kuwait and Saudi Arabia through the assistance of a general trading company. We did not buy on the spot as it was too risky. Besides, there was a foreign exchange risk, which we did not want to gamble on, although the president at that time (a former banker) showed some interest.

Our next alumnus returned from Australia in 1972 and became a group head (*shunin*) in charge of exporting household electric appliances to Central and South America (Case 2). Two years later, in 1974 he was promoted to manager of the television exporting section within a department covering a wide territory of Central and South America, Southeast Asia, the Middle and Near East, and Africa. Sections within the department were organized on the basis of products such as televisions, audio machines, and so on.

He recalls that, of the several regions, the Near and Middle East market expanded most rapidly—a reflection of the fact that the "oil money" started to contribute to an increase in purchasing power in the region. At the same time, he experienced difficulties doing business with people from certain African countries. According to him, "Their logic and time frame were very different from ours." He was very busy learning about local conditions, legislation, and contracts in the countries to which he was exporting television sets. He remained on the job for six years.

The third alumnus promoted to section manager was employed by a textile company (Case 3). After a five-year stay in New York, he returned to Japan in 1972 as deputy manager of a section in charge of exporting textiles primarily through general trading companies. In 1975 he was promoted to section manager. He was in the position for four years until 1979, when he was transferred to Malaysia. He recalls, "Promotion to the position of section manager is a happy memory in my life. I was thirty-eight years old. This was not really a quick promotion among my colleagues who joined the company in the same year [1963]."

According to him, the duties of the manager of this section included decisions on pricing policy and distribution routes, handling claims, and naming and discontinuing brand names. In regard to pricing he says:

> The section manager had the authority over transactions under ¥50 million (now ¥100 million). Sales policy was part of the annual budget worked out at meetings between the departmental general manager and section managers. The execution of the annual budget (or the achievement of sales goals) was the supreme order of the section manager. There was no input

into the annual budget from people below section managers. Monthly section meetings were conducted to follow up on sales performance and to discuss reasons if goals were not met. Countermeasures were decided by the departmental and section managers and conveyed to the section members. There was no consensus decision making or formulation of *ringi* proposals at the section level.

The fourth alumnus was promoted in 1975 to the position of deputy general manager in charge of exporting of substation parts within the International Sales Division of an electric machine company (Case 4). As mentioned before, sections had been abolished in this company; therefore, he was promoted from group head to deputy general manager. According to him, the business environment was such that the Middle and Near East boom after the oil crisis was producing almost an unlimited demand for both electrical power plants and their substations, as these countries invested their abundant oil money in infrastructures, and Japanese reputations were rising. He says:

> As deputy general manager of a newly established export group, I had seven subordinates under me. Since our group was new and our dealing was global, my subordinates were transferred from many different sections. Decisions on prices were made through discussions with our factory people as well as with customers. As we were a latecomer in a world market dominated by such European companies as the BBC and Siemens, we had to reduce our prices below those of our rivals to penetrate the market. We used about fifty percent of our energy for persuading our factory people, and the remaining fifty percent for negotiations with customers and competition against rivals like Mitsubishi Electric. As most of our customers were government agencies, such as the Ministry of Electricity and Water, the risk associated with the business was low and we were able to make good profits.

Our fifth alumnus was employed by a general trading company (Case 5). After five years of overseas assignment, he returned in 1977 to the original division (General Merchandise Division). He was appointed deputy section manager in charge of exporting paper and pulp products. Shortly thereafter, he was promoted to section manager, with ten subordinates (including one deputy manager).

In a sense, his new assignment was an extension of his previous work in Johannesburg. As mentioned in Chapter 8, he was exporting wood chips, the raw material for paper, to Japanese paper manufacturers. In this new assignment he exported one of the manufacturers' products (noncarbon papers) primarily to Europe. After the second oil crisis he substantially increased business with China.

In regard to decision making within his section, as much as possible, he delegated to his subordinates the authority to make an offer to customers. His role was to monitor the offers made by his subordinates to ensure an appropriate level of profits for each business transaction. Needless to say, when asked by his subordinates about the appropriateness of particular offers, he would provide the needed advice.

The next alumnus was employed by a marine products company (Case 6). After serving as the personal secretary to the president for eleven years, he was transferred to the Overseas Business Department in 1977. After a year and a half he was again transferred to the Marketing Control Department as manager of the Advertising Section, a position he held for eight years. The difficult international environment in which his company was operating has already been mentioned. The resource nationalism culminated in 1977 when the United States, Canada, the Soviet Union, and many other nations claimed "200-nautical-mile territorial waters" around their coasts. With a reduction in its whaling and fishing, the company diversified into food processing and the importation of marine products. However, strong competitors already existed in every area of the food processing industry. One way of gaining and increasing the market shares was through advertisement.

The Advertisement Section was a small one, with only one or two subordinates, and our alumnus had the final authority in deciding how to use the budget. Although he attempted to delegate his authority to his subordinates, they did not always come forward with good ideas. As a result, he made decisions almost single-handedly, even on such issues as commercials, posters, commercial films, and sales promotion materials. He recalls sponsoring musical shows in major cities produced by a famous musician/composer as a promotion campaign commemorating the company's one-hundredth anniversary. According to him, it was an early attempt by Japanese corporations to sponsor cultural activities.

Our next alumnus was promoted to the position of section manager in 1978 when he returned home from Vienna, where he had stayed for five years (Case 7). His new assignment was that of section manager in charge of tire cord sales. Synthetic fibers were used not only for textiles and garments but also for other industrial products. In particular, nylon and polyester fibers were widely used for the reinforcement of tires. With the increase in the sale of automobiles and trucks, the sale of these tire reinforcement fibers also increased. As a result of the rapid increase in sales and therefore in market shares, the company came to occupy a dominant position in the industry.

Despite the amount of sales, the section was a small one, with only four subordinates (including one deputy manager). Since the general manager of the department was in the Osaka office, the section enjoyed a relatively high degree of autonomy. Sales goals and the selling prices of the products of his section as well as of the department were determined at sales planning meetings attended by the general manager, section managers, and (where necessary) factory representatives. With advice from the deputy manager, our alumnus made virtually all decisions that were within his authority, including those on the sales goals of his subordinates. For effective communication with his subordinates he created a weekly news bulletin. Section meetings were held, not for decision-making purposes but for the subordinates to make reports.

An alumnus with a general trading company who had been assigned to the company's office in Houston came back to Japan in 1979 (Case 8). He was transferred to the Osaka branch as a section manager in a department in charge of steel exporting. He recalls that, by this time, the Japanese steel industry had reached maturity and its competitive power in the world market had begun to decline. Steel companies began to review the commission they paid to general trading companies more or less automatically. Within his company the steel division began downsizing by transferring employees to expanding areas such as information-related businesses.

His group's job was to export galvanized steel sheets produced by Osaka-based manufacturers to the United States and to Australia. He had three junior employees under him, but his role was more that of what he calls a "playing manager" than that of a supervisor. When necessary, he consulted a senior section manager about his business. He was on the job for less than two years before he was transferred back to the company's main office in Tokyo.

Our next alumnus also returned from abroad in 1979 after serving for six years as the CEO of the Canadian subsidiary of a ceramics manufacturer (Case 9). At the company's main office he was appointed deputy general manager of the Foreign Trade Department. The department consisted of approximately thirty people and was headed by a general manager who was also a member of the board of directors. According to him, the exporting of ceramics began to slow down partly as a result of the appreciation of the yen, and the company began to produce overseas. His department started to export knives, forks, crystals, and metal tableware in addition to ceramics. He assisted the general manager in making important decisions. After a year on the job, however, he quit the company to join his wife's family business.

Our next alumnus was employed by a petrochemical company and was engaged in sales, both domestic and foreign (Case 10). Between 1975 and 1979 he was transferred to the company's joint venture with a paper manufacturer, where he was in charge of selling synthetic paper. In 1979 he was transferred back to the parent company as a section manager in the Resin Sales Department of the Osaka branch. With seven subordinates, his section covered a wide territory in western Japan (excluding Kyushu). Although the industry was at a mature stage, sales were increasing. The general manager of the branch office was his immediate superior, but he was busy with ceremonial duties, and our alumnus reported to the general manager of the department in the main office in Tokyo. He was on the job until 1983, when he was again transferred to a subsidiary.

Our last alumnus worked for a brewing company (Case 11). He, too, spent several years in the company's soft drink subsidiary. After two brief stints in the parent company's branch offices, he was appointed manager of the Sales Section of the Sapporo branch. Although his company enjoyed a dominant market share nationally (well above 50 percent), its share in Hokkaido was only about 20 percent. He reported directly to the general manager of the branch and he had ten subordinates, including a deputy section manager.

Sales goals were discussed at weekly meetings of managers; the final decision on sales goals for the branch as a whole as well as for individual sections was made by the general manager. Section meetings were held when necessary, and at these meetings individual sales goals were discussed. Our alumnus believed that such meetings would have a positive effect on his subordinates' work motivation, and he encouraged all members to participate in the discussion. Our alumnus would make final decisions on individual sales goals taking into consideration the discussions held at these section meetings. He was on the job for four years before being transferred back to Tokyo.

This concludes our review of the roles of section managers in decision making. Next, we examine the extent to which decision making at the section level was of a "consensus," "group," or "bottom-up" nature, as is usually alleged, and, if so, why. With two exceptions (Cases 1 and 6), the alumni were engaged either in domestic sales (Cases 7, 10, and 11) or in exporting (Cases 2, 3, 4, 5, 8, and 9). These nine cases were similar in that sales goals and prices were the two most important items of decision making.

With regard to the determination of the sales goals of a section, the prevailing pattern appears to be that the decisions were made by the general managers of a department or a branch office in consultation with section managers, usually in a meeting. The general manager played a crucial role because the sales goals of a section were usually determined as part of the sales goals of the department or the branch office. Usually, input from the bottom (or rank-and-file members of a section) was nil or at most minimum. This pattern applied to Case 1, where the decision was made on the amount of purchase rather than of sales. This type of decision making cannot be considered consensus or bottom-up style as far as rank-and-file members were concerned. It is not group decision making either, because they were not directly involved. For section managers it may be called a group style because they were usually consulted in groups. From the standpoint of the general manager, this practice may be described as a "group consultative" style—the fourth one in the Vroom-Yetton model described in Chapter 2.

As for the sales goals of individual members of a section, section managers would make decisions with or without input from below. For example, in Case 11, the section manager would make final decisions by taking into account the comments of subordinates made at the meetings. In Case 7, in deciding individual sales goals, the section manager consulted his immediate subordinate (the assistant section manager), but not necessarily the individual subordinates under him. Still, in Case 3, the section manager made decisions unilaterally. Although section meetings were held, their purpose was to analyze the reasons for goals not being met. From the above, we see that there were certain differences among the companies as to the degree of subordinates' participation in decision making on their goals. Perhaps, as Vroom and Yetton state, the above differences were a result of factors related to the manager, the subordinate, and the situation. However, in spite of these differences, pure group consensus-based bottom-up decision making was not seen in any organization.

If we look next at decision making on prices, we see that final prices were determined only after negotiations with the customers (wholesalers, retailers, and corporate customers). As such, final outcomes reflected the relative bargaining power of the parties. Our concern here is with the locus of power of the negotiations, or who had the power of concluding a sales contract, formal or informal.

Our interview results suggest that, in companies dealing with bulky products and therefore involving a large amount of money, such as power plants and steel plates, decisions were made at the higher level, at least at the level of the section manager. On the other hand, in companies dealing with less bulky products such as textiles, plastics, papers, and ceramics, decisions varied according to the amount of money involved in each transaction. The statement of our alumnus in Case 3 that the section manager had the authority over transactions under ¥50 million, attests to this point. In addition, the statement of another alumnus, who was not involved in the sales function (Case 1), to the effect that, since they purchased the feedstock in large quantities, the decision was made through discussions with the general manager without involving his subordinates, supports the above conclusion.

There was one exception to the general rule, however. That is, the company in Case 11 was not involved in negotiations with customers because the brewing industry was an oligopoly consisting of only four companies, with this company playing the role of the industry's price leader. The company's price was determined on a cost-plus basis and was accepted by the wholesalers without negotiation. The main sales activity of this company consisted only of "allocating" the company's products (beer) to the wholesalers and large-scale commercial users such as restaurants, without regard to prices. Internally to the company, this may be called a very centralized pricing policy.

In conclusion, we can say that group and consensus decision-making styles were not reflected in the pricing policy of the companies under observation; only in transactions involving relatively small amounts of money did lower-level employees enjoy a certain amount of discretion—a form of bottom-up decision making. It must be added, however, that our conclusion is based primarily upon the observation of sales functions where individual responsibility is easily established and individual performance easily assessed. Different conclusions may be obtained in the case of other functions. To overcome this limitation, we will examine the same issue (the locus of decision-making power) at higher levels of management in Chapters 16 and 21.

We next address the issue of supervision of subordinates, another important function of the section manager. Training is an important element of supervision; therefore, we asked our alumni how they, as section managers, educated and trained their subordinates. Here are some of the typical answers on the overall severity of training:

> I trained my subordinates strictly so that they could see by themselves if they were meeting my expectations. I conducted the training on the belief that competent subordinates are those who are willing to learn, especially in regard to the technical aspects of their jobs. (Case 2)

> I conducted the education and training of my subordinates strictly, because I expected from them the same level of performance as the level of my performance when I was in their positions. I made every effort to train all of them to become outstanding performers. On reflection, perhaps I should have treated them differently according to the ability of each individual. (Case 7)

On the other hand, one alumnus says:

> I was not so strict. It was more like working together. (Case 8)

Thus, we see a significant difference between the first two answers and the last. Perhaps the difference is attributable to personality difference, but it could also be due to the different amount of supervisory responsibility required. While in the first two cases the responsibility was substantial, in the last case it was small.

As for the content of education/training, here are typical answers:

The group was newly created and the members (subordinates) were gathered from various departments within the company. As none of them had job knowledge about foreign trading, I taught them the basics of foreign trading. (Case 4)

As the subordinates' motivation for goal achievement was higher, I made them design strategies to achieve their individual goals. (Case 11)

The only thing I told my subordinates was to make efforts to become someone who could be trusted by others, or to provide the customers with the kind of service that would earn their trust, which I have been practicing. I also said that trading companies do not produce tangible products and that the only thing we provide is service. That is why the quality of service is all the more important. (Case 5)

Delegation was my way of training the subordinates. Although the final decision was my responsibility, I left the rest up to my subordinates. (Case 6)

Here again, the above answers appear to reflect not only personality differences but also differences in subordinates and situations. In spite of these differences, the answers obtained reflect certain tendencies. First, the answers are rather neatly grouped into the two categories of task orientation (Cases 2, 7, 4, and 5) and relations (or consideration) orientation (Cases 8, 11, and 6). Second, loyalty to the company, which is often pointed out as an important objective of on-the-job (OJT) training by Japanese companies, did not surface, at least at this level of training.

We will now look at assessment of the performance of subordinates, another important duty of a supervisor. Here are some answers:

Performance appraisal was conducted on the basis of two criteria: ability and results. Ability consisted of such items as motivation, job knowledge, and execution, and results consisted of the amount of sales and profits. For the evaluation of nonmanagerial employees, a heavier weight was given to ability factors. Appraisal was conducted by the section manager and reviewed by the general manager and the personnel department, but the section manager's appraisal was rarely altered. Evaluation of the results was difficult in the case of teamwork. (Case 3)

Performance evaluation was conducted twice a year—once for promotion and pay increase and once for the determination of semiannual bonuses. For the former, evaluation was made in terms of ability and results, with the relative weights of 30 percent and 70 percent, respectively. Initial evaluation was done by the section manager with input from the deputy section manager. The section manager's evaluation was reviewed by the general manager and also by the personnel department. In the process, a certain amount of adjustment was made on the basis of the general manager's subjective assessment and of the personnel office's effort to achieve uniformity across departments. (Case 10)

Performance evaluation was conducted using a standard form in which ability, efforts, and performance results were the three criteria. (Case 9)

In conducting performance appraisal the company-wide form was used. In actual appraisal "personality" was the most difficult criterion to deal with. (Case 11)

Needless to say, I tried very hard to make a fair evaluation. (Case 2)

"Since we conducted relative evaluation using a five-point rating form in which 1 means poor and 5 means excellent, there always were people whose overall score was close to 1. How to make best use of these people was a big problem. (Case 4)

Overall, then, the section manager played a key role in the evaluation of nonmanagerial employees. The two most popularly used appraisal criteria were ability (including potential ability) and performance (or results). The relative weight of these two factors varied among companies, but the general tendency seemed to be that, at the nonmanagerial level, ability was more important. We can also detect some vestige of Japanese paternalism, especially in regard to the treatment of the poorly rated employees.

12

Overseas Assignments, 1974–80

During this period (1974–80), a total of fourteen alumni were active in overseas assignments (Table 12.1). They are listed in the order of the commencement of their overseas assignments.

As shown in the table, several of them had been sent abroad prior to the first oil crisis of 1973 and remained in their assignments during this period. In addition, two alumni were transferred from one overseas assignment to another. In the table, Cases 1-1, 2, and 3 were partially discussed in Chapter 8, where Case 1-1 was rather fully treated and so needs no further discussion. Therefore, in this chapter we will cover the experiences of fourteen alumni in fifteen overseas assignments.

The table shows a wide variety of work assignments of the fourteen individuals, reflecting differences in the nature of the industries, in the stages of globalization of their companies, and in the level of responsibility of individual alumni. We saw in Chapter 8 that the general pattern of evolution in the business globalization of manufacturing companies in Japan was: exports through general trading companies, then direct sales through their own overseas sales offices, and finally, local production and sales.

Out of the fourteen alumni in whom we are interested here, three were working for general trading companies and involved in exporting and/or importing specific commodities. One alumnus (Case 6) was stationed in the main office of the company's wholly owned subsidiary headquartered in New York. The office employed about 70 Japanese and 200 American staff assigned to various departments organized on the basis of a line of commodities. Our alumnus was assigned to the Synthetic Resin Section, where his job was to sell the material exported from Japan to the U.S. market.

The second alumnus (Case 8) was stationed in the Houston branch office

Table 12.1

Overseas Assignments

Case	Industry	Duration	Place	Work
1	Construction machinery	(1) 1970–76	Sydney	Sales promotion
		(2) 1976–81	London	Sales promotion
2	Banking	1970–77	London	Lending and project financing
3	General trading	1972–77	Johannesburg	Trading (chemicals, wood, etc.)
4	Petroleum	1973–75	Houston	Regional strategy analysis
5	Ceramics	1973–79	Toronto	General management/ sales
6	General trading	1973–81	New York	Trading (plastics)
7	Textile	1973–78	Vienna	Sales promotion
8	General trading	1975–79	Houston	Trading (steel)
9	Trust banking	(1) 1975–77	Frankfurt	Market research
		(2) 1977–81	New York	Administration and accounting
10	Insurance	1976–80	Teheran	Casualty insurance
11	Economic federation	1977–80	Washington	Public relations
12	Airlines	1977–83	New York	Administration
13	Department store	1978–81	Singapore	General management
14	Textile	1979–82	Penang	Inter-department coordination

of the same U.S. subsidiary as the alumnus in Case 6. The Houston office employed about sixty staff, including twenty or so parent-country nationals (PCNs) from Japan. The main business of the office was the sale of steel products such as wires, plates, and pipes to U.S. oil companies. In addition, it sold machinery, chemicals, and textiles exported from Japan. Our alumnus specialized in the sale of steel plates. The oil crisis helped his business, as the U.S. oil drilling companies increased their production.

The experiences of our third alumnus (Case 3) were partially described in Chapter 8. Working in a small office with about twenty employees located in Johannesburg, our alumnus dealt with a variety of commodities including wood chips, chemicals, plastics, and textiles. In addition to the exporting of wood chips to pulp manufacturers in Japan, he was involved in other businesses as well. For example, during the oil crisis, local demands for chemicals and plastics were very strong; therefore, he imported those materials from Germany, Belgium, and the United Kingdom for resale to local dynamite manufacturers or for reexport to Japan. Here, too, the oil crisis helped our alumnus's business.

The five alumni working for manufacturing companies were given different assignments, largely depending on the stage of globalization of their companies and also on the location of their assignments. One alumnus employed by a textile company (Case 7) was sent to the company's office in Vienna that had been created two years prior to his assignment to act as a window to East European markets. It was a small office with four people—three Japanese and a locally hired secretary. Their mission was to promote the sales of textiles, textile products, and textile plant machinery to public textile corporations in East European markets.

As a general rule, they were not directly involved in actual sales, which took the form of exporting from Japan. Exporting was handled by general trading companies carrying out such activities as purchasing the company's products in Japan, shipping the products to an overseas market, and then selling the products in the local markets. Therefore, our alumnus worked in close collaboration with the sales representatives of trading companies who also operated from Vienna. To promote the company's products our alumnus traveled extensively in East European countries such as East Germany, Poland, Hungary, Czechoslovakia, and Yugoslavia. For example, he set up a display corner in "dollar shops" in six cities in Poland to advertise and sell certain products of his company, and he visited each city every week.

According to this alumnus, the economic policies of these countries were shifting from the importation of consumer goods, including textiles and textile products, to the importation of raw materials, the expansion of domestic production, and the domestic consumption and exportation of final products. However, things did not go according to plan because of obsolete plant facilities and a lack of well-trained manpower. Thus, they were beginning to import machinery and plant facilities from capitalist countries, including Japan.

On the side of Japan, there was a domestic oversupply of machinery and plant facilities after the oil crisis of 1973, and Japanese manufacturers needed overseas markets. East European countries were a logical market for Japanese machines, including textile machines. These countries purchased machinery and plant facilities as well as raw materials with loans from capitalist countries. However, the exporting industries were unable to generate sufficient foreign exchange due to their weak competitive power. As a result, they began to ask for the postponement of loan repayments. Our alumnus recalls, "The contradictions of socialism gradually became apparent and I felt the weakening of communism. However, I did not dream of the collapse of communism within the twentieth century."

Thus, although the products were shifting from textiles to textile machines, his company's operations in Eastern Europe remained the same: exporting through trading companies. The role of our alumnus was limited to sales promotion. As such, his company's operations represented stage one of the business globalization process.

The experience in Sydney of our alumnus working for a construction machine manufacturer (Case 1-1) has already been described in Chapter 8. This alumnus was transferred in 1976 from Sydney directly to London to head the company's liaison office there (Case 1-2). It was a small office with five people: our alumnus as the general manager, two local service staff, and two secretaries. As in Sydney, his role was to spearhead the company's exporting activity not only to the United Kingdom but also to Scandinavia and North Africa by a variety of means, including the building of a network of sales agents.

Prior to his assignment, the company's export activity to Europe was stagnant as a result of strong competition from U.S. and European companies. In fact, his company was a latecomer in the international market. In the 1960s the company's products were inferior in quality; this was compensated for by the price advantage due partly to lower wages and to exchange rates fixed at a low level. The company made every effort to upgrade the quality of their products, and their exports to the communist-bloc nations and to the Middle East expanded substantially, as competition from U.S. and European companies was less severe there. By the mid-1970s their continued efforts to improve quality resulted in their products becoming competitive against those of their U.S. and European counterparts, despite successive revaluations of the yen after 1970.

During the tenure of this alumnus, exports to the United Kingdom and to other European countries continued to increase, even though economic and political conditions were not very favorable. After the oil crisis, European countries continued to suffer from high unemployment rates, which resulted in protectionist policies, including dumping charges against imports from Japan. Despite these difficulties the ratio of exports to the company's total sales exceeded 50 percent by the late 1970s.

The third manufacturing company alumnus, who had highly successful achievements in Bangkok, was chosen in 1973 to head the company's Canadian sales base (Case 5). Prior to his assignment, sales of the company's products (ceramics) were stagnant because Canadian consumers had a strong preference for British ceramics. Therefore, his mission as the general manager was to rebuild the wholly owned sales subsidiary located in Toronto.

The first thing he did was to restructure the whole organization, including the replacement of top management and the reduction of sales staff. He says, "Compared with the operations in Thailand, it was much easier working in Canada since I could do business in English." The oil crisis did not adversely affect his business, because Canada was (and still is) an oil producing country, and therefore the sharp increase in oil prices brought large revenues to the Canadian economy. This in turn resulted in an increase in demand for goods and services, including imports.

Although the Quebec separatist movement caused political instability, it did not affect his business. As a result of favorable economic conditions and a successful restructuring of the company, sales gradually increased. As the brand name for his company's products began to attract the attention of Canadian customers, sales accelerated. And as his business improved, he increased the number of employees. Toward the end of his assignment, his sales company (a wholly owned subsidiary) consisted of approximately thirty employees: ten in sales, ten in warehousing, and ten in clerical or management positions. In this manner, he succeeded in increasing sales tenfold in the six years of his assignment.

While the above case (5) suggests that the company was at the second stage of business globalization, namely, direct sales by manufacturers, our next case represents yet another stage. In 1979 one alumnus (Case 14) working for a textile company was sent to Penang, Malaysia. This alumnus had spent five years in New York collecting information pertinent to the textile industry and also conducting the sales promotion described in Chapter 8.

In the early 1970s this company started overseas production because it became increasingly difficult to export textiles to the United States due to "voluntary" restraint and the successive revaluation of the yen. The company's strategy was to purchase a controlling share in a large Hong Kong-based multinational company that owned a number of spinning, weaving, dyeing, and garment production plants in several Southeast Asian countries. A large number of engineers and marketing and sales personnel were sent to these plants.

Our alumnus was assigned to one of these plants specializing in the dyeing and printing of textiles. The plant's products were sold to a number of garment companies headquartered in Hong Kong, with production facilities in Malaysia and Thailand. Virtually all garments produced by these customers were exported primarily to the United States and some to European countries via Hong Kong. In this way, his company was able to take advantage of lower wages and at the same time escape the need for "voluntary" restraint that would have been applied if the company had exported textiles to the United States directly from Japan.

The plant employed approximately 1,100 employees. Our alumnus was a general manager in charge of coordination between the production and sales departments of the plant. Specifically, on the basis of the orders from customers—how many meters of what textiles in what colors—when the orders were high, he discussed with people in the production department such matters as when to dye, with what colors, using which machines. On the other hand, when the orders were low, he went out to solicit customers for orders so that there would be no machines left idle. He continued to work in Malaysia until 1982, when he was transferred to Hong Kong.

The political environment in Malaysia was favorable then: the government had adopted a pro-Japanese "Look East" policy. In particular, Japanese-style cooperative labor management relations were held in high regard. However, our alumnus does not recall any preferential treatment for Japanese-owned companies. Socially, interracial relations were a sensitive issue, since Malaysia was a multiracial nation with Malays as the dominant group. Therefore, close attention had to be paid to employment policies and practices in regard to local employees.

Clearly, the operations at this plant suggest that the company was at the third stage of globalization, namely, overseas production and sales. However, the fact that sales were not directed to the local market (Malaysia) but to a third country (Hong Kong) suggests the company's orientation toward the final stage, that is, total globalization, if only on a regional scale. This contrasts sharply with Case 7 involving an alumnus stationed in Vienna and working for a different textile company whose operation was judged to be at stage one. Here we can see two different strategies pursued by two different companies but in the same industry. Faced with the same situation (difficulties in exporting textiles to the U.S. market), Case 7's company continued with its exporting strategy but sought a new market in East European nations. And when the demand for textiles and textile products declined, the company started to export textile machines and plant facilities. On the other hand, Case 14's company, faced with the same difficulties, took a different strategy of overseas production and total globalization.

We next turn to the overseas experience of our fifth alumnus working for a manufacturing company. Unlike all other alumni, this alumnus was employed by a petroleum company that was a wholly owned subsidiary of a major U.S.-based oil company. As mentioned in Chapter 8, he had obtained an MBA from the Wharton School on a company scholarship. In 1973, he was sent back to the United States, this time as an analyst working at the parent company's headquarters in Houston.

His work was to review annual investment proposals, including sales forecasts, from the four subsidiaries in Asia, Thailand, Malaysia, Singapore, and Hong Kong; to request additional information if necessary; and to prepare the final documents on which his superiors would base a decision. It was also his responsibility to convey the decision with comments to the subsidiaries, and also to monitor the progress of each investment project. He was on this assignment for a year and a half until January 1975, when he went back to Japan. To him this was more in the nature of training by the parent company under its global strategy than of an overseas work assignment by his immediate employer (the Japanese subsidiary).

As early as the 1950s, the predecessor to the parent company had developed global operations with subsidiaries all over the world. The predecessor company was so predominant worldwide that it was split into two in the early 1960s under the U.S. antitrust law. As a result, the Japanese sales subsidiary was also split into two companies, to one of which he belonged, while the refinery subsidiary remained as a single company. This refinery subsidiary was the exclusive supplier of gasoline and other kinds of oil to the sales subsidiaries. Thus, although Japan was the second largest oil consuming country after the United States by the early 1970s, our alumnus's company played (and still plays) a limited role within the global strategy of the parent company.

In the financial service sector, two alumni were involved in line duties. One alumnus working for a large bank (Case 2) was stationed in London before and after the oil crisis (1970–77). His experience up to 1973 has been described in Chapter 8. The oil crisis greatly affected the operation of the branch office he was working for. As a result of the oil crisis, funds were concentrated in a few major U.S. and European banks such as Chase Manhattan, Morgan, and the Bank of America; this caused a shortage of funds in the Euro currency market. Some German banks went bankrupt. He recalls that to deal with the situation his bank obtained an emergency loan of $1 billion from a Saudi Arabian bank with the guarantee of the government of Japan and with an annual interest rate of 16 percent.

During this period he continued to be a loan officer primarily for Japanese corporations. Lending to established British firms was difficult due to heavy competition with local banks that enjoyed long business relations with those firms. At the same time, lending to small and medium-sized firms was risky because information was not readily available on those firms. The nature of his work was gradually changing from trade financing to nontrade financing (mentioned in Chapter 8) and from corporate financing to project financing. (Project financing means lending a large sum of funds not to a single firm but to a group of firms involved in a large investment project.)

Since project financing involved a large sum of money, lending was done not by a single bank but by a group of banks, called a "syndicate." In the early 1970s the bank for which our alumnus worked was a minor participant in syndicates organized by U.S. or British banks. But over the years it came to play a leading role in organizing an international syndicate. This was a result of the bank's long tradition of international financing from prewar days, as well as a dramatic increase in the volume of its business (measured in monetary units), primarily as a result of the sharp increase in oil prices.

In 1976 an alumnus working for a marine and fire insurance company (Case 10) was sent to Teheran as the company's first representative there. His mission was to take charge of casualty insurance involving an international petrochemical project—a joint venture between a consortium consisting of several member companies of a former *zaibatsu* group and a national petrochemical company owned by the Iranian government.

Like the governments of other oil producing countries, the government of Iran, with a large amount of revenue obtained from oil royalties, initiated a number of national projects for the rapid industrialization of its economy with the use of foreign technology. The Japanese consortium members considered participation in this project to be a step toward securing stable sources of crude oil supply. Thus, this petrochemical project was the result of a meeting of minds of the Iranian and Japanese partners.

As a member of the consortium, the company employing our alumnus exclusively handled various kinds of insurance for several dozen Japanese contractors involved in the construction of a large-scale petrochemical plant. The total cost of the project was estimated to be ¥550 billion (or approximately U.S.$2 billion), and a total of 3,000 people were sent from Japan to work on the project.

Since he was the sole representative and had only one secretary working for him, our alumnus did everything himself, from drawing up contracts, to handling claims, to settling payments. Iranian legislation was such that, as a general rule, marine, fire, auto and other casualty insurance had to be handled by domestic insurance companies. And any businesses in which government agencies were involved had to be handled by the government-owned insurance company. Therefore, our alumnus operated as a sort of agent for this national insurance company.

When he arrived in 1976, Iran was under the regime of King Pahlavi, but Khomeini was leading the antigovernment movement from Paris, where he had fled. As early as 1976, our alumnus could feel the coming of the Islamic revolution, and social conditions gradually deteriorated. A series of violent antigovernment demonstrations were met with suppression by military forces. In the process, the office building where our alumnus was working was burned down. With the flight of the king and the return of Khomeini in early 1979, the revolution succeeded. However, it was not the revolution that seriously affected his insurance business, but the outbreak in September 1980 of the war between Iran and Iraq that was a fatal blow to the petrochemical project. A series of bombings of the plant, which had almost been completed by that time, forced the consortium to abandon the project, and with that our alumnus left Iran.

The fact that the above two alumni (one in London and the other in Teheran) came to be involved in the financial aspects of large overseas construction projects suggests that by the late 1970s an increasing number of Japanese manufacturing companies had begun overseas production or were entering into the third stage of business globalization. However, not all financial institutions were involved in project financing. Our third alumnus (Case 9-1) working for a trust bank was sent to Frankfurt in 1975 on a different mission. His brief stint in Düsseldorf in 1973 was touched upon in Chapter 8.

His employer sent two people to Frankfurt, our alumnus as the junior partner. Their immediate mission was to open and operate a new liaison office in Frankfurt with the following countries under its jurisdiction: West Germany, Austria, Switzerland, the Benelux countries, and the East European countries. In preparation for the opening of the liaison office they obtained assistance from some of the company's personnel from the London branch office as well as from the International Division of the headquarters. The objective of the liaison office, which consisted of the two representatives and a secretary, was to investigate the possibility of establishing a business office (or a bank branch) in continental Europe. To that end, they obtained financial and other relevant information (including country risks), had contacts with local banks and Japanese businesses operating in the region, and entertained potential customers from Japan.

West Germany was at the height of its economic prosperity, and political and social conditions were stable under the Social Democratic government. In terms of economic relations with Japan, however, there was not much of a complementary relationship, because the two economies were similar in structure. As a result, not enough Japanese companies were operating in the region to justify the opening of an additional Japanese bank. East European countries did not have a strong demand for loans, and the debt risks of these countries, particularly Poland, came to be recognized as problematic.

After these findings, it was decided not to open a branch office in the region, and the liaison office remained what it was—a place to collect pertinent information to be sent back to the headquarters in Tokyo. Specifically, our alumnus was engaged in the administration of the office, a monthly report on EC currencies, the translation of important news items, various surveys (such as one on the export reinsurance system of West Germany and one on forfeiture), as well as visits to local banks and Japanese companies in the region.

These activities of our alumnus in Frankfurt sharply contrast with those of the alumnus stationed in London (Case 2). Whereas in London both trade and project financing were done, in Frankfurt not even trade financing was done. This difference might be a reflection of the differences in the size and expertise of the two banks (a large and established bank with lengthy experience in international financing versus a much smaller trust bank without much experience in international financing) as well as a reflection of the two locations (London, the largest financial center in Europe, versus Frankfurt, the scene of a relatively small volume of business by Japanese companies).

After a two-year assignment in Frankfurt, our alumnus was transferred directly to New York in 1977, where he stayed for four years (Case 9-2). He was assigned to a branch bank with a total of approximately twenty employees, of whom nine were from Japan, including our alumnus.

The branch's businesses included the following: lending to South American companies as a member of international syndicates, lending to and carrying out trade transactions on behalf of Japanese companies operating from New York, and conducting funds and foreign exchange dealings. Our alumnus held the third highest position in the branch, and was in charge of administration, personnel, and accounting. Specifically, he was responsible for the planning and controlling of the branch's business plans, the establishment and execution of budgets, the administration of pay, the hiring, administration, and evaluation of local employees, and the safekeeping of important properties and documents. In addition, as a representative of the branch he would keep close contact with other member companies of the former *zaibatsu* group, participate in meetings with important customers, and attend various events and meetings for the general manager when the latter was not available.

When he was transferred in 1977, the U.S. economy was stagnant and the international prestige of the United States was at a low ebb, as symbolized by the seizure of the embassy in Iran in 1980. U.S. influence over South America was also weakening, resulting in economic confusion in those countries to which his bank would lend funds as a part of several bank syndicates. On the other hand, the business activities of Japanese companies were expanding, reflecting the increasing size of the Japanese economy. This was accompanied by an increased presence of Japanese banks in the United States, in sharp contrast to the situation in continental Europe. This suggests that globalization of a company does not proceed uniformly throughout the world; rather, the company adopts different globalization strategies depending on local conditions.

In the same year (1977) another alumnus was transferred to New York. For this alumnus in the employ of an airline company, it was the third overseas assignment (Case 12). He was assigned to the American regional headquarters that controlled the company's airport offices in the United States, Canada, Mexico, Peru, and other countries, in the following functional areas: administration of personnel, formulation of business policies, control of sales systems, and control of flight schedules and maintenance work. As personnel manager, our alumnus was responsible for the administration of personnel and wage systems, collective bargaining with the labor union organized by the local employees, and grievance handling.

He had to pay close attention to the guidelines of the Equal Employment Opportunity Commission (EEOC) created under Equal Employment Opportunity legislation. He recalls that the early retirement program introduced by his company was subjected to the EEOC's scrutiny as the program was alleged to be a form of age discrimination. The investigation lasted for a long time and a number of hearings were conducted. Although direct comparison with manufacturing companies may not be quite appropriate, it is safe to say that, by this time, his company had been fully globalized and was facing a typical labor problem that many Japanese manufacturing companies would come to face in later years.

Finally, one alumnus, working for one of the four national-level employers' associations, was sent to Washington, DC on yet another different mission (Case 11). As mentioned in Chapter 6, this alumnus had spent a year at Stanford University in his junior year and upon return to Japan in 1963 had done graduate study and had obtained an M.A. degree in economics in 1965. He was temorarily transferred out to the Japanese government public relations office located in Washington, DC, which dealt primarily with Japan–U.S. trade relations. This practice is called *shukko*, whereby an employee is transferred out to another company while retaining his or her employment relationship with the original employer. *Shukko* is used for a number of purposes, including the training of employees from the sending company, providing the receiving company with management and technical expertise, or trimming excess manpower at the sending company. When the first purpose is intended, the transferred employee returns to the original company after a certain period of time, while if the third purpose is intended, the transfer is permanent. In the case of the second purpose, however, the transfer may or may not be permanent (Nagano 1997: 124–137).

The office was staffed by about ten people, with only one employee from Japan. All others, including management personnel, were locally hired people, some Japanese and some Americans.

The objective of this office was lobbying to prevent, with the help of lawyers, bills unfavorable to Japan, such as export restraints on steel products, from being passed by Congress. By the time our alumnus arrived, the main emphasis was shifting from direct lobbying to indirect lobbying, by means of publications and public lectures. Exports of steel and automobiles were the focus of trade friction between the two nations. He recalls that dumping charges against automobile exports were narrowly defeated.

Since the office issued periodicals, as a member of the editorial staff, he wrote a number of articles to defend the Japanese position. In the late 1970s Japan was emerging as an economic giant, with the result that he received a number of requests for public lectures on the Japanese economy and management style. He used to make the point that a source of strength of the Japanese corporation is the lack of class conflict between labor and management, a situation that enables everyone to share information and goals and that gives management freedom to allocate workers without union opposition.

This concludes the outline of overseas assignments of fourteen alumni. Although most overseas operations were export-related, we could see the beginning of overseas production in certain industries, notably textiles. We now turn to the same issues that were analyzed in Chapter 8. These include failure rates, reasons for selection for overseas assignments, pre-assignment orientation and training, post-assignment assistance, ethnocentric staffing policies, the degree of autonomy of overseas offices, the methods of conducting business, the management of local employees, family adaptation to local cultures, and aftereffects of overseas assignments.

As mentioned in Chapter 8, length of stay is a crude indication of the success or failure of an overseas assignment. Of the fifteen cases under examination, the longest was seven years and four months in New York (Case 6) and the shortest was a year and a half in Houston (Case 4), with the average being four years and four months. Except for Case 4, only two alumni stayed overseas for less than three years (Cases 9-1 and 13). As mentioned earlier, Case 4 represents training rather than a job assignment; therefore, the duration of a year and a half is reasonable and should not be considered an indication of failure.

Case 9-1 was indeed a premature departure. This alumnus had been told by his superiors that his assignment in Frankfurt would be for four to five years. The fact of the matter was that a vacancy had suddenly been created in the bank's New York branch, and this vacancy had to be filled quickly. Our alumnus was chosen and was transferred directly from Frankfurt to New York. So this case cannot be called a failure either. Case 13 involves an alumnus who was the general manager of the company's wholly owned department store in Singapore. In the third year of his assignment a project team was created in the company's headquarters in Tokyo to study the feasibility of opening a store in Disneyland in the United States, and he was called back to become a project member. A year and seven months later he was sent to the United States as the general manager of the newly created store in Disneyland. Here again, our alumnus's relatively short assignment in Singapore does not represent a failure. We can safely say, then, that during this period none of our alumni failed in their overseas assignments.

Commenting on the reasons for their selection, the alumni whose overseas assignments started after 1973 voiced the following opinions.

> My predecessor in the London office made a serious mistake and lost the company's business in North Africa to a U.S. competitor. The company needed to replace him quickly. However, there was no appropriate candidate capable of conducting business in English. I was chosen and transferred directly from Sydney because of my successful work there for six years and above all for my superior English ability. (Case 1-2)

> The company's performance in Canada was poor and they needed someone to boost the sales there. I was chosen because of my successful experience in Thailand. (Case 5)

> My assignment to New York was a result of normal job rotation within the Synthetic Resin Department. In the 1970s, synthetic resin was one of the main export goods, and I had had more than eight years' experience with domestic selling, exporting, and importing of synthetic resin. (Case 6)

> I believe that my selection was a result of favorable evaluation of my overall performance up to that time, not only work performance but also labor union activities and cultural activities. With respect to work activities, my sense of responsibility was held in highest regard. Also, the preference of the chief representative (who was to become my immediate superior abroad) as well as my ability to adjust to local conditions might have been taken into consideration. As a result, I was chosen out of ten candidates. (Case 7)

> Timing was an important factor in that my predecessor's term was over and his replacement was needed. Since he was from the same department

(steel) and steel products were the major commodities that this overseas branch office was handling, and I had more than ten years' experience in the Steel Department, I was chosen. (Case 8)

My selection for the assignment in Frankfurt was a result of the fact that I had spent one year in Düsseldorf as a trainee learning German at the Goethe Institute and receiving on-the-job training (OJT) at a local bank. Or my selection as a trainee may have been made on the basis of the company's intention to send me to Germany on a job assignment. (Case 9-1)

Frankly, I do not know the reason for my sudden transfer to New York. My predecessor in New York was suddenly called back to Japan for some reason that was not explained to me. I was his replacement. (Case 9-2)

Several member companies of a former *zaibatsu* group were studying the feasibility of setting up a joint-venture petrochemical company with the Iranian national chemical company. I was selected as a member of the team set up within the company and studied the project for about a year, when the decision was made that this company would participate in the project handling insurance matters. As I was the only member on the team from the Foreign Business Department, I was selected for the assignment in Teheran. (Case 10)

Our organization was sending one of our staff to this office in Washington, DC. It was my turn then. (Case 11)

The reasons would have been my two previous assignments in the United States (a year in San Francisco, and four and a half years in New York), as well as my work experience in Japan in personnel administration and industrial relations. (Case 12)

Since English was needed in Malaysia, my English ability might have been a factor. Also, the final destination of the textiles produced in this Malaysian plant was the United States, so my familiarity with the United States and the U.S. market from my earlier assignment in New York for five years might also have been taken into consideration. (Case 14)

A review of the above responses reveals that job knowledge or work experience in the relevant field is the factor mentioned most often. English or other language skills are often mentioned by alumni in manufacturing, but not by those in general trading, airlines, or the bank with expertise in international finance. In the latter cases it is not that language skills are unimportant, but that they are taken for granted, while in the case of manufacturing, the availability of people with sufficient language skills was limited. Furthermore, in the latter cases, overseas posts were assigned more or less as a part of regular job rotation schemes, as these industries or companies were already fully globalized with branch offices in major cities of the world. In the case of manufacturing companies with a limited number of overseas offices, much closer screening could have preceded any overseas assignment.

What kind of pre-assignment training, if any, did our alumni receive? In Chapter 8 it was found that not many alumni received pre-assignment training. During this period, with the exception of the one alumnus sent to Vienna who received German language training for two months, no other alumnus received any training. The reason was that their work experience prior to overseas assignments was closely related to their work overseas, so that there was no need for special training in job duties. In regard to language training, with the exception of two locations (Frankfurt and Vienna, where the ability to speak German was needed), the overseas offices were located in English-speaking countries or countries where business was conducted in English, and the alumni who were sent to these countries did not need any language training. Overall, then, pre-assignment training does not seem to have played a significant role in the successful overseas assignments of our alumni.

Generally speaking, post-assignment assistance consisted of job-related assistance, assistance in getting settled, and financial assistance in the form of various allowances. Of the thirteen cases, substantial job-related assistance was given in only one case (Case 7). This was the case of the alumnus who stayed in Vienna for five years. His superior, the chief representative of the liaison office, helped him in all areas throughout his stay there. This superior had had a lot of overseas experience: he had opened the office two years prior to our alumnus's assignment and he stayed there after the return of our alumnus to Japan.

In other cases, assistance was limited to brief instructions from the predecessor on the nature of the jobs (Cases 6, 8, and 14). No assistance was given in cases where the mission was to open new offices (Cases 9-1 and 10) or the predecessors were replaced for poor performance (Cases 1-2, 5, and 9-2). A review of the above cases makes it safe to say that, on the whole, job-related post-assignment assistance did not play a significant role in the success of the overseas assignments of our alumni. Other forms of post-assignment assistance will be discussed later.

In order to address the question of the ethnocentrism of staffing policies, we now turn to a close examination of six of the fourteen cases. Other cases were excluded because certain overseas offices were owned and/or managed by host country nationals (Cases 4 and 11), certain offices were too small for this type of analysis (Cases 1-2, 7, 9-1, and 10), or sufficient information was not available (Cases 12 and 13). Key features of staffing in the selected six cases are summarized in Table 12.2.

Of the above six cases, three were located in the United States (Cases 6, 8,

Table 12.2

Number of Employees and Composition of Top Management

Case	Industry	Status of establishment	Number of employees	Number of Japanese nationals	Number in top management	Number of locals in top management
2	Banking	Branch bank	80	20	4	1
5	Ceramics	Sales subsidiary	30	3	4	1
6	General trading	Subsidiary company	270	70	20[a]	2
8	General trading	Branch office	60	15	2	0
9-2	Trust banking	Branch bank	20	9	3	0
14	Textiles	Joint venture	1,110	4	3	0

[a]Includes senior managers.

and 9-2), one in Canada (Case 5), one in the United Kingdom (Case 2), and one in Malaysia (Case 14). Case 6 was a wholly owned subsidiary of a general trading company with the lengthiest history in the industry. The U.S. subsidiary was headquartered in New York with branch offices in several locations in the United States, Case 8 being one of these branch offices. The main office in New York employed about 270 people, including seventy nationals from Japan. Approximately twenty people occupied senior management positions. Japanese nationals held the top management positions and senior management positions in line departments, while two U.S. nationals held senior management positions, one in legal affairs and the other in auditing. Virtually all middle and lower management positions were held by Japanese nationals, while local employees were in clerical and secretarial positions.

At the company's Houston branch (Case 8) a total of sixty people were employed. Two top management positions (branch manager and assistant branch manager) were Japanese nationals. In addition, all managerial positions were held by Japanese nationals. As in its main office in New York, local employees held the clerical and secretarial positions. But unlike its New York office, there was no senior manager in charge of legal affairs. Instead, legal matters were handled by a law firm with which the office had a contract.

The same arrangement (contract with a law firm) was made at a branch bank (Case 9-2) located in New York. It was a small bank with twenty employees. In this bank not only the three top management positions but also all lower management positions were held by Japanese nationals. The local employees were the ten or so clerks, all female, and a chauffeur.

At the sales subsidiary in Toronto, too, heavy reliance was placed on outside lawyers and accountants. The company's top management team consisted of four directors, including our alumnus as the CEO. One of the four directors was a Canadian national, while three others were Japanese nationals. In all, approximately thirty employees were evenly divided into sales, warehouse, and administrative departments. There were no Japanese nationals other than the three directors.

Case 2 was an overseas branch bank in London engaged in full-fledged banking operations. Top management consisted of the branch manager (or the general manager of the branch) and three assistant branch managers. Three of them, including the branch manager, were Japanese nationals, while one assistant branch manager was a United Kingdom national. The branch manager was also a member of the board of directors of the bank. The two Japanese assistant branch managers were in charge of corporate lending and foreign exchange, respectively, while the British manager was in charge of "operations," including deposits and personnel administration of local employees. The legal matters were handled through an external law firm.

The corporate lending department was divided into four sections (Japanese corporations, foreign corporations, securities, and trade financing), while the foreign exchange department was divided into two sections (foreign exchange dealing and international funding). All six section managers were Japanese nationals, and all "perpro" (or deputy) managers working under them (our alumnus being one) were also Japanese nationals. The local employees in these sections were engaged in clerical duties. The deposit and personnel sections, including the two positions of section manager, were staffed by local employees.

The dyeing and printing plant in Malaysia (Case 14) was a joint venture with the Hong Kong-based multinational company, with the Japanese side holding 70 percent of the ownership. The plant employed approximately 1,100 people, mostly in production jobs. The top management team consisted of the president and the two directors, one in charge of marketing and sales and the other in charge of production as the plant's superintendent. All three were Japanese nationals. Of the five general managers who would report to the directors, one was a Japanese national, three were from Hong Kong, and one, who was in charge of general administration (including personnel), was a local Malay. Although the company had to abide by the host country's racial quota on hiring so that the company's total workforce would consist of 60 percent Malays, 30 percent Chinese, and 10 percent Indians, most middle- and lower-level management positions were filled by local Chinese.

Although our sample is too small to make generalizations, we were able to observe certain tendencies. First, on the whole, overseas Japanese establishments adopted an ethnocentric staffing policy: all the highest positions (such as the president) as well as virtually all top-level management positions were held by Japanese nationals. Second, the degree of ethnocentrism was stronger in general trading and banking establishments than in manufacturing establishments.

In the former cases Japanese nationals occupied not only top management positions but also middle- and lower-level management positions, and in some cases nonmanagerial positions as well, while most local employees were in clerical and secretarial positions. In the case of the branch bank in London, although local nationals held certain senior-level positions, their functions were limited to relatively unimportant areas, and Japanese nationals held all managerial positions in important functional areas. On the other hand, in the ceramics sales office, one host country national was in a top management position, and major sales activities were conducted by local employees. At the textile plant, although all top management positions were held by Japanese nationals, many senior-level positions were held by nationals from the joint-venture partner, and virtually all middle- and lower-level management positions were held by local employees.

Ethnocentrism may affect not only managerial staffing but also the style of conducting business. Therefore, our alumni were asked whether in the overseas offices they followed the practices conducted at home offices in Japan or adopted typical practices followed in host countries. Below are some of the answers grouped by countries. First of all, two alumni who stayed in the United Kingdom answer as follows:

> I followed the local style. To do so, I hired a lawyer and sought his advice on many occasions. (Case 1-2, London)

> I followed largely the local practices due mainly to a big difference in legislation surrounding financial institutions in the U.K. and Japan. While in Japan financial institutions were tightly controlled by various types of legislation as well as "administrative guidance" from the Ministry of Finance and the Bank of Japan, in the U.K. much more freedom was allowed. For one thing, the lending rate was more or less fixed in Japan, but in the U.K. it had to be negotiated with the customer, which was an important element of my job. I followed certain Japanese practices only when dealing with Japanese customers, such as after-work socialization. (Case 2)

We have responses from four alumni who worked in North America, three engaged in trading/sales and one in banking.

> The procedures used in the head office in Tokyo were adopted in the New York office as well, but I am not sure if our company's procedures represent a typical Japanese style of business. (Case 6, New York)

> We could not always force Japanese methods on local employees or customers. When necessary, I asked the head office to recognize local practices and to make adjustments accordingly. (Case 8, Houston)

> To the extent that the particular job did not involve local employees or customers, I followed the procedures adopted in the head office in Japan. (Case 9-2, New York)

> I adopted both Japanese and Canadian practices. In the latter case I made frequent use of lawyers and accountants. (Case 5, Toronto)

We have responses from two alumni who worked in Europe, one engaged in sales promotion and the other, in information gathering.

> I made conscious efforts to adjust to local (East European) practices. At the same time, I explained to the local customers Japanese ways of business. Another role of mine was to inform the head office of local people's ways of thinking. In a sense, I played the role of a coordinator. (Case 7, Vienna)

Since I worked in a small liaison office, I followed local practices in dealing with local people. (Case 9-1)

Two alumni who worked in Asia, one as the sole insurance representative
in Teheran and the other as a senior manager in a textile plant, gave their
answers:

I followed the Japanese pattern. However, since the local legislation prohibited foreign insurance companies from engaging in full-fledged insurance
activities, I had to operate as a reinsurance business. (Case 10, Teheran)

I adopted Japanese methods as much as possible. The most important was
the adoption of a budget system that did not exist locally. I also changed to
Japanese ways such local practices as sales representatives not carrying
sample products, office workers not cleaning their own areas, or superiors
not educating and training their subordinates. (Case 14, Malaysia)

With the exception of the two Asian cases, our alumni said they followed
local practices more than Japanese practices. To the question of whether local practices were followed for legal and institutional reasons or cultural and
belief-oriented reasons, virtually all chose the former. The answer quoted
above from the alumnus assigned to the branch bank in London illustrates
this point. On the other hand, our alumnus in Malaysia answered that, although he tried to introduce Japanese practices, he made special efforts to
respect local religions and cultures.

The fact that conscious efforts were made to use Japanese practices at the
two Asian locations suggests that in those places Japanese methods were
"better" than, not simply "different" from, local practices. In a sense, the
same interpretation may apply, to a certain extent, to the practices involving
general trading companies, uniquely a Japanese institution, which possessed
more or less standard procedures that had been established over a long period of time. Simply put, in overseas offices of general trading companies,
the local example did not exist; therefore, they followed the company's own
methods subject to host country laws and regulations. Put differently, stronger ethnocentric business practices in the Asian establishments and the offices of general trading companies may have been for rational and functional
reasons rather than for value-based cultural reasons.

In terms of the management of local employees, all offices followed local
practices with varying degrees of Japanese elements. Here are some examples
for those establishments with at least a dozen or so local employees.

We followed local practices almost 100 percent. Local employees were
hired for the vacancies due to resignation or the creation of new positions.
(Case 6, New York)

Local employees consisted of male assistants/clerks and female secretaries. Following local practices, wages were negotiated on an individual basis. (Case 8, Houston)

Personnel administration of local employees was a part of my responsibility, and I followed local practices. In order to avoid conflict with local employees, I consulted lawyers on every important occasion, and, as a result, I was much influenced by local ways of thinking. In terms of actual practices, however, Japanese elements were unconsciously introduced, for example, small variations in the pace of promotion or in the amount of bonuses, and the payment of bonuses not contingent on the company's performance. (Case 9-2, New York)

Shortly after appointment as president, I dismissed a number of employees following local practices. After that I managed the employees in a family-like atmosphere, for example, by paying Christmas bonuses, which was appreciated by the employees. Employees were paid in annual salaries. Although I did not intend to formally adopt Japanese-style permanent employment, it turned out that many employees stayed with the company for a long time. (Case 5, Toronto)

Local employees were managed by a local personnel manager following local practices in all aspects of personnel administration including hiring, performance evaluation, and pay level and structure. (Case 2, London)

The treatment of local employees was made according to relevant local laws. For example, annual holidays and leaves were given as stipulated in legislation. That contrasted sharply with Japanese employees, who did not take holidays and leaves. (Case 3, Johannesburg)

Wages and other conditions of employment were determined by collective bargaining with the labor union conducted every three years. Pay structure consisted of the base rate and performance pay. Base rates were determined in the market consisting of a number of foreign companies, including our company, in the free trade zone. Different base rates were created on the basis of educational background and length of experience. (Case 14, Penang)

Although it is not clear from the above statement, Case 14 represents local (or non-Japanese) practices. For one thing, the general manager of the personnel department was a local Malay, as mentioned before. Furthermore, there was no Japanese employee directly engaged in personnel administration.

Common to all establishments reviewed is the fact that Japanese employees and local employees were on separate pay and other employment schemes. While Japanese employees were essentially on the domestic (Japanese) schemes with additional allowances associated with overseas assignments, local employees were on the schemes shaped largely by local legislation and labor market conditions.

This tendency of maintaining dual schemes was particularly evident in larger establishments (such as Cases 2, 6, and 14), where personnel functions were entrusted to host country nationals. Even in the smaller establishments, where personnel functions were performed by Japanese managers (such as Cases 5 and 9-2), there were apparently no attempts made to hire directly from schools, to provide substantial training, or to guarantee permanent employment, although some elements of Japanese practices were employed, such as the payment of bonuses and more or less uniform pay increases. It could be argued that this treatment of local employees was a rational response to local labor market conditions where labor mobility was typically high, which made it difficult to follow the above-mentioned Japanese practices.

It was stated in Chapter 8 that general trading companies were more centrally controlled than manufacturing and other companies. More or less the same tendency was observed for this period as well. For example, the alumnus working for a trading company (Case 6) says:

> Our office (as well as any other overseas office) was a miniature of the main office in Tokyo in terms of organizational structure. A department in an overseas office is within the jurisdiction of the department in the main office, whose general manager makes final decisions for all the departments of overseas as well as domestic offices. The general manager of an overseas office is very much like the host of an inn where guests come and go.

Another alumnus working for the same company (Case 8) says:

> The basic price guideline (of steel products) was set by the manufacturer and the final price decision was made at the main office in Japan.

On the other hand, overseas sales offices of manufacturing companies (Case 5) apparently enjoyed a higher degree of autonomy. As mentioned before, our alumnus working for a ceramics company was given full authority as its CEO to restructure the company's sales subsidiary in Canada. Likewise, another alumnus for a construction machine manufacturer (Case 1-2) made every effort to penetrate into the U.K. market as well as those markets where U.K. construction companies were operating. Although his official mission was "market research," he was given wide latitude in opening up new markets.

In Malaysia the textile plant where our alumnus was working (Case 14) was one of a number of spinning, weaving, dyeing, and garment factories that his employer owned. Apparently, for the smooth operation of his plant, the relationship with the Hong Kong-based customers was crucial; therefore, control from headquarters in Tokyo/Osaka was neither practical nor desirable. In this case, the role of headquarters was limited to making strategic decisions; operational decisions were left to individual establishments.

The difference in the degree of centralization between the two groups of companies parallels the difference in the degree of ethnocentrism in staffing practices discussed earlier. In a sense, this is a reasonable finding in that we can expect that the more Japanese employees there are in overseas offices, the easier it is for the headquarters to control these offices. Our earlier discussion of staffing practices of general trading companies attests to this point.

To return to the question of the failure rates of employees assigned to overseas posts, maladjustment of those employees and/or their family members to host country cultures is often mentioned as an important reason. We examine this point next. All twelve alumni who commenced overseas assignments after 1973 were married, most of them with children. In nine cases their families accompanied our alumni, while in three cases (Cases 1-2, 7, and 9-1) their families joined later, by a year, six months, and six months, respectively, due to company policies. In four cases very brief pre-assignment orientation was given to family members, while in other cases no orientation was given.

With the exception of the alumnus transferred to Vienna (Case 7), our alumni were not given much assistance in getting settled, such as in looking for a house or a school for their children, nor did they need much help since their assignments were in English-speaking countries or in countries where English was widely used. Case 9-1 (Frankfurt) was the only exception in this respect. As mentioned before, this alumnus's German was good enough for business purposes, and a priori for daily living.

As for financial assistance, our alumni obtained rather generous assistance in the form of overseas assignment allowances, housing allowances, educational allowances for their children, and so forth. One alumnus recalls their living conditions in New York as "comfortable" (Case 6). Another alumnus who stayed in Penang with his family could afford to hire a housemaid; this made life easy for them but at the same time caused some awkwardness since it was a new experience for them.

Most of our alumni were accompanied by children of elementary school age. While many alumni had their children enrolled in local schools (in London, New York, Washington DC, Houston, and Frankfurt), some opted for Japanese schools (in Johannesburg, Toronto, and Penang). While the former group of alumni apparently considered their overseas living as an opportunity for their children to learn different cultures, the latter considered a smooth transfer back into the Japanese school system after return to Japan more important. It should be noted, however, that even those alumni who sent their children to local schools made efforts to keep up their Japanese language ability by, for example, sending them to weekend Japanese supplementary schools or asking them to speak Japanese at home. Whichever may be the case, their children were still very young and they did not experience any difficulty adjusting to overseas living, including the schools.

To the question of the extent to which their families enjoyed overseas experiences, all but one alumnus answered that their families "enjoyed" or "enjoyed very much" their overseas experiences. Some of the reasons they gave were:

> We formed close family friendships during our stay in Houston that we have maintained up to the present. One of our daughters became bilingual and cosmopolitan from her experience in Houston and eventually she married an Australian. (Case 8)

> We sent our children to a local private school in London with many pupils from different countries. We were impressed with the school's capacity to accommodate to a variety of cultures. The school's cafeteria, for example, served many different ethnic dishes. (Case 1-2)

> German people, including our neighbors, were kind and we had a pleasant time while in Frankfurt. Also, I had more time to spend with my family than in Japan, so we enjoyed traveling to different places and also appreciated European culture. (Case 9-1).

In regard to their life in New York this same alumnus says:

> In the United States, too, we enjoyed traveling to different places. Our children were bigger and they began to enjoy a wide variety of things: ballet, musicals, the circus, and major league baseball; playing baseball and soccer; cycling, swimming, traveling, summer camps, home-stay exchanges, and dining at restaurants. (Case 9-2)

The only alumnus who answered in a negative way says:

> We did not enjoy our life in Teheran at all. When we arrived, it snowed a lot and we were unable to go out, and we spent "gloomy" days inside. Besides, local food was so different that we could not eat it. We missed Japanese food a lot. The children became frustrated and got sick. The only relief was travel to London (for health checkups!) every six months, which occasions we took advantage of for sightseeing in Europe. Fortunately or unfortunately, the law and order deteriorated so much that I had to send my family back to Japan after two years, though I had to stay in Teheran for another two years. (Case 10)

What is important in the above case is the fact that our alumnus stayed for two years after his family had left the country. The local conditions were not conducive to comfortable living: local foods were not agreeable to his taste and political and social conditions were unstable. What made him stay there? Dedication and loyalty to his company? Perhaps, but it is also true that, under permanent employment practices, it would have been extremely difficult for him to join his family in Japan by quitting the company if he felt he had to.

13
Lives of Alumnae, 1974–80

The purpose of this chapter is to describe the lives of our five alumnae—family life, social life, and work life, if any. This chapter will cover the period corresponding to child rearing (from their late twenties to early forties), and Chapter 18 will cover the period thereafter.

As we have seen in Chapter 7, in the section on female careers, by 1973, five of the six alumnae were married, did not hold a job, and were concentrating on their family lives. What were their family lives like? Most of our alumnae started their formal education immediately after World War II, when the ideal of sexual equality was especially emphasized in schools. At the same time, however, at home they were reared and educated by their parents who had prewar values.

In prewar Japan, the male-dominated, vertically structured society had been firmly established, and the lives of women were defined by such values as the maintenance of *ie* (the household), the superior status of men, and the inferior status of women. The ideal model of a woman as a "good wife and wise mother" was derived from Confucian ideology (Iwao 1993: 19). The good wife was expected to possess the "virtue of faithfully assisting the husband" (*naijo no ko*).

With the democratization of Japan by the Occupation forces after World War II, the "liberalization" of women was achieved (Ito 1990: 296). In the new Japanese Constitution, Article 14 stipulates that "all of the people are equal under the law" and that "there shall be no discrimination on the basis of sex." Thus, in the family a husband and a wife became equal. Sumiko Iwao makes the following observation:

> After marriage the women of the first postwar generation [defined as those who were born between 1946 and 1955—a few years younger than our alumnae] quickly realized that the roles of wife and mother

alone were not sufficiently satisfying. They began to question and attempt
to redefine their roles, especially after their youngest children entered
elementary school. Some found work as one path. . . . Others . . . found
new meaning in their lives by their involvement in . . . activities outside the
home. (Iwao 1993: 21)

Her remarks provide a useful framework to answer our central question:
To what extent were attitudes toward life and the behavior of our alumnae
affected by old (prewar) values or by new (postwar) values? In order to address this central question the following four questions were formulated on
the basis of Iwao's observation.

1. After marriage and up to forty-five years old or so, to what extent did
you practice the "virtue of faithfully assisting your husband?" To what extent did you find meaning in it?

2. During the same period, did you obtain a job? If so, for what reason(s)?

3. During the same period, were you involved in any social or volunteer
work, including PTA activities? If so, for what reason(s)?

4. During the same period, in what ways did your husband influence your
family life, social life, and/or work life?

These questions were answered by the five alumnae who were married.
No attempt was made to obtain information from the alumna who remained
single.

One alumna, who was married to a man who inherited a family business
(production and sales of incense products), provided the following answer:

Since it was a family business, I helped my husband by attending meetings
and entertaining foreign visitors. He was pleased with my efforts, so I was
able to find meaning in what I did. Besides, I learned the incense ceremony
for the first time.

Thus, for this alumna the virtue was practiced through assisting her husband
with his business rather than in family life.

A second alumna, married to a university professor of medicine, has this to
say:

To me marriage was a haven from a single life with stressful jobs. In the
faculty of medicine at my husband's university it was customary for faculty members to host parties on a regular basis, inviting a group of students
under his supervision. Also, I often entertained foreign scholars and did
research from my husband's laboratory, but I did not consider that I was
practicing the virtue of faithfully assisting my husband. I felt that the lifestyle
suited me. Also, I was good at collecting information I felt was necessary
for my husband through my contact with people here in Japan as well as
overseas. In this way, I think I assisted my husband.

This alumna, like the first one, identified activities related to her husband's job as a method of assistance.

The third alumna was married to an employee of a chemical company, who was to succeed to the family-owned company ten years after marriage. She says:

> Our common pleasure was to invite guests to our home, so I often entertained the staff from my husband's company. I think that our guests used to look forward to our invitations. I also think that my husband was satisfied with our comfortable home and family, and this had a positive influence on his interpersonal relationships in the company.

So this alumna, too, helped her husband by inviting and entertaining his company-related guests.

The fourth alumna was married to a man who was to change his job to become a picture dealer and owner of an art gallery ten years after they were married. She says:

> Perhaps my optimistic personality contributed to my husband's decision to change his job and try to become more independent. I worked diligently to help him obtain what he wanted. For the three years during which my husband was preparing for independence, I worked very hard to help him realize his dream. As I did this voluntarily, I would consider it just a wife's assistance rather than self-sacrifice.

Here again our alumna's assistance is related to her husband's job.

The fifth alumna, who had married a bank manager even before she graduated from the university, has this to say:

> I do not like the expression, "the virtue of faithfully assisting the husband." I made every effort to play the roles of daughter-in-law in the husband's family, wife, and mother perfectly—or in a way my husband wanted. I never asked questions about my husband's job; instead, I entertained my husband's guests in our home. I lived this kind of family life not out of a sense of faithfully assisting my husband but out of a sense of duty as a wife.

It seems that the family life of this alumna was the closest to the prewar model of a "good wife and wise mother" under the household system and that this alumna was not very happy with her family life.

Thus, with the exception of the fifth alumna, our female alumnae were content with assisting their husbands with their jobs either directly or indirectly. Although they might have had some reservations about the age-old expression, "the virtue of faithfully assisting the husband," they found meaningfulness in what they did for their husbands. Only in the case of the last one does it seem as if she felt that the traditional values were forced upon her.

In regard to the second question, which asked if they obtained any new jobs before they were forty-five years old or so, they gave various answers. Our first alumna (married to the incense manufacturer) answered that, between 1968 and 1982, she concentrated on family life and raising children. In her spare time she enjoyed her hobbies, including calligraphy. It was in 1982 that she went back to work at her husband's company. We will describe her case in detail in Chapter 18.

Our second alumna (married to the university professor of medicine) continued to help her husband as a secretary and advisor, thus involving herself in her husband's job rather than obtaining a job of her own. According to her, the most memorable experience during this period (1974–80) was accompanying her husband on his trip to the United States for three months in 1977. They made visits to a dozen universities and research laboratories, meeting their mutual friends and deepening their acquaintance. They were also invited to the homes of their friends and acquaintances. This was a very useful experience for our alumna, as she was able to learn about American families and society.

Our third alumna helped her husband to start an art gallery. After three years of preparation the gallery was opened in 1974 on the Ginza in Tokyo. She says:

> In addition to a regular housewife's work at home, I helped my husband as a business partner. I commuted to the gallery every day with our youngest child in tow. Aside from driving or sales, I did everything, including being a secretary, accounting, and buying at overseas auctions, as well as many other miscellaneous tasks.

The alumna married to the successor of the family-owned chemical company has this to say:

> As my husband did not want me to seek employment outside of the home, and he did not like the idea of my even studying, I stayed home during the time. Although I did not seek it, I ended up teaching English to junior high school and high school students twice or three times a week during the daytime when my husband was not at home. From time to time I did translation work at home. These activities satisfied my desire to stay in touch with the English language.

From her statement it sounds as if her husband held the prewar value of a "good wife and wise mother" whose role is to stay home and serve the needs of her husband and children.

The alumna married to a bank manager, who was trying hard to play the roles of a daughter-in-law, a wife, and a mother to perfection, has this story to tell:

> While living this kind of family life, I was yearning to discover my own place and position. I also hoped to become free from the stress of trying to balance the roles given to me. I searched for my place within the environment given to me and within the limits of the approval of my husband and/or his parents.

Here again we sense the influence of prewar values on the part of her husband and his parents.

She continues:

> I started an English conversation class for kindergarten and elementary school children twice or three times a week. I also started a cooking school for wives of my husband's colleagues who lived in the bank-owned houses nearby. The latter was an extension of my role as a wife, and therefore was not useful as a means to solve my "identity crisis." Finally, around the age of thirty, I found a solution in engraving, which was a kind of self-expression. It started as a hobby, but gradually became my work. After ten years, I held a one-man exhibition and started to sell pieces of my work. I did everything, from production to sales, all by myself. I was satisfied mentally, but it took a toll on me physically, as I was not allowed to neglect my housework. I became critically ill in my early forties. At the height of success, my illness forced me to stop engraving as a business. Since then, it has become my hobby.

A review of the above five cases suggests that the first three alumnae who closely identified themselves with the husbands' businesses or jobs did not seek their own jobs. Rather, they were content to play supportive roles for their husbands. On the other hand, the last two alumnae were not much interested in their husbands' jobs or perhaps they were not allowed to meddle in their husbands' jobs. Instead, their husbands and husbands' parents expected them to play the traditional "good wife and wise mother" role. Not satisfied with the traditional family life, they involved themselves in activities of their own as a means of self-fulfillment and self-expression.

We will now address the third question—social and volunteer work. In the 1970s Japanese society was as yet inadequately prepared to provide opportunities for socially active women. PTA activities were by far the most popular social activity, although limited in scope.

Our first alumna, who was concentrating on family life and raising children, was heavily involved in PTA activities together with her husband; these were their main social responsibilities. Both of them served as officers for a long time and her husband ended up being the president. Our alumna was also active in the female division of the university alumni and alumnae association and served as its manager. The alumna married to a professor of medicine said that, because they did not have children, she did not participate in PTA activities. Nor did she participate in any social activities. The main reason was that she had to take care of her senile mother-in-law, who was at home.

Our third alumna says:

> As our work [in the art gallery] consumed our lives, our children became latch-key children. That is why we took active roles in the PTA functions as a means to stay in touch with teachers.

She served on the PTA for thirteen years, from the time her oldest son started elementary school, as chairperson of many committees, as vice president, and finally as president. She also served on the Board of Education of Setagaya Ward in Tokyo as a member of its Juvenile and Youth Committee responsible for all nonschool activities with the school children, except the counseling work performed by professional counselors.

Her history contrasts sharply with that of the fourth and fifth alumnae. The fourth alumna says that she performed PTA activities unwillingly, and only as an obligation to the school. The fifth alumna said that she did not participate in any PTA activity as she sufficiently played her role as a mother at home and she was not particularly interested in her children's academic performance at school. She adds that, since her husband regarded his job as a quasi-civil servant type of job, he wanted our alumna to be moderate in social activities. He did not want her to go out by herself, so when she had to go out she did so when her husband was not at home.

Here again we see two types: those who were active in the PTA and other social activities and those who were not. It seems that those who were preoccupied with their own goals found less interest in PTA activities, which were really an extension of the mother's role. Second, the influence of their husbands seems to be an important factor. While some husbands were more accepting of their wives' involvement in outside activities, others were not. This leads us to the final question: husbands' influence on the family, social, and work lives of our alumnae.

Our first alumna (married to an incense manufacturer) says:

> After getting married, I was greatly influenced by my husband, as he was a man of strong personality. He did not compromise; he always got what he wanted—in his daily life, his hobbies, and his job. I always tried to meet his expectations. Also, through him I have learned the incense ceremony, which I enjoy very much. I appreciate him for that.

The second alumna, through her long acquaintance with her husband-to-be, which began in her teenage years and was followed by a long engagement period (four years), fully realized that her husband's work as a professor of medicine was special and valuable to society, and she strongly identified herself with his career. So after their marriage, she decided to find meaning in her life by helping him as a secretary and advisor throughout his career. She says:

> I was involved with my husband's work 80 percent of my time and 20 percent with the work of [taking care of] my mother-in-law.

The third alumna said:

> Running an art gallery was a joint business by my husband and me; for that reason it was "our" work. Our family life was increasingly centered around our work. However, flexible work hours made it possible for me to be involved in PTA and other social activities.

According to the fourth alumna:

> The nature of my husband's job [management of a family-owned chemical company] did not affect my family life or social life. However, his value orientation did greatly affect my life. That is, although we were only one year apart, he held a strong conviction that women should stay home. Although I resisted his ways of thinking, I gave in partly because I did not have a strong urge to get a job and partly because he agreed to let me teach English at home. After all, to stay in touch with the English language was what I really wanted in those days.

Finally, our fifth alumna (married to a bank manager) says:

> My husband did not pay much attention to family life, although he loved our children very much. He was not happy that I spent time with engraving, but he gave in finally. I was not very much interested in social life and activities. He was a serious person and our family life was formal. However, as I was raised in a similar atmosphere, I did not feel our family life too restrained.

Based on the above statements we can conclude that both the values and the occupations held by the husbands of our alumnae influenced the lifestyles of the alumnae. Although we did not interview their husbands, based on the remarks of our alumnae, we can sense that, perhaps with the exception of the art gallery owner/picture dealer, all held prewar values of the "superior status of men, and inferior status of women"—at least at the earlier stages of their marriages. However, not all of them forced their wives to stay home and just to serve the needs of husbands and children. Some "allowed" their wives to work. Why?

The occupations of the five husbands were: one self-employed business person, two owner/managers of family businesses, one professional, and one manager of a large organization. In all occupations except the last one, the scope for individual discretion was wide; therefore, they could involve their wives in their work if they so wished. Upon closer examination, it seems clear that the prewar value of the "good wife and wise mother" was limited to the family with the husband whose occupation was that of a salaried employee; in the family where the husband owned a family business, it was perfectly normal for the wife to work along with the husband.

On the part of our alumnae, some jobs were easier to relate to or even to learn than others. The artistic (or supposedly feminine) nature of art dealing and incense businesses may have been easy for our two alumnae to relate to. On the other hand, the masculine nature of the chemical company may have been the reason why our alumna was indifferent to her husband's management job. Besides, although the company was family controlled, it was a public company with 200 or so employees; therefore, there was no room for her to be directly involved in the company's business.

In the case of the alumna married to a university professor there was a broad scope for her to help him on the job because a professor's job, especially on a faculty of medicine, is very diversified. Moreover, it would have been easy for her to relate to the students as a sort of surrogate mother in view of the fact that she did not have children of her own. In the case of our last alumna, apparently her husband (the bank manager) did not talk about his job at home, nor did he want her to get involved in his job. In this case, naturally, our alumna was unable to relate to her husband's work.

The central question we posed at the beginning of this chapter was whether our alumnae were satisfied with the roles of wife and mother alone (a reflection of prewar values) or whether they also wanted to identify and achieve their own goals (a reflection of postwar values). Three alumnae identified with the work goals of their husbands, although the extent and methods of involvement differed among the three cases—from being an equal partner to playing a secretarial role. To the extent that they did so voluntarily, we can say that these were their own goals and that these alumnae possessed postwar rather than prewar values. The two alumnae who could not identify with their husband's goals clearly possessed postwar values and developed, despite their husbands' initial objections, goals of their own—studying/teaching English and engaging in engraving, respectively.

Summary to Part III

The first oil crisis of 1973 inflicted a deadly blow on the economics of the advanced industrializing nations that had depended on the supply of cheap oil. As we saw in Chapter 9, this led to the formation in 1975 of the Group of Seven Economic Summit Meetings to advance the economic prosperity of the free-world nations.

It has been a popular view that of the seven nations Japan most successfully tided over the two oil crises and emerged as an economic superpower in the 1980s. Although we do not deny this popular view, we also take note of the fact that the first oil crisis, with its strong influence on Japanese people's psyche, distorted the "normal" courses of economic development that Japan had followed up to that point into "abnormal" export-driven economic development.

That Japan is a resource-poor, fragile nation at the mercy of resource-rich nations was keenly felt by all Japanese. The fear that Japanese economic prosperity would collapse was so strong that "international competitive power" became the catchword of the industry, the government, and even the labor movement. In particular, cooperative labor management relations were considered the key to regaining international competitive power.

From our observations in Chapters 9 and 10 it is abundantly clear that this perception of the Japanese people was far from the economic reality. It is true that during the period such industries as textiles, steel, shipbuilding, and petrochemicals lost some of their international competitive power. With the exception of the last-mentioned industry, the decline of the above industries had nothing to do with the availability or lack of natural resources; it just followed the normal pattern of product life cycles in the course of economic development. The fact of the matter is that the productivity movement was so successful in strengthening Japanese competitive power that Japan started to register large trade surpluses.

Accelerating trade surpluses naturally put an upward pressure on the value of the yen. The appreciation of the yen became another source of worry to the Japanese people, a fear that yen appreciation would automatically increase the prices of Japan's exports expressed in foreign currencies, thereby weakening the competitive power of Japanese industries. This fear reinforced people's motivation to attain productivity increases by means of hard work, frugality, and labor-management cooperation, including wage restraint. QC circles, which became widespread in this period, were a result of such efforts.

It was against this background that our alumni worked hard and for long hours and moved up their managerial career ladders. During this period virtually all our alumni were promoted to the lower middle management position of *kacho* (or section manager), many in marketing and sales. From the interviews several findings emerged. First, pure group-consensus-based bottom-up decision making was not found in any organization; section managers possessed and exercised considerable power in determining the sales goals of individual members of a section. With regard to the determination of the sales goals of a section the general manager played a crucial role because sales goals of a section were determined as part of the sales goals of the department.

Second, with regard to the pricing policy neither group nor consensus decision making were adopted. Only in transactions involving relatively small amounts of money were lower-level employees allowed a certain degree of discretion.

Third, as for the training of subordinates by section managers, although the style of training varied, both job skills and interpersonal skills were emphasized. Loyalty to the company, which is often mentioned as an important objective of OJT by Japanese companies, did not surface.

Fourth, in performance appraisal of subordinates, the two most popularly used criteria were ability (including potential ability) and performance (or results). A simple notion that wages and promotion are determined by the length of service was not supported.

As mentioned in Chapter 12, a total of fourteen alumni worked in overseas offices. The "failure rate" was zero, again for the same reasons mentioned in the Summary to Part II—job knowledge, language skills, and eagerness to work overseas. Overall, neither preassignment training nor postassignment training played a significant role in the success of the overseas assignments of our alumni.

With regard to the question of ethnocentrism, on the whole overseas Japanese establishments in our sample adopted an ethnocentric staffing policy in that all the highest positions as well as top-level management positions were held by Japanese nationals. On a closer examination, the degree of ethnocentrism was stronger in general trading and banking than in manufacturing establishments.

On the question of the style of conducting business, responses were split between those who adopted local practices and those who followed practices in offices back in Japan. The former responses were given by those in sales offices of manufacturing companies, while the latter were given by those in general trading companies and establishments in Asian countries. This difference is understandable because the former type of offices directly deal with local consumers, while the establishments in Asian countries dealt with industrial customers who accepted Japanese practices as "superior." In the case of general trading companies, the institution was uniquely Japanese; therefore, there was no local model to follow.

In terms of the management of local employees, all offices followed local practices, a rational response to local labor market conditions where labor mobility was typically high. Japanese employees (PCNs) were essentially on the Japanese schemes.

Overseas offices of general trading companies were found to be more centrally controlled than those of manufacturing and other companies. This parallels the difference in the degree of ethnocentrism in staffing practices. This is understandable because the more Japanese managers there are, especially at the top level in overseas offices, the easier it is for the headquarters to control these offices.

To the question of the extent to which their family members enjoyed overseas experiences, all but one answered positively. As in the previous period virtually all were assigned to English-speaking countries or to Europe, whose ways of life were more familiar to our alumni than those in other areas. The only negative case involved an assignment in Teheran for reasons of unfamiliar culture and unstable social conditions.

At the end of 1973 twenty-five of the thirty alumni continued to stay with their original employers. During this period only one alumnus left the original employer (ceramics company) to join his wife's family business as a senior executive. These figures suggest that commitment to long-term employment was very strong on the part of both our alumni and their employers. Although the two oil crises adversely affected such industries as textiles, petrochemicals, and air transportation, the employment security of our alumni was not in danger.

By 1973 five of our six alumnae had been married, did not hold a job, and were concentrating on their family lives. One alumna remained single and held a full-time job. Our central concern was to see to what extent attitudes toward life and the behavior of our alumnae represented prewar values of "a good wife and wise mother" or postwar values of "equality of men and women." Our findings suggest that despite initial conflict between the two values all five married alumnae came to identify more strongly with postwar values either by sharing work goals with their husbands or by developing their own work goals.

Part IV

Period of Stable Economic Growth
to the Bubble Economy
(1981–1990)

14
General Environment, 1981–90

The decade of the 1980s was an epoch-making period in the twentieth century, featuring as it did the fall of the Soviet empire and the victory of the United States and its allies in the cold war.

At the beginning of the decade it looked as if the power of the Soviet Union under the firm leadership of Brezhnev was intact, as demonstrated by the holding of the Moscow Olympic Games, despite a boycott by the United States and many free-world nations, including Japan (Ministry of Foreign Affairs 1981: 158–62).

With the inauguration of Ronald Reagan as the U.S. president in January 1981, the United States stepped up its pressure on the Soviet Union (1982: 123–26). The U.S. defense budget, which had been cut during the Carter administration as a result of the Russian pretense of détente, was substantially increased. At the economic summit meetings held in Ottawa in July 1981, the Group of Seven (G-7) leaders reaffirmed the existence of a Soviet threat and their firm stand against Communist expansionism 1982: 492–94).

Inside Russia, however, the economy was turning from bad to worse, thanks to the inefficiencies of centralized planning and the heavy burden of large military expenditures. The war in Afghanistan turned into a civil war from which the Soviet Union could not pull out. The sudden death of Brezhnev in November 1982 led the Soviet Union into political instability 1983: 170–74). To the outside world it continued its highhanded politics. The world was appalled at the news that Russian fighter planes had shot down a Korean Airline passenger plane and killed a large number of innocent passengers for no reason but to "protect" their exclusive air space.

After a couple of short-lived administrations, Mikhail Gorbachev was named party leader of the Soviet Union in March 1985, and he started to take a new turn that the West had never expected (Ministry of Foreign Affairs 1986: 185–87). In July of the same year, he announced a unilateral suspension of nuclear tests for five months. In October 1986, a summit conference was held between the United States and the Soviet Union to discuss the reduction of their strategic defense arsenals.

In 1989 the East European nations that had belonged to the Soviet bloc achieved political freedom, one by one (Ministry of Foreign Affairs 1990: 233–40). In Poland, East Germany, Hungary, Czechoslovakia, Bulgaria, Romania, and the three Baltic nations of Estonia, Latvia, and Lithuania, communist governments fell, resulting in the transfer of political power to liberal groups. The Soviet Union under Gorbachev's leadership made no attempt to interfere militarily. The most dramatic moment was the destruction of the Berlin Wall that had separated East and West Berlin. When the wall was finally broken down in November 1989, twenty-eight years after its construction, the people of the world realized that the cold war was coming to an end.

After a series of events in Eastern Europe, a most momentous summit conference was held between George Bush, the newly elected U.S. president, and Gorbachev in December 1989 (Ministry of Foreign Affairs 1990: 183). At the end of the conference they issued a joint statement declaring the termination of the cold war, thus beginning a new era in world history.

The policies of the United States and its allies toward the Soviet bloc nations were directed toward promoting further liberalization and economic stabilization in these nations 1989 (Ministry of Foreign Affairs 1991: 257–58). And so it was that the West began to provide economic and technical assistance. Also, attempts were made to integrate these nations into the free-world economy. In 1990 the Coordinating Committee for Multilateral Export Controls (COCOM) ban on the export of strategic materials to Soviet-bloc nations was lifted. In May of the same year, the General Agreement on Tariffs and Trade (GATT) gave approval for the Soviet Union to join as an observer. The unification of West and East Germany in October 1990 was achieved at a massive cost to West Germany.

In Asia, after the death of Mao Zedong in 1976, China started to concentrate on economic modernization, and, by the early 1980s, its new economic policy was beginning to show positive results. In April 1984, U.S. President Reagan made an official visit to China and stated his support for Chinese modernization 1985: 109). In December of the same year the United Kingdom signed an agreement to return Hong Kong to Chinese sovereignty in 1997 (Ministry of Foreign Affairs 1985: 111). It looked as though China was following the footsteps of the Soviet Union in the direction of economic and political liberalization.

Then came the incident in Tiananmen Square in June 1989 (Ministry of Foreign Affairs 1990: 151–54). The Chinese government crushed student demonstrators who had demanded sweeping democratization. As a result of the incident, influential liberal political leaders lost power. Dismayed by the Chinese action, the United States and other Western nations expressed their disapproval of the Chinese position. But the Chinese government did not yield to international pressure and maintained its firm clamp on opposition. The world was reminded of the fact that in Asia, unlike in Europe, communism was intact in China, in North Korea, and in Vietnam.

In Japan the decade of the 1980s was marked by political stability and economic prosperity. It was also a decade in which trade friction with the United States and the EC nations became increasingly serious.

Yasuhiro Nakasone, who succeeded Zenko Suzuki in late 1982 as prime minister, stayed in power for five years, the longest tenure since Eisaku Sato's in the late 1960s through the early 1970s. Nakasone's long tenure and that of his successor, the veteran Noboru Takeshita, brought about political stability. Shortly after assuming the premiership, Nakasone mended a relationship with the United States that had been somewhat strained due to his predecessor's weak commitment to the Japan–U.S. military alliance. In fact, at the first meeting with President Reagan in January 1983, Nakasone quickly established rapport with the U.S. president by fully endorsing the latter's strong stance against the Soviet Union, which was still under a communist regime (Ministry of Foreign Affairs 1984: 149–51).

In the area of domestic policies, even before he assumed the premiership, Nakasone was engaged in administrative reform and privatization of public corporations (Jiyu Kokumin-sha 1992: 98). With the strong support of Toshio Doko, the president of the Japan Federation of Economic Organizations (Keidanren) and also the chairman of the Special Advisory Board on Administrative Reform, Nakasone achieved a series of privatizations—of the Nippon Telegraph and Telephone Public Corporation into NTT and of the Japan Monopoly Corporation into the Japan Tobacco Company in 1985—as well as the dissolution and privatization of Japanese National Railways into several JR companies. The latter reform met with strong resistance from both management and labor unions. Nevertheless, Nakasone pushed through his reform plan.

As we will discuss in more detail later, Japan registered large trade surpluses due partly to the "strong dollar" policy of President Reagan. A series of attempts to open the Japanese market were not very successful, although U.S. efforts to have Japan exercise self-restraint in its exports met with some success. Overall, though, these efforts failed and the United States was running huge trade deficits with Japan. As a result, in September 1985, finance ministers of the five major industrial nations met in the Plaza Hotel in New

York and agreed on joint action to devalue the dollar (Economic Planning Agency 1986: 12). Within a year, the dollar dropped dramatically, from over ¥240 to ¥160. Noboru Takeshita, representing Japan, pledged that Japan would curtail trade surpluses by stimulating domestic demand.

After two years, Takeshita succeeded Nakasone as the prime minister. By that time the economy was beginning to overheat and the bubble economy was swelling. It was against this background that the Recruit scandal came to light (Asahi shimbunsha 1990: 86). One of the Recruit Company's subsidiary publishing companies needed special favors from the ministries of Labor and Education, so before its stocks were traded on the open market the company sold or lent large amounts of them to high officials in the two ministries, as well as to such influential politicians as Takeshita, Nakasone, Miyazawa, and Abe, all of whom enjoyed handsome capital gains—when the stocks were finally traded on the open market—thanks to soaring gains on the stock market. All of these politicians, including Takeshita, were forced to resign from their positions. The next two prime ministers were not as competent and decisive as their predecessors, and this was one of the reasons for mismanagement of the economy and the subsequent growth of the bubble.

We will now review the overall performance of the economy during the entire period. Table 14.1 summarizes a few key economic indicators.

Unlike the first oil crisis, the impact of the second oil crisis was much milder. The annual rate of increase in the consumer price index fell from 8 percent in 1980 (from Table 9.1 in Chapter 9) to 4.0 percent in 1981. The gross national product (GNP) growth rate declined from 4.8 percent in 1980 (from Table 9.1 in Chapter 9) to 3.0 percent in 1981, a small decline. Relative to other countries that experienced more serious difficulties, Japan's performance may even be called a success.

Throughout the period, GNP grew at a respectable rate and inflation was under control. The trade balance was at a relatively low level in 1981 and 1982 but started to climb thereafter. However, it declined after 1987, partly as a result of self-restraint in exports and an increase in imports. Besides, the rapid increase in the value of the yen hit some of the traditional industries hard, such as the basic steel industry. In February 1987, five major iron and steel companies dismissed a total of 40,000 workers, nearly a quarter of the whole workforce of these companies.

On the other hand, new industries were emerging in areas such as communications, biotechnology, and electronics, leading to new economic growth. A communication satellite, "Sakura," was launched in February 1983 (Jiyu kokumin-sha 1992: 99). Personal computers and word processors became popular, resulting in the spread of office automation all over Japan.

The rapid appreciation of the yen forced Japanese export industries to

Table 14.1

GNP Growth Rate, Consumer Price Index (CPI), Trade Balance, Foreign Reserves, and Exchange Rate

Year	Increase in GNP	Increase in CPI (%)	Trade balance (nominal) (million USD)	Foreign reserves (nominal) (million USD)	Exchange rate (mid-year) (yen to USD)
1981	3.0	4.0	19,967	27,231	227.52
1982	3.1	2.6	18,079	24,015	249.64
1983	2.5	1.9	31,454	25,109	236.33
1984	4.1	2.2	44,257	26,538	244.19
1985	4.1	1.9	55,986	27,917	221.09
1986	3.1	0.0	92,827	58,389	159.83
1987	4.8	0.5	96,386	84,857	138.33
1988	6.0	0.8	95,012	99,353	128.27
1989	4.4	2.9	76,917	73,496	142.82
1990	5.5	3.3	63,528	69,894	141.30

Source: Economic Planning Agency, *Keizai yoran* [Summary Statistics on the Economy] (annual).

shift production to overseas plants. Industries in areas such as the automobile, electronics, and precision machinery industries started global operations. By the end of 1986, approximately one-third of industrial production came from overseas factories—a beginning trend that all industries would follow.

Table 14.2 shows the labor market trends in the period 1981–90. Again, the Japanese labor force continued to increase year after year. The unemployment rate was on the increase in the 1980s, reaching a peak (2.8 percent) in 1986–87 and then declining as the bubble economy headed toward 1990. Similarly, the active job opening rate was also on the increase, surpassing 1.00 in 1988–90.

Employment growth continued to be remarkable in the tertiary sector as well as in the female workforce. At the same time, the Japanese labor force was steadily aging and their job-opening rate kept falling.

On the other hand, technological innovations continued to be introduced into various industries. With the advent of new technologies in microelectronics (ME) and office automation (OA), more and more professional, technical, and skilled workers were needed, and they increasingly came to be in short supply.

In this period, various industries also required more full-time workers, and this led to a decrease in the number of temporary and seasonal workers. New openings for full-time jobs, however, increased less than those for part-time jobs,

Table 14.2

Labor Market Trends

Year	Labor force (thousand)	Unemployment rate (%)	Active job opening rate (%)	Wage increase (%)
1981	5.707	2.2	0.68	0.4
1982	5.774	2.4	0.61	1.5
1983	5.889	2.6	0.60	0.8
1984	5.927	2.7	0.65	1.4
1985	5.963	2.6	0.68	0.7
1986	6.020	2.8	0.62	2.3
1987	6.084	2.8	0.70	2.2
1988	6.166	2.5	1.01	3.0
1989	6.270	2.3	1.25	1.9
1990	6.384	2.1	1.40	1.5

Source: Ministry of Labor, *Rodo tokei yoran* [Summary Statistics on Labor] (annual).

especially in tertiary-sector areas such as services, transportation/telecommunications, and wholesale and retail trade. As a result, more and more female workers, especially housewives, and older workers entered the labor market.

We observe from the data in Table 14.2 that throughout this period wage increases were modest, well below GNP growth rates (see Table 14.1). This was a result of the deliberate policy of organized labor to moderate their wage demands in the annual *Shunto* wage negotiations. As mentioned before, the second oil crisis (1979–80) and the Plaza Accord brought about temporary setbacks to the Japanese economy. The "responsible" labor movement cooperated with management in tiding over the difficulties by restraining their wage increases.

In regard to international comparisons, the trends of the previous period remained. That is, among the five leading industrialized countries, Japan was the only country where the increase in productivity exceeded the increase in wages between 1980 and 1985 (Table 14.3). For the period 1985 to 1990, in Japan (as well as in the United States) productivity increased faster than wages, while in the United Kingdom, West Germany, and France wage increases exceeded productivity increases.

In reality, difficulties caused by the second oil crisis did not last long. Instead, wage restraints led to increased competitiveness of Japanese exports, which, in turn, resulted in huge trade surpluses. This put pressure on the yen to appreciate. With the appreciation of the yen, the Japanese wage level expressed in U.S. dollars increased exactly in step with the rate of appreciation. This, in

Table 14.3

Percentage Increase in Labor Productivity and Wages in Manufacturing in Five Countries

Year	Japan		United States		United Kingdom		West Germany		France	
	productivity	wages	productivity	wages	productivity	wages	productivity	wages	productivity	wages
1980–85	22	21	22	32	30	49	19	23	22	66
1985–90	29	18	26	15	23	51	8	23	18	20

Sources: For 1980–1985: Japan Productivity Center [Nihon seisansei honbu], *Katsuyo rodo tokei* [Practical Statistics on Labor] (1983, 1989); for 1985–1990: Japan Productivity Center for Socioeconomic Development [Shakai keizai seisansei honbu], *Katsuyo rodo tokei* [Practical Labor Statistics] (1995).

turn, put downward pressure on wage increases. Thus, the Japanese economy was trapped in a vicious circle of wage restraint resulting in the appreciation of the yen, which resulted in the need for wage restraint.

It was during this period that major legislative developments took place in female employment. After World War II, the protection of women was the most important objective of labor law. The Japanese Labor Standard Law, enacted in 1947, contained a protective clause created especially for working women, and it included restrictions on overtime work, nightshift work, and dangerous jobs. Except for a provision prohibiting wage discrimination, the law was silent on guaranteeing women equality with men in other areas of employment, including hiring and promotion.

In 1986, the Equal Employment Opportunity Law (EEOL) went into effect (Ministry of Labor 1986: 85–86). The EEOL encourages employers to provide equal opportunities in recruiting and hiring, job assignments and advancement, vocational training, and dismissal procedures. However, it does not contain any stipulation of penalties for any violation of the law. The only power of enforcement was social sanction, or the employer's wish to preserve a good corporate image in the eyes of women and the public in general.

After the enactment of the EEOL, many large companies began to offer women with university degrees one of two employment tracks: *ippanshoku* (general jobs) and *sogoshoku* (integrated jobs). The latter track treats women the same as men, including overtime work and transfers, as well as promotions. Although the number of openings for integrated jobs for women was generally small, and although the law itself has no teeth, it paved the way for highly motivated women to advance alongside their male colleagues. With favorable economic conditions in the latter half of the 1980s, it appeared that the EEOL had some effect in improving the employment status of women.

15
Industry-Specific Environment, 1981–90

The Iron and Steel Industry

The second oil crisis in 1979 caused renewed inflation, declining economic growth, and an increase in balance-of-payments deficits in industrialized countries, which were still suffering from stagflation. The sluggish economies of those countries resulted in a weakening demand for petroleum in 1981 and 1982, and this placed OPEC's current account balance in the red in 1982. The world economy simultaneously experienced a recession that was spread over the largest area ever. Then world economic recovery began when the crude oil price stabilized at a lower level.

Steel makers in Europe and the United States were in trouble because demand remained low, mainly due to the changing nature of demands for materials and because production facilities were not being sufficiently updated for more efficiency. Major U.S. steel makers went into the red in 1982 (total losses of the top ten being more than $3 billion). Manufacturers in the EC were also in the red. In the United States, the problem was dealt with on two fronts: the government provided relief measures, while the manufacturers themselves commenced (from the end of 1981) to restructure on a large scale. Obsolete equipment was scrapped, the number of factories was reduced, and employment was curtailed. Many integrated steel factories that had long been in operation were closed, scaled down, or sold.

Reacting to such developments, Japanese steel makers sank large investments into the United States. The following are some examples:

Nippon Steel—capital participation in Inland Steel for cold-rolled steel sheets/plates;

Nippon Kokan (NKK)—capital participation in National Steel;

Kawasaki Steel—acquisition of a Kaiser Steel factory;

Sumitomo Metal—a joint venture with LTV for galvanized steel sheets/plates.

In contrast to the steel makers in the United States or the EC, Japanese steel makers had been rationalizing from the time of the first oil crisis. They had introduced computers for automated or unmanned production lines, while at the same time tackling pollution issues. They upgraded the profitability target to "profitable even operating at 60 percent capacity" from the "profitable even operating at 70 percent capacity" target set after the first oil crisis. Furthermore, they implemented business diversification, expanded and intensified engineering operations, and went into such areas as coal chemistry, titanium, or new ceramics. (Earnings from engineering operations amounted to 10 percent of total sales of the five blast-furnace steel manufacturers in the 1982 accounting year.)

There was a sharp rise in the export of oil-well pipes in 1980 and 1981 in the midst of an oil-well drilling boom that began in 1979 and was taking place primarily in the United States. These exports contributed to improved profit performance for two years. After the boom was over, steel maker earnings, in spite of the efforts at rationalization, worsened again as a result of decreasing factory shipments, stagnant markets at home and abroad, and other adverse conditions. (Steel makers recorded ordinary losses for the 1982 and 1983 accounting years.)

With a view to transforming the Japanese economy into an economy led by domestic demand with an industrial structure free from trade frictions, the government launched emergency economic measures of ¥6 trillion in 1987 in order to overcome the recession caused by a strong yen. Demand picked up. Japan's iron and steel industry enjoyed the effects of these economic measures until the beginning of 1991.

The "heavy-thick-long-large industries," the products of which are heavy, thick, long and/or large, were designated structurally depressed industries. Their place in the strong-yen economy was bolstered by an emphasis on economic activities for domestic consumption instead of for exports. Shipbuilding started an upward swing. Plant and equipment investments and the creation of infrastructure led to revivals in the production of heavy electric equipment, machine tools, railway carriages, and construction machinery. It was the construction boom more than anything else that contributed to a rise in demand for iron and steel.

Reflecting the lively demand, a halt was called to planned cessations of plant operations as part of rationalization processes. Several blast furnaces, due to be closed down, were kept in operation. Japan's economy plunged into the bubble economy. Annual crude-steel production, which had been hovering around 100 million metric tons since 1981, returned to 110 million metric tons in 1990 after nine years below that figure (Table 15.1). A year earlier, all the major steel manufacturers had recorded their largest profits ever.

Imports of products of ordinary steel began to rise rapidly in 1987, with Korea at the head of the exporters and Taiwan and Brazil next in line. Imports reached a peak of 7.5 million metric tons in 1991. Exports, on the other hand, declined, falling below 30 million metric tons in 1987, and below 20 million metric tons in 1990 (Table 15.2). The primary reason for the decline was that the active domestic demand reduced export capacity and high-grade products were selected for exports under a globally strained demand-supply situation.

Even though the U.S. Trigger Price Mechanism was suspended in 1982, pressure was continuously put on imports from Japan. The United States and Japan reached a Voluntary Restraint Agreement in 1985, and it would be in effect until March 1992.

Synthetic Fiber Manufacturers

Synthetic fiber manufacturers continued the process of qualitative improvement of corporate structures that they had started in the previous period, and to this they added reviews of their overseas operations.

The strong yen in the latter half of the 1980s made the labor-intensive apparel industry look to China and other cheap-labor countries as bases for the production of garments for mass sales. Spinning, dyeing, weaving and/or sewing companies, in cooperation with the synthetic fiber makers, also commenced to transfer their operation bases overseas. Japan was far ahead of other Asian countries in high-value-added fibers, but demand for these was at a low level in Asian markets. Korean and Taiwanese fibers replaced multipurpose fibers, which could be mass produced. Imports of middle- and low-grade garments rose sharply. These imported products, domestically produced items of higher qualities, and goods of the highest quality imported from industrialized countries shared the domestic market, with each product jealously guarding its own territory against the others (Table 15.3).

To strengthen their grip on the domestic market, textile manufacturers aimed toward applying their products to use in high-grade garments and widening nongarment uses. To this end they transformed themselves from an orientation toward mass production to an orientation toward products with high value added.

In the field of products for high-grade garment purposes, manufacturers

Table 15.1

Basic Statistical Data on the Iron and Steel Industry

Year	Shipment amount (billion yen)			Number of employees (thousands)			Crude-steel production (thousand metric tons)		
	Iron and steel (A)	All industries (B)	(A)/(B) (%)	Iron and steel (%)	All industries (D)	(C)/(D) (%)	Production capacity	Output	World market share (%)
1980	17,896	214,700	8.3	433	10,932	4.0	158,724	111,395	15.6
1981	17,228	224,712	7.7	423	10,568	4.0	158,390	101,676	14.4
1982	17,447	229,931	7.6	417	10,481	4.0	157,989	99,548	15.4
1983	16,073	235,527	6.8	407	10,651	3.8	156,262	97,179	14.7
1984	17,298	253,030	6.8	396	10,733	3.7	156,377	105,586	14.9
1985	17,754	265,321	6.7	388	10,890	3.6	152,365	105,279	14.7
1986	14,783	254,689	5.8	369	10,893	3.4	150,731	98,275	13.8
1987	13,800	253,515	5.4	349	10,738	3.2	152,158	98,513	13.4
1988	15,621	274,401	5.7	338	10,911	3.1	143,233	105,681	13.5
1989	17,269	298,893	5.8	337	10,963	3.1	141,596	107,908	13.7
1990	18,269	323,373	5.6	338	11,173	3.0	136,896	110,339	14.3
1991	18,631	340,835	5.5	340	11,351	3.0	137,353	109,649	14.9

Sources: Adapted from MITI, *Census of Manufacturers* (annual); and Japan Iron and Steel Federation, *Handbook for Iron and Steel Statistics* (annual).

Table 15.2

Exports and Imports of the Iron and Steel Industry

| Year | Total exports | Exports of all iron and steel products (thousand metric tons) | | | | Imports of steel products [ordinary steel] (thousand metric tons) | | | |
		To the United States	To the EC	To Asia (including China)	To China	Total imports	From Korea	From Taiwan	From Brazil
1980	30,327	5,185	634	13,074	3,215	696	N/A	N/A	N/A
1981	29,134	6,168	303	11,545	2,219	1,345	1,197[a]	137[a]	20[a]
1982	29,474	4,152	361	12,179	2,930	1,894	1,332[a]	315[a]	137[a]
1983	32,012	4,602	368	17,048	7,249	2,613	1,504[a]	516[a]	387[a]
1984	32,841	6,418	387	17,529	8,614	3,723	1,287[a]	455[a]	424[a]
1985	33,342	5,245	376	19,233	10,934	2,503	1,437[a]	477[a]	407[a]
1986	30,323	3,952	469	18,803	9,244	2,889	1,386[a]	263[a]	352[a]
1987	25,685	4,342	127	15,351	5,848	4,436	1,960	323	393
1988	23,652	4,276	246	14,044	4,929	6,208	2,697	463	713
1989	20,197	3,426	320	12,895	3,940	6,404	2,785	537	623
1990	17,021	3,220	442	10,301	1,754	5,978	2,694	627	499
1991	18,027	2,780	318	11,954	2,064	7,505	3,086	672	665

Source: Japan Iron and Steel Federation, *Handbook for Iron and Steel Statistics* (annual).
[a]These figures are for the accounting years (from April to March of the following year).

Table 15.3

Export and Import of Textile Products (million US$)

Year	Total Export (A)	Total Import (B)	Trade balance (A) – (B)	Materials Export	Materials Import	Yarns Export	Yarns Import	Fabrics Export	Fabrics Import	Secondary products Export	Secondary products Import
1965	1,576	904	672	155	847	183	5	760	34	478	18
1975	3,719	2,834	885	466	1,524	587	197	1,715	408	951	705
1985	6,263	6,041	222	635	2,195	1,000	715	3,122	758	1,507	2,414
1986	6,874	6,890	(16)	695	1,863	1,152	651	3,460	905	1,565	3,471
1987	6,917	10,326	(3,409)	708	2,702	1,117	977	3,481	1,091	1,611	5,556
1988	6,908	13,940	(7,032)	847	3,309	1,108	1,245	3,359	1,548	1,593	7,838
1989	6,862	16,620	(9,758)	827	3,337	1,109	1,104	3,316	1,885	1,610	10,293
1990	7,195	15,447	(8,252)	838	2,643	1,117	1,004	3,564	1,727	1,675	10,073

Source: Japan Chemical Fibers Association, *Kasen nenpyo* [Chronological Table of the Chemical Fibers Industry] (annual).

succeeded in the creation of "new synthetic fibers" by cooperating with petrochemical companies in the upgrading of materials, with machine makers in developing high-speed spinning machines, and with weaving and/or dyeing companies in the creation of properties, appearances, and textures different from those of natural fibers. Their success in new synthetic fibers led to their largest profits ever in 1990.

In regard to nongarment uses, the manufacturers went into industrial materials. Special properties, which multipurpose products for use in garments were not able to satisfy, were required for this purpose. This business was possible only in a large economy such as Japan's, where all the industrial fields were represented. Products covered use in a wide range of industries, for example, the semiconductor, engineering, and medical industries. Automobile makers were especially big buyers, and fiber manufacturers codeveloped new fibers for them.

The Petrochemical Industry

Facing slackening business conditions and excess capacity after the second oil crisis, petrochemical companies determined for the first time to reduce production facilities. On the basis of the Industrial Restructuring Law, a new law promulgated and taking effect in 1983, a government-led reduction plan was put into effect; according to this plan, from 1983 to 1986, the ethylene capacity was to be curtailed by 20 percent (from 6.15 million metric tons per year to 4.69 million metric tons per year), and a reduction of 10 percent to 40 percent was to be made in its derivatives (vinyl chloride resin, polyethylene, polypropylene) and intermediate materials (ethylene monomer and ethylene oxide).

But then the crude oil price began to fall in 1982. Production costs fell; demand recovered. The demand-supply situation improved remarkably, and the ethylene manufacturers' business enjoyed an upswing. The number of factories in operation, after hitting bottom in 1982, rose globally, and ethylene was in short supply in 1987 and 1988. In Japan the price of the raw material (naphtha) went down in 1987. There was a large demand from the electric appliance and automobile industries in the midst of heightening domestic demand as the bubble economy began in the latter half of 1987. The production of ethylene exceeded 5 million metric tons in 1988 (JPCA 1998: 39). The twelve ethylene manufacturers enjoyed an increase in profits.

The weakening competitiveness of Japan's petrochemical industry, evident in increasing reliance on imports of naphtha, forced manufacturers to change their product line. Two possible directions to take were considered: (1) enhancing high-value-added products, in particular, special resins like engineering plastic (EP), which were highly heatproof, wearproof, and shock-proof; and

(2) developing new business areas like medical supplies, biochemical products, semiconductors, or electronic materials.

In actual fact, they entered the field of special resins, which were used for electronic machinery and equipment, and for automobiles.

By way of developing new fields of business, petrochemical manufacturers linked up with several giant U.S. and European enterprises. Major foreign enterprises also attached importance to the Japanese market. A few examples of cooperative ventures that Japanese makers hoped would differentiate them from their competitors were:

Mitsui Toatsu Chemicals joined BASF for sales of polyestersulfone;

Asahi Chemical linked with Du Pont for nylon 66 materials;

Asahi Chemical joined Dow Chemical for polystyrene business in Asia; and

Kureha Chemical united with Cellunese for production in the United States of PPS resin.

In other action, Sumitomo Chemical founded an ethylene production base in Singapore, while Showa Denko set up an ethylene and polyethylene production base in Indonesia.

The Industrial Machinery Industry

Japan recovered from the second oil crisis comparatively early because of its high productivity and technological innovations. Trade gaps with the United States and Europe widened in Japan's favor, and trade imbalance emerged as an issue. A construction machine dumping charge raised in the United Kingdom in 1983 had repercussions across all of Europe. Another factor worsening export environments was the strong yen after the Plaza Accord of 1985.

Machine Tools

Lively demand had a widespread ripple effect that extended outward over subcontractors, other industries, and medium and small enterprises. The industry was excited by a backlog of orders equivalent to a few years' work. The NC-type machine tool share of total machine tool production amounted to 66.9 percent in 1984.

Reduced production costs realized by greater mass production strengthened international competitiveness. Exports increased rapidly, especially to the United States; 49 percent of all exports went to the United States in 1981. This was the cause of trade disputes. Even more serious was the fact that the munitions industry was based upon machine tools, and the sharp rise in these imports became a political issue in both the United States and European countries. In 1981 President Reagan launched a policy for defense purposes that requested machine-tool exporting countries to exercise self-restraint in exports. It was virtually a curb on imports from Japanese manufacturers. The issue developed into government-level talks and then into a Voluntary Restraint Agreement (VRA), whereby quantitative restrictions would be imposed on Japanese makers for five years, beginning in 1986. The value of exports to the United States in 1987 declined 54 percent from the year before. The VRA was later extended for two more years.

The yen went on an upward curve after the Plaza Accord of 1985. Domestic demand as well as exports declined for once. Local production of machine tools overseas was expanded in order to avoid trade disputes. In 1987 Toshiba Machine Co. was blamed for having broken the restrictions of the Coordinating Committee for Multilateral Export Controls (COCOM). Things went so far that the chairman and president of Toshiba, the parent company, took responsibility and resigned. This shows that Japanese machine tools were strategically important items during the cold war and that the technological level of Japanese machine tools was at a world standard (Takamura and Koyama 1994 [vol. 4]: 82).

Construction Machines

Construction machines were becoming smaller and more labor-saving, reflecting an aging labor force and a shortage of young manpower. Fuel-economical engines were developed for energy-saving purposes.

The production of construction machines amounted to a record ¥1.8 trillion in 1990, when it seemed that demand had reached a ceiling.

Exports of construction machinery grew, keeping pace with quality improvement. They reached a peak of ¥680 billion, with an export ratio of 58 percent, in 1982. They stayed in the range of ¥400 billion to ¥500 billion thereafter (JSIMM 1998: 8).

The Electric Machine Industry

Heavy Electric Equipment (HEE)

The two oil crises constituted a turning point in the Japanese economy. It was transformed from an energy-consuming to a knowledge-intensive economy in which assembly industries gained stature as key industries and continued to enjoy stable growth.

In the electric power industry, nuclear power was playing an increasingly important role in the diversification of power resources. The HEE industry advanced technical developments aimed at higher efficiency in equipment, systems enhancement, higher reliability, and so forth.

The recession that followed the strong yen after the Plaza Accord in the autumn of 1985 reduced the facility investments of export-intensive manufacturing industries like steel. For a short time, this affected the HEE industry. It made a remarkable recovery when the bubble economy brought about double-digit growth in plant and equipment investments from 1988 to 1991 (Nihon Kogyo Shimbunsha: 659; Takamura and Koyama [vol. 4] 1994: 89).

Electrical Appliances (EAs)

The domestic EA market was divided into an increasing number of sectors. Products were regarded as a means for achieving enjoyable lives and self-satisfaction rather than as status symbols or something fashionable. Consumers who were once multifunction-oriented and high-grade-oriented now wanted products appropriate to the quality they sought in their daily lives, and they selected products in a sound and prudent manner.

The strong yen after the Plaza Accord rapidly worsened the business performance of the EA industry, which is highly dependent on exporting its products. EA manufacturers, while pushing forward with globalization by further transferring production bases overseas, switched their domestic business from export-led to domestic-demand-led.

When the economy entered the bubble stage, domestic demand expanded so much that it made up for the declines in exports (Takamura and Koyama [vol. 4] 1994: 91-92).

General Trading Companies (GTCs)

The recession after the second oil crisis bottomed out early in 1983. GTCs, however, continued to be in "winter." During the first half of the 1980s, exports led the growth of Japan's economy (Table 15.4). But the export business of GTCs did not keep pace.

The nation's total amount of exports (on custom basis) increased by 35 percent during the period, while GTC exports (sales amounts) rose only 25 percent (Table 15.5).

The slackness of GTC exports was attributed to:

(1) a shift from GTC export staples such as steel or ships toward durable consumer goods or other items that manufacturers could export directly (Table 15.6);

Table 15.4

Factors in the Increase in Gross National Expenditure (1980–85)
(as percent)

Private consumption	40.6
Government consumption	6.8
Domestic fixed capital formation	22.1
Increase in inventory	2.0
Exports	37.7
Imports	(9.2)
Gross national expenditure	100.0

Source: Ryouichi Miwa, *Gaisetsu Nihon keizai-shi, kin/gen-dai* [A Short History of Japan's Economy: The Modern Age] (Tokyo: University of Tokyo Press, 1993), p. 198.

Table 15.5

Increase in Exports (1980–85)

	1980	1985	Increase (%)
Japan's exports	$129,807 million	$175,638 million	35
General trading company (GTC) exports	¥14,662 billion	¥18,358 billion	25

Sources: For Japan exports: Japan Foreign Trade Council, Inc., *Nihon boekikai 50-nen-shi* [Fifty Years' History of the Japan Foreign Trade Council] (Tokyo, 1998), Statistical appendix, p. 8; for GTC exports: adapted from Shigetaka Asuka, *Sogo shosha ron* [A Treatise on GTCs] (Tokyo: Chuo keizai-sha, 1998), p. 210.

(2) less scope for GTC exporting activities because of the trend for manu-facturers to transfer factories overseas; and

(3) a serious drop in plant exports because oil producing countries were gaining less revenue, because of the growing risk of countries with accumu-lated debts, and because of increasingly keen competition among exporting countries (JFTC 1998: 73, 79).

GTC business operations deteriorated as a result of a strong yen, cheap

Table 15.6

Major Export Items and Their Market Shares (as percent)

Items	1980	1985	1990
Machines	62.8	71.8	74.9
Office machines	1.8	4.4	7.2
Audiovisual machines	—	—	6.9
Telecommunications equipment	6.3[a]	7.0[a]	2.1
Electronic parts, including semiconductors	1.8	2.7	4.7
Automobiles	17.9	19.6	17.8
Scientific and optical equipment	3.5	3.9	4.0
Ships	3.6	3.4	1.9
Metals	16.4	10.5	6.8
Steel	11.9	7.7	4.4
Metal products	3.0	2.0	1.6
Chemicals	5.2	4.4	5.5
Textiles	4.8	3.6	2.5
Foodstuffs	1.2	0.7	0.6
Others	9.5	9.0	9.6
Total	100.0	100.0	100.0
(Amount: billion yen)	(29,383)	(41,956)	(41,457)

Sources: Adapted from Shigetaka Asuka, *Sogo shosha ron* [A Treatise on GTCs] (Tokyo: Chuo keizai-sha, 1998), p. 80; Japan Foreign Trade Council, Inc., *Nihon boekikai 50-nen-shi* [Fifty Years' History of the Japan Foreign Trade Council] (Tokyo, 1998), Statistical appendix, pp. 8–9.
[a]Televisions and radios are included.

oil, and the recession following the Plaza Accord in September 1985. It was the bubble economy from 1987 to 1990 that put an end to the "winter."

> This expansion was domestic-demand-led. Businesses were doing a brisk trade in housing construction, plant and equipment investment, the construction of office buildings, and real estate transactions. Expensive consumer goods were greeted by eager demand [Table 15.7]. Each GTC did good business in the fields it was strong in. (JFTC 1998: 107)

During the period in question, the government's trade policy already stressed imports rather than exports in order to avoid trade frictions. At the government's request, GTCs endeavored to increase imports in the form of

Table 15.7

Total Amount of Sales and Distribution Ratio in Four Categories

Distribution ratio

Accounting year (March to April)	Total sales (billion yen)	Domestic (%)	Export (%)	Import (%)	Offshore (%)
1981	80,112	41.4	21.2	24.0	13.4
1982	83,151	40.2	21.5	24.1	14.2
1983	84,052	40.3	20.0	23.6	16.1
1984	92,892	38.6	19.6	23.9	17.9
1985	98,173	39.0	18.7	22.8	19.5
1986	82,739	44.7	19.5	17.8	18.0
1987	91,182	44.9	16.3	18.9	19.9
1988	98,327	46.6	14.8	18.7	19.9
1989	129,860	38.6	16.1	22.1	23.2
1990	126,626	42.4	12.2	18.2	27.2

Source: Shigetaka Asuka, *Sogo shosha ron* [A Treatise on GTCs] (Tokyo: Chuo keizai-sha, 1998), p. 210.

finished goods. On the whole, they did not live up to expectations in this regard. This proved that they were weak in end-user-oriented businesses and forced them to start strengthening this area in order to create new business opportunities. The following were worthy of notice:

(1) grouping with major food wholesalers;

(2) joining with volume sales stores such as supermarkets and convenience stores; and

(3) entering into the leisure industry (development of resorts, marinas, ski slopes, golf links, etc.) (JFTC 1998: 80, 108, 111; Shimada 1991: 260).

During this period, GTCs pursued the development of new business fields (high-tech or service industries) and investment in manufacturers or related firms in order to strengthen supply capacity. There was a substantial increase in "jigyo toshi" (enterprise investment) for the same purpose; in these schemes GTCs not only invested in but also participated in the management of a particular company (Kawahara and Hayashikawa 1999: 51–52).

GTCs raised funds at low interest rates for such investments either through bond issues in overseas capital markets or equity finance. They also wrote off bad debt losses caused by investments in the past. In addition, they entered the financial business in the latter half of the 1980s by establishing financial subsidiaries at home and abroad (JFTC 1998: 109; Shimada 1991: 256–57).

The strategic issue of the GTCs throughout the 1980s was how to cope with a changing industrial structure in which high-value-added products were growing in demand and technology-intensive industries were becoming stronger. They entered the following business areas:

• new materials—electronic materials, ceramics, carbon fibers;
• new media—communications, satellite-related business, CATV, videotex, VAN, information and communication services; and
• biotechnology—investments in venture businesses, the seed business.

New media businesses were emphasized, with major projects commencing primarily in the latter half of the 1980s (JFTC 1998: 82–83, 109).

The Banking Industry

The United States urged the Japanese government to deregulate its financial and capital markets as well as voluntarily to curb exports. Japanese manufacturers took various measures in reaction to U.S. pressure on them to exercise self-restraint in exports. Nissan Motors and Honda built plants in the United States; Toyota founded a joint venture with General Motors. Major electrical appliance manufacturers such as Toshiba, Mitsubishi Electric, Matsushita, and Sony established production centers in the United States.

Liberalization of the financial and capital markets was accelerated, with a more rapid relaxation of interest rate restrictions than originally scheduled, an expanded Euro-yen market, and the promotion of investments in overseas businesses. Japanese banks expanded their overseas profit center networks: Fuji Bank acquired a major U.S. finance company, and Mitsubishi Bank and the Bank of Tokyo acquired a major U.S. bank each.

A review of the postwar financial system got under way. A Financial System Research Council was formed by the Ministry of Finance in 1985 to review the system of restricting financial institutions to specific categories of financial services. In regard to the capital market, the Securities and Exchange Council began in 1989 to review securities businesses. These reviews led to the Financial System Reform Law enacted in 1993.

In the bubble economy, most demand for money came from securities investors and the three sectors of real estate companies, construction companies, and finance companies, all of which were enthusiastic about land speculation. Prices of land, stocks, and other asset items rose sharply. To counter this abnormal state of the economy, the Ministry of Finance and the Bank of Japan took one measure after another (examples were a rise in interest rates in May 1989, restrictions on loans for land purchases in October 1989, and a ceiling set on such loans in February 1990). Business reached its peak in April 1991, when the upward trend ceased. The bubble economy was to lead to economic turmoil and a slump in the 1990s.

Meanwhile the "Big Bang" was set in motion in the United Kingdom in October 1986 and the securities market was drastically deregulated. The "Big Bang" aimed at reinvigorating the London capital market. It consisted mainly of a liberalization of capital participation in the Stock Exchange and a liberalization of brokerages.

The Air Transport Industry

U.S. President Carter launched a policy of deregulation of air transportation in 1978. The U.S. domestic air transport industry had turned into an oligopoly in which three airlines (American, United, and Delta) dominated the market. In the field of international air transport, the United States resorted to its greater strength in bilateral negotiations with second parties, in order to pressure them to accept deregulation. The International Air Transport Association (IATA) and civil aviation agreements obstructed U.S. moves in this regard.

Negotiations over a revision of the Japan–United States Civil Aviation Agreement, carried on between 1976 and 1981, were inconclusive. The controversial issues included rights to routes, rights beyond, and volume of transportation. Japan tried to discuss the agreement itself, while the United States was inclined to introduce individual airline companies' interests. Then Yasune Takagi took over the presidency of Japan Airlines (JAL) in 1981, the first president promoted from JAL regular staff.

A Tentative Japan–United States Civil Aviation Agreement was concluded in 1985. Settlement of the question of a Japan Cargo Air flight to the United States was put off until 1990. It was decided that each side would allow three additional airlines to enter the Pacific route. This decision was inconsistent with the Japanese government's basic policy up to that time, which allowed only JAL to operate on international routes.

In 1985 the Council for Transport Policy submitted to the Minister of Transport recommendations that more than one company be allowed to service international routes, that each domestic route be open to any airline, and that JAL be privatized. JAL was thrown into managerial confusion in 1985, when the number of its labor unions increased from four to six. The greater number of unions hindered quick decision making and any restructuring plans from that year on.

The year 1986 was called the first year of the deregulation era. Japan's airline companies were required to adapt themselves to changing business environments in both international and domestic air transportation. Demand was picking up. Japan's three airlines enjoyed good performance. On the Pacific route, United Airlines made Tokyo the hub of its operations after 1986, establishing a network that linked the Pacific region, the United States, and Canada. It was very strong. The other two companies, American and Delta, flew into Japan in 1987. On the "moneymaker" Japan–U.S. mainland route, the U.S. airlines, including Performing Arts Abroad and Northwest, took 74 percent of the market share and left the Japanese airlines (JAL and All Nippon Airways) with only a 26 percent share.

JAL was 100 percent privatized in 1987. Until then the government had owned one-third of its stocks. Deregulation had nullified the government's basic air transportation policy, and it no longer made sense for the government to keep JAL a special public corporation. Besides, JAL officials themselves had been eager to be independent of the government (JAL 1985: 448).

All Nippon Airways (ANA) joined international airlines in 1987. It was quite capable of getting along with its labor unions and ran a close-knit business. Japan Air Systems (JAS), on the contrary, was weak-kneed before its labor unions, and labor-management relations were behind the times.

The Gulf War in 1990 and the burst of the bubble affected the air transport industry seriously. JAL's ordinary profits plunged to ¥53.8 billion in the red in 1992, from being ¥52.7 billion in the black in 1989.

The Beer Industry: Distribution

After the second oil crisis, the beer industry moved from high growth to a period of moderate growth. To expand shares, brewery companies competed intensely in developing new products. The time came when large numbers of products were on the market. Some were hits, but most products disappeared like the foam at the top of the glass. Hits were beginning to affect market shares. Good products became more important than strong sales staff at breweries or agencies. Brewers endeavored to promote sales by working directly on retail stores as well as agencies and by suggesting promotion plans to them. In addition, brewers employed dedicated female part-timers to communicate to retailers the brewers' messages, requests, and other information, to collect information on retailers' activities, to check the production dates of merchandise on sale, and so forth. Brewers thus took over some of the functions of agencies.

Beer was sold at the same price across the whole nation, regardless of brewer, even though pricing was liberalized in 1964. The Fair Trade Commission (FTC) inquired into a price revision in 1990, suspecting that brewers had colluded in a concerted price increase. The issue was settled when the FTC accepted the brewers' proposal that each brewer place a Declaration of Free Prices in national newspapers. This settlement is thought to have encouraged liquor discounters, who by now were increasing in number (Kirin 1999: 212).

During the bubble economy, when there was an unprecedented shortage of labor, agencies, whose work was still labor-intensive in some regard, had a hard time finding staff and faced sharp rises in labor and distribution costs. They managed to control these costs as long as sales were increasing, but when the bubble burst they were left with high costs. Agencies were hard hit in terms of management.

Department Stores

Consumer spending weakened further for the first half of this period, with annual growth rates of 3.6 percent at department stores, 6.7 percent at supermarkets, and 4.8 percent at retailers overall (Table 15.8). The figures seemed to indicate that the retail industry was in a period of moderate growth. In the latter half of the decade, however, sales improved, with growth rates of 7.0 percent, 6.3 percent, and 5.5 percent at department stores, supermarkets, and retailers overall, respectively. Department stores recovered, while supermarkets slumped slightly.

In the latter half of the period, consumer behavior changed as the bubble economy took off. People who benefited from sharp rises in the value of stocks and/or real estate lavished a great deal of money on expensive articles other than the necessities of life. It was department stores, which had a lot of rich people and corporations as their clients, that enjoyed an advantage in such a business environment. Supermarkets took a sharp drop into sluggishness. "Bubble," however, was a skillful metaphor. Retailing as a whole grew at an average annual rate of only 5.5 percent. In other words, the general public did not loosen their purse strings; only a minority of consumers was being extravagant. The high growth rate at department stores, therefore, did not mean that department stores had once again taken over as leaders in the retail trade. Another factor that must be considered was the consumption tax introduced in 1989; it threw cold water on the spending boom of the bubble economy.

At this time, all the major department stores competed in building enormous stores. Some typical examples were Sogo (in Yokohama), Matsuzakaya (in Nagoya), and Tobu (at Ikebukuro, Tokyo). Other department store companies vied with one another in making huge investments in fixed assets. Huge stores had available a large selection of merchandise in each category of goods and offered shoppers the convenience of finding almost any article they wanted within a single store. The system used in running such a huge store, however, remained to be reviewed.

Table 15.8

Growth of Sales by Style of Business

Year	Growth of sales (%)			Consumption elasticity		Share of nationwide retail market (%)	
	Dept. stores	Supermarkets	Retailers overall	Dept. stores	Supermarkets	Dept. stores	Supermarkets
1980 (base)	100.0	100.0	100.0	1.00	1.02	7.1	10.0
1981	105.8	108.9	108.5	0.98	1.00	6.9	10.0
1982	109.1	115.0	116.9	0.96	0.98	6.6	9.8
1983	111.3	122.4	120.1	0.99	1.04	6.6	10.2
1984	115.1	130.8	123.4	1.01	1.04	6.6	10.6
1985	119.4	138.8	126.6	1.01	1.03	6.7	10.9
Average annual growth	3.6	6.7	4.8				
1985 (base)	100.0	100.0	100.0	1.01	1.03	6.7	10.9
1986	104.6	104.0	104.3	1.00	1.00	6.7	10.9
1987	109.6	109.0	108.6	1.01	1.01	6.8	11.0
1988	117.0	116.4	112.9	1.03	1.03	7.0	11.3
1989	129.7	127.1	121.9	1.03	1.01	7.1	11.4
1990	140.7	136.0	130.9	1.01	1.00	7.2	11.4
Average annual growth	7.0	6.3	5.5				

Sources: Adapted from Japan Department Stores Association, *Sales Statistics* (annual); Japan Chain Stores Association, *Sales Statistics* (annual); and Ministry of International Trade and Industry, *Census of Commerce* (annual).

Table 15.9

Housing Starts

Year	Number of houses	Year-on-year change (%)
1980 (base year)	1,268,626	85.0
1981	1,151,699	90.8
1982	1,146,149	99.5
1983	1,136,797	99.2
1984	1,187,282	104.4
1985	1,236,072	104.1
Average year-on-year-change	—	101.4
1985 (base year)	1,236,072	104.1
1986	1,364,609	110.4
1987	1,674,300	122.7
1988	1,684,644	100.6
1989	1,662,612	98.7
1990	1,707,109	102.7
Average year-on-year change	—	108.4

Source: Ministry of Construction, *Housing Statistics* (annual).

The FTC pointed out that Mitsukoshi had repeatedly pressured suppliers into buying merchandise by abusing its stronger position over them in business relations. Mitsukoshi had rejected the FTC's recommendation in 1979 that it eliminate this practice. This time, however, it admitted in 1982 that it had violated the Anti-Monopoly Law and accepted the FTC judgment. Department stores lost their prestige. Mitsukoshi's main store, the Mitsukoshi flagship that had long been the individual store with the largest amount of sales in Japan, yielded pride of place in 1982 to the Ikebukuro store of Seibu. Furthermore, Mitsukoshi slipped into the red for the accounting year ending February 1983. This showed that Mitsukoshi, however proud it might be of its history, could not manage its business without the support of consumers. The period threw new light on the fact that a department store exists as a member of the community (Koyama 1997: 205).

Building Materials: Distribution

Housing starts continued to decline slightly, but then turned upward in 1985, when the process of business adjustment after the second oil crisis was over (Table 15.9). In the latter half of this period they recorded an average growth

Table 15.10

Share of Imported South Sea Logs (as percent)

Year	Philippines	Indonesia	Malaysia				Others	Total
			Subtotal	Sabah	Sarawak	West Malaysia		
1981	9.6	28.1	56.9	37.1	19.8	0.0	5.3	100.0
1982	8.7	16.2	69.4	42.6	26.8	0.0	5.7	100.0
1983	4.7	15.2	74.3	44.9	29.4	0.0	5.8	100.0
1984	7.2	10.3	75.2	42.4	32.9	0.0	7.3	100.0
1985	3.9	1.1	86.9	45.3	41.5	0.0	8.1	100.0
1990	0.2	0.0	91.6	30.8	60.8	0.0	8.2	100.0

Source: Japan South Sea Timber Council, *Chronological Data on Imported Logs* (annual).

of 8.4 percent with 1985 taken as the base year; this result was their second-highest, after their 11.3 percent growth in the period of high economic growth. During the bubble economy, consumers pursued high quality, and high quality was also expected in houses. A sharp rise in land prices, however, meant the houses had to be smaller. A small house was compared to a "rabbit hutch."

Indonesia ceased supplying South Sea logs (Table 15.10). Instead of logs it exported plywood processed from logs. Malaysia made up for Indonesian logs. In Malaysia, the State of Sabah was initially the main supplier, then gradually the State of Sarawak took its place. The reason for this was that Sabah, whose resources were being depleted, passed a law prohibiting the export of logs. (Sabah's logs were superior in quality to Sarawak's.)

In looking back over the history of imported South Sea logs, we see that there were changes in the main suppliers, with the Philippines being followed by Indonesia, which was followed by Malaysia. These imports were an example of the development-and-import formula applied to natural resources. Frequently criticized, they were inclined to be heavily concentrated in a relatively small number of resource-rich countries. It can also be pointed out, however, that exporting countries have consistently sought demand for their resources in order to obtain foreign currencies or to create employment.

16
Career Progress and Change, 1981–90

The third subperiod (1981–90) represents the mid-career stages of the thirty alumni, covering the age span from their early forties through to the age of fifty or so. According to Schein, this stage is characterized by career stabilization and/or a mid-career crisis. Career stabilization means that one establishes a clear identity in the organization and accepts higher levels of responsibility. At the same time, for many people, this is a period of crisis in which a major reassessment of one's progress is made relative to one's ambitions. Decisions are made to level off, change careers, or forge ahead to higher challenges.

In 1981, at the beginning of this period, twenty-four of the thirty alumni were with their original employers. Of these twenty-four alumni, seven were engaged in overseas assignments, many of them in senior management positions. The overseas experiences of these seven alumni as well as of several others who were transferred overseas later in this period will be discussed in Chapter 17. Virtually all of the remaining fourteen alumni had held the position of section manager (*kacho*) or above, for example, deputy general manager (*bucho-dairi*), by the beginning of the period. During this period many were promoted to the next and the highest middle management position of "bucho," or general manager of a department. Therefore, in the first section of this chapter we will examine the work of a *bucho*, who plays a pivotal role within the Japanese organization. The second section will study the experiences of those alumni who changed their jobs and/or careers.

The *Bucho*: The Linchpin in the Japanese Corporation

Management decision making in the Japanese corporation is often characterized by practices such as *ringi* (proposal submission and deliberation), *nemawashi* (prior consultation before meetings), as well as frequent and long meetings allegedly unique to Japan. Thus, Japanese-style management decision making is labeled as "bottom-up decision making," "group decision making," and "consensus decision making." The main focus of this section, therefore, is to examine the extent to which the above practices actually took place in the offices run by those of our alumni who held the key position of *bucho*.

A total of a dozen alumni were promoted to the position of *bucho* in their main offices during this period. However, the study in this section is limited to ten cases involving nine individuals, and the reasons for this are the following. First, as discussed in Chapters 14 and 15, the economic environment of this period drastically changed after the Plaza Accord of September 1985; therefore, only the appointments made after that time will be studied, in order to control for the environmental effects. Two appointments that were made prior to 1985 will not be considered. In addition, one appointment was made toward the end of this period (1990). However, the tenure of this alumnus extended into the mid-1990s, by which time economic conditions again changed drastically, so this appointment will not be included either. In addition, several alumni held a *bucho* position more than twice. However, with the exception of an alumnus who experienced very different jobs, only one experience per individual will be studied, in order to avoid duplication. With these qualifications in mind Table 16.1 was prepared. The alumni are listed in the order of the commencement of their appointments.

The table shows two distinctive features. First, none of our alumni in general trading companies is on the list, although, as will be discussed in Chapter 17, one alumnus with a general trading company held the position of general manager of an overseas office, a position that was considered equivalent to that of a department in the main office. Six of the nine alumni included in the table were in manufacturing, two in banking, and one in air transport. These figures may be compared to those at the time of initial employment mentioned in Chapter 6: fifteen in manufacturing, two in banking, two in air transport, and six in general trading companies.

Second, of the ten cases, six involved departments engaged in sales (including exporting), with two in administration, and one each in inspection and public relations. No alumnus was in charge of other functions such as accounting, finance, or, above all, production. For this reason we cannot claim that our sample represents the overall organizational structure and processes of large Japanese corporations. Nevertheless, our sample gives a vivid idea of the most dynamic sector (sales, both domestic and overseas) of Japanese corporations at the time they accelerated the speed of globalization.

Table 16.1

Key Features of General Managers

Case	Industry (or business)	Duration	Function	Size	Superior	Subordinate
1	Construction machine parts	1985–89	Export	100	Division general manager	Section manager (7)
2	Synthetic fiber	1986–88	Sales	47	Division general manager	Section manager (6)
3	Petrochemicals	1986–89	Sales	16	Division general manager	Deputy general manager (1)
4	Textile	1986–89	Export	57	Division general manager	Deputy general manager (1)
5	Electrical machinery	(1) 1986–87	Export	25	Office general manager	Deputy general manager (1)
		(2) 1989–91	Administration	30	Division general manager	Deputy general manager (3)
6	Trust bank	1988–92	Inspection	7	Managing director	Deputy general manager (1)
7	Petroleum	1989–96	Public relations	8	Managing director	Deputy general manager (1)
8	Air cargo transport	1989–91	Administration	20	Division general manager	Section manager (3)
9	Bank	1989–91	Lending	20	Managing director	Deputy general manager (1)

Notes: Size refers to the total number of members of the department. Figures in parentheses in column 7 (Subordinate) represent the number of immediate subordinates.

As regards the organizational structure of the departments, it can be noted that their size varied, ranging between 100 members and seven members, with an average of thirty-four members. In seven out of the ten cases, the departments our alumni headed were parts of larger units, in virtually all cases called *honbu* or divisions. In those cases our alumni would report to the general manager of the division, called the *honbucho*, who was a member of the board of directors.

In only three cases there was no higher-level work unit of which the department was a subunit (Cases 6, 7, and 9). In two of the three cases, the departments were small, with seven and eight members each, and were engaged in special duties (inspection and public relations, respectively). In these three cases, our alumni directly reported to a managing director who would normally be responsible for more than one department.

In seven of the ten cases, the position of our alumnus's immediate subordinate was that of a deputy general manager, called either a *bucho dairi* or a *jicho*. In the remaining three cases, the immediate subordinate's rank was that of a section manager (*kacho*). The proportion of managers (deputy general managers, section managers, and group heads) to the total number of subordinates within the department ranged from 12 percent (Case 1) to as high as 50 percent (Cases 7 and 8).

In seven of the nine cases, the authority of a *bucho* was clearly documented and observed. In only two cases (Cases 2 and 3), there was a delegation of authority to the general managers (our alumni), who in turn delegated their authority to their immediate subordinates. In the latter case both our alumni requested reports from their subordinates, and approved the reports after revision, if necessary. The above findings suggest that, contrary to general belief, a job description was in existence at the *bucho* level and the line of command was firmly established.

Next, our alumni were asked how they would allocate their working time to (1) functional tasks (of the department), (2) decision making, and (3) supervision of their subordinates. The results are shown in Table 16.2 (information was not available for Case 4).

A wide variation was found among the alumni for the first two items. The time allocated to the functional tasks (as a percentage of the total working time) varied from 87 percent (Case 6) to a low of 10 percent (Case 9), with an average of 49 percent. Although the Case 6 alumnus reported an allocation of 45 percent to the "other" item, on closer examination these activities should really come under the first item. We shall have to explain the wide variation in the time our alumni allocated to the functional duties. At this point, however, the following remark may suffice. That is, the general belief that the Japanese manager is a generalist and as such he does not perform

Table 16.2

Time Allotted to Different Activities

Case	Functional tasks	Decision making	Subordinate supervision	Other	Total
1	50	20	30	0	100
2	80	10	10	0	100
3	70	20	10	0	100
5-1	30	50	20	0	100
5-2	30	50	20	0	100
6	42	3	10	45	100
7	50	20	20	10	100
8	10	70	10	10	100
9	80	10	10	0	100

functional duties specific to the work unit he is responsible for is an overgeneralization and not supported by our data. In many cases our alumni were specialists in their functional areas.

Naturally, the functional duties our alumni cited varied from case to case. The alumnus who gave the highest figure (87 percent) was a general manager in charge of inspection of a trust bank's international operations (Case 6). His functional duties included: supervising on-the-spot inspection of overseas offices as well as those work units of the home offices engaged in international operations; reporting the inspection results to his superior (a managing director); providing guidance to the inspected offices and work units; and developing inspection instruments (or manuals) and methods (this last activity he placed in the "other" category).

Two alumni gave 80 percent to the first item. One of them was with a textile company and was engaged in the following activities: domestic sale and exporting of synthetic fiber materials to industrial users such as automobile manufacturers, building construction contractors, and interior decorators; collaboration with the processing manufacturers (of his company's materials); attendance at board meetings of affiliated companies; and participation in activities (such as joint promotion campaigns) of the industrial association of which his company was a member (Case 2). The functional duties of the other alumnus, a bank manager, included negotiations of the loan contracts with major corporate customers in the petroleum, energy, gas, and electric power industries as well as with public corporations, and the monitoring of his department's profits (Case 9).

The Case 3 alumnus, in charge of the sale of petrochemicals, gave the next highest figure of 70 percent. His functional duties included the domestic sale and exporting of basic petrochemical materials, such as ethylene, to large industrial users, as well as the domestic sale of such materials as styrene monomers and BTX. He was directly involved in sales activities (negotiation of sales contracts) because a large amount was sold to a limited number of corporate customers, and, therefore, each transaction involved a large amount of money.

On the other hand, the alumnus who gave the smallest figure (10 percent) for the first item (Case 8) described the major functions of his department, which was in charge of administration of a division dealing with air cargo transport, as being the establishment of the department's annual plans; the establishment of the department's annual budget; transfers of personnel involving his department; and the establishment of basic policies for affiliated companies. Table 16.2 shows that this alumnus spent a large amount of time on decision making.

A review of the above five cases suggests that the three line managers (Cases 2, 3, and 9) spent far more time on functional duties than the typical staff manager (Case 8). Case 6 (inspection) was a special case in that, although inspection might be classified as a staff function, it operated more like a line department with independent goals than a staff department providing services to line departments.

Unlike functional duties, decision making involved more or less uniform activities. It typically included attendance at meetings and individual consultation and negotiation, both formal and informal. There were four types of meetings: (1) higher-level (or top management-level meetings), where a general manager was invited to participate as an observer or to accompany his immediate superior; (2) interdepartmental meetings attended by general managers of different departments for liaison, coordination, and information-sharing purposes; (3) managerial meetings of a department attended by all managers of the department and chaired by the general manager; and (4) departmental meetings attended by all members of the department and chaired by the general manager.

Formally, individual consultation would involve individuals connected by the chain of command, namely, superiors and subordinates. However, informal consultation would involve practically anybody in the organization who occupied key positions influencing the smooth running of the department. ·

Table 16.2 shows that the time allocated to decision making varied widely from a low of 3 percent (Case 6) to a high of 70 percent (Case 8), with an average of 28 percent. As can be expected, there appears to be a negative correlation between the first and the second items. This means that the more time one spends on functional tasks, the less time one spends on decision making, and vice versa.

The alumnus in Case 8 spent proportionately the longest time on decision making and the shortest time on functional tasks. As mentioned before, this alumnus lists the following five as the most important items of decision making: (1) the annual plans of the department, (2) the annual budget of the department, (3) transfers and promotions of personnel, (4) basic policies for affiliated companies, and (5) the basic policy of the department.

He describes how decisions were arrived at for each item. First, the annual plans of the department were discussed at departmental meetings and proposals were formulated. The proposals were discussed and approved at division meetings attended by general managers of all departments within the division. Second, a proposal for the departmental budget was originally formulated at the division level. It was forwarded to the Management Planning Office for consultation and negotiation, after which the final budget was determined. Third, as regards personnel issues (transfers and promotions), discussions were made by involving administration departments of other divisions and a proposal was forwarded to the Personnel Department for final approval. Fourth, basic policies for the affiliated companies under the control of the division were first discussed at meetings within the division and a proposal would be formulated. The proposal was discussed at the top level of the division and the final decision was made. Finally, the basic policies of the department represented the only item over which our alumnus had almost complete authority to decide. The above description of decision-making processes clearly indicates that virtually all decisions made were carried out through meetings of all kinds, so that our alumnus spent a lot of time not only attending but also preparing for such meetings, including informal prior consultation and negotiation (*nemawashi*).

The next highest figure (50 percent) was given by an alumnus who was a general manager of two different departments in this period (Cases 5-1 and 5-2). The first department was in charge of exporting industrial machines and components such as robots, controllers, various factory automation machines, and air conditioners. He lists the following five as the most important decision-making matters: (1) establishment of the order budget and the cash receipts budget, (2) personnel staffing, (3) establishment of the expenses budget, (4) selection and termination of overseas dealers, and (5) performance evaluation of subordinates and their transfer to overseas offices.

Our alumnus used the following methods of decision making for the above issues. First, in regard to sales and receipts budgets the decision was made by intradepartmental deliberation. Next, personnel staffing was decided in consultation with the three deputy general managers. For the third item, the expenses budget, he had his three deputy general managers make proposals, which he would discuss with them, and then he would make the final decision. Fourth, the selection and termination of overseas dealers were determined on the basis of their quarterly performance as measured primarily by their share of sales in the markets for which they were responsible. For this reason, he often traveled to visit overseas dealers, but he did not visit end users. Finally, the performance evaluation of his nonmanagerial subordinates and their transfer to overseas offices were determined in consultation with his three deputy general managers. Based on the above description, we can see that our alumnus spent a lot of time consulting with his immediate subordinates; he rarely made quick decisions on his own.

His second department was in charge of administration of the International Business Division. Here again he spent 50 percent of his working time on decision making. The five important decision-making matters were: (1) the determination of the division's order budget, (2) the determination of the division's expenses budget, (3) the determination of the division's personnel evaluation policies, (4) personnel transfer and revision of the position hierarchy, and (5) control of overseas offices and personnel.

First, in regard to the division's order budget, proposals from individual sales departments were collected and considered in meetings before the final decision was made. Exactly the same method was adopted for the determination of the second and the fourth items. The third item, personnel evaluation policies of the division, was determined in consultation with his superior, the division's general manager. The last item, the control of overseas offices and personnel, was determined in consultation with relevant departments of the division. He says that he had to attend "innumerable" meetings with line departments to determine the division's order budget.

The smallest figure (3 percent) was given by the alumnus in charge of inspecting the international operations of a trust bank. According to him, decision making involved three issues: (1) inspection schedules, (2) inspection items, and (3) overall evaluation. Intradepartmental meetings were held to decide on the above issues. Needless to say, items one and two were decided at meetings held prior to inspection, while the third issue was decided at meetings after inspection. Our alumnus chaired these meetings and took the initiative in the deliberations.

Approximately fifteen meetings per year were held, at a rate slightly more than once a month—much lower than was the case for other alumni, who held weekly meetings. Since all important issues were determined at the department meetings, there was no need for individual consultation. Furthermore, because of the nature of the duties of his department, there were no interdepartmental meetings for information sharing and coordination/collaboration. This is the reason that he spent very little time on decision making.

The next lowest figure (10 percent) was given by two line managers (Cases 2 and 9). The alumnus of Case 2, who was in charge of selling synthetic fiber materials, provided only two duties as important decision-making matters: (1) the department's mid- and short-term sales plans and (2) the department's sales strategy. When dealing with the first matter, a departmental proposal was formulated and forwarded to a staff department controlling and coordinating various businesses within the division. The final decision was made at the division meetings. The second issue was determined by the general manager of the department (our alumnus), in consultation with section managers. According to him, although intradepartmental meetings were held regularly (weekly with section managers and twice per quarter involving all members of the department), the purpose of those meetings was more information sharing than decision making.

For the alumnus with a bank (Case 9), the only important issue for decision making was the terms and conditions of making loans. He says that, according to the bank's rules, certain cases were decided by him in consultation with a deputy general manager, while certain other cases were forwarded to a higher level of management for decision making.

Based on the above observations, we note that two of the three alumni who spent a proportionately great deal of time on decision making headed staff departments, while two of the three alumni who spent a proportionately small amount of time headed line departments. A line manager who spent a great deal of time on decision making (Case 5-1) represented a unique case in which, as a part of company policy, *ringi* decision making was not used; therefore, it is suspected that he had to spend a much greater amount of time on other forms of decision making that were more time consuming. A staff manager who spent little time on decision making was in charge of inspections, which required decision making on only one issue: evaluation of inspection results. With these qualifications, it is safe to say that, on average, staff managers spent more time on decision making than line managers.

Regardless of the length of time our alumni spent on decision making, their frequent use of meetings and individual consultations (*nemawashi*) tend to support the general belief that Japanese-style decision making is group decision making and consensus decision making. We address the third characteristic, bottom-up decision making, later in this section when we study in detail the *ringi* system practiced in our alumni's offices.

Returning to Table 16.2, we see that the time our alumni spent on the supervision of their subordinates did not vary as much as it did for the first two items. The greatest figure given was 30 percent (Case 1). This is under-standable, in view of the fact that this alumnus headed the largest of the ten departments under study. The total number of subordinates was 100, includ-ing seven section managers directly under our alumnus, as there was no deputy general manager to assist him. Indeed, he says that supervision of his subor-dinates was "very time-consuming." With the exception of this alumnus, others spent either 10 percent or 20 percent on subordinate supervision.

In answer to a question on what methods were used to supervise immedi-ate subordinates, such as deputy general managers and section managers, the answers given were:
- "give directions in writing" (Case 1);
- "have them report on the problems they encountered" (Case 2);
- "give directions based on their reports" (Case 3);
- "have them report periodically" (Case 5-1);
- "give directions and have them report when necessary" (Case 5-2);
- "provide policies and have them report; also give directions when neces-sary" (Case 6);
- "give directions and have them report when necessary" (Case 7);
- "give directions and have them report; also, communicate closely" (Case 8); and
- "case by case" (Case 9).

As expected, in controlling the subordinates, six of the nine superiors took the initiative by giving directions and demanding reports. In only two cases the superior relied on a subordinate's report.

Performance evaluation of subordinates is an important element of the supervisory functions of the general manager. In all ten cases studied the general pattern was that the general manager would directly evaluate the performance of his subordinates in managerial positions (deputy general man-agers and section managers), who in turn would evaluate the performance of their nonmanagerial subordinates. In the latter case the role of the general manager was to review the recommendations of the section managers and to make decisions. In many cases general managers' decisions were subject to further review by their superiors and the personnel department when the decisions involved promotion and transfer.

In all ten cases evaluation was conducted regularly with varying fre-quencies among the companies—from once per year to three times per year. In two cases involving one company (Case 5) self-evaluation was conducted in addition to three evaluations by superiors. Self-evaluation was conducted in another organization (Case 9), too. Evaluation was con-ducted for decisions on promotion and annual pay increases as well as for decisions on the amounts of semiannual bonuses. Although an annual pay increase was granted to every employee (the reason the Japanese pay system is said to be "length-of-service" oriented), the amount differed among employees, thus reflecting evaluation results. Some companies conducted just one evaluation for all the above purposes (Cases 7 and 8), while some others conducted three evaluations, one for each of the above three purposes (Cases 2, 3, and 5).

Criteria for evaluation differed somewhat among the ten cases and between the evaluation of managers and the evaluation of nonmanagers. Our alumni were asked to rank the following three criteria in order of importance: (1) effort (including work habits and interpersonal relations), (2) ability (including potential ability), and (3) results and performance. The most important criteria for the evaluation of managers were: results (6), ability (2), and effort (2). For the nonmanagers, the rankings were also results (5), ability (4), and effort (1). There are reasons to believe that the above figures represented the policies of individual companies rather than the preferences of individual evaluators. The above findings appear to contradict the general belief that Japanese companies value such factors as an employee's loyalty and commitment to the company, which might have shown up in the criterion "effort."

In five of the ten cases the results of evaluation were conveyed to individual employees, while in four cases they were not, and in one case the normal practice was not known. This result also contradicts the belief that Japanese companies adopt a more participatory approach than their counterparts in the West. In fact, the most "progressive" of the ten cases was a wholly owned subsidiary of a U.S. company where not only the results were conveyed but also individual counseling was conducted.

We will now examine to what extent and in what manner our alumni, as general managers, were involved in the *ringi* decision-making system. As we said in Chapter 2, the *ringi* system is considered to be a uniquely Japanese process of consensus-building and bottom-up decision making, whereby a lower-level employee writes up a proposal on an issue of concern to him, and this proposal is circulated from the bottom of the organization to the top. In the process, the document needs the approval of all the management personnel concerned with the issue. The entire decision-making process is completed with top-management approval.

In actuality, however, the *ringi* is not standardized; rather, it varies from one company to another in terms of structure and processes—what issues are to be decided, what groundwork needs to be done even before the drafting of a *ringi* proposal, who is to write the original draft, to whom the document is to be circulated, who is to give the final approval, and, most important, who decides if the entire process will be used. In fact, the *ringi-sho* is a generic term; it is called by various names: *hatsuan-sho* (a proposal), *shinsei-sho* (an application), *ukagai-sho* (an inquiry), "kessai-sho" (a decision-seeking document), and *ketteishinsei-sho* (an application for requesting decision making), to mention a few.

In three of the ten cases (involving two companies) the *ringi* system was not adopted (Cases 5-1, 5-2, and 7). One of the two companies was a wholly owned subsidiary of a U.S. corporation. The other was a large electric machine manufacturer, and this suggests that the *ringi* is not universally adopted in Japanese corporations. In seven other cases the *ringi* system was used.

In two cases the *ringi* originated at the section manager's level (Cases 1 and 8). In Case 1, where our alumnus was in charge of exporting construction machine parts, the following issues were subject to *ringi* decision making: (1) consignment of machine parts, (2) buying back and disposing of unsold parts, and (3) establishment of overseas depots. The decision to use the *ringi* system was made by a section manager, who would order one of his subordinates to write up the original document.

It was circulated upward and back to the section manager, laterally to another section manager in charge of parts planning, upward to the general manager (our alumnus), laterally to another general manager in charge of administration, and upward to the general manager of the division—who would give the final approval. The role of our alumnus as general manager, prior to the formulation of the document, was to negotiate with sales departments about the necessity and profitability of the intended proposal. His role after the circulation of the document was to explain its need to his fellow department manager(s) and his superior.

Case 8 involves an alumnus who headed the administration department of an airline's cargo business. According to him, a variety of issues were deliberated by the *ringi* method. Among the more important issues were: (1) new investment projects and (2) the establishment of new subsidiaries. He says that the decision to initiate the *ringi* process would come either from above or below him. Whichever the case might be, the *ringi* document required the consent of all relevant departments before it was circulated upward for final approval.

The role of our alumnus, therefore, was to conduct prior consultation (or *nemawashi*) with the relevant department(s) and obtain its consent prior to the formulation of the document. Since most groundwork was conducted beforehand, once the document was circulated, not much work was left for him except to answer questions when asked.

In the case of a third alumnus, who was in charge of inspecting the international operations of a trust bank, the most important item for *ringi* deliberation was the planning of annual activities (Case 6). The role of the general manager (our alumnus) prior to the formulation of the document was to hold intradepartmental meetings to solicit members' ideas about annual activities and to formally assign the task of preparing the document to his deputy general manager, who in turn had one of his subordinates write the first draft.

The document, when formulated, would be circulated upward from the deputy general manager to our alumnus, and then to a managing director in charge of inspection, who would give the final approval. Our alumnus's role in the process was to modify the content and expression of the document in order to obtain the managing director's prior consent to the document before its formal approval.

Some *ringi* proposals would originate at a higher level—the general manager's level. Our alumnus in charge of sales of petrochemical materials says that major issues for *ringi* deliberation included matters related to the industrial association, and the disposition of and investment in plants and machinery (Case 3). In this company the formulation of a *ringi* proposal was the responsibility of the general manager. Prior to the formulation of the document, our alumnus, as general manager, would make necessary adjustments with the departments concerned and would also strive to obtain the prior consent of the senior officers concerned.

The proposal would be forwarded to the division's general manager for approval, then laterally to other relevant divisions, to the president, and finally to the *jomukai* (or the top management level committee, consisting of managing directors and above) for formal approval. It was the responsibility of our alumnus to "sell" the proposal to relevant individual senior officers as well as to attend *jomukai* meeting(s) and its subcommittee meeting(s) to speak for the proposal.

Case 4 involves an alumnus in charge of the exporting of textiles. In his company the authority to make routine decisions was well defined for each of various management positions. *Ringi* decision making was used for nonroutine and strategic issues. For the department that our alumnus headed, the creation of joint ventures and the conclusion of technical licensing agreements were examples of strategic issues that were subject to *ringi* decision making. The formulation of the proposal was the responsibility of the general manager (our alumnus). This proposal was forwarded to the meeting of senior officers within the division attended by directors and above, and, if successful there, further forwarded to the *jomukai* for final approval. The decision-making mechanism of this company at the top management level will be discussed in Chapter 21 along with other cases.

A third alumnus who was directly responsible for the formulation of the *ringi* proposal was the one in charge of sales of synthetic fiber materials (Case 2). He says that while a number of issues were determined by the *ringi* method, the most important of these issues were new investments and loans. According to him, for certain cases a direction to initiate a *ringi* process would come from above, that is, from his superior, who was the division's general manager and also a member of the board (a director), or even from a higher-ranking officer.

In other cases a *ringi* was jointly proposed by his department and the administrative department of the same division. It was the responsibility of our alumnus to formulate a *ringi* proposal, and, prior to its formulation, he would "sell" the ideas behind the proposal to any key individuals in other relevant departments. The proposal was forwarded to the business administration department and then to the top management meeting attended by senior officers concerned with the issue, at which meeting the final decision would be made.

The final case involves a bank where our alumnus headed a department in charge of corporate lending (Case 9). In the bank there were detailed rules and regulations regarding decision-making authorities. Two types of decision making were specified: individual decision making, which was based on the authority entrusted to each management position, and decision making by the *ringi* process. As for the latter, detailed procedures were specified for different kinds of issues, covering such items as who would initiate the *ringi* process, which route of circulation would be followed, and who would give the final approval.

Generally speaking, the *ringi* process started with an intradepartmental meeting. Then a nonmanagerial member of the department would draft a document, which was circulated upward to the section manager, to the deputy general manager, to the general manager, and finally to corporate headquarters. Depending on the nature of issues, lower-level steps would be skipped. The role of the general manager (our alumnus) before the formulation of a *ringi* document included negotiation with the customers, collection of relevant external information, as well as a check of legality. In forwarding the document to a higher level, our alumnus had to make an operating as well as a strategic assessment of the document.

The above description of the seven cases presents very diverse ways in which a *ringi* method was used for decision making. First, in a certain case it was used primarily for routine and operating decisions (Case 1), while in another case it was used for nonroutine and strategic decisions (Case 4). In other cases it was used for both routine and nonroutine decisions. Second, a *ringi* process was initiated by managers at different levels—by a section manager (Cases 1 and 8), by a deputy general manager (Case 6), by a general manager (Cases 2, 3, and 4), and even from above (Cases 2 and 8). Third, final approval for important issues of a department was given either by an individual officer or by a group of officers at different levels—by a division's general manager (Case 1), by a senior officer (Case 8), by a managing director (Case 6), by a group of senior officers concerned (Case 2), and by the *jomukai* (Cases 3 and 4).

Despite the above variations, we notice certain common tendencies. First of all, the role of the rank-and-file members of a department in the *ringi* decision-making process was minimal. Although a junior employee might draft a *ringi* proposal, such an act was not initiated by himself but at the direction of his superior, often a section manager. Second, the role of the general manager was crucial in the entire process. Often he would write a *ringi* proposal. Even before the drafting of a *ringi* proposal, the general manager would "sell" the proposal to relevant departments. While a proposal was being circulated he would attend higher-level meetings to speak in favor of the proposal and also approach individual senior officers for their support at the relevant meetings.

The above observation tends to support the argument of Yoshimura and Anderson stated in Chapter 2 that real decisions in the *ringi* process are made by division managers rather than by junior members of a department as originally suggested by Ouchi stated in Chapter 2. Furthermore, based on the remarks of two alumni (Cases 2 and 8), we have reason to believe that for certain (very important) issues real decisions were made at an even higher level.

In discussing whether the *ringi* method represents bottom-up decision making or not, we argue that the person who initiates the process is far more important than the person who writes the first draft. Viewed this way, the *ringi* methods as practiced in the seven cases cannot be said to represent a genuine bottom-up decision making about significant issues from the standpoint of the rank-and-file members. And for that reason it could hardly be called a form of consensus-building decision making. Only in two cases (Cases 6 and 9) were intradepartmental meetings held before the drafting of a *ringi* proposal, and even in these cases apparently no attempt was made to build a consensus among all members of the department. In five other cases rank-and-file members were not even consulted.

On the other hand, from the standpoint of the general manager the *ringi* system may be called a form of bottom-up decision making as long as the general manager possesses the power to start a proposal for higher-level management on those issues that are not completely within his authority. It may also be called a form of consensus-building decision making in that he has to "sell" the proposal to his fellow general managers of the relevant departments and that each of them has a veto power to block the proposal. What happens to the *ringi* proposal that is circulated upward to higher-level management is the subject of Chapter 21.

Career Change

As mentioned at the beginning of this chapter, at the outset of this period, twenty-four of the thirty male alumni were still with their original employers. With the exception of one alumnus who was with an economic association, all others were employed by private corporations. It seems from the interviews that they were anchored both in managerial competence and in security, as they were rising to higher levels of management within a single organization and they were happy with this progress. During this period a total of five of the twenty-four alumni changed their jobs or career anchors.

One alumnus quit a large chemical company in 1987, after serving the company for twenty-five years, to join the Japanese subsidiary of a British-based worldwide chemical company. He did so not because he was dissatisfied with the original employer but because he was eager to pursue greater challenges. In fact, he had been very successful in the original company—by the time he left the company he had been promoted to the position of *bucho* or general manager, just one step below the level of *torishimariyaku* or board member. According to him, the original company, although one of the largest in Japan, is a dwarf compared to major U.S. or European chemical companies.

So, when the job offer was made, he thought it would provide him with an opportunity to test to what extent his experience with the original company would be equally valuable in a truly worldwide company. Besides, the terms and conditions of the offer, including the salary, were very attractive. In his case, it is clear that he has been anchored in management competence, an anchor that was formulated while he was working for the original employer.

Among the remaining twenty-three alumni who stayed with their original companies, two changed their careers without quitting the original company. One alumnus was working for a major brewing company in such areas as accounting, enterprise union leadership, sales, and sales management. With the broadening of his experience he moved to a higher level of management—an indication that he was anchored in management competence. In 1987 he was deputy general manager of the Marketing Department, when he was asked by the company if he wanted to continue with the sales/marketing career or switch to a newly created job that provides management advice to affiliated wholesalers on business strategy, sales, and finance—a sort of intrafirm consulting job. He chose the second option.

Then the company sent him for a three-month executive extension course on business management at his alma mater. This was followed by a year's study at the Japan Productivity Center. Upon completion of the study in 1988, he obtained a management consultant certificate issued by the Center. In addition, in 1989 he obtained a registered management consultant certificate issued by the national government. Since then, he has continued in the consultancy job for the company. Thus, his career anchor changed from management competence to technical/functional competence.

Another alumnus was working for a major petrochemical company primarily in the areas of distribution and purchasing. In 1982 he was temporarily transferred out (*shukko*) to JICA, a semigovernmental organization involved in international economic cooperation and assistance. He was stationed in Jakarta, Indonesia, for two and a half years as a JICA advisor for the government of Indonesia in one of its energy development projects. His temporary transfer (*shukko*) was a result of the company's policy of reducing, even if only temporarily, its manpower, because the petrochemical industry was hard hit by the two oil crises of the 1970s.

He returned to the original company in 1985. However, after a two-year stint as deputy general manager of the International Marketing Department, he was transferred out again—this time to a consulting company that was newly created and wholly owned by the original company.

The above-mentioned consulting company provided services to the governments of Southeast Asian countries who were recipients of any Japanese government overseas economic assistance. As a result, our alumnus worked on various assistance projects between 1987 and 1991, when he was sent to Jakarta to work on human resource development projects in the capacity of resident senior management consultant. His primary responsibility was to select and place young government officers in graduate programs overseas (mostly in Japan and the United States). Thus, his career orientation was anchored in management competence until 1982 or so. However, realizing that chances for advancement to higher managerial positions had become slim, he opted for a new career: consulting, which is anchored in technical/functional competence. Looking back upon his career change, he says:

> It was a good decision for me to switch to consulting, because I find the present job interesting and rewarding. Staying with the original company would mean just doing mundane jobs until retirement. In this sense, the experience in Jakarta for two and a half years prior to the permanent *shukko* in 1987 was extremely valuable for brushing up my rusty English, learning survey and research skills, and obtaining firsthand information about Indonesia.

Toward the end of this subperiod, two more alumni were transferred out by *shukko* to subsidiaries. In 1989 one alumnus, who had been working for a large electrical machine manufacturing company primarily in exporting with long overseas assignments in Australia and the United States, was transferred out by *shukko* to a newly created subsidiary. Prior to the *shukko*, he was working at the Lighting Products Exporting Department of the original company. When this department was separated and formed into a subsidiary together with several other affiliated companies dealing with lighting products, all members of the department were transferred out by *shukko* to the new company for a fixed period of two years and at the same pay level as they had at the parent company. At the end of the two years, everyone was asked to choose between two options: returning to the original company, or staying with the new company for a fixed period of three years by severing ties with the parent company (a practice called *tenseki*). Our alumnus chose the second option and stayed with the subsidiary as Deputy General Manager of the division responsible for the exporting of lighting products all over the world. It is apparent that he anchored his career in general management competence up to that point.

In 1990 another alumnus, who had been working for a general trading company specializing in the exporting and importing of steel and related products, was transferred out by *shukko* to a small subsidiary of the original company to be its vice president. It was actually a joint venture owned not only by the trading company our alumnus had worked for but also by two other companies. Its business was the planning and carrying out of trade exhibitions. It was difficult to manage the company because of the composition of its workforce. Besides, the company was too small to compete with giant advertising agencies. When the company went out of business two years later, he retired from the original company, which, in turn, referred him to a nonprofit organization. It is not very clear whether his career with the original company was anchored in managerial competence or in technical/functional competence.

17

Overseas Assignments, 1981–90

As mentioned in the preceding chapter, twenty-four alumni remained with their original employers at the beginning of this period (1981). Of the twenty-four, a total of fifteen alumni were assigned to various overseas offices during this period (1981–90). Of these fifteen, the case of one alumnus who stayed in New York from 1977 through 1983 has already been discussed in Chapter 12. A second alumnus was transferred out to a nonprofit organization (NPO), which in turn sent him overseas for an assignment in an area entirely different from that in which he had been engaged up to that time. From a third alumnus detailed information was not available. Therefore, in this chapter we will study the overseas experiences of the remaining twelve alumni. They are listed in order of the commencement of their overseas assignments (Table 17.1).

The average duration of the fourteen appointments was three years and six months, somewhat shorter than those in the previous two periods. Perhaps the following two factors accounted for this. First, all alumni had at least one previous overseas experience (some as many as three) prior to this assignment; therefore, they needed less "start up" time, or time to get settled. Second, as the table shows, many of our alumni held top management positions in the overseas establishments, and thus did not require much time for learning or adjusting functional skills to local conditions.

This period may be divided into two subperiods, with the Plaza Accord in September of 1985 as the dividing line. As we saw in Chapter 14, the first subperiod was characterized by the "strong dollar" policy of the Reagan administration, while the second subperiod was characterized by the reversal of that policy, resulting in rapid appreciation of the yen. In this sense, it is interesting to note that nine out of the fourteen appointments were made

Table 17.1

Overseas Assignments

Case	Industry	Duration	Place	Previous experience	Position
1	General trading	(1) 1979–84	Portland	1	Deputy general manager,
		(2) 1986–89	San Francisco	2	Administration and accounting
		(3) 1989–92	Seattle	3	
2	Electric appliances	1980–87	Chicago	1	Senior vice president, U.S. subsidiary
3	Airlines	1981–84	Honolulu	1	Deputy general manager, administration
4	Banking	1982–86	New York	1	Senior vice president, U.S. subsidiary
5	Textile	1983–85	Hong Kong	2	Vice president, joint venture
6	Trust banking	1983–86	Frankfurt	3	Chief representative, liaison office
7	Economic federation	1984–86	London	1	Economist, embassy in the United Kingdom
8	General trading	1984–89	Seoul	2	Manager, steel export and import
9	Casualty insurance	1984–89	Sydney	1	Chief representative, liaison office
10	Construction machinery	1986–88	Frankfurt	2	President, German subsidiary
11	General trading	1986–91	Seattle	1	General manager, branch office
12	Electric machinery	1987–89	New York	1	General manager, sales division

before 1985, while only five appointments (involving four individuals) were made after that year.

As shown in the table, four of the nine alumni were sent to the United States in the late 1970s through the early 1980s. Of these four, the first two (Cases 1-1 and 2) had arrived in the United States prior to this period, but their cases were not discussed in chapter 12 because most of their assignment took place during the period now under discussion. The first alumnus had been employed by a major general trading company (Case 1-1). He started his career in the company's Accounting Department, where he received basic training in accounting for two years. Afterward, he worked in three operations departments, including the Melbourne office, before being transferred to the Portland branch office in 1979. Thus, this was his second overseas assignment. By this time, he had broadened his areas of expertise to include other staff functions such as finance, personnel, and general administration.

When he arrived in December 1979, the United States was in an economic slump under the outgoing Carter administration. The Portland branch was a small office staffed by four Japanese and six local employees. The main business of the branch was the importation of grain: purchasing grain (primarily wheat) produced in the Western United States and Canada from grain companies and selling it to the Food Agency of the Ministry of Agriculture, Forestry, and Fishing back in Japan. Under the Japanese general manager of the branch office, our alumnus was in charge of all staff functions. In addition, foreign exchange risk hedging was an important part of his job, since the office was purchasing from Canada as well. This office was not engaged in exporting activities, that is, selling Japanese products to local customers. He worked in the office for four years and nine months, at which point he was transferred back to Japan.

Another alumnus was a bank employee (Case 4). After returning from London, this alumnus was engaged in large-scale project financing in the bank's international investment department. The project financing in which he was directly involved was energy-related, such as the construction of petrochemical plants in Iran and in Singapore (the outcome of the Iran project was discussed in Chapter 12.

In 1982 he was assigned to the bank's U.S. subsidiary, which was headquartered in New York and had four offices including the main office. A total of 250 employees including forty Japanese were employed in these four offices. Like our first alumnus (Case 1-1), this alumnus, too, found the United States in an economic slump symbolized by the near bankruptcy of the Chrysler Corporation. It appeared to our alumnus as if American people had lost confidence in themselves. On the other hand, an increasing number of Japanese companies began to make their presence known by building factories, creating joint ventures with American companies, and acquiring American companies. U.S. federal and state governments were receptive to the advances of Japanese companies, as it was believed that Japanese investment in the United States would help its economy out of the prolonged recession.

Our alumnus, as a vice president in charge of business development, was engaged in project financing and financing involving mergers and acquisitions (M&A). He was also approached by many state government officials to help them attract Japanese companies to their states, and he took an active role in assisting them as an advisor. He was also active in coordinating M&A by Japanese manufacturers. For example, he was instrumental in M&A transactions by an undergarment manufacturer and by an electric parts manufacturer. He recalls how, in assisting a Japanese client to purchase a factory, he and his lawyer helped the client successfully negotiate revision of a collective agreement with UAW representatives.

He also recalls vividly the day when the Plaza Accord was achieved in September 1985. Even before the accord, his colleagues in the bank were busy repositioning in the foreign exchange market. He says, "In retrospect, the historical accord was the origin of the Japanese bubble economy in the late 1980s, because the appreciation of the yen against the U.S. dollar created excess funds in the hands of Japanese corporations and financial institutions." After his three-year assignment in New York he was transferred back to Tokyo in early 1986 to engage in a special mission. Three years was somewhat on the short side. However, if his talent had not been needed in his next assignment (rebuilding a major client company that had ended up in financial difficulty), he would have stayed in New York much longer.

Our third alumnus (Case 2), who had been employed by an electric machine producer, was sent to Chicago in April 1980. This was the second overseas assignment for this alumnus, too, the first one being an assignment in Sydney/Melbourne in the late 1960s through early 1970s. After his return from Australia he was engaged in the exporting of electric appliances to various parts of the world. The Chicago office was the headquarters of the company's wholly owned sales subsidiary in the United States, and had approximately 200 employees including twenty Japanese. The main function of this subsidiary was to sell the company's two types of products to the U.S. and Canadian markets: household electric appliances to individual consumers, and electric and electronic machine parts to corporate customers. The demand for original equipment manufacturing (OEM) was particularly strong, according to our alumnus. As a senior vice president of the subsidiary his main job was to supervise his subordinates, the sales representatives. Although he met customers on occasion, he was not directly involved in sales activities.

He recalls that trade friction between the United States and Japan intensified during his stay, and this had a negative impact on their sales activities. The most damaging was the "COCOM violation" (Coordinating Committee for Multilateral Export Controls) incident of 1987 involving his company. In the previous year one of the company's subsidiaries specializing in the manufacturing of machine tools exported to the Soviet Union a machine tool included in the list of items whose export to the Soviet Union was prohibited. Officially, the tool was exported for use in the production of power generators, but it was later discovered to be capable of use for the production of screws for nuclear submarines. Since the cold war was not yet over, this alleged COCOM violation was taken as a serious act of betrayal by a company of an allied nation.

Although our alumnus's company argued that it was totally unaware of and therefore not responsible for what one of its subsidiaries did, its appeal was to no avail. The nationwide boycott campaign started against his company's products. He recalls that two major automobile companies quickly cancelled contracts to purchase certain parts from his office. The incident affected not only his business but also his family, as family members suffered unpleasant experiences. Shortly after the incident he and his family left the United States because he was transferred back to Japan.

Our fourth alumnus was employed by an airline company (Case 3). After a series of job rotations, primarily in the operating departments, this alumnus was assigned to the company's Honolulu airport branch in 1981. The branch was under the control of the general manager's office of the company's American regional headquarters in New York. It was staffed by approximately 230 employees (many being Japanese Americans), of whom six were Japanese nationals from Japan.

According to the alumnus, the main business of Hawaii was tourism, and the promotion of tourism was an important job of the governor. Eighty percent of the tourists were from Japan, so without Japanese tourists, tourism, and, therefore, the economy of Hawaii, would be on shaky ground. For that reason, Japanese people were well received, at least on the surface, but inside, some Hawaiian people had mixed feelings about Japan from their memories of World War II, so our alumnus was very careful not to hurt any feelings.

This was the second overseas assignment for this alumnus, the first time being one year of training at the company's Rome airport branch in the late 1960s. As deputy general manager in charge of general administration and industrial relations, his specific mission was to rationalize the branch operation by downsizing the workforce of full-time regular employees of the company. During his tenure of three years he was able to outsource two departments (maintenance and cargo loading/unloading), and to dismiss several older employees by giving them extra severance pay. It would be more accurate to say that it took him the full three years to accomplish his mission. In this sense, his relatively short stay should be interpreted as an indication of success, rather than of failure.

The alumnus with a casualty insurance company who had a hard time in Teheran (Case 9) was working in the company's main office in Tokyo as a section manager in charge of corporate casualty insurance in the early 1980s. In 1984 he was transferred to Sydney as the sole representative of the company's liaison office. It was his job to sell insurance and handle claims through local agents. He was responsible for a large territory covering Australia, New Zealand, and Papua New Guinea. Many of his customers were Japanese companies operating in these areas, such as Mitsui and Co. and Toyota Motor Company.

He found Australia committed to multiculturalism and the number of Asian immigrants was increasing. The friendly nature of Australian people made the life of our alumnus and his family very comfortable. As a market, however, his territory was rather small, since the entire population of Australia was about the same as that of Tokyo. His clients were scattered all over the territory, which meant he had to do a lot of traveling. In Papua New Guinea he still could see, after forty years, remnants of World War II, and this visit left him with a lasting memory. He stayed in Sydney for five years, until his return to Japan in 1989 to head a newly created team dealing with overseas M&A.

In the first half of the 1980s, two alumni were assigned to Asian countries. One alumnus (Case 5), whose assignment in Penang was discussed in chapter 12, was transferred from Malaysia directly to Hong Kong in 1983; this, according to him, was a normal route of job rotation. He says that Hong Kong was in great turmoil when he arrived, because it was shortly after the United Kingdom–China agreement on the return of Hong Kong to China in 1997. Some of his customers (garment manufacturers) were preparing to leave Hong Kong, while others opted to stay. At the same time, some overseas Chinese, who had once left Hong Kong, were returning home. Generally speaking, those people who originally came from Shanghai were anti-China, while those from Canton (Guangzhou) were pro-China. As a result, the proportion of the company's customers originally from Southern China, including Canton, increased.

The office to which our alumnus was assigned was a joint venture in which his employer held 70 percent of ownership, while the remaining 30 percent was owned by local Chinese. But a year later, in 1984, his employer bought the remaining 30 percent to become the sole owner of the former joint venture. It employed fifty-five people including four Japanese. The main business of the subsidiary was to sell the textiles produced in various factories owned by the company in Southeast Asia to garment manufacturers in Hong Kong.

As the vice president of the subsidiary, our alumnus was responsible for:

(1) following up on sales performance in terms of quantity, price, and the date of delivery; (2) determining sales policies; and (3) evaluating the performance of section managers (to him, the most difficult of his responsibilities). According to the alumnus, the above were the usual duties performed by a general manager of a department back in Japan.

The alumnus reports that a crisis occurred when the affiliated company became the wholly owned subsidiary in 1984. That is, although an offer was made to all local employees to continue employment under the existing terms and conditions of employment, nineteen out of fifty-three employees demanded severance pay in addition to continued employment. Instead, he dismissed ten (including two section managers) of the nineteen, giving them severance pay, while the remaining nine opted for reemployment without severance pay. As a result, the office was ten people short, a situation that created difficulties in business operations. Through this experience he learned the importance of possessing accurate information about subordinates if one is to manage them effectively.

Our next alumnus (Case 8), who had been engaged in steel-related business in a general trading company, was transferred to the company's Seoul branch office in 1984. After Moscow and Houston, this was his third overseas assignment. Because of Korean legislation, which, according to our alumnus, was intended to protect local trading companies, the company's Seoul office was not allowed to engage in full-fledged trading activities because it was prohibited from signing a contract. Its official status, therefore, was as a liaison office (between Korean customers and the company's main office in Tokyo), although, in practice, business negotiations were conducted with local customers up to the point of signing a contract. It was a large office with approximately 130 employees including thirty Japanese. Our alumnus was the manager in charge of exporting and importing metal, mostly steel, as in his previous assignments.

Nearly forty years after World War II, our alumnus found that the Korean people were still resentful about prewar Japanese colonialism. According to him, there were suppressed anti-Japanese feelings as well as a manifest spirit of competing against Japan among people in general, and among his office subordinates in particular. Furthermore, when he arrived, Korea was in the process of shifting from a military dictatorship to a democracy. The democratization movement was accompanied by a series of major labor disputes involving large conglomerates such as Hyundai and Daewoo.

The anti-Japanese feelings of the local employees, combined with the aggressive labor movement, resulted in a "reverse" lockout against his branch office in the summer of 1988. According to the alumnus it started as normal collective bargaining in which the enterprise union demanded a substantial wage increase. The bargaining was quickly broken off and the union not only called a strike but also occupied the office premises, from which Japanese managers and employees were barred. Our alumnus recalls that he and his Japanese subordinates operated from a hotel room during the dispute, which lasted for nearly three months before it was settled following a major concession by the employer.

Two alumni were transferred to Europe during this period. One alumnus (Case 7) served at the Japanese Embassy in London in the mid-1980s on loan from the economic association that employed him. His mission was to gather information and to give lectures with a view to improving economic relations between Japan and European countries, including the United Kingdom. According to this alumnus, a number of instances of economic friction surfaced in the 1980s. For example, he recalls that Prime Minister Thatcher protested against the successful bidding of Japanese companies over British counterparts for the construction of the Bosporus Bridge in Turkey. Overall, though, Japan–United Kingdom relations were favorable, and the British government welcomed Japanese direct investment in the United Kingdom. As a result, Japanese automobile and electric appliance manufacturers started production there. Relations with other countries, notably France, were more difficult.

The embassy was staffed not only by officials of the Ministry of Foreign Affairs but also by those of other ministries, as well as those from nongovernmental organizations, as was the case of our alumnus. One of his duties was to prepare, as a member of the economic analysis group, quarterly reports on the British economy. The interest of the official from the Ministry of Finance was limited to national budgets and foreign exchanges; all other items were left to our alumnus and an individual sent from a bank. After two years of assignment, this alumnus returned to Japan in 1986 to resume his duties with his original employer.

The other alumnus (Case 6), working for a trust bank, was transferred in 1983 back to the liaison office in Frankfurt he had been instrumental in establishing and where he had served for a couple of years in the 1970s. As the chief representative of the office our alumnus was responsible for gathering information on the bond markets in Germany and surrounding countries as well as for negotiating loans on behalf of branch offices in London, Geneva, and other cities (i.e., those offices with appropriate licenses to make loans).

According to this alumnus, the West German economy, although the most powerful in Europe, was beginning to fade, with, for example, unemployment rising to approximately 9 percent. There were also signs of political and social instability, such as the emergence of the Green Party and conflicting views on the status of second-generation foreign guest workers. In the financial field, too, German bond markets were not as active as Swiss bond markets. On the other hand, Japanese banks were active and reaped profits in Europe, including Germany. Our alumnus recalls, "In retrospect, that was about the time when Japanese banks attained their maximum presence in Europe." Although the reunification of Germany came about only three years after he left the country in 1986, our alumnus did not detect any hints of the fall of the Berlin Wall during his stay in West Germany.

Within a month after this alumnus left Frankfurt, another alumnus (Case 10), working for a construction machine manufacturer, arrived in 1986 in Gross-Gerau, a small town near Frankfurt. This was the third time this alumnus would head one of his company's overseas offices (he had previously managed offices in Sydney and London). Unlike the two previous times, when he headed relatively small liaison offices, this time he was appointed president of the company's wholly owned sales subsidiary in Germany, where approximately 100 employees were on the staff. The subsidiary's function was to import the parent company's products from Japan and resell them to local dealers and end users on its own account and risk. Unlike his two previous overseas assignments, no Japanese trading companies were involved in any way in the process.

Most of the company's employees were engaged in sales, with some in customer service, some in parts supply, and some in accounting departments. As president, our alumnus was responsible for sales, customer service, and managing the dealers, as well as supervising the employees. He was busy day and night. In the daytime, in addition to general administrative duties, he was directly engaged in sales activities, often traveling on the Autobahn (at a speed of 200 km an hour!) to various parts of the country. At night he had to keep in close touch with the main office in Tokyo.

He recalls that the economy of West Germany was not as dynamic as it had been. As a result, sometimes his customers (end users) went bankrupt with accrued liabilities. In such cases he would retrieve the machine(s) sold them. He also felt income taxes were very high (as was his salary, by German standards). He held this position for two years until 1988, when he returned home to become deputy general manager of the overseas division. This alumnus, too, did not see any signs of the fall of the Berlin Wall that would take place only a year after his departure. He says, "Perhaps things would have been different in Berlin, but in Frankfurt there was no sign of any imminent exodus of people from the East European countries."

After the Plaza Accord of 1985, three alumni were transferred to offices in the United States. Two of them were employed by general trading companies, the third, by an electric machine manufacturer. The experience in Portland of one of the two alumni working for a general trading company has already been discussed earlier in this chapter (Case 1-1). After a brief stint in the company's branch office in Osaka, this alumnus was sent back to the United States, first to San Francisco (Case 1-2) from 1986 through 1989 and then to Seattle (Case 1-3) from 1989 through 1992, for a total of six years.

The two branches were similar in size, employing about fifteen Japanese and twenty to twenty-five local employees. In both branches he held the position of deputy general manager in charge of administration covering such functions as accounting, finance, and personnel. The office in San Francisco was engaged in importing from Japan steel, chemicals, machinery, and electronic parts, and reselling them to local companies such as ALMAX. Receiving VIPs from Japan was also an important role of the branch, as San Francisco was considered a gateway to the mainland United States. With the rapid appreciation of the Japanese yen after the Plaza Accord, an increasing number of Japanese companies started to invest in overseas real estate. As a result, negotiating real estate purchases on behalf of Japanese clients became an important business of the branch.

The main business of the Seattle branch was exporting lumber, marine products, and other raw materials to Japan. Although the office was also engaged in importing from Japan, the commodities were limited to such items as steel and used cars, and the volume of imports was much smaller than that of the exports. According to our alumnus, this was the time of peak presence of Japanese corporations in the United States, and this was symbolized most by the start-up of the GM-Toyota joint-venture plant in Fremont.

The second alumnus working for a general trading company was also active in the Seattle-Portland region about the same time (Case 11). After returning from Johannesburg in 1977, this alumnus was engaged in importing wood chips and exporting paper and pulp. In 1986 he was assigned to the company's Seattle branch as its general manager. From there he was also responsible for the running of the Portland branch. The Seattle branch employed about twenty people, while the Portland branch employed about ten people.

According to this alumnus, the Seattle branch was the company's largest gate for exports to Japan, while other branches in the United States were engaged in the importing of various processed commodities. The main items of export to Japan included lumber, wood chips, wheat, and marine products. Since Japan was in the midst of the bubble economy, exports to Japan quickly increased, and the branch registered large profits.

In addition to running two branch offices, he was actively engaged in community relations. While the Japanese companies were prospering, the U.S. economy was depressed. Fully realizing the importance of corporate citizenship, representing the company, he donated to various charity programs and actively participated in community activities. He reported that his policy was not necessarily popular among his Japanese subordinates. They regarded such donations as wasteful, but our alumnus persuaded them otherwise by pointing out that, in trimming the large expense account peculiar to the Japanese corporation, a sufficient amount of money could be saved for donations.

Realizing that the purchase of U.S. real estate by Japanese corporations was unpopular among American people, he refrained as much as possible from business involving real estate investment. He says he tried very hard to sell his belief to the office staff that friendly relations with the local community would result in long-term business gains, although the creation and maintenance of friendly relations might be costly in the short term.

The third alumnus to be transferred to the United States was working for the international division of an electric machine manufacturer, where his job was to export power plants and substation parts worldwide (Case 12). In 1987 this alumnus was transferred to New York as the general manager of the Industrial Components Division of the company's wholly owned U.S. subsidiary. This subsidiary was a large one engaged in the importing and wholesaling in the United States and Canada of all products produced by the parent company except household electric appliances. It consisted of seven divisions organized on a product basis: telecommunication equipment, heavy machinery, industrial machinery, computers, auto parts, electronic products, and OA machines. Approximately 1,000 employees including fifty Japanese were scattered in sales offices in major U.S. cities including New York, Chicago, Detroit, Atlanta, Los Angeles, and San Francisco. Our alumnus was general manager of the Industrial Components Division headquartered in New York. The division was staffed by about thirty local employees along with two Japanese (our alumnus and an accounting manager). The division's objective was to sell industrial electric components and air conditioners in the U.S. and Canadian markets.

This alumnus, too, found the U.S. economy depressed, and the "American dream"—hard work with a bit of luck would make one a millionaire—no longer existed. On the other hand, the appreciation of the yen pushed up his salary, which made life in New Jersey, where he and his family reside, very comfortable.

However, the high value of the yen and the depressed U.S. economy made his job extremely difficult. The value of the yen doubled between 1985 and 1987, when our alumnus arrived in the United States. That would mean that the prices of his company's products had to double in terms of U.S. dollars to maintain the gross margin. Of course, the products could not be sold at those prices. On the other hand, if the price levels were to be maintained in terms of U.S. dollars, sales revenue in terms of Japanese yen for the company's factories back in Japan would have to be halved, a proposition not acceptable to them. The solution adopted was to sell substantially fewer units of products for somewhat higher prices. Nevertheless, some of these products remained unsold. He struggled under unfavorable conditions for two years until 1989, when he was transferred back to Tokyo.

Reviewing the above fourteen cases we can make certain observations. First of all, in terms of the stages of globalization of manufacturing companies, the textile company (Case 5) was at the most advanced stage; that is, there were overseas production and sales on a regional level. Electric machine manufacturers (Cases 2 and 12) as well as the construction machine manufacturer (Case 10) were at the stage of exporting directly without involving general trading companies. On the basis of information from the alumni in general trading companies, industries such as steel and paper manufacturers still depended on general trading companies for the export of their products.

Second, the rapid appreciation of the yen after 1985 and the slowing down of the U.S. economy made the Japanese export of certain products to the United States sluggish. Although hard evidence is lacking, more or less successful operations before 1985 (e.g., Case 2) are in sharp contrast to the hardships associated with Case 12 after 1985. Case 10 involves exporting to West Germany, whose currency was strong; in that instance, exporting was still a viable form of business even after 1985.

Third, "service" industries, including general trading companies, banks, and the casualty insurance company, adjusted their businesses to changing economic environment. After 1985, general trading companies sought and exploited business opportunities in importing from and investing in the United States instead of concentrating on exporting. Banks shifted from trade financing to project financing and to M&A financing. And the casualty insurance company benefited as a result of the shift from exporting to direct investment by manufacturing companies, as the latter required more insurance protection.

We shall now address the question of the reasons for their selection for overseas assignments. Six of the twelve alumni replied that the overseas assignment was part of regular job rotation. For example, the alumnus who was assigned to three different locations in the United States from the late 1970s to the early 1990s (Cases 1-1, 1-2, and 1-3) simply says: "These assignments were parts of normal job rotation within the staff section (accounting, finance, and personnel) of the company. Since our company is a general trading company, working overseas is expected of any employee, although I experienced more overseas assignments than most of my colleagues and I enjoyed them very much."

Another alumnus (Case 8) working for the same company as the Case 1 alumnus says, "It was part of normal job rotation within the steel division of the company." As for the location of assignment, he says, "I had no idea why I was transferred to Seoul, because I had no experience doing business in or with Asian countries." Apparently he was not happy with the assignment, as he had to leave his family in Japan for a reason that will be described later.

In the manufacturing industry, the alumnus who stayed in New York for a relatively short period of time in the late 1980s (Case 12) says, "It was an extension of my two successive assignments prior to the transfer to New York, namely, the exporting of industrial machines and air conditioners." As mentioned in Chapter 6 (Career Entry), this alumnus was hired by the overseas business division of a large electric machine manufacturer, a rather unique hiring policy for large Japanese corporations. As a result, those in the export departments within this division worked either in the main office in Tokyo or in overseas sales offices.

For the alumnus working for a textile company (Case 5), transfer from Malaysia to Hong Kong was part of normal job rotation. He elaborates:

> Since textiles produced in Malaysia were sold in Hong Kong to local garment manufacturers, a sales executive with a substantial amount of knowledge thanks to experience in the dyeing factory in Malaysia was most suitable for the position. Also, in cases of emergency in business relations with customers in Hong Kong, it was easy to make certain requests to the Malaysian factory through the interpersonal network that had been established in Malaysia.

The alumnus who was assigned to the liaison office in Frankfurt for the second time (Case 6) simply says, "It was about time for a second overseas assignment for those who had work experience in the German language region." The economic association for which one of our alumni (Case 7) was working would send, through the Ministry of Foreign Affairs, its staff members to overseas Japanese embassies on a regular basis. Since he had been engaged primarily in overseas economic cooperation up to that point, an overseas assignment was considered part of normal procedure. In the late 1970s this alumnus had been sent to Washington DC for three years.

The remaining six alumni did not refer to "normal job rotation." Instead, they gave specific reasons. The alumnus with a construction machine manufacturer who stayed in Germany (Case 10) answers, "The reason was probably because of my English skills, although after two years I had someone with German skills take over the job." The alumnus with an electric machine manufacturer (Case 2) says, "The export of OEM parts to the United States was increasing and the local sales subsidiary needed a manager in charge of selling OEM parts in the United States."

The alumnus with a bank (Case 4) who stayed in New York provides the following answer:

> I believe that the reason for my assignment to New York was my job experience in project financing up to that point. I had been engaged in major petrochemical projects—one in Singapore and another one in Iran. At that time the relative weight of project financing quickly increased in the Japanese financial circles.

The alumnus with a casualty insurance company (Case 9) says:

> In casualty insurance companies, the supply of managers capable of operating abroad is limited. In our company, the term for the chief representative in Sydney was about to be over. I think I was chosen because I was thought to be familiar with working and living abroad."

The case of the alumnus with a general trading company who was transferred to Seattle to head the branch office there is rather unique (Case 11). About five years after his return from Johannesburg, this alumnus requested an overseas transfer. His request was not accepted then because business in his department was not going very smoothly as a result of the turbulent conditions after the second oil crisis. After another five years, by which time his department's business had stabilized, he made another request, and this time it was approved. This is very unusual in large Japanese corporations, because transfer decisions are made more or less unilaterally by the employer in the form of a "jirei" or assignment order. In substance, however, the transfer was from the general merchandise division to an overseas branch office dealing primarily with general merchandise. Therefore, in a sense this transfer can be seen as part of normal job transfer.

Our final case (Case 3) involves an alumnus with an airline company who was sent to Hawaii. He said that he was sent to the Honolulu Airport branch with the specific mission of downsizing its workforce. But he did not elaborate on why he was chosen for the mission. Up to that point, he had had no work experience in personnel administration and industrial relations, and so he was not particularly equipped to perform the mission. Perhaps this assignment was intended to broaden his area of expertise, a stepping stone to becoming general manager of an overseas airport branch. Indeed, twelve years later he was made the general manager of the Saipan Airport branch.

The above answers of our alumni suggest that overseas assignments were not a special type of assignment, but rather were closely related to assignments in Japan. It seems that under the system of lifetime employment each company had well-defined routes of job rotation, such that one's current assignment would serve as a preparation for the next assignment, including overseas assignment.

For the above reason, virtually all alumni said that they did not receive any education or training prior to the overseas assignment. One alumnus (Case 6) elaborates:

> It was not exactly training; however, for a year and a few months between the return from New York and the commencement of the assignment in Frankfurt, I was assigned to the bank's securities department in order to study securities operations. This was because one of my intended duties in Germany was to survey total fund raising plans of prospective customers in the region.

Only one alumnus (Case 2) replied that he received special education/ training prior to his overseas assignment. Since he was expected to be in charge of selling a variety of household electric appliances as well as OEM and parts, he deliberately set out to obtain technical knowledge about those products. Furthermore, he was given detailed briefing about the products that various divisions wanted to export to the United States.

Next, in order to examine the extent of any ethnocentric staffing policy, Table 17.2 has been prepared in such a way that the case numbers correspond to those in Table 17.1. Note that certain cases are missing. They were intentionally dropped: Cases 6 and 9, because both were liaison offices with very few employees, and Case 7, because it involved a Japanese embassy and was thus deemed inappropriate for studying ethnocentric staffing policy.

On the basis of Table 17.2, we note that eight of the eleven overseas establishments were located in the United States, and one each in Hong Kong, South Korea, and West Germany. It is also worth noting that all manufacturing establishments were wholly owned sales subsidiaries, while all general trading company offices were branch offices. This distinction is reflected in the size of the two groups of companies in that, on average, the sales subsidiaries of manufacturing companies were much larger than the branch offices of general trading companies, except in Cases 5 and 10. Another important difference between the subsidiary companies and branch offices relates to the definition of "top management." In the former cases top management consisted of those on the board of directors with titles such as president and vice president, while in the latter case it included not only the branch office's general manager (*shitencho*) and deputy general manager (*jicho*) but also heads of functional units (usually called *bucho* or general manager). Therefore, the numbers in Table 17.2 relating to top management positions cannot be directly compared between the two types of establishments.

Table 17.2

Staffing of Overseas Offices

Case	Industry	Country	Status	Total number of employees	Number of Japanese	Number of top managers	Number of locals in top management
1-1	General trading	United States	B	10	4	3	0
1-2	General trading	United States	B	40	15	5	0
1-3	General trading	United States	B	35	15	N/A	0
2	Electric appliances	United States	H	200	20	4	1
3	Airlines	United States	B	230	6	N/A	0
4	Banking	United States	H	250	40	4	1
5	Textile	Hong Kong	H	55	4	2	0
8	General trading	South Korea	B	130	30	7	0
10	Construction machinery	West Germany	H	100	2	2	1
11	General trading	United States	B	20	6	6	0
12	Electric machinery	United States	H	1,000	45	8	3

Note: Status B denotes the branch office and status H denotes the headquarters of a subsidiary.

With these differences in mind, we can observe certain tendencies. First of all, general trading companies continued to adopt an ethnocentric staffing policy in that in all five offices, Japanese nationals held the positions of general manager, deputy general manager (when such a position existed), and functional manager as well as nonmanagerial positions. Typically, local employees were assigned to assistant, clerical, and secretarial jobs. As to the reasons for this ethnocentric policy, one alumnus (Case 1) says:

> Activities of general trading companies are closely related to Japanese government regulations and business practices; therefore, it is impossible for a non-native Japanese employee to master all those intricacies. He simply could not function effectively, especially in line positions.

Although no local employee held top management positions, the airline branch office adopted a less ethnocentric policy. Here, our alumnus (Case 3), as deputy general manager in charge of administration and industrial relations, appointed local employees to middle management positions in operation departments such as passenger transportation and cargo claim handling. He also allowed those local middle managers to participate in meetings regarding performance evaluation of their subordinates.

Overall, sales subsidiaries of manufacturing companies appear to have adopted even less ethnocentric policies. In three of the four cases, local employees occupied top management positions. Moreover, on average, the proportion of Japanese employees within the total number of employees was much smaller. Take, for example, Case 12, which was a large sales subsidiary. The ratio of Japanese to total employees was 4.5 percent. The board of directors consisted of five members: the president, an executive from the parent company, and three external members. The president and the parent company representative were Japanese, while all three external members were Americans. The top management of the subsidiary consisted of eight members: the president and the seven vice presidents who were general managers of the seven divisions. Four of the seven vice presidents, including our alumnus, were Japanese, while the remaining three were Americans. Under division general managers there were department managers, many of whom were Americans. As mentioned before, in the main office of the division where our alumnus was general manager, all but one department manager were Americans.

We observe more or less the same trend in the sales subsidiary of another electric machine manufacturer (Case 2). The top management team of this company consisted of four people, including the president, an executive vice president, and two senior vice presidents (one of whom was our alumnus). The president was Japanese, while the executive vice president was American. Both senior vice presidents were Japanese. Under the two senior vice presidents were several vice presidents (equivalent to *bucho* in the parent company), a majority of them Americans.

In West Germany, the top management team of the sales subsidiary of a construction machine manufacturer (Case 10) consisted of only two people: the president (our alumnus) and the vice president (a German). Under the vice president were several general managers, one of whom was Japanese (in charge of accounting). All the others were Germans. Our alumnus remarks:

> Since the unit price of our products was high, it was important to possess accurate credit assessment of the dealers and end users. In this regard, we needed someone who was well versed in the market conditions involving construction machines. Our vice president was such a person.

The company's entire sales force was made up of local employees. Perhaps this was the least ethnocentric of all the companies being studied here.

In Hong Kong, the sales subsidiary of a textile company (Case 5) was run by two Japanese top managers, the president and vice president (our alumnus). However, under our alumnus, a number of the general managers were Hong Kong Chinese.

The case of the subsidiary bank in New York (Case 4) provides an interesting example. This bank was incorporated under the laws of the state of New York. It had four internal directors and four external directors. The external directors were the chairman of the American Insurance Company, a former president of Caltex Corporation, a prominent university professor, and a lawyer. According to our alumnus the appointment of external board members was required under state legislation. The internal directors were the general manager, the president, and two executive vice presidents. One executive vice president was American, while the other three internal directors were Japanese.

According to our alumnus, because the majority of board members were Americans, this bank was at a higher stage of "indigenization" at the highest level of organization. However, the fact that a relatively large number (forty) of Japanese were working in various managerial and nonmanagerial positions suggests that an ethnocentric staffing policy was adopted at a level below top management.

The above discussion demonstrates that the degree of ethnocentric staffing differed from industry to industry and was perhaps affected by local legislation. This raises another question. Why is it that general trading companies adopted a seemingly more ethnocentric policy than the sales subsidiaries of manufacturing companies, despite the fact that both were involved in selling? There are two possible reasons. First, while manufacturers sell their own products, general trading companies sell the products of other companies. As a result, work associated with importing would be much simpler for the manufacturing companies than for the general trading companies. The latter's job would be affected, for example, by things such as long-term relations with the manufacturers whose products they were selling, factors that were beyond the comprehension of foreign employees in overseas offices.

Furthermore, general trading companies, through their Japanese sales representatives overseas, had long accumulated market information for each commodity they dealt with. On the other hand, manufacturing companies, which were relatively new to selling overseas, did not have much information. As a result, when attempting to penetrate a foreign market, they had to depend on local dealers. Even when a sales company was created, they needed support from local people for local market information. This was more applicable to a recently acquired market (Europe) than to an established market (the United States). Case 10 attests to this point.

We will next examine to what extent the so-called Japanese-style business procedures were followed in the overseas offices. Here, again, differences were found between general trading companies and other companies. As mentioned before, individual departments of overseas offices of general trading companies were under the strong control of corresponding departments in the main office. According to the alumnus who was assigned to three different branch offices in this period (Case 1):

> To achieve the budget established by the relevant department of the main office was the supreme goal of each department of an overseas office. To achieve the goal, standard business procedures of the main office were followed, subject to the laws and institutions of the host country.

Another alumnus who was employed by the same company and who worked in Seoul (Case 8) added another constraining factor: culture or national feelings. He says:

> In large Korean companies, decision making was top-down and the superior–subordinate relations were authoritarian. However, if we adopted that approach, it would not work, because of the underlying anti-Japanese feelings of Korean employees. The treatment of subordinates was a very delicate matter. I made the utmost efforts to make final decisions in a manner that did not offend the feelings of my subordinates.

To communicate better with his subordinates and local people in general he worked very hard to learn Korean and soon mastered the language.

In the two small liaison offices (Cases 6 and 9), home office procedures were followed, since no local people other than a secretary were employed. The alumnus who was the chief representative of a trust bank's liaison office in Frankfurt (Case 6) says, "My most memorable experience was the successful sale of fund and trust to a reinsurance company in Munich using purely Japanese sales methods." In the other liaison office in Sydney (Case 9), our alumnus attempted to conduct business in a Japanese way. He says, however:

> It was difficult to follow the Japanese practices. Although I wanted our agents to pay claims promptly, as in Japan, to my important customers, such as Toyota Motor Company and Mitsui and Co., they simply did not do so. As communication improved, they began to understand what I wanted, and in the end we were able to enjoy very good relations.

In six other offices, local methods were used (Cases 2, 3, 4, 5, 10, and 12). Four of the six offices were located in the United States, and one each in West Germany and Hong Kong. Furthermore, four of the six were offices of manufacturing companies, one was the office of an airline company, and one the office of a bank.

Here are the remarks of three alumni working in the United States (Chicago, New York, and Honolulu, respectively). An alumnus with the sales subsidiary of an electric machine manufacturer (Case 2) says, "We adopted the U.S. methods, because it wouldn't work otherwise. In particular, methods mixing Japanese and American elements were not operative." An alumnus with a subsidiary bank (Case 4) says, "We made conscious efforts not to introduce Japanese methods, because they wouldn't work. Rather, they were a source of trouble." An alumnus with an airline company (Case 3) says:

> We adjusted to local methods, because Japanese methods wouldn't work. However, there were cases where Japanese methods were accepted when we said, 'This is the way things are done in Japan." Cleaning the desk and serving tea were among such examples.

An alumnus with a sales subsidiary in Hong Kong (Case 5) makes the following remarks:

> We did not follow Japanese practices; rather we adopted local methods, which are patterned after the U.K. practices, including emphasis on the role of written contracts. One problem with the local practices was connected with payment by the customers. There were cases when payments were not made even after the due date. Their idea was to pay for materials purchased only after their products were sold. This practice was neither British nor Japanese.

It is interesting to note that this same alumnus had introduced Japanese methods to the factory in Malaysia, while he followed local business practices in Hong Kong that were basically British.

Closely related to business practices is the style of management of local employees in forms such as hiring directly from school, substantial on-the-job training (OJT), pay increase and promotion on the basis of length of service, and long-term employment. As in the two previous periods (1962–73 and 1974–80), the above elements were largely absent in the overseas offices as far as local employees were concerned.

Here are some remarks from those alumni who worked in the United States:

> Under an American personnel manager our office adopted an entirely American system for local employees (Case 2).

> Since employees' mobility was high, the Japanese style was not suitable; therefore we followed local practices (Case 4).

> We hired local people for positions in general administration and accounting, in addition to trading. We encountered a lot of problems in employment and promotion. Sometimes we had to discharge employees, some of whom sued us. We handled all personnel problems in consultation with lawyers. In this sense, it was important to hire good lawyers (Case 11).

> We hired employees through newspaper ads and private recruitment companies. We encountered some difficulty with the Equal Employment Opportunity Commission (EEOC), especially in regard to racial discrimination. Also, I don't think we were able to fill the quota for handicapped people" (Case 12).

In Hawaii and in San Francisco our alumni encountered unique situations. As mentioned before, the Honolulu branch office of an airline company (Case 3) was under the control of the American regional headquarters in New York. Uniform personnel policies, including hiring practices and wages that were typically American, were enforced, with minor modification, throughout all branches in the United States. According to our alumnus, many employees were Japanese Americans whose ways of thinking were American but who were, at the same time, receptive to Japanese culture and customs. After initial resistance, they absorbed the corporate culture of this company that was based on the strong points of Japanese culture. Our alumnus introduced such practices as bottom-up communication through the suggestion box and leading by doing (a manager cleaning his own desk, etc.). According to him these Japanese American employees were transferred to various airport branch offices on the mainland as "model employees."

If the above Hawaiian experience was a happy one, the case in San Francisco involving a general trading company's office was the opposite. In this office, too, many Japanese Americans were employed. According to our alumnus they had been valuable assets to the branch in earlier years, for example, in establishing business contacts with local companies. As a result, they had been treated more like Japanese employees from Japan: pay according to the length of service, semi-annual bonuses, and long-term employment. By the mid-1980s their role had diminished, while their payroll cost continued to increase. It was our alumnus's biggest headache to control payroll costs.

In Hong Kong, our alumnus with the textile company (Case 5) found the Hong Kong people much closer in mentality to the British than to the Japanese, in that they preferred a written contract. In wages they preferred pay on the basis of performance rather than pay based on the length of service. Therefore, our alumnus did not adopt Japanese practices at all. Employment was for a fixed period of one year (subject to renewal). Recruitment was done through open advertisement or recommendation whenever vacancies arose. Finally, in Seoul, according to our alumnus (Case 8), wage increases were negotiated with the enterprise union that was affiliated with a national federation. Initial terms and conditions of employment were negotiated with individual job applicants. Although the company for which our alumnus was working was not committed to long-term employment, terminating employment was extremely difficult because of union pressure.

Based on the above observations, it is safe to say that the so-called Japanese-style management was not applied to local employees in overseas offices. with the exception of Japanese Americans in a general trading company's office in San Francisco.

Finally, we examine the family lives of our alumni who were overseas in the 1980s. By 1980, our alumni were in their early forties, with some of their children entering their teens. As such, the single most important issue was their education. The first question they faced in transferring to overseas offices was whether or not they should be accompanied by their children, and if not, what they should do. As can be expected, those alumni with younger children of elementary school age had less of a problem. Thus, those who left Japan in the early 1980s took their entire families with them (Cases 1, 2, and 3). The first alumnus, who lived in the United States from 1979 to the early 1990s, except for a brief stint in Japan, had his three children educated almost entirely in the U.S. education system. He says:

> We had our children enrolled in local public schools, which they enjoyed very much. In addition, we sent them to a Japanese supplementary school open only on Saturdays to keep up with their Japanese. The U.S. education that our children received was a great asset to them.

Another alumnus (Case 2) remarks:

> Since we lived in a nice community north of Chicago, the public school our child attended provided an excellent education."

On the other hand, the third alumnus (Case 3) points out a few problems:

Our child experienced no difficulty learning English and in keeping up with the class. Instead, we were afraid that the level of education in the public school was low by Japanese standards. So, like many other Japanese families in Honolulu, we had our child enrolled in a Japanese correspondence course using Japanese educational materials, in preparation for the "examination hell." That must have been a heavy burden on our child.

The situation was more serious for the fourth alumnus (Case 4). When he was ordered to transfer to New York, his two sons were aged fifteen and thirteen. The elder son had already started high school, so it was decided to leave him alone in the company's dormitory for employees' children. His wife and younger son accompanied our alumnus. During their stay in New York he and his wife had a difficult time supervising their elder son from a distance. On the other hand, the younger son adjusted well to the U.S. school system and enjoyed his life in New York.

Not all alumni with young children took their entire families to the overseas posts. One alumnus with a textile company opted to live overseas by himself (Case 5). This alumnus was transferred from Penang directly to Hong Kong. In Penang this alumnus had his three children enrolled in a Japanese school, although when the eldest son started junior high school he went back to Japan and enrolled in a boarding school. When our alumnus was ordered to transfer to Hong Kong, he sent his entire family back to Japan so that his children could receive a Japanese education. Our alumnus was lucky enough to join his family in two years, when he was transferred back to Japan.

Another alumnus who opted to leave his family in Japan was the one who was transferred to the Seoul branch of a general trading company (Case 8). In the previous overseas assignment in Houston, he had no hesitation in taking the whole family and in having his two daughters enrolled in a local public school. The daughters enjoyed their school life very much. This time, however, the situation was different. The elder daughter had been enrolled in a prestigious private junior high school and the younger one was preparing for admission to the same school. He did not want to disrupt the school life of his daughters, so he decided to live in Seoul by himself. In his case, the overseas assignment lasted five long years, although during this time he could occasionally visit with his family.

It may not be a coincidence that the above two cases of temporary family separation involve assignments in Asian countries. Generally speaking, sending their children to a local school in an Asian country was not a viable option for a Japanese family living abroad temporarily. Sending children to an overseas Japanese school would not be very attractive, either, because such schools only went up to grade nine and they were regarded as less effective than their counterparts in Japan in preparing students for admission into "good" high schools (grades ten through twelve). For this reason, assignments in Asian countries were not well received by business people with children of junior high school age or above.

The third alumnus who left his family in Japan was the individual transferred to Frankfurt for the second time (Case 6). In his first assignment there, he took his whole family: his wife and three small children (one son and two daughters). He had their children enrolled in a local (German) elementary school and kindergarten, where they quickly adjusted. After only two years, he was transferred to New York. This time, too, he took his whole family with him. With some initial difficulties, all the children adjusted to American school life. Three years later they had to make another adjustment, this time to Japanese school life, when our alumnus was transferred back to Japan. So when he was ordered to transfer to Frankfurt for the second time, he thought that the additional adjustment would be too disruptive to his teenaged children, so he left for the assignment without his family.

For a child of high school age, adjusting to a foreign school system is not an easy task because to learn the language in use (English, for example) requires a higher level of grammatical knowledge and a much larger vocabulary than required at an elementary school level. In addition, the content of many subjects can be very different from that of subjects taught in Japanese high schools.

As an example, our alumnus with a casualty insurance company (Case 9) was accompanied by his family (wife and two teenaged daughters) when he was transferred to Sydney. He had his two daughters enrolled in a nearby private high school. Although the school was very receptive to the newcomers, his daughters struggled to catch up with the class. He had to hire three or four private tutors for each daughter, and the cost was partially subsidized by his employer. In spite of these efforts, the elder daughter could not catch up and she went back to Japan by herself. The younger daughter managed to survive the initial difficult period and adjusted well to school life. By the time the family left Sydney after five years she spoke perfect Australian English.

In the case of another alumnus with a general trading company (Case 11), when he was appointed general manager of the Seattle branch, his four children were at different stages of school education. The elder daughter was a university student; the younger daughter was in grade twelve, the elder son in grade eleven, and the younger son in grade six. Our alumnus says:

> For a moment, I thought about leaving the entire family in Japan, because from the standpoint of school education, it was risky to take high school children overseas. However, we decided against that idea because family ties were of utmost importance to us. Besides, we felt that overseas experience would be beneficial to our children.

So they decided to leave only the elder daughter in Japan so that she could continue her college education. As expected, the two high school children had a hard time keeping up with academic work. Our alumnus says of his elder son:

> He was enrolled in the grade eleven class, but he could not understand what was being taught in class at all. So, at the suggestion of his class adviser, he spent most of his time taking English as a Second Language (ESL) classes instead of taking as many academic subjects as his classmates. It took him an extra year to graduate from the high school. Again, at the suggestion of the adviser, he entered a community college with a view to transferring to a university instead of applying directly to a university. He worked very hard at the community college for two years and succeeded in transferring to a university, from which he graduated in two years.

Our alumnus concludes:

> From the experiences of our children's education, I am very appreciative of American society in general and educational institutions in particular. They not only accepted foreign(-born) children with an open mind, but they also provided various assistance, for example, ESL programs. In contrast, Japanese society is closed, although individual Japanese are kind on average.

His latter point (the closed nature of Japanese society) is illustrated in the experience of the alumnus who spent two years at the Japanese embassy in London (Case 7). He was accompanied by a daughter of high school age and a son of junior high school age as well as by his wife. After two years in a local public high school and a Japanese school, respectively, the two children returned to Japan where they faced difficulties in transferring to Japanese high schools. Our alumnus says of the daughter:

> Since she left Japan on leave from a public high school, we wanted her to transfer back to the original school. After a series of transfer tests in various subjects designed for transferees from other domestic high schools, she was not allowed to return to her original class. So we had her enrolled in a private high school with a more flexible transfer policy.

The hardship experienced by the above alumnus and his children after their return to Japan was just one of tens of thousands of similar cases that occurred at the time (the mid-1980s). It was about then that the "overseas returnee student problem" was recognized as a significant social problem. Ironically, the greatest problem faced by our alumni with teenaged children was associated more with the closed nature of the Japanese education system than with the differences of foreign education systems.

18
Work Lives of Alumnae, 1981–90

As of 1981, when our alumnae were about forty years old, only two of the six held full-time jobs. Within the next decade, three went back to work or started to work either full-time or part-time. The remaining alumna continued to help her husband more extensively as the scope of his work expanded over the years. The purpose of this chapter, therefore, is to provide a picture of the lives of our six alumnae, focusing on their work lives from their early forties up to their early fifties. We will present their experiences in the order in which they started or resumed their work lives.

Our first alumna, after a three-year stint with her father's company, started her lifetime career in 1967 with a foreign educational and cultural mission in Tokyo. In her first assignment, she was assistant to an English education officer. In 1979 she was promoted to assistant to the chief representative of the mission. The mission's aim has been to promote long-term educational, scientific, and cultural cooperation with other countries. It is a worldwide nonprofit organization with offices in 109 countries. To achieve its aim, the organization has been engaged in activities such as facilitating academic and professional visits, exchanges, and research projects, arranging cultural events and seminars, providing information and advice, and, more recently, English language teaching, testing, and teacher training.

As assistant and secretary to the chief representative, our alumna was involved in all of the above activities. For example, in the area of academic visits, she assisted the chief representative in planning and executing a program to invite Japanese university administrators to the United Kingdom to study university reform in that country. She accompanied her superior on visits to a couple of national universities in northern Japan. When one of the two universities accepted an invitation, she made all the arrangements for its president and the dean of the faculty of education to travel to the United Kingdom and to visit universities and government agencies.

In the area of cultural exchange, she was involved in a number of projects: inviting an actor who performed plays for solo actors to Edinburgh; building a hall in commemoration of Father Weston in Kamikochi, Nagano Prefecture; building a British garden in Nagano to popularize old roses; and sending a group of junior high school students from Yakushima Island in Kagoshima Prefecture to the United Kingdom to observe rare rhododendron flowers from Yakushima that had been successfully transplanted in the United Kingdom.

As secretary she prepared monthly lists of events and visitors, or itineraries when VIPs visited from the United Kingdom. It was also her job to translate English speech manuscripts into Japanese when the chief representatives gave a speech in Japanese. She usually took home translation work. As a secretary, she did not have a subordinate, so her working hours were intense, so much so that after eight hours of work she was exhausted. For that reason she never worked overtime. Besides, there was no payment for overtime work.

According to the alumna, top-down decision making was practiced in the organization. Although a management committee existed, it was more for window dressing—real decisions were made by the chief representative. The chief representative, however, was not given much autonomy by the main office in the home country, which apparently kept overseas offices under tight control. As a result, when there was a major policy change at the head-quarters, it directly affected local operations, including operations in the Tokyo branch office.

Throughout the period, this alumna remained single and lived with her mother. In her spare time, she enjoyed singing as a member of a choir, as well as water painting. However, more recently, she stopped participating in the choir, because she had to look after her aging mother.

The second alumna, who started an art gallery and picture-dealer business with her husband in 1974, continued with this business into the 1980s and 1990s. Their business was running smoothly in the 1970s and 1980s, but the burst of the bubble economy made the business more difficult and they moved their gallery into their house.

From the beginning they specialized in dealing with Western paintings by Western artists. According to our alumna, there were guild-like relationships among Japanese art dealers, so that paintings of a particular Japanese artist were handled only by a particular dealer who had a longstanding relationship with the artist; there was no room for newcomers like our alumna and her husband to enter into such a market with Japanese paintings.

Essentially, their business was to purchase, on behalf of their customers, Western paintings from art dealers or at auctions in Europe or the United

States. According to her, the art dealing business is relatively simple. When the deal is made, transactions are made on a cash basis and arrangements for insurance and shipping are made through an air cargo transportation company. She and her husband took turns traveling abroad to purchase paintings their customers wanted. So she was always alone when she made overseas trips. Negotiation was usually done in English. Back in Japan they would sell the painting for an amount that covered the purchase price, insurance, shipping, and other costs incurred, plus a modest profit.

She recalls that, at the height of the bubble economy, a lot of Japanese money flooded the market, with the result that Japanese dealers offered exorbitant prices. Japanese banks were more than willing to lend large amounts of money to the dealers, some of whom purchased high-priced paintings for speculation purposes—in anticipation of even higher prices in the future.

The burst of the bubble changed all this. Art dealers with a large stock of paintings purchased through bank loans went bankrupt because they could not repay the loans. Banks that took unsold paintings as collateral ended up with bad loans because the value of the paintings was now much lower than the amount of outstanding loans. The collectors who purchased the paintings for "investment" also suffered because of a substantial decline in the price of paintings. Naturally, they began to blame art dealers for having charged them high prices.

Our alumna and her husband survived the post-bubble crisis because they purchased paintings only on orders from the customers and because they did not charge the customers very high prices; in other words, they were not involved in speculative purchasing and selling of paintings. Besides, she says that most of their customers were real collectors who would not sell their paintings once they had them, so they do not feel they have lost money.

Another area in which this alumna was substantially involved in the mid-1980s through the mid-1990s was social (volunteer) activities. As mentioned in Chapter 13, this alumna served on the Juvenile and Youth Committee of the Board of Education of Setagaya Ward in Tokyo. The committee organized community activities and helped with various cultural activities for youth groups. The two activities she considered most successful were rice-cake making and bus hikes, which were conducted annually for ten successive years. She says:

> Through my association with children and youth my views have broadened. Also, it was a very rewarding experience for me to observe that they enjoyed those activities and kept coming back in successive years to participate in them.

The above description shows this alumna to be a person who was committed not only to her occupation but also to community activities.

In the meantime, our third alumna, married to the president of an incense manufacturing company, went back to work after fifteen years away from active participation in the family business, although during that time she had continued to help her husband by entertaining business guests at home. In 1982, she participated in a cultural mission to introduce and popularize the incense ceremony (*kohdo*). The mission performed incense ceremony demonstrations, with our alumna acting as spokesperson, at the United Nations, Columbia University, and the University of California, among other places. Her debut on the international scene was sensational, as the mission was highly successful: the events were broadcast nationally by ABC News and reported in articles in the *New York Times*. In addition, the Japanese Broadcasting Corporation (NHK) reported on the events in its news programs.

After a series of incense ceremony demonstrations, she participated in a sales promotion campaign for her husband's company. She visited a number of branches of a major department store headquartered in New York with the objective of opening up a specialty shop in the branch locations to sell the company's products. At each branch, they performed incense ceremonies, thereby attracting shoppers' interest in incense products. They also gave advice to sales staff on sales techniques. Also, they were successful in having the company's products selected for exhibition at the Japan Fair held at the department store Bloomingdale's in New York that year. Looking back, our alumna recalls that as the beginning of the globalization of the company's business.

After returning from a highly successful U.S. tour (both in terms of introducing the Japanese culture of the incense ceremony and in terms of promoting the products of her husband's company—incense powder and sticks), she decided to resume working for her husband's company. Her duties included entertaining an increasing number of foreign buyers and taking charge of business correspondence with overseas customers. In 1985, when her husband established a store specializing in the sales of goods needed for the incense ceremony and providing advice on selecting incense wood, our alumna was made a director of the company.

On the international front, whenever her husband made overseas business trips, our alumna accompanied him to meet business customers and acquaintances and to make presentations of and/or to demonstrate the incense ceremony. On average they spent about eighty days a year abroad, until very recently. As late as 1995, she accompanied her husband to the United States when the company opened "KOH HOUSE," an incense specialty store at Disney World. The following year they went to Paris to commemorate the acquisition of a famous company. They were accompanied by the master of the *Oieryu* incense ceremony school and his wife. Our alumna performed a ceremony to which a number of journalists were invited. Thus, her job has been to contribute to the company's international sales by heightening the image of their products through the introduction of Japanese traditional culture (the incense ceremony).

As regards social activities, this alumna continued to work for the female division of the alumni association. In recent years, she has been particularly active in international cultural exchange by providing various kinds of services to foreign students. She has done this because of her experience as a summer exchange student at Stanford University in 1961, when she received a very warm reception from American people. Since that experience formed the basis of her ways of thinking and a happy life thereafter, she felt that now it was her turn to do what she could for foreign students in Japan.

On her relationship with her husband she says:

> Ever since I went back to work, my husband has expected me to perform at a high level. So I have had to work hard to meet his expectations, and, through my efforts to do so, my job skills have improved. I think that my husband appreciates my contribution to the success of his work on a global basis.

Unlike the above two alumnae, some alumnae did not have a husband's job or a family business to turn to for a job. Two such cases will be discussed next.

The alumna who had become seriously ill because of conflicting roles stopped being a perfectionist after she recovered from the illness. She decided not to overwork and not to hold back from speaking her mind in front of her husband and his mother. Her role as a mother also became less demanding. As she could no longer spend sufficient time on engraving, she began to develop an interest in areas that were less physically demanding. Haiku, or seventeen-syllable Japanese verse, was the answer.

She began to attend a haiku class in a culture center. At the center she attended classes on Japanese literature and language as well. She says:

> In the meantime, at the suggestion of a friend who said that my voice and way of speaking would make me a good Japanese language instructor, I enrolled in a program to train instructors of Japanese as a second language. I took courses on linguistics, phonetics, and grammar as well. When I completed the program in 1982, I became a Japanese language instructor.

In the same year (1982) her husband changed his job—from bank manager to senior manager with a manufacturing company. Our alumna says about him:

> With the job change, my husband seemed to appreciate a more relaxed lifestyle. His values also changed—he placed less emphasis on formality. As for me, he must have thought that it would be difficult to keep me home all the time.

In 1986, after a few years of experience as a Japanese language instructor, she became an instructor in the Japanese language instructor training program at the culture center where she had been a student. Almost every day, she taught courses such as teaching methods, grammar, the history of the Japanese language, and the history of Japanese language studies. Her identity crisis was finally over. In addition, by that time, her husband, who was exposed to and becoming used to a new, relaxed work life, supported her decision to become an instructor at the culture center. In 1993, however, he died suddenly. She was fifty-three years old at the time.

A year after her husband's death, our alumna went back to work. This time she joined a small language school on a full-time basis. She not only taught Japanese language classes for foreign students, but also performed administrative work, with which she had no previous experience. But a year later she resigned because the business was slow.

In 1996 she was urged by a friend to start up a joint business covering foreign language instruction, interpretation, and translation. By investing in the business, our alumna has become a co-owner/manager of the business. The two did not employ any workers, instead dividing all the work between themselves. Our alumna was made responsible for management, accounting, and clerical work, while her partner was responsible for personnel and line work. Instructors and translators were hired from a temporary employment agency on an hourly basis. Advertising was done through the Internet.

For the fifth alumna, who was married to the successor of a family-owned chemical company, her early forties were the most difficult time of her life. First, her husband became ill and subsequently died in 1987, when she was forty-six years old. Second, about the same time, her son and daughter each had serious problems with their lives that caused her many headaches as a mother. It was very difficult for her to maintain mental balance. Ironically, however, she gained freedom through the loss of her husband. As we have seen in Chapter 13, he had been very authoritarian and had strongly objected to her seeking employment outside the home, or even to her studying outside the home. So, within a year of her husband's death she began the study of English through private lessons from an American teacher once per week. She also started social dancing as a hobby, as she had seriously practiced classical ballet until her high school days. These activities freed her from the stress she had suffered in trying to balance her role expectations—that of a good wife and that of a wise mother. And soon she felt like a new person.

Now that her husband was gone, she wanted to seek her own career by making use of her English language skills. To that end she planned carefully and proceeded methodically. First, she attended a word processing school in order to improve her "marketability." Then, through an acquaintance at the school, she joined a nonprofit organization, a Japanese branch of a world-wide organization involved in international aid programs on the basis of donations primarily from corporations. There, she composed English letters and did translation and other clerical work. In addition, she learned personal computer skills on the job—through the creation of a directory of donor corporations. She felt she was lucky because she was able to gain the useful work experience she had wanted and because her superior was a very respectable person.

During this time she attended an intensive Japanese language instructor training course at a certain language school in preparation for still another career, when she came upon the notice of an opening for an English instructor position. She applied for and obtained the position, quitting her work for the nonprofit organization. Since then, she has been a part-time English instructor at the language school. In addition, she has kept up the private English teaching at home that she had begun shortly after marriage.

This brings us to our sixth alumna, who is married to a professor of medicine. The amount of her work increased as the scope of her husband's work expanded. In 1977 her husband became involved in the management of a private foundation established in the same year by an industrialist, who, through his own experiences, realized the importance of international exchange at an individual level. The basic objective of the foundation was to deepen international understanding by sponsoring an international symposium in eighteen academic areas every year. The eighteen areas included philosophy, history, folklore, mathematics, and physiology, all of which are important but not very popular areas. The symposium was to be attended by Japanese and foreign scholars for a period of five days during which the participants and their spouses were to stay in the same hotel. In this way, the participants could not only exchange their academic opinions but also deepen their personal friendships.

Between 1977 and 1989 our alumna's husband served as the coordinator for one of the divisions, physiology. Every year he selected ten participants each from Japan and abroad. It was the responsibility of our alumna to help him with correspondence and with the organizing of cultural and social activities for the participants of the division for which her husband was responsible. When the symposium was held abroad, she accompanied her husband to participate in international exchange activities. Since 1989 her husband has served the foundation as chairman of the organizing committee for all eighteen divisions, and with that our alumna's supporting role has become even greater.

When her husband retired from the university in 1991, he took a part-time teaching job as well as the position of adviser to the Japanese Association for the Removal of Discrimination against Color-Blind People. In an attempt to abolish discrimination and regulations against color-blind people, her husband has been involved in negotiations with government agencies, corporations, and publishers, as well as in keeping in touch with overseas academic associations and organizations sharing the same objective. Again, our alumna has played the role of secretary for her husband in all these activities.

After his retirement, she no longer needed to look after the students under her husband's supervision. Instead, as her husband has come to spend more time on writing and public lectures, her role has shifted more toward being a director and agent for her husband.

It is apparent from the above descriptions that all our female alumnae were eager, through various means, to identify and pursue their own goals beyond being "a good wife and a wise mother," and that they were successful in their pursuits.

Summary to Part IV

The decade beginning in 1981 and ending in 1990 was an epoch-making period in international politics, as it witnessed the final victory of the free-world nations in the Cold War that had lasted for four decades. In the process of the dissolution of the Soviet empire Japan, under the strong leadership of Prime Minister Nakasone, reaffirmed close military alliance with the United States. Nakasone's firm foreign policy was also instrumental in bringing about domestic political stability.

In contrast, Japan experienced further economic turmoil during this period. The "productivity-first" mentality of the Japanese people, both management and workers alike, continued into this period. Japanese bureaucracy continued to exercise a protectionist trade policy, despite Nakasone's international pledge to make the domestic market more accessible to imports.

As a result, Japan continued to register large trade surpluses. This meant that most of Japan's trade partners, notably the United States, registered large trade deficits. Self-restraint in exports exercised by individual industries including iron and steel, textiles, industrial machines, and electric machines were, as we saw in Chapter 15, not very effective. Thus the G-5 finance ministers met in New York in 1985 and agreed to devalue the dollar that had been maintained at a high level due to the "strong dollar" policy of President Reagan. The resultant rapid appreciation of the yen put pressure on the Japanese export industries to further increase productivity on the one hand, and on the other hand to accelerate overseas production not only in Asia but also in the United States and Europe.

The more immediate effect of the yen appreciation was a sharp decline in Japan's exports, causing a mini recession. With a view to helping economic recovery, the government and the central bank adopted major fiscal and monetary measures consisting of a substantial decrease in the official discount rate, substantial spending on public works, and a substantial reduction in income tax.

These measures were successful in stimulating both investment and spending. For example, as we saw in Chapter 15, between 1985 and 1990 new housing starts grew at an average annual rate of 8.4 percent, as against 1.4 percent between 1981 and 1985. This resulted in a sharp increase in land prices, thus triggering the bubble economy. Thanks to the "land myth" that land prices will never decline, land speculation began, followed by stock market speculation. Corporations and individuals spent large sums of money in speculative purchasing of land, stocks, memberships in golf clubs, expensive foreign art works, etc. "Japan money" started to purchase foreign assets as well.

This was the background against which our alumni and alumnae pursued their careers. They were now in their 40s and most alumni were promoted to the upper middle management position of *bucho* (or general manager of a department) just below the top management position of *torishimariyaku* (or member of the board of directors).

As discussed in Chapter 16, *bucho* plays the role of linchpin in the Japanese corporation. Contrary to the popular belief, our findings revealed that job description did exist for this position in all organizations studied and that our alumni followed it more or less closely in performing their work. Functional tasks were an important element of their work, again contrary to the "generalist" image of Japanese managers. Generally speaking, general managers in line departments spent more time on functional tasks than those in staff departments. On the other hand, general managers in staff departments spent more time on decision making than their counterparts in line departments.

Ringi, allegedly another unique Japanese decision-making instrument, was used in all but one case. However, contrary to the popular view, it was not a tool for bottom-up decision making in the sense that rank-and-file members initiate this process of decision making. Rather, general managers were found to play a crucial role in the *ringi* process. In this sense, Japanese-style decision making may be more accurately called "middle-up" rather than "bottom-up." Other features of Japanese-style decision making, namely group decision making and consensus decision making, were found to be actively in use at this level of management.

Supervision of subordinates, both managerial and nonmanagerial, is another important job of the general manager. Systematic evaluation of subordinates was conducted in all cases. Here, the single most important criterion of performance evaluation was "results or outcomes." Loyalty to the company, allegedly an important feature of Japanese-style management, did not surface as an important criterion of performance evaluation.

In terms of career anchors, of the twenty-four alumni who were with the original employers in 1981, only one quit the company to accept a job offer from another company during this period. This suggests that our alumni were strongly anchored in organizational security, as originally expected.

Toward the end of this period three alumni were transferred to subsidiaries of the original employers as a result of corporate restructuring/downsizing.

They were employed in the steel division of a general trading company, lighting products division of an electric machine manufacturer, and marketing division of a petrochemical company. These were the industries or divisions thereof whose international competitive power declined, as we saw in Chapter 15. Another alumnus changed his career from sales to consulting within the same company, which helped him obtain new skills. He was given leave with pay for more than a year to attend educational/training programs at the company's expense.

The four cases suggest that paternalistic employment policies, allegedly a distinctive feature of Japanese-style management, was indeed in actual use. In particular, in the first three cases involving restructuring, a typical U.S. firm would simply have terminated the employment of such redundant managers.

Also during this period a dozen alumni were assigned to various overseas offices where they held top management positions. After the Plaza Accord of 1985 overseas sales offices, mostly in the United States, experienced difficulties due to a rapid appreciation of the yen. Hardest hit were the two U.S. offices of electric machine manufacturers. General trading companies began to shift their emphasis from exporting to importing. Banks shifted from trade financing to M&A financing.

In the staffing of overseas offices, general trading companies continued to adopt ethnocentric policies, while manufacturing companies adopted less ethnocentric policies. Likewise, general trading companies adopted Japanese-style business practices, while manufacturing companies followed local practices. This distinction may be explained by the fact that general trading companies were a uniquely Japanese institution. In the management of local employees, Japanese-style management was not practiced in any office studied, including those of general trading companies. Overall, then, it appears that an ethnocentric staffing policy and Japanese-style business and management were practiced to a less extent in overseas offices than is generally believed.

When it came to family living associated with overseas assignment, the education of teenage children was the most difficult problem our alumni experienced. At the secondary school level, adjusting to host country schools was difficult. However, adjusting back to the Japanese school system was found to be even more difficult. It was ironical that Japanese culture, which emphasizes uniformity and conformity, posed the biggest challenge for our alumni.

Finally, as of 1981 only two of the six alumnae held full-time jobs. By 1990 an additional three went back to work or started to work. They did not simply follow "a good wife and a wise mother" model; they sought and found their own goals in work. It is important to add that they did not take their jobs out of economic necessity. It was the intrinsic nature of the jobs themselves that attracted our alumnae.

Part V

Post Bubble Period
(1991–2000)

19

General Environment, 1991–2000

The last decade of the second millennium was characterized by a series of events symbolizing the end of the cold war. Following the unification of West Germany and East Germany on October 3, 1990, the Warsaw Treaty Organization (called the Warsaw Pact), with the Soviet Union as the leader, was dissolved on July 1, 1991 (Ministry of Foreign Affairs 1991: 314). The dissolution of this organization drastically weakened the international position and influence of the Soviet Union. It no longer could rival the United States, which became the only superpower. The Soviet Communist Party had to terminate its existence on August 22, after an unsuccessful coup d'état by conservative communists (Ministry of Foreign Affairs 1992: 276–77).

The three Baltic states declared their independence from the Soviet Union, as they were convinced that there was no longer a chance of military invasion. Finally, the federal state of the Soviet Union itself was brought to an end on December 21, 1991, when each member state became independent (Ministry of Foreign Affairs 1992: 278).

Earlier, in April 1991, President Mikhail Gorbachev made an official visit to Japan at the invitation of the Japanese government (Ministry of Foreign Affairs 1991: 316–21). The purpose of the visit was to discuss the long-awaited peace treaty between the two nations. There was no major break-through, because of the dispute over the four northern islands. One positive outcome of the meetings was that the Soviet Union allowed former residents of the islands to visit their homes without a visa issued by the Soviet Union.

A major topic of discussion at the economic summit meetings held in London in July 1991 was assistance to the Soviet Union (Ministry of Foreign Affairs 1991: 5–6). Although there was no financial commitment to the

Soviet Union, the summit leaders agreed to accept it as an associate member of the International Monetary Fund (IMF). In less than a year, the IMF officially admitted Russia as a full member, as the country was judged to be making economic reform in the right direction.

At the 1992 Group of Seven (G-7) summit conference held in Munich, it was agreed to extend support to Russia in order to achieve economic stability in that country and also to secure the safety of its nuclear power plants (Ministry of Foreign Affairs 1992: 1–3). Russia, led by President Boris Yeltsin, was an official invitee to the following summit meetings held in Naples. The fact that former foes of Russia accepted it as a member of their club was a clear indication that the cold war era was over.

The dissolution of the cold war brought about a number of side effects in international politics. In Asia both North Korea and South Korea were admitted to the United Nations in September 1991 (Ministry of Foreign Affairs 1991: 209–11). These two countries had been denied entry to the United Nations (U.N.) for nearly half a century after their independence, because North Korea had been regarded by the UN as a hostile nation during the Korean War. Naturally, both the Soviet Union and China had objected to the admission of South Korea to the UN.

The end of the cold war had a favorable effect on Cambodia, which had been plagued by civil war long after the termination of the Vietnam War. The peace treaty was signed in Paris in October 1990 (Ministry of Foreign Affairs 1991: 234–36). Ideological conflict ceased to be a cause of war in the post–cold war era.

It was precisely for this reason that South Korea made a series of drastic diplomatic moves representing a clear departure from past policy. In August 1992, South Korea normalized diplomatic relations with the People's Republic of China, terminating its long-cherished bond with Taiwan (Ministry of Foreign Affairs 1992: 175–76). In November of the same year, South Korea signed a basic agreement to normalize diplomatic relations with Russia. This was followed by a similar agreement with Vietnam a month later. The Republic of Korea thus drew world attention through what they called "northern diplomacy."

In Europe the twelve nations of the European Community (EC) decided to join together at the end of 1992 into one economic unit consisting of 320 million people (Ministry of Foreign Affairs 1992: 245–53). The so-called EC 92 referred to the elimination of tariffs and customs as well as financial and commercial barriers among member nations, effective January 1, 1993. In terms of mutual defense, Western Europe under NATO proposed a cooperative treaty with former East European nations at the very beginning of 1994.

In the United States, the inauguration of Bill Clinton as the forty-second president in January 1993 marked a new era of domestic economic prosperity as well as political dominance in the world (Ministry of Foreign Affairs 1993: 35–37). Shortly after the inauguration of the new president, the U.S. government announced that its GDP had increased by 3.8 percent from the previous year, a recovery after four years of stagnation. At the end of the same year, the U.S. government declared a recovery in the job market, as the unemployment rate decreased by 0.4 percent.

One year after the creation of the EC, the United States, Canada, and Mexico signed the North American Free Trade Agreement (NAFTA). It was an extension of the free-trade agreement between the United States and Canada in order to include Mexico. This trading bloc of 360 million people laid the foundation for faster growth and more jobs as a result of increased exports and trade.

Economic recovery soon turned into economic prosperity (Economic Planning Agency 1994: 10–11). The Dow Jones stock index of the New York Stock Exchange, which was around 3,000 in early 1993, exceeded 4,000 in February 1995, 6,000 in October 1996, and 7,000 in February 1997. The U.S. economic boom was led by the "high-tech" industry. Microsoft was the most symbolic case. When it put Windows 95 on the market in August 1995, it became an instant hit, not only in the United States but all over the world (Asahi Shimbunsha 1996: 300). Windows 95 was a brand new version of the basic operating system used in personal computers (PCs) produced by all manufacturers. It meant that U.S. software came to dominate the world PC market; no other firm could outdo Microsoft.

The economic prosperity of the United States sharply contrasted with the economic stagnation of Japan. The aftereffects of the bursting of the bubble economy were so significant that successive governments were unable to put the economy back on track. While the economy was turning from bad to worse, political debate revolved around issues such as Japan's role in [U.N. Department of] Peacekeeping Operations (PKO), electoral reform, and scandals involving political and business leaders.

Japanese politics have always been plagued by money scandals—the Lockheed scandal in the 1970s and the Recruit scandal in the 1980s are only two such examples. In the early 1990s, it was the Sagawa Kyubin scandal (Asahi Shimbunsha 1993: 74). Sagawa Kyubin was a relatively new but fast-growing courier service company. For a young and innovative company like Sagawa, the administrative "guidance" of bureaucrats was a problem because such guidance tended to maintain the status quo, which would favor old and established companies.

Sagawa Kyubin contributed a "political donation" of ¥500 million to Shin Kanemaru, then deputy president of the ruling Liberal Democratic Party

(LDP), with the alleged motive of getting Kanemaru to wield influence over the transportation ministry so that it would loosen control over the company. Kanemaru and Sagawa managers were arrested for bribery. Shortly afterward Kanemaru resigned from the LDP (in October 1992). This incident further tarnished the dirty image of the LDP, which had already been seriously damaged by the Recruit scandal of only a few years earlier.

While the opposition parties (socialists and communists) continued to advocate a ban on political donations from corporations, a different approach was suggested from within the LDP. Ichiro Ozawa, then secretary general of the party, articulated the problem. According to him, an electoral reform would be the most effective method of eliminating money scandals. Under the multi-seat district system then in force, several candidates from the same party would run in the same district. They could not effectively compete on the basis of policies because they belonged to the same party, which forced them to compete on the basis of the amount of "services" they would provide to the voters. These services included throwing parties for (would-be) supporters, inviting them on free trips to Tokyo (from rural electoral districts), and attending weddings, funerals, and other gatherings. These activities were so expensive that politicians, especially those of the LDP, were always in need of money.

The solution, according to Ozawa, was a single-seat electoral system, so that only one candidate would run from the same party. Candidates could now compete on the basis of the policies of the parties in which they were members. This system would lead to a two-party system in which a change of power between the two parties would likely take place, thereby putting an end to the long-term domination of the LDP, a hotbed for scandals.

It was ironic that a high-ranking official of the LDP proposed a system intended to end LDP rule in Japanese politics. However, for Ozawa and his associates, political reform was more important than staying in power. Therefore, they split from the LDP in early 1993, and, when opposition parties proposed a vote of nonconfidence in the Miyazawa cabinet, Ozawa and his group voted with them, thus bringing down Miyazawa (Asahi Shimbunsha 1994: 108–9). At the general election held in August 1993, the LDP was unable to obtain a majority. A coalition cabinet representing eight parties was formed, with Morihiro Hosokawa as the prime minister and Ozawa as the secretary general, ending thirty-eight years of domination by the LDP since 1955.

The Hosokawa cabinet was well received by the Japanese people in general, who had been frustrated under LDP rule. It was hoped Japan would finally rid itself of outdated political and economic laws, regulations, and administrative guidance of all sorts to become a true democracy. Unfortunately, the eight-party coalition was so fragile that the LDP came back to power in June 1994, less than a year later (Asahi Shimbunsha 1995: 236–37). It formed a coalition with the Japan Socialist Party (JSP), the LDP's long-time foe, with Tomiichi Murayama of the JSP becoming prime minister. Since then the LDP has managed to stay in power by forming coalitions with one or two minor parties. During this time, the political and economic reforms advocated by Ozawa and his associates have been sabotaged, and Japan has been left in the dark.

It was disclosed during this period that corruption, a moral hazard, was not a monopoly of politicians, and it became abundantly clear that business leaders and bureaucrats were equally guilty of corruption.

The collapse of the stock market that began in 1990 cast its shadow on securities firms and investors. In June 1991, it was reported that four major securities firms had engaged in improper compensation for losses suffered by their large corporate customers (Asahi Shimbunsha 1992: 136–40). Perhaps, from the standpoint of top managers of the securities firms, these acts might not have been considered criminal or unethical; rather, they were considered a normal part of business practices to maintain long-term close relations with important customers. However, from the standpoint of individual investors, who had sustained heavy losses in the stock market and who were not compensated, these were acts of discrimination. When the list of the names of corporations that had benefited from such compensations was revealed, the public was doubly appalled to find the names of many leading Japanese corporations. It was rumored that the names of politicians, high-ranking bureaucrats, and gangsters were intentionally withheld.

The rapid decline in land prices inflicted much more serious damage on banks and nonbank financial institutions (Asahi Shimbunsha 1996: 268–70). From the end of World War II through the bubble period, the Japanese people had maintained strong faith in the "land myth," holding that land prices keep rising, thus making land the most preferred method of investment. During the bubble period, banks and other financial institutions made easy loans to customers with land as collateral. (It must be added here that large Japanese city banks do not lend to real estate developers directly but indirectly, through their subsidiary "nonbank" financial institutions.)

With the collapse of the real estate market, real estate developers were the first to go under, followed by nonbanks, each with a lot of pieces of now-devalued land on their books. Through investigation of many bankruptcy cases, it became clear that city banks had improperly engaged in pressuring the nonbanks to grant loans even though it was obvious that the collateral was worth less than the amount of the loan. *Boryokudan* (organized crime syndicates) and *sokaiya* (professional troublemakers at stockholder meetings) lost no time in threatening the city banks that they would reveal information to the public about the banks' wrongdoings (Asahi Shimbunsha 1995: 321). Thus, major city banks and other nonbanks made illegal payments to them. The case of Daiichi-Kangyo Bank was among the most widely known.

The problem was the total amount of bad debts held by banks and other financial institutions and their attempts to conceal this information until such time that they either went bankrupt or were ordered by the Ministry of Finance to liquidate (Asahi Shimbunsha 1999: 152–53). Yamaichi Securities, the Long-Term Credit Bank of Japan, and Hokkaido Takushoku Bank were among the major financial institutions that went under in this way.

Thus, when Keizo Obuchi assumed the premiership in August 1998, Japan's financial system was on the verge of a total breakdown. In March of the following year, the government set aside approximately ¥7.5 trillion (U.S. $70 billion) to be used to purchase the stock of fifteen major banks, thereby saving Japan's financial system (Asahi Shimbunsha 1999: 151).

Throughout this period, mismanagement of the economy by government agencies, especially the Ministry of Finance (MOF), was appalling. To begin with, a direction issued in April 1990 by the director of the Banking Bureau of the MOF triggered collapses in both the stock market and the real estate market (Asahi Shimbunsha 1991: 126). In order to stop further increases in land prices, the bureau issued directives to major banks to restrain lending for the purpose of purchasing real estate, causing a "crash" landing instead of a "soft" landing. Second, the MOF did not function as an effective monitoring agency over the activities of financial institutions. There is every evidence to suggest that the MOF tacitly consented to the financial firms' practice of concealing bad loans in the hope that, when the market improved at some time in the future, the bad loans would turn into healthy loans. Third, and related to the second point, some MOF inspectors were corrupt (Asahi Shimbunsha 1999: 238). In exchange for overlooking improper practices by financial firms, corrupt officials received expensive gifts, played golf at company expense, and were wined and dined, if more discreet about receiving cash donations as well.

This last point, a series of individual acts of corruption, jarred the nerves of the Japanese people, as they had assumed that MOF officials were the cream of the elite: not only the brightest of all bureaucrats, but also those with the highest moral standards. Their trust in bureaucrats was thus shattered. This realization has given support to reform-minded politicians calling for deregulation.

Against the above background, we will review the performance of the economy. Table 19.1 summarizes a few key economic indicators.

Based on the table, it appears that the effect of the collapse of the stock market and the real estate market did not affect the growth of the Japanese

Table 19.1

GNP Growth Rate, Consumer Price Index (CPI), Trade Balance, Foreign Reserves, and Exchange Rates

Year	Increase in GNP (real, %)	Increase in CPI (%)	Trade balance (nominal, 10 million USD)	Foreign reserves (nominal, million USD)	Exchange (year end, yen to USD)
1991	3.0	2.9	9,608	68,230	125.25
1992	0.7	1.4	12,476	70,045	124.65
1993	0.3	1.1	13,942	101,737	111.89
1994	0.6	0.2	14,419	141,523	99.83
1995	3.1	–0.4	13,179	203,951	102.91
1996	4.7	0.1	8,356	219,357	115.98
1997	0.0	2.2	10,160	223,593	119.92
1998	–1.9	0.1	12,239	222,523	115.20
1999	0.5	–0.6	12,332	288,080	102.08

Source: Economic Planning Agency, *Keizai yoran* [Summary Statistics on the Economy] (annual).

economy until 1992. Even then, many politicians were optimistic about Japanese economic performance and kept themselves occupied with debates over PKO and electoral reform. However, Prime Minister Miyazawa, an expert on the economy, was different. Concerned about the stagnant economy, in August 1992, he enacted special legislation to spend ¥10.8 trillion to prop up the economy (Economic Planning Agency 1993b: Appendix 4). Realizing that this amount was not sufficient, in April of the following year, he undertook another spending program of ¥13.2 trillion. At the same time, during his tenure of two years the Bank of Japan decreased the official discount rate six times, from 5.5 percent in November 1991 to 2.5 percent in February 1993 (Economic Planning Agency 1994b: Appendix 4).

Miyazawa's economic policy was followed by the non-LDP government of Morihiro Hosokawa, who introduced a special spending program of ¥15.2 trillion in February 1994 (Economic Planning Agency 1995b: Appendix 4). Also during his tenure, the official discount rate was decreased from 2.5 percent to 1.75 percent in September 1973. Three years of efforts by the Miyazawa and Hosokawa Cabinets showed positive effects in 1995 and 1996 when GNP growth rates were 3.1 percent and 4.7 percent, respectively. The coalition government of Murayama, himself a socialist, did not adopt any measure to stimulate the economy. However, during his tenure, the Bank of Japan decreased the official discount rate twice, from 1.75 percent to 1.0 percent in April 1995 and from 1.0 percent to a mere 0.5 percent five months later (Economic Planning Agency 1996b: Appendix 4). This low interest rate, called the "zero interest policy," remained in force until August 2000.

Thus, when Ryutaro Hashimoto assumed the premiership in January 1996, it seemed as if Japan had finally recovered from the post-bubble recession. With an optimistic view of the future of the Japanese economy, Hashimoto undertook a number of reform measures, one of which was fiscal reform. Because of the expansionist economic policies of the governments before him, the ratio of yearend outstanding national debt to GDP in 1994 was 41.2 percent, much higher than that in all other advanced nations except the United States (Economic Planning Agency 1995a: 26).

After one year's preparation, in April 1997, he increased the consumption tax from 3 percent to 5 percent and increased income tax rates from the previous year (Economic Planning Agency 1998: Appendix 4). In June of the same year, medical fees under various medical insurance plans were substantially increased. These measures were sufficient to dampen the economy; the GNP growth rate declined to zero percent in 1997 and to −1.9 percent the following year. The economy obviously had not fully recovered from the post-bubble recession. It was during this period that the failures of large banks and securities firms took place. In July 1998, Hashimoto resigned and

Table 19.2

Labor Market Trends

Year	Labor force (thousands)	Unemployment rate (%)	Active job opening rate (%)	Real wage increase (%)
1991	6,505	2.1	1.40	0.2
1992	6,578	2.2	1.08	0.1
1993	6,615	2.5	0.76	−0.6
1994	6,645	2.9	0.64	1.3
1995	6,666	3.2	0.63	2.1
1996	6,711	3.4	0.72	1.6
1997	6,787	3.4	0.69	0.4
1998	6,793	4.1	0.50	−2.1
1999	6,779	4.7	0.49	−0.7

Source: Ministry of Labor, *Rodo tokei yoran* [Summary Statistics on Labor] (annual).

was succeeded by Keizo Obuchi, who suspended fiscal reform and switched to an expansionist economic policy.

One side effect of the prolonged recession was the fact that, throughout the period, prices were stable. In 1998, it was feared that Japan was on the verge of a "deflation spiral," which it narrowly escaped thanks to Obuchi's big-spending policy.

In addition, throughout the period, Japan continued to register large trade surpluses, resulting in an increase in foreign reserves. This means that whatever economic growth Japan was able to achieve depended to a considerable extent on exports. It was fortunate for Japan that the U.S. economy was strong enough to absorb imports from Japan.

We will now turn to a review of conditions in the labor market (Table 19.2).

In Table 19.1, we observe a time lag of about one year before the effect of the decline in the stock and real estate markets showed up in the national economy. In Table 19.2, we see that in the labor market the time lag was two years. For example, the active job opening rate, or the ratio of job openings to job seekers, was 1.40 in 1991, meaning that there were more job openings than job seekers. Even in 1992, the number of job openings exceeded the number of job seekers, although the margin was very small. The situation quickly changed in 1993, when the number of job seekers far exceeded the number of job openings; this condition has continued to date.

The same tendency can be observed in the unemployment rate. The rates for 1991 (2.1 percent) and for 1992 (2.2 percent) were as low as, or even lower than, the figures for the 1980s (see Table 14.2 in Chapter 14). However, since 1993, the rate has been consistently on the rise; in 1998, it exceeded 4 percent and continues to rise.

The size of the labor force has continued to increase; however, the increase is a reflection of increases in unemployed workers and in part-time workers, especially among females. In an attempt to improve the status of women in the job market, the Equal Employment Opportunity Law was modified and put into effect as of April 1999. However, without penalties for violation of the law, its effectiveness in the current difficult economic climate remains questionable.

20
Industry-Specific Environment, 1991–2000

The Iron and Steel Industry

Japan's economy faced a serious situation as the result of a recession after 1990 and a strong yen. A slowdown in processing industries with assembly plants (such as the automobile and electric appliance industries) and expanding imports reduced domestic demand for iron and steel (Tables 20.1 and 20.2). The steel makers with blast furnaces fell deep into the red in the 1993 accounting year. In order to recover international competitiveness, they carried out further restructuring, which, this time, involved not only producing departments but also the administrative departments of head offices.

It seemed that the postwar business cycle had basically, or structurally, changed. Public investments, which used to be effective as pump-priming measures, did not lead to quick recovery of demand for steel, because construction companies were in a serious crisis following over-investment during the bubble economy and their own scandals. Moreover, emphasis in public investments was shifting from engineering works to infrastructure for daily living or information/communication purposes, from which vigorous demand for iron and steel could not be expected.

Assembling manufacturers in the automobile and electric machinery and appliance industries had been good customers of steel makers since the pe-

Table 20.1

Basic Statistical Data for the Iron and Steel Industry

Year	Shipment amount (billion yen)			Number of employees (thousands)			Crude-steel production (thousand metric tons)		
	Iron and steel (A)	All industries (B)	(A)/(B) (%)	Iron and steel (C)	All industries (D)	(C)/(D) (%)	Production capacity	Output	World market share (%)
1990	18,269	323,373	5.6	338	11,173	3.0	136,896	110,339	14.3
1991	18,631	340,835	5.5	340	11,351	3.0	137,353	109,649	14.9
1992	16,588	329,521	5.0	331	11,157	3.0	140,283	98,132	13.6
1993	14,974	314,787	4.8	326	11,477	2.8	137,950	99,623	13.6
1994	13,574	299,027	4.6	308	10,416	3.0	147,475	98,295	13.5
1995	14,111	309,437	4.6	301	10,880	2.8	149,828	101,640	13.4
1996	13,928	316,436	4.4	289	10,647	2.7	149,733	98,801	13.1
1997	14,603	326,515	4.5	277	10,473	2.6	149,775	104,545	14.3
1998	12,988	309,305	4.2	265	10,399	2.5	149,758	13,548	12.1

Sources: Adapted from MITI (Ministry of International Trade and Industry), *Census of Manufacturers* (Tokyo: Annual); and Japan Iron and Steel Federation, *Handbook for Iron and Steel Statistics* (Tokyo: Annual).

Table 20.2

Exports and Imports of the Iron and Steel Industry

Year	Exports of all iron and steel products (thousand metric tons)					Imports of steel products [ordinary steel] (thousand metric tons)			
	Total exports	To the United States	To the EC	To Asia (including China)	To China	Total imports	From Korea	From Taiwan	From Brazil
1990	17,021	3,220	442	10,301	1,754	5,978	2,694	627	499
1991	18,027	2,780	318	11,954	2,064	7,505	3,086	672	665
1992	18,980	2,629	315	12,708	2,368	5,389	2,655	687	324
1993	23,506	1,825	231	18,172	6,911	5,578	2,643	801	442
1994	23,953	3,637	255	17,427	4,406	5,189	2,649	756	357
1995	22,988	2,334	293	17,894	3,843	6,143	2,933	609	258
1996	20,615	2,049	380	16,067	2,538	5,150	2,812	625	357
1997	23,501	2,704	346	17,615	2,659	5,665	2,893	1,028	574
1998	27,649	7,020	733	15,556	2,477	4,489	2,779	934	388

Source: Japan Iron and Steel Federation, *Handbook for Iron and Steel Statistics* (Tokyo: Annual).

riod of high economic growth, but they had been transferring a substantial part of their production bases overseas during the preceding twenty years (in what is called "industrial hollowing"). Therefore, any increase in demand stimulated by public investments would lead to minimal purchases of steel products by such manufacturers.

The predicament of the iron and steel industry is seen in the collapses of Toa Steel, a major electric furnace steel manufacturer, Okura Trading, and Tsuda Steel Products, a wholesaler dealing in steel.

Trade disputes were renewed. When the Voluntary Restraint Agreement (1985) expired in 1992, major U.S. steel makers filed an ambitious suit against twenty-one major iron and steel manufacturing countries, including Japan. The suit concerned antidumping and countervailing duties against four items belonging to the sheets/plates category of ordinary steel. The investigations into losses suffered by U.S. makers proved that, with minor exceptions, the suit was not applicable to Japanese products. Yet, after 1997, antidumping actions against Japanese makers were introduced one after another. Some similar developments were seen recently outside the United States.

What Japanese steel makers are expected to do under these circumstances in order to survive into the twenty-first century as world enterprises might be the following:

(1) implement further restructuring and strengthen competitive power so that they can compete against overseas makers at home as well as abroad;

(2) strengthen overseas operation bases by establishing sales centers in local markets;

(3) further diversify businesses and diversify sources of profits so that they can reduce dependence on steel business; and

(4) have a good supply of raw materials stored for future use (a tight demand-supply in scrap is expected in the future).

Synthetic Fiber Manufacturers

In 1992 the Japan Chemical Fibers Association advocated "globalization" during a forum at which the future of the industry was discussed in an international meeting attended by people in this field from the United States, Europe, Japan, Korea, and Taiwan (Table 20.3).

In the same year, a law for the textile industry with a limited period of validity (the Textile Law) was revised so that the government could assist the textile industry to improve itself. Each company was well aware that self-help was indispensable. Each maker went its own way. Restructuring advanced.

Table 20.3

Production Capacity of Polyester (thousand metric tons)

Year	World	The Americas	%	Europe and Russia	%	Japan	%	China	%	Asia (excl. Japan and China)	%	Korea (out of Asia)	%	Taiwan (out of Asia)	%
1970	1,877	921	49	654	35	253	13	0	0	37	2	17	1	12	1
1975	4,375	2,034	46	1,347	31	505	12	0	0	417	10	117	3	199	5
1980	6,346	2,698	43	1,743	27	691	11	115	2	855	13	181	3	398	6
1985	7,988	2,499	31	2,016	25	775	10	567	7	2,262	28	428	6	814	10
1990	10,560	2,430	23	2,184	21	852	8	1,245	12	3,607	34	894	9	1,679	16
1995	14,258	2,928	21	2,142	15	910	6	2,020	14	5,812	41	1,889	13	2,223	16
1996	17,101	2,796	16	2,317	14	922	5	2,400	14	6,677	39	2,162	13	2,561	15

Source: Japan Chemical Fibers Association, *Kasen nenpyo* [Chronological Table of the Chemical Fibers Industry] (annual).

Mitsubishi Rayon pulled out of the polyester business and Unitika pulled out of polyamide paper. Two joint ventures ended.

Among the major spinning companies, Toyobo entered the area of high-tenacity fibers in cooperation with a Dutch company. Unitika penetrated the French market by setting up a joint venture, and expanded its production of nylon films in Indonesia and Italy. Kanebo went into joint ventures for polyester and nylon in China in 1994.

Kuraray, a synthetic fibers manufacturer that had already gone into dental materials and optical disks, entered into a partnership with Ube Industries for polybutylene terephthalate (PTB).

Asahi Chemical substantially scaled down its production of polyester, an area it had entered rather late. It withdrew from its spandex (elastic fiber), carbon fiber, nylon carpet, and acrylic business in Ireland. In place of its contracted textile businesses, it pushed diversification with an emphasis on building materials and housing construction. The ratio of nontextile businesses to all of its businesses rose from 77 percent in 1987 to 87 percent in 1993. It also proceeded to strengthen its medical supplies business by merging Toyo Brewery, a subordinate, in 1991. It shifted from being a textile manufacturer to being a chemical company. Its name finally reflected the type of business in which it was engaged.

Teijin entered the markets of resin, films, and medical supplies. Its ratio of nontextile businesses reached 41 percent in 1993. It gained a market share of more than 80 percent in oxygen concentrator for home health care. With regard to textile businesses, it promoted the production of textile fabrics through joint ventures in Thailand, China, and Italy. In 1995 it set up a joint venture for tire cords in Indonesia, expecting that products there would someday replace exports from Japan of textiles for industrial use. Teijin demonstrated its positive stance toward cooperation with giant chemical companies in the United States and the United Kingdom by entering into a joint venture with ICI for a substitute for Freon, and joining with DuPont for film manufacturing in the United States and Europe. With DuPont it also set up a joint venture in Japan for nylon.

Toray, the largest manufacturer of synthetic fibers, increased its ratio of nontextile businesses to a 49 percent maximum by engaging in businesses dealing with resin, electronic materials, and medical supplies. It also had ambitious plans in textile businesses, such as investing ¥35 billion in China, Thailand, and Indonesia for an Asian production base for integrated operations from chips to dyeing (by 2000). It invested in the United Kingdom in 1992 (for an integrated operation from weaving to dyeing), and in the Czech Republic in 1996. It was in the process of establishing global operations.

In June 1999, the Textile Law was abolished. Relief measures directed exclusively toward the benefit of the industry, which had a long history dating back to 1956, can no longer be expected. The manufacturers are expected to, and are ready to, survive on the basis of the principle of self-help.

The Petrochemical Industry

Around 1990, at the last stage of the bubble economy, the petrochemical industry, which constitutes half of the entire chemical industry, and companies oriented toward processed goods recorded their largest-ever profits.

Lively investment in equipment, however, peaked in July 1991. After the bubble burst, the total profit of the twelve ethylene companies, major players in the petrochemical industry, plunged into the red from ¥250 billion in 1991. The petrochemical industry, a materials industry, suffered from the unfavorable business conditions that were a big reaction to the boom of the bubble economy: sluggish domestic demand, falling prices due to weak international markets, and competition with imports from Korea and Taiwan under a strong yen. Moreover, assembly industries, for example, the automobile and electronics industries, normally their good customers, were transferring their production bases overseas to take advantage of cheap labor. (Even the chemical industry had commenced in the latter half of the 1980s to move overseas, mostly to places in Asia, as mentioned in Chapter 15.)

While the materials-oriented industries were in trouble, processed goods manufacturers, whose products were close to final products (such as photographic film, cosmetics, toiletries, and floppy disks), were developing consumer markets. Fuji Photo Film, Shiseido, Kao, and Maxell were examples of such companies.

In the field of automobile tires, alliances or groups were formed to survive worldwide competition. Bridgestone acquired Firestone (United States), Okamoto joined with Michelin (France), Yokohama Rubber, Toyo Tire and Rubber, Continental (Germany), and General (United States) joined together, and Sumitomo Rubber linked with Goodyear (United States).

Production of pharmaceuticals was also expanding, despite the fact that drug price standards (prescribed under the Health Insurance System) were being lowered every two years. The market was lively, penetrated by players from other industrial fields such as synthetic fibers manufacturers, in addition to original pharmaceutical companies like Takeda or Sankyo.

The production of ethylene, after it exceeded 6 million metric tons in 1991, decreased in 1992 and 1993 as a result of the worsening business climate. The Ministry of International Trade and Industry (MITI) proposed a measure to export excess capacity of 1 million metric tons to China. The government was no longer in a position to protect domestic manufacturers, because it had already (in 1987) made the Industrial Restructuring Law inapplicable to the petrochemical industry, because foreign countries were being sharply critical of Japan's regulation/protection barriers, and because the government was tackling the differences between domestic and overseas prices. Manufacturers had been restructuring and were succeeding in reducing fixed costs, by means of steps such as reduction of the workforce.

According to the government's business forecast announced in April 1994, only some "weak sunny weather" lay ahead. Yet the U.S. boom and European recovery stimulated Asian economies, causing inquiries into Japan's products to increase despite the strong yen ($1 = ¥100). Some petrochemicals, for example, synthetic materials and resins, improved enough to ease production curtailment.

On the other hand, there was increasing pressure on the automobile industry, a large user of chemical products, to purchase imported parts. The domestic market share of the chemical companies grew increasingly precarious. The strong yen was favorable to imports, and this seemed to work in support of the government, which had to make an international pledge to deregulate.

The Great Hanshin Earthquake of 1995 resulted in huge losses to Japan's industries, including the petrochemical industry. Its business activities were restored in the latter half of that accounting year (October 1995 through March 1996) with easing of the strong yen. Profits rose in that period. The general feeling, however, was not so bright although investments in equipment increased for the first time in four years. That was because sales prices were going down in the midst of ongoing deflation after the bubble economy, and stock prices were plunging. (Chemical companies, like other Japanese big businesses, held stocks.)

The production of ethylene exceeded 7 million metric tons in 1996. Total world production capacity was 90 million metric tons per year as of the end of May 1998, as shown in Table 20.4, and it is expected to surpass 100 million metric tons in 2000 (JPCA 1998: 20).

How can Japan be competitive with only an 8 percent share? Its current production size seems insufficient to beat the United States or the Middle East region, which use natural gas for materials.

The 1994 merger of Mitsubishi Chemical Industries and Mitsubishi Petrochemical Co. created Mitsubishi Chemical Corp., which ranks among the top ten in the world, with annual sales exceeding ¥1 trillion. In the field of polystyrene, the shipment of which had decreased due to the transfer of production bases overseas by electric appliance manufacturers, Showa Denko transferred its goodwill to Asahi Chemical and withdrew in 1994. Ube Industries consigned production of linear low density polyethylene (L-LDPE) to Sumitomo Chemical. The largest and the second largest producers of styrene monomer,

Table 20.4

Production Capacity of Ethylene by Region (million metric tons per year, as of May 1998)

Region	Capacity	Share (%)
The Americas	33.5	37.2
Western Europe	20.0	22.2
Eastern Europe (including Russia)	7.2	8.0
Middle East and Africa	7.0	7.8
Korea and Taiwan	5.9	6.6
China	4.0	4.4
Japan	7.5	8.3
World	90.0	100.0

Source: JPCA (Japan Petrochemicals Industry Association), *Sekiyu kagaku kogyo no genji* [The Present State of the Petrochemicals Industry] (1998), p. 20.

Mitsubishi Chemical Corp. and Asahi Chemical, planned to unite their productions beginning in April 2000. Thus the chemical industry commenced restructuring at the industry level, leaving behind the period of government protection and a succession of government-encouraged cartels (Table 20.5).

The entire chemical industry is now required to tackle environmental protection, in the form, for example, of measures to combat global warming and reduce Freon gas. An especially urgent issue is the establishment of a recycling process for waste plastics.

The Industrial Machine Industry

After the bubble burst, more and more Japanese manufacturers transferred their production bases overseas and industrial hollowing progressed. A sharp rise in imports due to the strong yen started to create mayhem with price mechanisms.

Machine Tools

Decrease in domestic demand and sluggish exports were inflicting damage upon the machine tool industry. Though the amount of production remained number one in the world, it was below half of what it was at peak level. The automobile industry, a key domestic client, had excess capacity and a structural problem to solve. Transferring production bases overseas was popular

Table 20.5

Major Chemical Company Sales and Employee Numbers (million USD/ thousand, 1977)

Country	Company	Sales amount	Number of employees
United States	DuPont	41,304	98
	Dow Chemical	20,018	43
	Monsanto	9,457	22
	Union Carbide	6,502	12
Germany	Hoechst	33,839	148
	BASF	32,410	103
	Bayer	32,298	142
United Kingdom	ICI	16,428	63
France	Rhône-Poulenc	16,774	75
Belgium	Solvay	8,812	35
Japan	Mitsubishi Chemical	14,006	12[a]
	Asahi Chemical	10,355	15[a]
	Mitsui Chemica	7,920	7[a]
	Sumitomo Chemical	7,724	6[a]

Source: JPCA (Japan Petrochemicals Industry Association), *Sekiyu kagaku kogyo no genji* [The Present State of the Petrochemicals Industry] (1998), p. 22.
[a]As of 1998.

among manufacturers, including machine tool makers. The machine tool industry, on which the whole of Japan's industrial world is based, was seriously affected by the structural depression of the entire economy.

The spread of NC-type machines homogenized not only the products of all the makers but also production structures. Asian countries like Korea and Taiwan, as well as the United States and European countries, were catching up with Japan. The yen remained strong. Japan's status, like that of Japanese manufacturers, was not secure in the world market. All companies were racking their brains for ways to survive (Takamura and Koyama 1994 [4]: 85).

Construction Machines

The transfer of productions overseas cut domestic production down to around ¥1.1 trillion. Machines were upgraded in size and horsepower for higher productivity. In consideration of energy conservation and environmental protection, factors such as energy efficiency, noise prevention, and design became key elements in production. Product quality was ranked highest in the world. Decline in domestic demand and lively overseas demand caused exports to recover to ¥650 billion, with an export ratio of 48 percent in 1997.

Japanese construction manufacturers globalized their operations through overseas production and linking with overseas makers. As they carried out their business activities, they watched world market developments, as can be seen in the recent (intended) adoption of international standards, for example, those of the International Organization for Standardization (ISO) (JSIMM 1998: 14).

The Electric Machine Industry

Heavy Electric Equipment (HEE)

The burst of the bubble did not affect the HEE industry as seriously as it did other industries, because demand for HEE was sustained by stable investment in power supply and in public works for infrastructure such as sewerage—this latter type of activity expanded as a result of pressure under the Structural Impediments Initiative (Japan–United States talks over deregulation by Japan) with a view to expansion of domestic demand. What was worthy of notice about the HEE industry in the midst of a strong yen were the establishment of overseas production bases and increasing procurement of materials from abroad.

In the post-bubble period, social environments are changing, as seen in low economic growth, environmental and energy issues, and an aging society. Individual value systems are being diversified. The role of the HEE industry is expected to expand qualitatively as well as quantitatively, for example, by contributing to energy saving, or by responding flexibly to the changing social system (Takamura and Koyama 1994 [4]: 90–91).

Electrical Appliances (EAs)

The burst of the bubble drastically reduced domestic demand for EAs after 1991. In March 1992, the Fair Trade Commission made on-the-spot inspections of twenty sales agencies affiliated with four major EA manufacturers, suspecting that the agencies had broken the Anti-Monopoly Law by forcing volume sales stores to accept the prices set down by the manufacturers for retail prices. The Commission issued a recommendation to these agencies that they put an end to their conduct (interference with prices). After that it was difficult for manufacturers to dictate retail prices.

Price competition intensified in the midst of an oversupply and consumer preference for lower priced goods.

Each EA manufacturer implemented restructuring and reviewed its policy toward sales agencies. Operations were globalized in such a way that the most appropriate area/market was selected for production or sales, whether it was in Asia, the United States, Europe, or Japan.

A new product (area) has not yet been found that appeals strongly to consumers, because demand is almost filled for EA products that constitute the base of people's daily lives.

In any discussion about the future of the EA industry, it will be important for information-related businesses to participate. A trend toward multimedia-related EA products is emerging, based on recent technological progress in software as well as hardware. The EA industry is expected to contribute to our information-oriented society by supplying products that are required by the community, ranging from terminal equipment to products responding to new services expected to be offered in the future (Takamura and Koyama 1994 [4]: 93–98).

General Trading Companies (GTCs)

GTC business, as a whole, was quite sluggish in the first half of the 1990s as a result of the collapse of the bubble economy and the strong yen, then it took a turn for the better, but was hurt in 1998, most of all by a domestic financial crisis and plunging Tokyo stock prices (which resulted in appraisal losses), and to a lesser extent by the Asian turmoil. Throughout the period, the trading companies sought new profit centers and shed poor performers (JFTC 1998: 136–41, 163–67, 185–87; Nihon keizai shimbun 1999: 126).

They reviewed their organizations, assets, and investment undertakings, all of which had expanded excessively during the bubble period. For better earning power they began streamlining operations by liquidating unprofitable subsidiaries, reducing employment, and writing off bad debts (JFTC 1998: 164–65; Nihon keizai shimbun 1999: 126).

While Japanese manufacturers were losing export competitiveness and transferring their production bases abroad as a result of the super-strong yen, GTCs had to put more emphasis on importing or offshore businesses than on exporting ones (Table 20.6). As regards offshore businesses, they established profit centers mainly in increasingly stronger Asian countries, including China. As regards import businesses, they aggressively engaged in importing finished goods, with a significant expansion in food items in particular (JFTC 1998: 139, 163–66, 186–87).

Positive long-term and medium-term investments were made in Asian countries in the creation of infrastructure or in oil development projects. In Russia and the East European region, GTCs made investments in the devel-

Table 20.6

Total Amount of Sales and Distribution Ratio into Four Categories of Six Major General Trading Companies (GTCs)

Accounting year March to April	Total amount of sales (billion yen)	Distribution ratio			
		Domestic (%)	Export (%)	Import (%)	Offshore (%)
1991	119,198	44.3	13.1	16.8	25.8
1992	111,226	45.1	13.8	16.4	24.7
1993	103,178	48.8	13.3	14.5	23.4
1994	99,773	46.8	12.6	14.9	25.7
1995	96,789	47.9	12.1	14.8	25.2
1996	84,549	45.9	14.7	18.3	21.1
1997	84,741	43.3	16.0	17.8	23.0
1998	71,138	44.9	17.0	17.7	20.3

Sources: Shigetaka Asuka, Sogo shosha ron [A Treatise on GTCs] (Tokyo: Chuo keizai-sha, 1998), p. 210; JFTC (Japan Foreign Trade Council), Nihon boekikai 50-nen-shi [Fifty Years' History of the Japan Foreign Trade Council] (Tokyo: 1997). p. 35.

Note: The offshore transactions above include only those booked by the parent companies (in Japan). Such transactions booked in overseas subsidiaries recorded a big increase in this period. Their total amounts increased from ¥3,986 billion in 1988 to ¥6,896 billion in 1995, or an increase of 73 percent (Shigetaka Asuka, Sogo shosha ron, p.110).

opment of oil fields, petrochemical projects, hotels, and passenger car factories (JFTC 1998: 138–39, 166, 187).

GTCs continued to be active in communication and information-related businesses, an area in which they had been placing strategic emphasis, and they
turned out to be one of the major players in Japan (Table 20.7). This industry
requires large initial investments and long lead times. Cooperation with leading
overseas enterprises is also important in international communications. GTCs
coordinated enterprises in related industries by putting to use their wide range of
business relationships, and they diversified risk in their investment (Asuka 1998:
82; JFTC 1998: 140, 166–67, 186; Kubo 1997: 82–89).

Positive investments by GTCs resulted in the growing importance of financial incomes (i.e., interest or dividends received) from their affiliated companies (Table 20.8). "Actually, the GTC ratio of Operating Profit to Ordinary
Profit tends to fall . . . mass media refer to it as GTC transformation to venture capital" (JFTC 1998: 186).

The general trading companies are said to be in their second "winter." They
grew in step with the pace of Japan's economy in the postwar days, but gradually their growth has gone out of step with the growth of the economy as a
whole. They have not managed to adapt themselves to a surge in mass
consumption or to the distribution revolution. In other words, they did not
get solid footholds in new-growth industrial sectors such as the automobile
industry or the electric appliance industry, while their old customers, such
as the iron and steel industry, shipbuilding, and chemicals, waned in importance in the economy as a whole. They could not throw off their conventional status as wholesalers. It was not until the mid-1980s that they
decided to stake their future on penetration of the new-growth business
sectors of communications and information.

In their conventional business their commissions have been getting thinner and thinner. They have not fully recovered from the bursting of the
bubble—not mentally or financially. How to survive this severe "winter" is a
problem to which they must find an urgent solution (Kawahara and
Hayashikawa 1999: 3–12, 33–34, 63–69; JFTC 1998: 185–86).

The Banking Industry

The liberalization of interest rates on deposits, which began with the introduction of certificates of deposit in 1979, was completed in October 1994
with the liberalization of demand deposit interest.

As for lending rates of interest, Mitsubishi Bank abolished the regulation
of interest rates based on the official discount rate in January 1989 and introduced its own prime lending rate for a short-term loan. Other banks followed

Table 20.7

Amounts of Investments of Six Major General Trading Companies (GTCs) in Communication and Information Business
(billion yen, as of January 31, 1996)

Item	Company name					
	C. Itoh	Sumitomo Corp.	Mitsui and Co.	Mitsubishi Corp.	Nissho-Iwai	Marubeni
Communication via satellite	10.5	13.8	8.5	12.6	13.8	0.4
International communication	5.5	1.8	1.8	1.8	1.2	1.2
Domestic communication	1.3	3.5	11.7	12.0	0.9	1.6
CATV	12.9	20.4	2.0	0.9	0.5	1.6
Portable telephone	2.1	1.2	5.3	5.0	2.9	1.1
Picture software	4.3	2.7	1.9	0.4	1.1	0.4
Overseas	3.5	0.9	4.3	0.3	2.0	1.8
Others	60.7[a]	1.7	1.9	1.1	1.3	2.5
Total	100.8	46	37.4	34.1	23.7	10.6

Source: Shigetaka Asuka, *Sogo shosha ron* [A Treatise on GTCs] (Tokyo: Chuo keizai-sha, 1998), p. 89.
Note: [a]Includes the stake in Time Warner ($600 million).

Table 20.8

Latest Ordinary Profits of Six Major General Trading Companies (GTCs)
(billion yen)

Accounting year	Operating profit (A)	Nonoperating profit (B)	Ordinary profit (A) + (B)	Financial profit[a] included in (B)
1995	153.1	115.6	268.7	—
1996	165.3	167.7	333.0	—
1997	171.4	158.6	330.0	162.9
1998	123.7	192.5	316.2	169.9

Source: Adapted from Nihon Keizai Shimbun, *Japan Economic Almanac 1999* (Tokyo: July 1999).
[a]Financial profit = interest received + dividends received – interest paid.

suit. As regards long-term loans, city banks put an end to the bank (i.e., long-term credit bank) prime lending rate linked to the debenture interest rate and introduced their own lending rates for long-term loans.

The capital-adequacy requirements set by the Bank for International Settlements were applied to Japanese banks in March 1993. "If a bank with international operations had a capital-to-assets ratio of less than 8 percent or a domestic bank had one of less than 4 percent, the Financial Supervisory Agency was allowed to order restructuring and business shutdown" (Nihon keizai shimbun 1999: 18).

A Financial System Reform Law was enacted in April 1993; this permitted banks and securities companies to enter the capital market and the financial market, respectively. The first financial institutions to enter the capital market were the Industrial Bank of Japan, the Long-Term Credit Bank of Japan, and Norinchukin Bank, which established subsidiary securities companies in July 1993.

With the bubble's burst, the sharp fall in real estate prices changed banks' loans to the Three Sectors into a huge mass of bad loans collateralized by real estate. The plunge in stock prices reduced the capital-adequacy ratios of banks. Thus, bank management was basically affected.

At first, mortgage finance companies and some small financial institutions collapsed as a result of bad loans. But in November 1997, Hokkaido Takushoku Bank, a city bank, failed. A package of bills was enacted in October 1998 to put a safety net in place in case of the collapse of a major bank. Under the package, the Long-Term Credit Bank and Nippon Credit Bank were nationalized in October 1998 and December 1998, respectively. The bad loan problem refused to go away.

The postwar financial system functioned efficiently under the given economic conditions and contributed to high economic growth (Enkyo 1995: 82). As Japan became money-affluent and increased its presence in the international community, the financial system and financial market were increasingly liberalized and internationalized. The Japanese financial system is now in the process of reforming itself into a system that is more market-oriented and that can bring about efficiency in the market, on the one hand, while it protects depositors and prevents a systemic meltdown, on the other hand.

To survive intensifying competition, alliances were formed and intra-industry restructuring took place. Following the merger of Mitsui Bank and Taiyo Kobe Bank (creating Sakura Bank) in April 1990, Kyowa Bank and Saitama Bank merged (creating Asahi Bank) in April 1991. In April 1996, Mitsubishi Bank and the Bank of Tokyo merged (creating the Bank of Tokyo-Mitsubishi). Alliances are scheduled for the Industrial Bank of Japan, Daiichi Kangyo Bank, and Fuji Bank, between Sumitomo Bank and Sakura Bank, and between Mitsui Trust and Chuo Trust. Further alliances or restructuring can be expected, involving not only Japanese institutions but also foreign institutions.

The Air Transport Industry

Demand remained weak. Measures were taken against oversupply. Deep discount air tickets increased, so much so that a large market emerged in which air travel agencies specializing in such tickets grew remarkably. Since the strong yen (weak dollar) allowed foreign airline companies room for cutting airfares, Japan's air transport market held out advantages for foreign airlines.

In 1994, the Ministry of Transport approved a new airfare system based on the concept of price ranges, in an attempt to narrow the gap between the official tariff and market fares. Competition in overall services intensified among airline companies.

Kansai International Airport opened in 1994. Expected to be a hub airport in the future, it was the first airport in Japan to be available twenty-four hours per day, and it charged airlines the highest landing fees in the world. Japan's airlines faced higher costs than other airlines in the world, partly because of the strong yen. Labor costs were twice as high as those in Southeast Asia, and higher than those in the United States. Japan's airlines were too slow in denominating costs in foreign currencies, and all kinds of work for repairs and maintenance were done in Japan. This was one of the major reasons for the high costs.

The Council for Civil Aviation submitted to the Minister of Transport a recommendation for further deregulation in 1994. Japan airlines (JAL) announced a restructuring plan that emphasized cutting the workforce by 5,000 people. ANA and JAS followed suit. The three seemingly competed in restructuring in order to survive the deregulation era.

In order to correct excess supply, the Japan–United States Civil Aviation Agreement (1952) needed a basic review. Despite repeated negotiations between the two nations, the agreement remained unequal. U.S. airlines were permitted rights beyond Japan for unrestricted regions, while the rights of Japanese airlines were severely restricted. U.S. airlines were making the best use of rights beyond and established networks in rapidly growing Asian markets. Another round of Japan–U.S. Civil Aviation talks began in January 1997 and ended a year later. A new agreement came into effect in April 1998, whereby inequality was finally eliminated: rights beyond were equally permitted to Japanese and U.S. airlines and the number of airlines with substantial freedom was equalized to three each (Ministry of Transportation 1999: 9, 221–23).

Two new domestic airlines were founded on the occasion of the completion of the new runway at Haneda Airport in 1997, creating room for more flights. Skymark Airlines Co. and Hokkaido International Airlines Co. (Airdo) started flights in 1998 on trunk lines, charging about 40–50 percent less than the standard fares of the existing major airlines. Although their shares were very small, fare competition heightened and was cutting into the profits of the existing major carriers.

The regulation for adjustment of demand and supply, on which Japan's civil aviation policy had been based, was to be abolished in 1999. This deregulation is part of the Big Bang in the air transport industry, and it aims at encouraging Japanese carriers to survive the growing competition in the international market as well as at home. Each airline must restructure itself quite intensively, while it has to maintain quality of services and reduce costs drastically. Otherwise it will not have a future, as can be seen in the history of rises and falls of airlines around the world (Takamura and Koyama 1994 [4]: 153).

The Beer Industry: Distribution

Deregulation proceeded in the Japanese economy. It was easier for major supermarkets (or volume sales stores) as well as convenience stores to obtain liquor licenses. Discounters took root. Multiple merchandise in small quantities, a self-service system, and cash sales are characteristic of these retailers with new business styles (apart from liquor stores). They are called new-business-style enterprises or growing-business-style enterprises. Such enterprises have been expanding their shares in regional markets, and it is said that they will take over majority shares. They made good use of the negotiating power that they gained through information strategy, and they eliminated interference from manufacturers and agencies in decisions about what to put on shelves in stores. Beer prices went up on May 1, 1994, because the tax included in beer prices was increased. Daiei, the biggest supermarket operator, had implemented a price cut the previous month, anticipating the price increase in May. It froze its beer prices after May. A margin arose between Daiei's prices and the retail prices considered to be standard. Other volume sales stores and discounters followed suit. Retail prices, which had remained unchanged even under the free price system, were destroyed at a stroke. Neither the brewers nor the agencies were able to take effective measures against destruction of the conventional price mechanism because of the principle of a free-price system and because of the relatively greater leverage enjoyed by new-business-style stores over themselves (Kirin 1999: 268).

The chain operators of volume sales stores demanded that brewers and agencies unify the complex distribution channels into a single one in which all kinds of beer and all the brewers' beers could be delivered together. The distribution system was streamlined. This resulted in a reduction in the number of cars and trucks involved in delivery and turned out to be an effective antipollution measure. There are now movements on the part of agencies to introduce joint deliveries of the beer products of all four brewers, for the same ecological purpose (Miyashita 1997: 102).

Agencies have to accept the strategies of new-business-style stores. They are in the process of transforming themselves into (computer-)system-oriented wholesalers. New-style stores place severe conditions on deliveries. Small and medium-sized agencies have already lost business relations with such stores. Only major agencies making desperate efforts to survive and those that have succeeded in reducing distribution costs by computerization can meet the requirements of the new-business-style stores.

As for small and medium-sized agencies, their primary clients are ordinary retail stores other than growing-business-style stores, and service-industry-related stores, both of which are inferior to growing-style stores in competitiveness. Therefore, their business performances are affected unfavorably. Their sales quantity stagnates, and their clients urge them to grant discounts on the grounds of the destruction of the conventional price mechanism. Their sales and their profits are declining. These agencies more or less downsize themselves in their eagerness to be productive. An increasing number of agencies are involved in mergers and acquisitions (M&A) or retire from the business.

Supermarkets were given partial liquor licenses that permitted them to deal for an initial three years in Western liquors and imported beer. Afterward, the licenses were changed to full licenses that authorized them to handle any kind of alcoholic beverage. A certain chain operator did business with an agency belonging to a brewer's distribution channel under a partial license. (It did not yet handle beer.) Immediately after it obtained a full license, it demanded that the agency deliver the (beer) products of all four brewers to all the stores in the region that belonged to the chain operator. Although the agency accepted this ultimatum, the chain operator still severed business relations with it. Another agency delivered to the distribution center of one of the major convenience store chains. It was forced to make deliveries to increasingly more distant distribution centers, until finally the business relations were severed. The growing-business-style stores are now in a position to select the wholesalers with whom they want to deal.

Though these changes have taken place in regard to the distribution and sale of beer, the liquor license system remains unchanged. The three-tier framework within the beer industry, consisting of brewers, agencies, and retailers, is still in place. What has been happening is that consumers are tending to buy beer more frequently in new-business-style stores than in conventional retail stores. Brewers supply products. Agencies responsible for distribution will remain, but their functions have been declining. It appears that delivery and finance will remain their only functions. Brewers and their agencies should cooperate to improve agency sales capacity by recovering the functions of sorting products and promoting sales. When brewers are strengthening their own sales function by putting more emphasis on dealing with growing-business-style stores than with agencies, they are required to adopt a policy that will increase the number of innovative agencies and help such agencies introduce computer systems for stronger cost-competitiveness. An appropriate distribution system might allow brewers, agencies, and retailers to coexist, while meeting consumers' requirements.

Department Stores

The bubble economy was over all too soon. The annual growth rates of sales between 1991 and 1997 with 1990 as the base year were only 0.5 percent at department stores, 2.1 percent at supermarkets, and 1.5 percent at retailers overall (Table 20.9). It is obvious that the retail industry entered a low-growth era.

Sales of money-making articles in department stores, items such as paintings, jewelry and ornaments, and furniture and interior decorations, stalled. Sales in department stores continued below the level of the previous year for the forty-four months from March 1992 through October 1995. Consumption elasticity for the same period was below 1.0.

It finally dawned on everyone that department stores were obviously doing something wrong. The Japan Department Stores Association tackled busi-

Table 20.9

Growth of Sales by Style of Business

Year	Growth of sales			Consumption elasticity		Share in nationwide retail market	
	Dept. stores	Supermarkets	Retailers overall	Dept. stores	Supermarkets	Dept. stores	Supermarkets
1990 (base)	100.00	100.0	100.0	1.01	1.00	7.2	11.4
1991	104.10	106.0	106.9	0.97	0.99	7.0	11.3
1992	102.00	107.7	107.1	0.98	1.01	6.9	11.4
1993	96.00	109.2	107.4	0.94	1.01	6.5	11.6
1994	94.00	108.0	107.6	0.98	0.99	6.3	11.4
1995	91.80	110.1	108.8	0.97	1.01	6.1	11.5
1996	94.70	115.5	109.9	1.02	1.04	6.2	12.0
1997	100.40	116.0	111.0	1.05	0.99	6.5	11.9
Average annual growth (%)	0.05	2.1	1.5				

Sources: Adapted from Japan Department Stores Association, *Sales Statistics* (annual); Japan Chain Stores Association, *Sales Statistics* (annual); and MITI (Ministry of International Trade and Industry), *Census of Commerce* (annual).

ness process reengineering for all its members. Mitsukoshi took the initiative as the leading store. Gift certificates (vouchers) available for use in all department stores across the country were put on sale in 1991. Until then each member company had issued only its own gift certificates. These continued to be sold, but the common certificate was a big hit. The sales for the first year came to ¥300 billion. Department stores were finally beginning to think of things that might meet consumers' needs. For instance, they developed hangers that could be used in all stages of the distribution process, starting with a manufacturer's shipment and ending with a display of the merchandise in a department of a store. Until then, different types of hangers had been used at each stage. The introduction of new hangers reduced the number of hanger types in use from 700 to 7. It contributed to cutting labor costs by decreasing the number of people employed at each stage to replace hangers. Furthermore, actions to reduce the number of items returned by the department stores to the suppliers, or co-deliveries, though limited in number, began to be taken (JDSA 1998: 1).

In addition to business reforms, managerial reforms were carried out as well. These were exemplified by shifting finances from bank loans to capital markets, breaking away from management by family partners to management by directors, enhancing representative directors' power, and establishing a monitoring function over directors.

Meanwhile, supermarkets went through their second restructuring and new business-style retailers with chain operators became overwhelmingly strong. They were allied with some manufacturers who were aiming at diversified small-quantity merchandise lines. Their business advanced so much that they were able to adopt collective distribution by establishing distribution centers. Consumer distrust of prices picked up as discounters and specialty retailers took root. A distinction arose between the business styles of retailers who participated in and those who could not participate in the overthrow of the conventional price mechanism. Department stores belonged to the latter group.

Department stores could not overcome their cost disadvantage and found it hard to compete with their rivals. In other words, while their gross profit ratio is merely 25 percent, the labor cost ratio is high, at 10 percent. As a result their breakeven point is as high as 97 percent. Their financial structure is such that even a slight stagnation in sales puts them into the red. Moreover, they maintain conventional business practices that work against them. Suppliers reserve the right to decide merchandise lines and to decide prices in exchange for accepting returned articles. Costs related to returned articles and the costs to suppliers of employing salespersons are included in buying-in prices. In addition, these practices keep department stores from grasping consumers' needs. Thus, they lack the most basic function of retailers. Other

Table 20.10

Housing Starts

Year	Number of houses	Year-on-year change (%)
1990 (Base year)	1,707,109	102.7
1991	1,370,126	80.3
1992	1,402,590	102.4
1993	1,485,684	105.9
1994	1,570,252	105.7
1995	1,470,330	93.6
1996	1,643,266	111.8
1997	1,387,014	84.4
1998	1,198,295	86.4
1999	1,214,601	101.3
Average year-on-year change		97.4

Source: Ministry of Construction, *Housing Statistics* (annual).

problems include: there is a lack of parking space for stores located in down-town areas; sales personnel working on out-of-store sales are inclined to resort to discounts; and competition to increase credit card holders results in lower profitability.

Mitsukoshi and Takashimaya, companies with long and illustrious histories, do business primarily on the basis of their reputations and prestige. But consumer behavior has changed, affected by American material civilization. Consumers now buy whatever they want, wherever they can buy it, whether at home or abroad. As things are going now, the mission of Mitsukoshi or Takashimaya may become a thing of the past (Koyama 1997: 89).

Building Materials: Distribution

The bubble burst very suddenly. Housing starts fell in 1991 to 1.37 million, or 80.3 percent of the previous year's level, reminding people of the nightmares that followed the oil crises (Table 20.10). Supported by measures to stimulate and promote business for housing construction, housing starts rebounded to 1.64 million in 1996, meeting the industry's criterion of 1.6 million. The industry, however, fell into a serious slump in 1997 when housing starts sharply declined to 1.39 million, 84.4 percent of the previous year's

Table 20.11

Supply of Plywood (thousand square meters)

| Year | Domestic production growth | % | Import | | | | | | |
| | | | Total import growth | % | Major suppliers | | Total supply growth | % | Import's share (%) |
					Indonesia	Malaysia			
1990	997,693	100.0	417,699	100.0	407,383	1,943	1,415,392	100.0	29.5
1991	960,209	96.2	447,879	107.2	434,000	4,280	1,408,088	99.5	31.8
1992	880,191	88.2	442,451	105.9	423,690	8,053	1,322,642	93.4	33.5
1993	788,986	79.1	581,766	139.3	507,551	51,992	1,370,752	96.8	42.4
1994	719,629	72.1	512,705	122.7	420,812	67,986	1,232,334	87.1	41.6
1995	655,799	65.7	601,582	144.0	436,343	133,122	1,257,381	88.8	47.8
1996	643,487	64.5	683,517	163.6	460,624	180,466	1,327,004	93.8	51.5
1997	571,631	57.3	720,562	172.5	435,993	211,147	1,292,193	91.3	55.8

Sources: Adapted from Ministry of Agriculture, Forestry, and Fisheries, *Report on Demand for Timbers* (annual); and Ministry of Finance, *Monthly Report on Exports and Imports.*

level. In the midst of the recession in the nation's economy, they sank to 1.19 million in 1998. There is no sign of this declining trend turning upward. The slump is more serious than those following the oil crises—so serious that increasing numbers of small distributors have been going bankrupt. People have lost any hope that there will be a recovery bringing the level back up to the industry's criterion.

Of the total supply of plywood, domestically produced material has been diminishing, while imported plywood has been increasing, as indicated in Table 20.11. Imported plywood took a majority share of the market in 1996; it is usually less expensive than domestic products. Prices are inclined to drop as total demand decreases. The slump is worsening.

The industry has some structural difficulties. The major problems are:

(1) demand within the whole economy, including demand for houses, is weakening, with no sign of recovery;

(2) domestic plywood producers are inferior in cost competition to overseas competitors;

(3) distributors are burdened with price collapses and narrow margins;

(4) government has been subsidizing plywood producers that scrap facilities, and this reminds people of the situation with textile manufacturers, who used to resort frequently to such subsidies;

(5) import duties were reduced by 50 percent in January 1999, in accordance with the Uruguay Round Accord, thus giving imported materials more advantage over domestic products; and

(6) the outlook for South Sea log imports is bleak, for environmental reasons. Japan has been switching its major suppliers, as we have seen in the previous chapters. It is now looking to new suppliers such as Papua New Guinea, the Solomon Islands, or African countries, for future supply. An environmental issue, however, may come up at any time. It is also being deliberated whether or not to switch from broad-leaved trees to conifers, which grow faster. Conifers, however, have some quality problems that need to be solved.

In the face of all these structural difficulties, the viability of plywood distributors is precarious.

21
Top-Level Decision Making

The objectives of this chapter are twofold: (1) to describe decision-making processes at the highest level within Japanese organizations with specific reference to the use of *ringi*, and (2) to analyze how the decision-making power is shared, if at all, among various positions within the organization. To find answers to these questions, we obtained data through intensive interviews of those who had the position of *torishimariyaku* (member of the board of directors [to be called "director"]) or above and who were directly involved in top-level decisions.

As mentioned in Chapter 2, the board of directors, whose legal function is to represent stockholders' interests, has become a de facto executive body with most members having a position that carries specific functional responsibilities, such as president of major subsidiaries, including those abroad, and general manager of major branch offices, divisions, and even departments. Thus, board members are usually called "yakuin" or officers and constitute the top management in a well-defined hierarchy: president, vice president, senior managing director (*senmu torishimariyaku*), managing director (*jomu torishimariyaku*), and director (Figure 21.1). Nearly half of the thirty alumni belonged to this category. Of these, data from ten individuals are used for this chapter.

A separate description/analysis will be conducted for four different categories of organizations: large corporations, subsidiaries, medium-sized companies, and small family-owned business organizations. Profiles of the ten companies are provided in Table 21.1.

Large Corporations

One alumnus works in the position of managing director in charge of overseas operations for a large diversified synthetic fiber company with approxi-

Figure 21.1 **Top Management Hierarchy in Japanese Organizations**

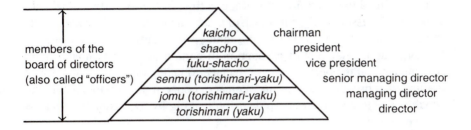

	kaicho — chairman
members of the	*shacho* — president
board of directors	*fuku-shacho* — vice president
(also called "officers")	*senmu (torishimari-yaku)* — senior managing director
	jomu (torishimari-yaku) — managing director
	torishimari (yaku) — director

Table 21.1

Profile of Ten Companies

Company	Main business	Number of employees
L-1	Synthetic fibers	50,000
L-2	Retailer	600
L-3	Retailer	12,000
S-1	Airport service	3,000
S-2	Plant engineering	2,200
S-3	International trading	40
M-1	Ink manufacturer	430
M-2	Trading	390
F-1	Plywood wholesaler	170
F-2	Bedding manufacturer	250

mately 50,000 employees both at home and abroad. He joined the company in 1963 upon graduation from the university after one year's study at Stanford University in the United States. During his thirty-five-year tenure with the company he has been appointed to increasingly important managerial positions primarily in the international area, including assignments in New York, Penang (Malaysia), Hong Kong, and London.

The company is the largest in the industry and one of the few truly globalized companies in Japan. For top-level decision making, four levels of senior management groups are involved. They are (from the top): (1) the vice presidents liaison meeting, (2) the management meeting, (3) the managing directors meeting, and (4) the board of directors meeting.

The vice presidents liaison meeting, while informal, is the most important decision-making body; it consists of the five top managers of vice president level or above (the chairman, the president, and three vice presidents). The meeting is held twice per month without a time limitation. Any and all subjects are discussed freely and decisions are made on the direction or the courses of action to be taken by the corporation. An example would be whether the corporation should start production of certain textiles in Great Britain. Any manager at the *bucho* (general manager of a department) level or above is allowed to bring a matter of his interest or concern directly to the meeting, which is an attempt to speed up decision making by bypassing deliberation at lower levels.

Below the vice presidents liaison meeting is the management meeting; it consists of those officers of *senmu torishimariyaku* (senior managing director) rank or above. This body meets once per month and makes decisions on corporate business policies or strategies. An example would be, given the corporation has decided to start operations in Great Britain, whether a new plant should be built, an existing plant should be purchased, or a joint venture should be established with a local company. Any board member is allowed to propose a policy or strategy-related issue to the meeting.

When the decision is made to build a new plant, for example, the line department that will be responsible for the operation of the plant is involved. Relevant members of the department, usually headed by a board member, write up a formal proposal (called "hatsuan-sho" rather than "ringi-sho") spelling out detailed plans for building the plant, occasionally in consultation with staff members of the management planning office.

The document is discussed at the managing directors meeting, which consists of all senior officers of *jomu torishimariyaku* (managing director) rank or above. The head of the line department in question, who is also a member of the managing directors meeting, presents the proposal before the members of the meeting. If the proposal is approved, it is forwarded to the board of directors meeting for formal approval. Although the board is the only formal decision-making body under the law, any proposal approved by the managing directors meeting obtains more or less automatic approval from the board.

In this corporation the *ringi-sho* is used, but its function is very different from what is described by Ouchi (1981) or Yoshimura and Anderson (1997). First of all, it is not a consensus-building document; rather, it is a document that spells out the plans for implementing a decision that has already been made. It does not mean, however, that implementation plans are unimportant. In fact, much time is spent on their deliberation. Second, it is written not by the lowest-working-level employee of a line department affected by the proposal, but by a staff specialist with long years of experience in the area dealt with in the proposal.

With respect to the locus of decision-making power, then, it is safe to say that in this corporation the power is centralized, in the sense that the most important decisions are made at the highest level, although inputs are accepted from middle managers and up. No formal mechanism exists for the lowest-working-level employee to participate in the corporate-wide decision-making process.

Another alumnus works for a company in the retail business. It belongs to a large conglomerate with businesses in the transportation, retail, real estate, and recreation industries. His position is managing director in charge of planning. Before joining this company he had worked for a major bank for nearly thirty years in various managerial capacities both in Japan and abroad. His initial assignment with the present company was to oversee international operations, but later his assignment shifted to planning or corporate strategy.

In this company the top-level decision-making body is called the policy meeting, which is held once per week and attended by the chairman, the president, the director of the planning office (our alumnus), and head(s) of line departments concerned with the issues to be discussed. Agenda items are determined in two ways. Top management (the chairman and the president), in consultation with the planning office, make a proposal. In this case, it is the responsibility of the planning office to collect pertinent information regarding the issues to be discussed. The line department may also bring up an issue, again after consultation with the planning office. Some of the typical issues that are discussed at the policy meeting include the starting of a new business, the opening of a new store, and the issuance of corporate bonds. In many cases issues for discussion are proposed by the top management rather than by line departments.

At the policy meeting open discussion is conducted. No formal document is prepared in advance. The purpose of the meeting, then, is to identify the pros and cons of the issue in question rather than to arrive at any decision. After an issue is reasonably well delineated, it is forwarded to the managing directors meeting (*jomukai*), a formal decision-making body of the company. A formal proposal prepared by the department concerned is presented at the meeting. Full discussion takes place and a decision is made. Among the decisions made at the managing directors meeting, important ones are forwarded to the board of directors meeting for formal approval, while less important ones do not require the board's approval. Decisions about budgets, borrowings, and credits are examples of important decisions.

When a proposal is approved at the managing directors meeting, the department concerned prepares implementation plans in the form of a *ringisho*. It is prepared by the lowest-working-level employee of the department and works its way upward. The level in the managerial hierarchy at which final approval is given depends on the amount of money involved—the larger the amount, the higher the level.

Thus, in this organization, as in the first organization discussed, top management is involved in the decision-making process from the very beginning. According to the alumnus interviewed, the decision making is "top-down," not "bottom-up." Here again, the role of the *ringi-sho* is secondary in that it is used only for making implementation plans after major decisions have already been made.

Our third alumnus also works for a large retailer that owns a chain of department stores throughout Japan. In fact, it is the oldest and largest of its kind, with over 10,000 employees. Like many other rival companies in the department store industry, this company was run by the chairman of the board almost in a dictatorial manner for a long time. Important decisions were made by the chairman and were rubber-stamped by a board of directors composed of many members handpicked by the chairman. As a result, this company was plagued by factionalism and internal turmoil.

At the time of the interview (January 1998), our alumnus was a managing director responsible for the reform of both the company and the industry, because the industry had experienced forty-four consecutive months of declining sales. Shortly thereafter, an overhaul of the company's highest-level decision-making system was completed and the new system was put into effect in March 1998. Therefore, additional information was collected in October 1998, by which time our alumnus had become an internal auditor of the company.

The main thrust of the reform was to make the decision-making process more formal and open, thereby increasing accountability to the stockholders. To that end, two new bodies were created—the management meeting and the management planning office. First of all, the management meeting was given the supreme decision-making power that had earlier been monopolized by the chairman. The meeting consists of eight top officials (the president, the senior managing director, four managing directors, and two directors) and the auditor as an observer. The management planning office is the staff organization whose main function is to prepare agenda items for the management meeting.

The head of the office (a managing director) serves as chairman of the management meeting. Proposals from line departments are forwarded to the management planning office for processing. Those proposals with corporate-wide implications are directed to the management meeting, while more specific proposals are directed to individual executives with the authority to approve them.

Proposals from line departments take the form of *ringi-sho*. They are drafted by the lowest-working-level employee of the department concerned and work their way upward to the general manager, who, in turn, brings them to the management planning office. Thus, in this company the stereo-typical *ringi* method is used more or less.

It is the responsibility of the auditor (our alumnus) to report to the president whether the management meeting was conducted in a proper manner, and, if necessary, to make recommendations on how to improve deliberations at the meeting. Decisions at the management meeting are conveyed to the board of directors meeting, some for formal approval and others simply as reporting items. Here, the auditor's job is to make all information available to the board of directors meeting.

Thus, in this company attempts have been made to decentralize the power that, until recently, has been monopolized by the chairman and is now shared by the eight senior officers. In addition, as a means of bottom-up decision making, the *ringi* method in the traditional sense has been implemented. To what extent these mechanisms are effective remains to be seen.

Subsidiaries

One alumnus has been working for a subsidiary of a major airline company since 1992, first as managing director and later as senior managing director in charge of corporate planning. Prior to the transfer (or *tenseki*, to be explained in chapter 22) to this subsidiary, this alumnus had worked for the parent company for thirty years in the areas of cargo marketing and industrial relations both at home and abroad. His last position with the parent company was general manager in charge of cargo marketing.

The main business of this subsidiary is to provide ground services at airports to the parent company in three areas—loading baggage and cargo onto the airplane, unloading them from the airplane, and cleaning the airplane both inside and out—which are highly labor-intensive operations. The company employs approximately 3,000 people working in five major domestic airports, with the headquarters at Haneda Airport. The parent company owns 85 percent of its stocks, and 95 percent of the company's sales are to the parent company, indicating very heavy dependence on the parent company. The parent company controls this subsidiary through its Affiliated Businesses Division.

Four bodies are involved in the top-level decision making in this company. They are the Affiliated Businesses Division of the parent company, the board of directors meeting, the internal directors meeting, and the general managers meeting. First of all, the parent company's Affiliated Businesses Division, acting on the basis of the company's mid-range plans to make the group companies' operations more cost competitive, gives the subsidiary directions to follow in major areas such as corporate restructuring. These directions are studied by the department in charge of the matter in collaboration with other departments that will be affected by the direction when it is implemented. The major objective of such an exercise is to identify problem areas, if any, when a change is introduced in individual work units.

These matters are fully discussed at the internal directors meeting, consisting of the chairman, the president, and ten other top executives, all internal members of the board of directors, and this meeting makes the de facto decision. This group meets once a month on a regular basis. Some matters are forwarded to the full board of directors meeting for formal approval, while others are not. The board of directors consists of twelve internal members and two external members, the latter sent from the parent company. The board meets once every three months on a regular basis.

Another body that plays an important role in decision making on the issues that originate internal to the subsidiary is the general managers meeting. They meet twice per month to deliberate on issues that are brought up from individual departments and that have company-wide implications. When an agreement is arrived at on the policies for each issue, they are referred to the internal directors meeting for approval. As mentioned above, some issues are forwarded to the full board meeting, while others are not. For example, the creation of, or additional investment in, a subsidiary needs the approval of the full board, while the budget does not.

With respect to the *ringi* system, it seems that the traditional method is used in that the lowest-working-level employee drafts a proposal that works its way upward. It is used for three different purposes. If the impact of the proposal is largely limited to the department in question, it is eventually approved by a single executive with the authority to do so. If the proposal has company-wide implications, it is forwarded to the general managers meeting through the head (general manager) of the department where the proposal originates. Finally, when a decision is made at the internal directors meeting, a proposal for implementation is drafted by a junior member of the relevant department and works its way upward for approval.

It appears that the basic directions for this company are determined by the parent company. What the top management of this subsidiary does is to translate those directions into specific policies and to strike a balance between the demands of the parent company and those of the rank-and-file members of the company. In this sense, the *ringi* system works as a useful bottom-up communication channel.

The second alumnus works as managing director in charge of marketing and sales for a wholly owned subsidiary of a major chemical company. This subsidiary was created in 1996 as a result of the merger of two subsidiary companies, one of which was owned by a chemical company, the other by a petrochemical company, both belonging to the same former *zaibatsu.* So when these two parent companies merged, the two subsidiaries also merged. At the time of the merger, the new company's corporate philosophy, mid-range plans (three years), and long-range plans (five years) were created after lengthy deliberation. Since then, the company has been operating within these frameworks.

Our alumnus had worked for one of the parent companies (the petrochemical company) for thirty years, primarily in the area of marketing and sales. His last position was general manager of the company's Nagoya branch. In 1992 he was transferred (by *shukko*) to the company's engineering subsidiary before the merger as director in charge of marketing and sales.

Asked about the reasons for his transfer to the subsidiary, our alumnus replies:

> The real reason is unclear. My guess is that since this company's management consisted entirely of those with engineering backgrounds, there was a need for someone with a different expertise. Also, there was a need to become somewhat more independent from the parent company, with stronger marketing and sales functions. Since I had wide experience in sales and general management dealing with both plastics and chemicals, as well as assignments in Tokyo, Osaka, and Nagoya, I was chosen to head the marketing and sales department of the subsidiary.

The main business of this subsidiary is to provide customers with engineering and maintenance services. Approximately 40 percent of its business is with the parent company and its group companies, while the remaining 60 percent is with other companies. The company has about 2,200 employees—800 in engineering, 1,200 in maintenance, and 200 in various functions covering both areas. In terms of sales, however, three-quarters are from engineering, and the remaining one-quarter, from maintenance.

The company's top management team consists of sixteen members: chairman, president, vice president, five managing directors, and eight directors. Major decisions are made by the *jomukai* (or managing directors meeting), consisting of eight members who are managing directors or above managing director. Our alumnus, overseeing the company's marketing and sales functions, is a member of this group; it meets once per week. Agenda items are proposed by four line departments—two engineering, maintenance and construction, and marketing and sales—each headed by a managing director. Proposals are forwarded to the general administration department, which is also headed by a managing director. This staff department makes adjustments among the proposals and prepares agenda for weekly meetings.

At the weekly *jomukai* participants freely express their views on agenda items. When it comes to decision making, no vote is taken; rather, a consensus style is adopted. In reality, however, the president's voice carries heavy weight. It appears that in this company the president makes final decisions in consultation with the members of the top management team.

There is no representative from the parent company at the managing directors meeting. In fact, there is no attempt by the parent company to interfere with the subsidiary's business operations. The former's interest is limited to financial matters, as they adopt a consolidated balance sheet system together with a number of subsidiaries, including this subsidiary. Figures on items such as profits and retained earnings need to be approved in advance by the parent company.

In this company, *ringi* proposals do not play an important role in decision making at the top management level. Instead, informal discussion/negotiation (or *nemawashi*) is used for the adjustment of positions on agenda items among *jomukai* members. After a decision is made, a formal *ringi-sho* is circulated to iron out details, including the amount of money to be spent on each approved item. Thus, a *ringi-sho* is used to spell out implementation plans on the issues that have already been decided.

Our third alumnus heads a small trading company that is a wholly owned subsidiary of the largest construction (or the so-called earth-moving) machine manufacturer in Japan. This subsidiary is staffed by several dozen employees, virtually all of whom have been transferred out (by *shukko*) from the Overseas Operations Division of the parent company. Our alumnus had been working for the parent company for more than thirty years, primarily in the international area, including assignments in Sydney, London, and Frankfurt. His last position with the parent company was general manager of the Plastics Business Department of the New Businesses Creation Division. When the Plastics Business Department was dissolved in 1994, he was transferred (by *shukko*) to the present company as its president. The usual practice of the parent company was that those who have reached fifty-five years of age without having been promoted to membership of the board of directors are transferred, either by *shukko* or *tenseki*, to a company's subsidiary. Such practices were considered necessary to keep the senior management relatively young in age while, at the same time, maintaining the seniority-based pyramidal management structure of the company.

The subsidiary to which our alumnus was transferred as president is a trading company that had been created in the mid-1980s. It was created to seize increasingly attractive importing opportunities due to increases in the value of the yen, as well as to make use of increasingly redundant personnel involved in exporting and importing, which were quickly replaced by offshore production. Its main business was the overseas procurement of supply materials, the export of diesel engines, and the export and import of parts and components of earth-moving equipment. At one point, the company imported items that included luxury sailboats, paintings, and apparel. However, such businesses did not make any profitable contribution; therefore, when our alumnus took over the company, it stopped handling such items and instead concentrated on its main items: attachments to construction machines and maintenance goods.

Being a small company, the top management team consists of six people, including the president, vice president, and four external board members who are general managers of related departments of the parent company. This group (the board of directors) meets twice per year to prepare annual reports and business plans within the framework of the mid-range plan, which is formulated on the basis of the long-range plan established by the parent company. The company's mid-range plan or objective is to increase sales and profits every year. To that end the company either expands the territory in which existing commodities are traded or introduces new commodities in existing territories.

The company's performance is monitored by the parent company through a department whose function is to oversee the operation of affiliated companies or subsidiaries. Thus, although this subsidiary's formal decision-making body is its board of directors, as mentioned above, its financial statements for the current year as well as the budgets for the next year require prior review by the parent company before they are formally approved at the subsidiary's board meeting. Furthermore, the company is required to submit to the parent company a mid-year report, including the prospects for the second half of the year. If a profit is expected, the company is allowed to proceed with the annual plans established at the beginning of the year. However, if a loss is expected, revisions to the annual plans are required so that a profit may be achieved at the end of the year.

The parent company's concern is limited to the financial outcomes of the subsidiary; it does not extend to the internal operations of the subsidiary, including the formulation of annual business plans. Since board meetings are held only twice a year and each meeting lasts for only about half an hour, major decisions are made by the president in consultation with individual external director(s) directly concerned with the issue(s) in question. Their interest is limited to matters related to the operation of the parent company departments that they head.

Proposals for annual business plans originate both from the president and from below (managers). Usually, proposals for such matters as new customers (or business connections), new merchandise, new territories, organizational changes, and personnel issues are made by the president. In particular, proposals for downsizing have to come from the president. Managers may propose any new business so long as it is judged profitable. It is, however, the responsibility of the president to formulate a proposal and obtain a formal approval at a board meeting.

The *ringi-sho* is used in this company for the purpose of documenting decisions that have already been made, or of spelling out monetary transactions—the amount of money that each manager is authorized to handle, that is involved in contracts with customers and agents, or that is transmitted to overseas offices of the parent company. The *ringi-sho* starts from the department managers, not the lowest-level employee, and is approved by the president. Such documentation is required for auditing by tax authorities and also by the parent company.

Thus, the internal decision-making mechanism of this company is such that the president takes an active role. He makes important decisions in consultation with individual board member(s) and by taking into consideration proposals from managers when deemed appropriate. The *ringi* system is used not for decision making but for the documentation of decisions, primarily for external auditing purposes.

Medium-Sized Companies

One of the two companies to be examined in this section is engaged in the manufacture and sale of ink. Our alumnus joined this company after a stormy career experience. Like most other alumni covered in this study, this alumnus also joined a large corporation—an electric machine manufacturer—upon graduation from the university. But after a few years he quit this company to succeed to his father's business. He diversified the business to found a plastic modeling company. However, the company became a victim of the first oil crisis of 1973 and it went bankrupt in 1976. It took him a year and a half to liquidate the company. After a year's stint with a consumer loan company, he joined this ink manufacturing company in 1979 through the introduction of a friend—one of the thirty alumni involved in this study.

He decided to join the company because it possessed unique technologies and had succeeded in developing EV ink suitable for offset printing—a niche market that large companies had neglected to penetrate. When he joined, the company employed slightly less than 300 employees and had a sales share of approximately 10 percent in the paste-type ink market. It was a private company owned and run by a family. For the first year he was assigned to a planning office where he was given the opportunity to study the overall operation of the company. He was soon promoted to section manager in charge of raw material procurement and foreign operations.

The company owned joint-venture plants in Hong Kong, South Korea, and Indonesia. In 1983 he was sent to Indonesia to head the joint-venture plant as its president. He successfully introduced Japanese-style factory management, which the local employees readily accepted. Upon returning to Japan in 1989, our alumnus was promoted to general manager in charge of material procurement and overseas operations. In 1995 he was appointed a member of the board of directors as director in charge of international operations, a position he has held to date.

In 1997 the company became an open corporation whose stocks have come to be traded on the over-the-counter market. The top management team of this company consists of the chairman (the founder), the president (the chairman's son), a senior managing director (formerly with a bank), and two managing directors—one in charge of sales and the other in charge of technology and plants—as well as a dozen directors, each in charge of a specific function (such as overseas operations in the case of our alumnus).

There are two methods of decision making with respect to issues that are of major importance to the company. The first is an informal officers meeting that is called by the president and attended by the officers (directors) for whom the issue is relevant. A thorough discussion takes place and a decision is reached. This method is used when the issue and the decision on it need not be documented. These informal meetings take place when necessary, with the frequency ranging from once every two to three months to twice a month.

On the other hand, if documentation is needed, the *ringi* system is used. A *ringi* proposal is initiated by one of the general managers, most of whom are directors, or someone of a higher level. Section managers and below are not involved in the *ringi* process. Often an important issue cuts across more than one department. As a result, it is more usual that two or more departments, instead of one, propose a joint *ringi*. Sometimes the president gives an order to a relevant officer to study an issue with company-wide implications and to formulate a proposal in a *ringi* format. The final authority to approve a *ringi* proposal rests with the president. The board of directors meetings are held three times a year to formally approve the decisions already made by the methods mentioned above. The *jomukai* meetings are held once a month, primarily for information exchange.

As a director and the general manager in charge of overseas operations, our alumnus is responsible for the following activities: (1) production in joint-venture plants in South Korea, Indonesia, and Hong Kong, and sales in the local markets as well as exports to other Southeast Asian countries; (2) monitoring local production by a British company and a New Zealand company conducted by cross-license agreements and their sales in the local markets, as well as exports to European countries and to Australia; (3) providing technical assistance to the end users (adjustment of the ink mixture to suit their printing machines and papers) through the overseas joint ventures and local dealers; and (4) purchasing raw materials on behalf of the overseas licensees.

Our alumnus makes decisions by himself on the above matters if they are routine in nature. For nonroutine matters he consults the president (his immediate superior). If an issue involves technical elements he consults the managing director in charge of technology. He recalls:

> With regard to cross-licensing with a British and a New Zealand company, my proposal was not approved for the first year or so because of strong opposition from the technical people. But gradually they came to understand the advantages of cross-licensing and agreed to my proposal. Now they enjoy associating with foreign engineers and exchanging technical ideas with the help of my interpreting!

In regard to bottom-up management and consensus management, he has this to say:

> In a medium-sized company like ours it is important for top management to have clear-cut ideas about the future direction and to build a consensus around it. It is unrealistic to expect a good idea with company-wide implications to emerge from the bottom and to build a consensus as it moves upward.

In contrast to this alumnus, another alumnus had worked for a large general trading company for thirty years or so, specializing in the synthetic resin business, and had smoothly moved up the ladders of promotion. In 1992, when he was deputy general manager in a department dealing with synthetic resin, he was scouted and offered a senior management position with a medium-sized trading company dealing primarily with chemical products. It was a difficult decision for him, but with strong urging from a close friend, he decided to take the offer.

The company, headquartered in Fukui City, started as a wholesaler of dyes whose end users were small and medium-sized textile companies in the north-central region (called Hokuriku) of Japan. The company expanded its lines of business to include all kinds of chemical products, both nonorganic and organic, including synthetic resin and (more recently) computer hardware and software. The company has also expanded geographically by establishing branch offices in large cities such as Tokyo, Osaka, and Nagoya, as well as overseas offices in Hong Kong, Singapore, Shanghai, Bangkok, and Jakarta. When our alumnus joined the company, it employed approximately 330 people (now it has about 400). It, too, was (and still is) an open corporation whose stocks are traded on the over-the-counter market.

He was first appointed general manager in charge of chemical products and also of the Tokyo office. The following year he was elected to the board of directors, and since 1995 he has been a managing director in charge of the Pacific coast side (i.e., not the Sea of Japan side) of domestic operations as well as all overseas operations.

The top management team of the company consists of the chairman, the president, a senior managing director, two managing directors, and five directors, all with functional responsibilities. All directors except our alumnus operate from the company's headquarters in Fukui City; our alumnus oversees the above-mentioned operations from the branch office in Tokyo.

The company's highest decision-making body is the board meeting (usually called the *yakuinkai,* or officers meeting), because all directors possess functional or operating responsibilities as general managers of divisions or departments. The officers meeting is held on a weekly basis for two purposes: reporting and decision making. Agenda items are rather loosely set. Some are set by the chairman and the president, while some others are proposed from below in the form of *ringi.* According to the alumnus, officers meetings last many hours, sometimes degenerating into a less formal meeting. As a rule, each issue is thoroughly discussed until a decision is reached. Although the chairman and the president do not take a strong position from the beginning, a meeting of these two persons' minds is a precondition for decision making.

The *jomukai,* consisting of the chairman, the president, a senior managing director, and two managing directors, meets less frequently and in a more informal manner. Topics are limited to key company issues such as appointments of directors and major investments. No decision is made at a *jomukai* meeting.

In this company the *ringi* system is widely used, recently by means of the e-mail system. Depending on the nature of the issue, a *ringi* proposal may be initiated by a nonmanagerial employee, a section manager, a general manager, a director, or even a managing director. Final approval is made at different levels of management, again depending on the content of the *ringi* proposal. Usually a *ringi* proposal involving a lower level of management is of a routine nature; for example, a section manager may request approval for concluding a sales agreement involving an amount of money exceeding his authority. On the other hand, in the case of an issue important to the company, for example, a major investment project abroad, the president directs a general manager of the relevant department to formulate a *ringi* that is to be fully discussed at an officers meeting.

As a managing director in charge of the chemical product division, our alumnus is responsible for domestic sales, exporting, importing, and trading between third nations of chemical products. For him the most important issues for decision making include overseas investment and the opening up of overseas offices. He seeks approval on these issues by submitting *ringi* proposals to an officers meeting.

From his experiences with the two companies where he has worked, this alumnus rejects the argument that Japanese-style decision making is characterized by consensus decision making and bottom-up decision making. He concludes:

> Decision-making methods vary according to the issues involved and the circumstances surrounding the issues; therefore, it is wrong to assume that there is a uniform and uniquely Japanese style that is applicable to all cases.

Small Family-Owned Companies

One alumnus, since graduation from the university in 1962, has worked for a family-owned business that had been founded by his uncle. The company, which employs about 170 people, is a wholesaler of plywood and other construction materials. At the time of the interview in 1997, this alumnus was senior managing director of the company assisting the president (his cousin) and overseeing the entire operation of the company.

For a wholesaler, sales plans are the most important objective of strategic decisions. On the basis of a five-year plan, annual plans are formulated and the degree of achievement is monitored. The format of the annual sales plan has been developed over the years by a working group led by the managing director in charge of sales. The forms are distributed to fourteen branch offices throughout the eastern half of Japan (the company's business territory) and filled out by the branch managers of those offices.

The fourteen sales plans are sent to the managing director and scrutinized by him, by the senior managing director (our alumnus), and by the president. After this, they are integrated into a single corporate sales plan, which, in turn, is forwarded to the full board of directors meeting, consisting of the three top managers mentioned above and three directors in charge of sales in three districts. At the board meeting, a full discussion takes place until a consensus emerges. If the group has failed to arrive at a consensus, the president has the final authority to make a decision. Although the former president (the founder) sometimes exercised this authority because he had charismatic power, the current president highly values consensus decision making or decisions by agreement of all members.

Once the annual sales plan is formally approved by the board, it becomes the responsibility of three directors, who serve as district general managers, to achieve the plan. To that end they closely monitor sales performance within their own districts and solve problems when they occur. In spite of these efforts, sometimes sales goals are not met. It is the view of our alumnus that the reason is not poor planning but the lack of sales abilities of the people who carry out the plan. The solution, then, lies in the constant upgrading of employees' abilities by means of company-sponsored education and training.

It appears that in this company annual sales plans are used in similar fashion to the *ringi-sho*. They originate somewhere around the branch managers' level and work their way upward. However, they are different from a *ringi-sho* in that the lowest-level employees are apparently not involved in their formulation, because under the ideal *ringi* system they should have no serious difficulty in achieving the goals to which they are committed.

It is also apparent that, at the top management level, decisions are made by consensus, while under the former president, this was not necessarily the case. It is interesting to note that our alumnus implies that consensus decision making takes place due to the lack of charisma on the part of the second-generation president.

The second alumnus started working for his wife's family business in 1980 after eighteen years of work experience with a major ceramics company, primarily in international sales. It was a bedding manufacturer/wholesaler with a 100-year history, and one of four major companies in the industry with about 250 employees.

One year after joining the company, he became director in charge of planning and development in 1981, managing director in charge of merchandising in 1987, and senior managing director in charge of sales in 1991. In 1994 he left the company when his nephew took over the company presidency.

During this time, as a member of the top management team, he was involved in the formulation of the company's mid-range strategies every two to three years so as to provide organization-wide directions. The management planning office, with a staff of ten, was responsible for the formulation of strategies. Since the office was short-staffed, individual strategies were formulated on a project basis in which not only the management planning office staff but also those outside the office with expertise on the issues in question were asked to participate. When necessary, consulting companies were used as well.

The company's management planning office had the authority to formulate individual strategies or projects, and our alumnus, who was director in charge of this office, had the final power to make decisions. In arriving at a formal decision he had his project members spell out their opinions, thereby enabling him to find the common ground. Then, by adding his own ideas, the project plans were finalized.

It was important to fully explain the plan to the line manager responsible for its implementation so that he would thoroughly understand and implement the plan without any reservations. The most effective way of explaining, according to our alumnus, is an informal talk on a personal and individual basis; formal explanation in meetings is not effective and results in only superficial acceptance. Therefore, occasionally it took a long time, even several months, before his explanation was fully accepted. But it was worth the effort, according to our alumnus.

The process of implementing the projects was closely monitored and reported to the board meeting, which in turn would evaluate each case. Those projects whose progress was judged to be poor were terminated. It was considered important to make a decision either to continue with or terminate a project after a certain period of time.

In this company a staff department plays an important role in strategy formulation wherever the *ringi* system does not seem to be used. However, an important element of *ringi* is utilized; that is, abundant time is spent on "selling" a project to the people responsible for its implementation. This practice assumes a certain psychological principle: the internalization of a decision is a strong motivator for people to perform. This means that the mere ordering of a higher-level decision does not ensure successful implementation of the decision at the lower level of the organization.

The *ringi* system was extensively used, however, for different purposes. It was used, for example, for the approval of any expenses in excess of ¥100,000 or for the approval of the conclusion of a contract involving a certain amount of money or less, specifying terms and conditions of the contract such as methods of payment and/or collection. Thus, it appears that the company used the *ringi* primarily for routine decisions.

In the preceding sections we have examined decision making at the top management level in ten organizations—three large companies, three subsidiaries, two medium-sized companies, and two family-owned companies. There are a number of findings on the use of *ringi*.

First, the *ringi* system was used in nine out of ten cases; information was not available from one organization. Thus, it may be said that the use of *ringi* is quite widespread. Second, it appears that different types of *ringi* are used at different levels of an organization. The *ringi* may be differentiated in terms of who writes it and who makes the final approval. Thus, some *ringi* documents are written by a lower-ranking employee and approved by a general manager of the department, while others are written by a manager of the section and approved by a director. Still other types are written by a staff specialist and approved by a senior-level decision-making body such as a managing directors meeting.

In spite of these differences, one thing is common among all types of *ringi*, that is, whoever actually writes it, a decision to initiate a *ringi* comes from the higher-level management or management group. They also provide the general directions as well as the specific framework within which a *ringi* is written. These practices tend to support the argument of Yoshimura and Anderson that a *ringi* is a form of "window dressing."

Third, the *ringi* is used for different purposes. It seems that a large number of *ringi* are used for routine decisions, while a relatively small number of *ringi* are used for nonroutine decisions. The *ringi* is also used to spell out the plans for implementing a decision that has already been made. Rarely is the *ringi-sho* used for making major decisions with company-wide implications, for example, decisions on corporate strategy.

The use of *ringi* for routine decisions supports neither the consensus-building function suggested by Ouchi nor the motivational function suggested by Yoshimura and Anderson. Rather, the main function seems to be documentation or record keeping. In the Japanese corporate culture, where informal and verbal communication is highly valued, the *ringi-sho* is a useful device for documentation that is necessary for future review or audit of various decisions, especially those involving monetary transactions.

In only two cases is the *ringi* system used as a method of genuine participation in nonroutine decision making by lower-level employees. But these two cases represent a rather unique situation in that both organizations need a sort of "countervailing power" against dominance from above— in one case the Chairman of the Board and in the second case the parent company.

The above discussion suggests that the *ringi* plays a rather limited role in making company-wide decisions at the top management level. Instead, various kinds of executive meetings (or committees) play a dominant role. Although the board of directors meeting is the only legally sanctioned body, its decision-making power is severely curtailed for the following reasons.

Because the separation of ownership and management has gone to an extreme in Japan, the appointment to membership on the board of directors is made by the president, who is the chief executive officer in most Japanese corporations. The president's decision is more or less automatically approved at the annual stockholders meeting. The chairman of the board often becomes a nominal position that is usually filled by the retired former president. Board members usually carry functional responsibilities. Thus, the board meeting becomes a de facto executive body that is under the control of the president.

In large corporations the size of the board is disproportionately large, often consisting of several dozen members. Such a large board cannot function as an efficient executive body. Therefore, several layers of executive meetings (or committees) are created with increasingly restrictive (and therefore smaller) membership, such as meetings with managing directors and above (*jomukai*), with senior managing directors and above, and with vice president(s) and above.

A useful frame of reference in analyzing the decision-making style in the above regime is the decision tree model, first proposed by Vroom and Yetton in 1973 (see Chapter 2). In the model, they identify five types of decision-making styles on the basis of the degree of subordinates' participation. Among them the following two are directly relevant: (1) the manager shares the problem with subordinates as a group, obtaining their collective ideas and suggestions, and then makes the decision himself (to be called "consultative style"); and (2) the manager shares the problem with subordinates as a group, and serves in the role of a chairman engaging the group in consensus, seeking to arrive at a decision, which decision he is willing to accept (to be called "consensus style").

Although Vroom and Yetton identify a set of conditions to determine the best solution, in our interviews it was not possible to obtain information on a decision-by-decision basis. Instead, the following two factors seem to account for the difference in the decision-making style: the type of industry and the power of the president in the top management team.

It seems that the consensus style is used in manufacturing and transportation industries, while the consultative style is used in trading and service industries. This may be a reflection of differences in how much time is required for decision making. Faster decision making is required in trading and service; therefore, the consultative style, which is less time consuming, is preferred. Furthermore, if the president has charisma or some other sources of power such as age and seniority, the consultative rather than the consensus style is adopted. The size of the organization does not seem to have any bearing on the decision-making style.

In conclusion, this chapter shows that bottom-up decision making by using the *ringi* system is an oversimplification of decision making at the top-management level. Top-level decisions are made by top-level managers with or without input from below. The companies studied use a variety of mechanisms and arrangements, both formal and informal, in an attempt to make the "best" decisions and to implement them effectively and efficiently. A *ringi-sho* is only one such device, and its primary objective had more to do with the implementation of a decision that has already been made than with decision making itself.

22
Late Career Diversity

This chapter deals with the late career stages of our alumni covering the eight-year period beginning in 1991 and ending in 1998. It corresponds to the age range of the early to late fifties of our alumni. This period is somewhat shorter than the one suggested by Schein (1978)—age forty until retirement. This is because, under the Japanese length-of-service system, managers' late career stages begin rather late, a reflection of the fact that managers' career progress continues, on average, through their forties and into their early fifties, and that during this period managers' work involvement remains very high.

According to Schein, late career stages consist of two substages—the late career stage in a narrow sense and the decline and disengagement stage. At the first substage, some people may fulfill leadership roles such as general manager, officer, senior partner, or senior staff, while others may fulfill nonleadership roles such as key member and individual contributor.

By 1990, a total of ten alumni had left their original employers at various stages of their careers. The experiences of some of them have been given in earlier chapters. As of 1991, they held the jobs shown in Table 22.1. They are listed in the order of resignation from their original employers.

With the exception of Case 6, resignations took place either in the early career stage, when the alumni were in their twenties or early thirties, or in a late stage after more than twenty-five years of service with the original employers. In the last three cases (Cases 8, 9, and 10) they were transferred out (by *shukko*) to subsidiaries, thereby maintaining a connection with the original employers, as mentioned in Chapter 16. All alumni except Cases 2 and 8 held various management positions with private companies. Cases 4 and 7 were employed by foreign-owned firms in Japan, while Cases 5 and 8 were working overseas (Manila and Jakarta, respectively).

Table 22.1

Status of Leavers

Case	Original employer	Year of resignation	Occupation in 1991
1	Electric machine company	1966	General manager, international operations, chemical company
2	Petrochemical company	1966	Academic
3	Steel company	1969	Founder and president, employment agency
4	University	1970	General manager, personnel, foreign food company
5	General trading company	1970	General manager, overseas subsidiary
6	Ceramics company	1980	Senior managing director, family business
7	Chemical company	1987	General manager, planning, foreign chemical company
8	Petrochemical company	1987	Educational consultant, subsidiary
9	Electric machine company	1989	Assistant general manager, subsidiary
10	General trading company	1990	Vice president, subsidiary

The remaining twenty alumni were still working for their original companies in various managerial capacities. The breakdown of these twenty alumni by the positions they held at the beginning of 1991 is shown in Table 22.2.

Of the nineteen alumni working for private corporations, three were top managers (including the one working for a family business), while the remaining sixteen were upper middle managers. As mentioned above, the three alumni (Cases 8, 9, and 10 in Table 22.1) had been transferred out by *shukko* to subsidiaries of their original employers. As we will see later in this chapter, this tendency accelerated during this period. While some were transferred to subsidiaries as senior officers (directors and above), others changed jobs either to pursue general management positions of higher responsibility or to settle for positions with limited responsibilities.

We will provide a few typical cases for each of the following three types of male careers: (1) careers with foreign-owned firms, (2) overseas careers, and (3) later careers of stayers (as of 1998).

Table 22.2

Status of Twenty Stayers

Position in 1991	Number
Member of the board of directors	3
General manager of a department in the main office	7
General manager of a domestic branch office	2
General manager of an overseas branch office	1
Deputy general manager of a department in the main office	3
Deputy general manager of an overseas branch office	1
Unspecified middle management position	2
Other (executive counselor with an economic association)	1
Total	20

Careers with Foreign-Owned Firms

In this period five alumni were working for foreign-owned subsidiaries in Japan in various managerial capacities. The first alumnus was general manager of public relations with a wholly owned subsidiary of a U.S.-based oil company that he had joined upon graduation from the university. He was the only one of thirty alumni who opted to work for a foreign company. As to his reasons for choosing this company he recalls: "I had an aspiration to become an international business person. Besides, the high starting salary was very attractive. The foreign ownership of this company did not bother me at all."

This company was one of a few wholly owned subsidiaries of foreign companies that were established shortly after World War II, when the Ministry of International Trade and Industry did not exercise strong control over foreign investment. Being a well-established foreign company in Japan, business and management practices of this company were a blend of U.S. and Japanese practices. The company followed U.S. practices in reflecting stockholders' interest in the management of the company—seeking a high return on investment. Naturally, the parent company's control over the Japanese subsidiary was based on the latter's performance measured in terms of return on investment. This means that, as long as performance met the level acceptable to headquarters, the subsidiary was allowed a high degree of autonomy.

For this reason, there were elements of Japanese-style management practiced in this subsidiary. First of all, although the *ringi* system was not adopted in decision making, there were elements of bottom-up and consensus decision making. For example, as a general manager in charge of public relations, our alumnus held weekly departmental meetings in which he shared information with all members of his department and followed up on work progress. He met with his subordinates who were in managerial positions whenever necessary to share information and to discuss methods of implementation of the decisions already made. Second, long-term employment was customary. In fact, our alumnus worked for this company for thirty-four years until 1996, when he took an early retirement.

Through his thirty-four years of services with the company, this alumnus had accumulated experiences in a number of functional areas, including sales, marketing, finance, and public relations, suggesting that he was anchored in management competence. However, it seems more appropriate to classify him as having been anchored in technical/functional competence, for the following two reasons. First, he spent a total of eleven years in public relations, including the final seven years as a general manager, thereby establishing himself as a specialist in public relations. Second, after an "early retirement" from the original employer, he took a job with a consulting company that specialized in providing advice to corporate clients on how to deal with mass media.

The second alumnus followed a very different career path from that of the first alumnus. As mentioned in Chapter 7, this alumnus had started an academic career, switched to a research job with the Tokyo branch of an international organization, and then to a consulting company specializing in international human resource management, before joining a foreign firm in 1986. The latter was the Tokyo branch of a major U.S.-based bank, and his job as personnel manager involved him in hiring a large number of employees to expand the operation (until the "Black Monday of October 1987"), and afterward in firing about an equal number of employees. Our alumnus quit the job after two years, as this bank was "too short-term oriented" and its employment policy too "cold-blooded" for him.

In the early 1990s, he worked for another foreign company—a wholly owned subsidiary of a large U.S. food processing company. As an assistant to the president, he was primarily responsible for personnel administration. General administration including contract administration was also part of his job. According to our alumnus, this company represented the traditional type of U.S. multinational company, with a long chain of command and centralization of the decision-making authority.

The chain of command originated in the U.S. headquarters, through the regional director in Sydney (a Canadian), to the chairman of the Japanese subsidiary (British), and to the president (Japanese), and layers of management. The key decisions were made in the U.S. headquarters; the Japanese subsidiary was not given autonomy to conduct "local marketing," for example. Prices of the company's products in Japan as well as in other countries were set by the U.S. headquarters. Our alumnus was frustrated by the fact that prices in Japan were set at such a high level that the Japanese subsidiary was unable to compete with rival Japanese companies.

After four years he left this company for another foreign firm—this time a subsidiary of a British manufacturer of lubricants, where he was director in charge of general administration and personnel, as well as assistant to the president. Although the parent company was a manufacturer of lubricants, the Japanese subsidiary was not involved in the production, which was consigned to Japanese petroleum refining companies. The Japanese consignors produced lubricants according to a specification (or formula) provided by the company, and the products were shipped from the consignors' plants directly to the customers. In this way, the Japanese subsidiary did not have to own production facilities or storage tanks.

According to our alumnus, this type of operation was typical of certain multinational corporations. He found that the company followed the British colonial style of management—complete indigenization of management by locals as long as the local operation was profitable. His specific responsibility was to build an organizational structure in such a way as to reflect the goals and objectives of the parent company, and, at the same time, to function smoothly under Japanese legislation and customs. According to him, it would take about three years to build a personnel system. He says, "Building a new system is fun. But maintaining one is not so exciting." He worked for the company for four years until 1996, when relocation of the company's office made it necessary for him to spend two and a half hours commuting. After a two-year stint with a Japanese consulting company, he joined another foreign company, this time a subsidiary of a Canadian-based company.

Asked about the reasons for his frequent job changes, primarily among foreign companies, he replied:

> In a foreign company there is no promotion from within at the general manager level or above. Therefore, in order to obtain a higher salary, one has to move to a new company that makes a higher salary offer. I never attempted to "join" a company; instead, I chose an occupation, that of human resource specialist, and attempted to upgrade and sell my marketable skills to any company interested in making use of my skills.

Throughout his professional history, following eight years of graduate work in industrial relations in both Japan and the United States, his career has been anchored in technical/functional competence in the field of human resource management. His career pattern is in sharp contrast to the typical pattern characterized by strong orientation toward general management and organizational security.

The earlier career history of the third alumnus was briefly discussed in Chapter 16. This alumnus quit a large chemical company in 1987 after serving the company for twenty-five years. When an offer was made by a British-based worldwide chemical company, he did not hesitate to accept it, because it would give him a challenging opportunity to test his abilities in a truly worldwide company. Our alumnus worked primarily in the company's Japanese subsidiary as general manager of the planning department. He was engaged in the formulation of long-range (ten-year) strategic plans as well as in market research related to plastic resin products.

He was with this company for five years until 1992, when he was scouted again: this time to become president of the Japanese subsidiary of a European-based multinational company engaged in manufacturing and selling consumer and industrial containers, including steel drums. The parent company had been planning to start production in Japan of steel drums to be sold to chemical and petroleum companies. To head the Japanese operation, they had been looking for someone who had experience in the chemical and/or petroleum industries, and who was also familiar with the organizational cultures of foreign companies. He was the perfect candidate for the position. An offer was made through a friend, and he accepted the offer.

His immediate responsibility was to establish a Japanese company whose business was to conclude original equipment manufacturing (OEM) agreements with Japanese companies to consign the production of steel drums under the parent company's license and to sell the drums to Japanese customers. His next job was to build a plant for the company to produce steel drums on its own. The plant was recently completed, and, according to the alumnus, the company's business has been going well. His career experiences suggest that he has been anchored in management competence but not in organizational security—a typical career pattern in Japan. It may well be that his managerial success was achieved at the expense of organizational security.

The fourth alumnus had been working for a trust bank for thirty years until 1992. His last position with the bank was general manager in charge of international operations (his experience was discussed in Chapter 16). In 1992 he took early retirement from the bank and joined a wholly owned subsidiary of a major U.S.-based trust bank. Earlier (in 1986) this alumnus had been on temporary loan to the same subsidiary, established a year earlier, to help them start trust bank operations in Japan. In two years he built from scratch a strong organization to conduct trust banking operations, and then he returned to the original employer. When he was about to leave the original employer permanently, he looked for a job with a foreign bank where his international experience would be of value. So when he was asked to return to the Japanese subsidiary he had earlier helped to build, he accepted the offer.

As general manager in charge of marketing management, he was responsible for all private sector trust businesses. This was after the burst of the bubble economy, and the business environment in which the bank found itself was not very favorable. The only bright aspect was financial deregulation, which meant that business restrictions on foreign banks were beginning to ease. However, this was counterbalanced by the entry into the market of foreign investment companies.

Within his trust bank, conflict broke out between the traditional trust operations for which our alumnus was responsible and the emerging derivative businesses toward which the U.S. headquarters was shifting emphasis on a global basis. As a result, our alumnus was eventually "kicked upstairs" to become an auditor (part-time) in 1993 and then an adviser (part-time) in 1995.

From his own experience, our alumnus notes the following factors of the internal operation of the foreign-owned bank: (1) absolute control of headquarters; (2) excessive sectionalism and individualism resulting from work specialization; (3) control of subordinates by providing rewards; (4) the achievement of short-run results as the supreme goal, often resulting in troubles to co-workers and inconvenience to customers; (5) manipulation of interpersonal relations for the purpose of promotion; (6) subjective performance evaluation by superiors, resulting in extreme fluctuations in subordinates' fates.

The U.S. headquarters' switch to the derivative business, which our alumnus had opposed, failed after a few years and resulted in a large loss for the bank and forced it to merge with a stronger financial group. At any rate, it is clear from the above description that this alumnus was anchored in management competence with reduced responsibility at the decline and disengagement stages. The fact that he left the original employer in his early fifties suggests that he was not anchored in organizational security.

As stated in Chapter 16, the fifth alumnus in this group had worked for a large electric machine manufacturer for twenty-seven years until 1989, when he was transferred (by *shukko*) to a newly created subsidiary (Case 9 in Table 22.1). In 1994 he retired from the subsidiary and started to look for a general management position with a foreign company. Through his long experience with overseas operations he had come to feel more comfortable with U.S.-style management. He landed the kind of job he had hoped for through his personal network of connections outside the original company. It was a wholly owned Japanese subsidiary of a large U.S.-based electrical machine manufacturing company, with 85,000 employees working in seventy-five divisions.

The Japanese subsidiary consisted of twenty-three divisions, one of which had been newly created for the introduction of garbage disposal units into the Japanese market. The division consisted of only two people, including our alumnus as the general manager. Unlike in the United States, where kitchen garbage may be ground up and washed down into a sewer, in Japan, such a practice is prohibited by regulations of the Ministry of Construction. Therefore, at the time of the interview (October 1997), the job of our alumnus was to find ways to circumvent the regulations, for example, by devising a biochemical treatment before garbage disposal.

This alumnus was clearly anchored in management competence while he was working for the original employer and its subsidiary. However, in the foreign subsidiary his management skills did not seem utilized much; rather, his work required liaison skills with division headquarters in the United States, Japanese government agencies, and other companies interested in the garbage disposal unit market. Apparently he enjoyed meeting different kinds of people and exchanging ideas about the new business in which he was involved.

Overseas Careers

In this period a total of five alumni worked in overseas offices. While two of them stayed for a relatively short time, the remaining three apparently made a career out of overseas operations. In this section we will concentrate on the latter three alumni.

The first alumnus had enjoyed substantial overseas experience—New York (five years), Penang (three and a half years), and Hong Kong (two and a half years)—before being assigned in 1989 to London, where he worked for five years. The synthetic fiber company for which this alumnus worked experienced a sharp reduction in the volume of exports after the Plaza Accord. As a countermeasure, the company adopted a strategy of increased overseas production. Negotiations started in 1988 with a British company over its acquisition. Our alumnus participated in the negotiations at the final stages, which were settled in early 1989. He was assigned to the newly acquired plant in late 1989 as one of the directors.

The plant, a wholly owned subsidiary of the alumnus's company, was engaged in the weaving and dyeing of polyester fiber. Half of the textile was sold to the British market, while the remaining half was sold to other European countries in the form of apparel. The plant employed 600 people, including six from Japan: two directors, one accountant, and three engineers (two in production and one in maintenance). The top management team consisted of six people: the chairman (Japanese), the president (British), and four directors. Three of the four directors were British, in charge of sales, production, and accounting, respectively, while the remaining one was our alumnus in charge of management planning.

Our alumnus recalls that, although the British economy was still in a prolonged recession, the policies of the ten-year-old Thatcher administration were beginning to produce some positive results. Trade unions became more moderate and Japanese direct investment was well received, while exports from Japan were declining. To counterbalance the export decline, the subsidiary built a new polyester production plant, completed in 1993. Three hundred people were newly hired. The raw materials—polyester fiber—were imported from Japan.

In managing the subsidiary our alumnus attempted to introduce good aspects of Japanese-style management as practiced in the Japanese main office; these included budget control and harmonious labor-management relations. Budget control meant that he compared performance with goals, and if the goals were not met, he analyzed why they were not met, then found and implemented solutions. He had to dismiss the president, who refused to adopt the budget control system.

In regard to relations with the union, he found the labor movement too depressed and inactive. So he took the initiative in meeting with union representatives for information sharing. In the management of local employees he followed the practices of the predecessor company, because the employer enjoyed a high degree of freedom, for example, in dismissing employees. Hiring was done by a local personnel manager. The only new element that was introduced to the pay system was assessment of worker competence based on an appraisal of workers' performances and their potential ability.

He was on the job for five years, until the end of 1994, when he was transferred back to Japan as general manager of a newly created division in charge of all overseas operations, including export and import trade. He was soon promoted to the rank of managing director, and in 1998 he was transferred back to London as the chairman of a subsidiary overseeing the company's entire European operation, a position he still holds.

His late career experiences suggest a number of things. The company's operation in the United Kingdom represents a typical process of business globalization as described in Chapter 2. First, in an attempt to make up for the decline in exports, the company started overseas production, first by acquiring a local firm and then by building a new plant. Second, the company no longer adopted an ethnocentric staffing policy, in that a majority of the top management positions were held by host country nationals and the number of Japanese nationals was kept to a minimum. Third, there was a blend of headquarters (Japanese) and local (British) management practices in order to achieve the two goals that any global corporation has to achieve: the universal goal of efficiency, and adjustment to local conditions.

As for the career pattern of our alumnus, it is clear that his career has been anchored in management competence, and he has been very successful in climbing the ladder of general management. Perhaps the key to his success is what Schein calls "centrality." That is, as the company shifted its emphasis from exports to local production, his job changed from exporting to the management of overseas operations that were of central importance to the company.

While the above alumnus established his general management career in the process of the globalization of his company, our second alumnus (Case 5 in Table 22.1) made a different career out of his long overseas experience. As we see in Table 22.1, this alumnus had started his career with a general trading company, which he quit in 1970 to join a major airline company. This was a rather unusual job change, because large companies would hire directly from schools and universities. But this airline company was rapidly expanding, and, by way of exception, it hired some "mid-career" people. At any rate, this alumnus worked for the airline company for a total of nearly twenty years, including five years in Anchorage, Alaska.

In 1989, he was transferred (by *shukko*) to a company subsidiary that was a travel agent, from which he was again transferred to an affiliated company in Manila to be the chairman and managing director. In the beginning, this company, incorporated under the laws of the Philippines, benefited from strong protection by the parent airline company. But soon after his appointment, the parent company withdrew all assistance. As a result, our alumnus had to run the company on his own, in competition with many rivals in the travel agent industry.

The company employed about fifty people, all Filipino except our alumnus. In running the company he adopted the local management style, and, needless to say, abided by local laws and regulations. The top management team consisted of five directors: our alumnus and four Filipinos. In addition, there were five external directors: four Filipinos and one Hong Kong Chinese. He successfully ran the company for four years. During that time, he found Filipinos very friendly and that it was easy to work with them. Aside from business, he became interested in the history of the Philippines, including the country's relations with Spain, the United States, and Japan. He became particularly interested in the betterment of Filipino-Japanese relations in all aspects.

Desirous of studying more about the Philippines and Filipinos, he took an early retirement from the parent company in 1993, which automatically resulted in the termination of the job with the local company he headed. With a hope of bettering Filipino-Japanese relations, he established a business consulting company providing various kinds of services to Japanese companies interested in doing business with, or in, the Philippines. As a first step, he started a travel and tour arrangement business, drawing on his experience up to that point. He maintains the business to this date.

The career pattern of this alumnus is very different from that of the first one, although for both of them overseas experience played an important part in their career formation. (1) While the first alumnus faithfully and competently carried out the company's global strategy in his overseas assignments, the second alumnus ran overseas operations with much more freedom. (2) While the first alumnus closely identified with the goals of the company, the second one developed his own goals while overseas and created his own company to achieve them. Thus, despite his long service with an airline company, we can safely say that the career of this alumnus was anchored in autonomy.

Later Careers of Stayers

By March 1998, a total of fourteen alumni had left their original companies (Table 22.3), while the remaining six stayed on with their companies. Among those who left, eight were transferred to subsidiaries, three as presidents and five as senior managers, by means of either *shukko* (six people) or *tenseki* (two people). The exact terms and conditions of these transfers differ from individual to individual. The common elements are that in the case of *shukko*, employment relations with the original employer are retained and the transferred managers are on the same salary scales as they had with the original employers. In the case of *tenseki*, however, the transferred managers "retire" from the original company and are placed on a salary scale in the new company that is usually lower than the original employer's.

As an example of *shukko*, one alumnus (Case 11), who had been working for a large textile company primarily in sales functions, switched to the Medical Products Division in 1988 as general manager in charge of sales. When the business of one department within the division dealing with a particular product line was transferred to a joint venture newly created with a Japanese subsidiary of a European-based pharmaceutical company in 1996, he was transferred out to the new company as its president. The terms and conditions of the transfer (*shukko*) were such that he would be placed on the same salary scale as that of the parent company and would abide by the same mandatory retirement rule (at sixty years of age) as that of the parent company. His career pattern clearly shows that he has been anchored in managerial competence. At the same time, the transfer to a subsidiary may represent an element of the security anchor, in the sense that he accepted what was required of him by the employer in order to maintain job security, a decent income, and a stable future. (This applies to all alumni who obtained their second jobs through *shukko* or *tenseki*.)

A case of *tenseki* is illustrated in the career pattern of an alumnus who was working for a major airline company in the areas of cargo handling and labor relations (Case 6). The company had a career selection system for its managerial employees. Under that system, *bucho,* or general managers, who

Table 22.3

Profiles of Late Leavers

Case	Original employer	Year left	Method of job change	New employer	Business	Position
1	Electric machine company	1991	Transfer	Subsidiary	Plant construction	Managing director
2	Bank	1991	Job offer	Unrelated company	Deptartment store	Director
3	General trading company	1991	Transfer	Subsidiary	Trading company	President
4	General trading company	1992	Job offer	Unrelated company	Trading company	Director
5	Petrochemical company	1992	Transfer	Subsidiary	Plant engineering	Director
6	Airline company	1992	Transfer	Subsidiary	Airport service	Managing director
7	Trust bank	1992	Job offer	Unrelated company	Trust bank	Auditor
8	Construction machine company	1994	Transfer	Subsidiary	Trading company	President
9	Casualty insurance	1994	Referral	Related organization	Industry association	General manager
10	General trading company	1995	Transfer	Subsidiary	Travel agent	Director
11	Textile company	1996	Transfer	Subsidiary	Medical products	President
12	Petroleum company	1996	Job search	Unrelated company	Public relations	Managing adviser
13	General trading company	1996	Job search	Unrelated company	Real estate	General manager
14	Airline company	1997	Transfer	Subsidiary	Airport security	General manager

have reached fifty-six years of age and who have not been selected to be members of the board of directors have two options. One option is to step down from the position of *bucho* and stay with the company as a nonmanagerial employee. The second option is to retire from the company with severance pay and work for a subsidiary as a senior manager at a reduced pay level until sixty-two years of age. Our alumnus chose the second option. Here again we can see a career anchored in management competence coupled with an element of the security anchor.

Of the six alumni who moved to different and unrelated companies, three did so by accepting attractive job offers (Cases 2, 4, and 7). All of them took "early retirement" from the original companies, one in general trading and two in banking, and have served the new companies as senior managers. Their careers have been anchored in management competence alone, without an element of security.

The remaining three also took "early retirement" and found their second jobs with varying degrees of assistance from the original company. One alumnus landed the second job through referral by the personnel department of the original company (Case 9). The second alumnus obtained the company's assistance in that the company paid the cost of a job search conducted by a job placement company (Case 12). The third alumnus found the job on his own without any assistance from the original company (Case 13). The common thread among the three is that they found the new job on the basis of their functional skills—casualty insurance handling, public relations, and accounting, respectively—which they had gained through long service with the original employers. Their careers, therefore, have been anchored in technical/functional competence.

As of March 1998, six alumni were still working for their original employers. Two alumni were managing directors of a major textile company and a department store, respectively. One alumnus was general manager of marketing in a food processing company. The fourth alumnus is the only one who opted not to work for a large organization upon school graduation. Instead, he joined his uncle's company, a wholesaler of construction-related materials, with the clear goal of reaching the top management of the company. He has achieved his goal: he is senior managing director. The career anchors of these four alumni can easily be identified as managerial anchors.

The case of the fifth alumnus, working for a brewery company, was already mentioned in Chapter 16. As of 1998, he continued the consultancy job on behalf of the company holding the title of deputy general manager of the Marketing Development Department. The sixth alumnus continued to work for an economic association as executive counselor in charge of environmental issues. It can be said that those two alumni were anchored in technical/functional competence.

After reviewing the entire work careers of our thirty alumni, several questions may be posed. They include the following. To what extent is permanent employment, or the guarantee of employment until the mandatory retirement age of sixty, practiced by major Japanese corporations? How do Japanese corporations trim their managerial employees, while maintaining permanent employment? What happens to those who leave the corporation at various career stages? To what extent are Japanese university graduates biased toward managerial and security anchors?

First of all, with respect to permanent employment, six out of thirty alumni have stayed with their original companies for thirty-six years, until approximately their sixtieth birthdays. Another fourteen were still with their original companies after twenty-eight years, when they were in their early fifties. In view of this, it would be more accurate to call the Japanese employment system "long-term" employment, rather than "permanent" employment.

Second, Japanese corporations trim their managerial employees by means of *shukko*, *tenseki* and job referral or some other assistance. A total of twelve employees were transferred out of the company—eight by *shukko*, two by *tenseki*, and two by job referral.

Third, those who leave the company at various career stages do so for a number of reasons, including: to do graduate work (one case), to succeed to a family business (three cases), and to work for a different company (eight cases). It is worth noting that many of these leavers anchor their careers in areas other than managerial competence.

Fourth, although the sample itself is heavily biased toward managerial and security anchors, nevertheless, variations were observed. Of the thirty alumni, career anchors other than managerial competence were observed in twelve cases—four autonomy/independence anchors and eight technical/functional anchors. There was no case that was anchored in creativity. Also, security anchors were observed as secondary anchors for those whose primary anchors were managerial competence and who were transferred out by means of *shukko* or *tenseki* at the late stage of their careers.

Finally, although Schein hypothesizes that career anchors remain stable throughout a person's career, several cases were observed in which career anchors changed—for example, from managerial to technical anchors. In that case, can we say the second anchor is the real one? Furthermore, as the age of retirement approaches, the security factor surfaces as a need, if not an anchor. Or is it possible that a person possesses more than one anchor and that one or the other becomes dominant depending on career stages and circumstances? More rigorous study is needed on individuals' talents, abilities, motives, needs, attitudes, and values in order to answer these questions.

Careers of Alumnae

Although Schein's study did not extend to women's career anchors, our study is not complete without reference to the work lives of our alumnae. Therefore, we assemble here brief reports and some comments by the alumnae themselves on their most recent work experiences.

The alumna who started her career with a foreign educational and cultural mission still works for the same organization as an assistant to the chief representative (as of January 1999). Since 1994 she has spent about 60 percent of her time on the alumni association of Japanese who once studied in the United Kingdom on scholarships from the organization. As the executive secretary of the association, she provides support to the association's various activities. In 1998, for example, in an attempt to attract Japanese youth to British universities, a reception was held by the ambassador, who was the honorable chairman of the association. One of our alumna's duties was to invite the Minister of Education and several presidents of universities to the reception. To carry this out, she had to write a number of letters and make a number of telephone calls.

Commenting on her thirty years of service with the organization, she says:

> When I started to work thirty years ago, I was told that international educational and cultural activities should not be considered a business. However, since the mid-1980s the organization's policy has changed—to making money out of our activities such as English language teaching, testing, and teacher training. With that change we were sent to marketing seminars to learn techniques to effectively compete with private language schools, and our work has become more stressful. I will be retiring soon as the mandatory retirement age is sixty years old. I certainly feel a lot has changed over the thirty-year period.

She has devoted most of her life to her career. In terms of Schein's categorization, we can say that she was anchored in technical/functional competence (secretary/assistant). It is difficult to determine if this was the result of her own choice or of the workings of the "glass ceiling."

Our second alumna, engaged in the art dealership jointly with her husband, says that Japan's economic slump has been adversely affecting their business. Their regular customers no longer purchase as many paintings as before. However, she has never thought of quitting her work, because she loves it very much. She says that she feels blessed for having the chance to meet renowned artists and to see many rare antique works of art. Moreover, she views her job not simply as the selling of paintings for profit but also as the building, jointly with her customers, of fine collections of paintings. In this way, she feels that she is contributing to the enrichment of art collections in Japan. She says:

> Whenever I go abroad to purchase paintings, I stop in at art museums. There I usually find a group of school children led by a teacher freely exchanging their impressions about famous paintings on display. Japanese children don't spend their time that way. For one thing, they are too busy with some other things. And then there are not many good paintings easily accessible to children. I feel sorry for them. My dream is that there will be as many art museums with good paintings as in European or American cities so that school children could appreciate those paintings.

As a final note she says:

> Our oldest son recently resigned from the company where he had been employed for several years and started the same business as his father's. This suggests to me that he must have felt our business and lifestyle something on which to model.

Here we find a happy and contented alumna who has been successful in balancing her work, social, and family lives. In regard to her work life we can perhaps say that she has been anchored in autonomy.

Our third alumna, who has been married to the president of an incense manufacturing company and who herself manages one of the stores owned by the company, continues to work as before. She has this to say:

> Looking back on my work life, I feel that I have contributed to the globalization of my husband's company. However, recently, my husband and I have been trying to curtail the amount of work in preparation for our rich but quiet remaining years. We travel abroad less often now, because traveling is physically very demanding. Instead, we play golf together. It becomes even more important now to have good friends and hobbies.

As for her work, she adds:

> These days I spend more time on the incense ceremony than on sales-related activities. Since three years ago, under the guidance of a famous poet, I have been working on a project to translate into modern Japanese and publish documents from the Edo era on the incense ceremony.

After a very successful and fulfilling work career, this alumna seems to be preparing for happy retirement with her husband. It appears that her career, although interrupted for fifteen years, has been anchored in technical/functional competence (English language skills).

Our fourth alumna, now widowed and with her daughters grown up, is devoted to the business that she started in 1996 with a friend. Their business consists of language classes, interpretation, and translation. She says:

> Our business strategy is to aim at the high-quality and niche market. We also attempt to maintain close and long-term relations with our customers. In 1996 our business was in the red, but the following year it went into the black. Our foreign language classes, dealing with fourteen different languages, are doing particularly well. It is interesting that minor languages such as Thai, Vietnamese, and Indonesian are popular, especially among students sent from corporations.

She continues:

> My biggest headache is how to deal with the taxation office. We are amateurs, so we go by "honesty is the best policy." In these tough economic times, we are prepared to close our business when it becomes unprofitable. But it will be difficult to determine exactly when is the time to do so.

We do not find in her a trace of the young married woman trying to balance her roles as daughter-in-law, wife, and mother as she struggled to seek her own identity. However, it is still premature to determine her career anchor.

Our fifth alumna, also widowed, enjoys her life teaching English and practicing social dancing. As a part-time English instructor in a private language school, she teaches students of all kinds either on an individual basis or on a small-group basis. For example, she teaches grammar to a junior high school student, conversation to a housewife, and TOEFL-taking skills to business people.

Teaching English is not only a job for her but also a source of pleasure and self-fulfillment. She says:

> I find my work rewarding, especially when junior high school students who had done poorly in their school English discovered that through my instruction English learning was interesting or pleasurable, or when students who had completed a course with me came back to the school for another course, saying that they liked my class so much they did not want to discontinue English lessons with me. . . . I learned the importance of professionalism from my employer, herself an English instructor as well as the owner/manager of the school. For example, according to her, inability

to answer students' questions properly is an indication of a lack of professionalism. Teachers have to maintain professional dignity. Mere friendliness or honesty is not enough!

Here we observe a process in which a woman who started to teach English to children just out of love for it is developing into a professional teacher.

Since her husband is long gone and her children grown up, she lives alone. She feels that by maintaining a good balance between her work life (English teaching) and social life (social dancing) she will be able to experience a fulfilling life. Her career anchor is clearly in technical/functional competence (English language skills).

Our sixth alumna, after her husband's retirement from the university, has suggested a new lifestyle to him. According to her suggestion, he is to spend one-third of his time on work (part-time teaching and writing), one-third on lectures and speeches (both academic and public), and the remaining one-third on volunteer work (with the foundation and the association to help color-blind people). That is more or less how she allocates her time other than the time she spends on housekeeping. Through assisting her husband, she has come to identify even more strongly with the social cause of his activities.

Of particular importance to her is the annual international symposium. She says:

> Many Japanese corporations, as part of their global cultural activities, are engaged in such activities as awarding prizes to renowned foreign scholars and artists, holding exhibitions of paintings by famous foreign artists, and sponsoring concerts by famous foreign musicians. However, although such activities may be eye-catching, they do not have long-lasting effects. In this sense, the kind of activities in which my husband has been involved—the organizing of international symposia—have a lot to offer in promoting international understanding at the grassroots level.

It is not certain to what extent Schein's concept of career anchor applies to our alumnae, especially to the one without a job of her own. However, it is clear that their life histories do not conform to the prewar values of "good wife and wise mother." Their work lives clearly are an important element of their total lives.

Summary to Part V

The last decade of the twentieth century witnessed the continuation of the process of dissolution of the Soviet empire. Former satellite nations in East Europe regained political independence and were integrated into the Western market economy. Russia itself was democratized and transformed into a market economy under the leadership of Yeltsin, who succeeded Gorbachev. In Asia, too, tension was eased; the civil war in Cambodia ended, and South Korea actively sought to improve diplomatic relations with former foes. It is important to note, however, that communism was and still is intact in Asia—in China, in North Korea, and in Vietnam.

In the international economy the formation of the EC in 1992 and the creation of NAFTA in 1994 accelerated regional economic integration. At the same time, the transformation of GATT into the WTO in 1995 symbolized the increased commitment of major industrial nations to free trade on a global scale. The United States, now the only superpower, began to show signs of economic recovery after the inauguration of President Clinton in 1993. The U.S. economic recovery soon turned into economic prosperity.

Japan, which had enjoyed domestic political stability for three decades, experienced major turmoil in this period. The problem, which started as another money scandal, led to the split from the LDP of a reform-oriented group led by Ichiro Ozawa, former Secretary General of the party, and to the eventual downfall of the LDP government in 1993.

The Hosokawa coalition cabinet was formed with eight former opposition parties, thanks to the skillful manipulation of Ichiro Ozawa, a firm advocate of sweeping political, administrative, and economic reform. The Hosokawa cabinet was well received by the Japanese people in general, who hoped that Japan would finally rid itself of outdated laws, regulations, and above all "administrative guidance" of all kinds, to become a true democracy.

Unfortunately, the coalition was so fragile that it collapsed when the LDP lured the Socialists away from the coalition into their camps. Thus, in less than a year the LDP came back to power by forming a coalition with the Japan Socialist Party, with the latter's chairman Murayama serving as the prime minister (June 1994). Since then the political, administrative, and economic reform that Ozawa and his associates advocated has been sabotaged by the hands of the LDP, leaving Japan in the dark.

Meanwhile, the bubble economy burst as a result of mismanagement of the economy by the Ministry of Finance and the Bank of Japan. Alarmed by the so-called bubble phenomenon symbolized by skyrocketing land prices, the Bank of Japan increased its official discount rates five times between mid-1989 and mid-1990, from 2.5 percent to 6 percent. The Ministry of Finance issued "directives" to major city banks to restrain lending for purchases of real estate.

The combined effect of these measures was immediate; both stock prices and land prices, which had already started to decline by the end of 1989, took a nosedive. The collapse of the stock market and the real estate market brought about a chilling effect on the whole economy. Big public works spending by the Miyazawa and Hosokawa cabinets from 1992 to 1994 as well as the Bank of Japan's six consecutive discount rate reductions from six to 0.5 percent between 1991 and 1993 contributed to temporary economic recovery in 1995 and 1996.

However, fiscal reform measures aiming at the reduction of government debts adopted by the Hashimoto cabinet in 1997 once again dampened the economy to zero growth in 1997 and to negative growth in 1998, on the verge of a deflationary spiral. Keizo Obuchi, who replaced Hashimoto in July 1998, switched back to a big-spending policy. Obuchi's policy has been faithfully followed by his successor, Yoshiro Mori, after the former's sudden illness in April 2000 (and subsequent death a month later). The Bank of Japan, however, in August 2000 adopted an erratic policy of increasing the call rate by 0.25 percent in the midst of continued economic recession.

Today the Japanese economy is experiencing a demand-deficit recession in which the "paradox of thrift" is actually in operation. After all, thrift is what employers and the government have preached for the last three decades. Now the government's plea to spend more falls on the deaf ears of consumers who are worried about their employment in the face of rising unemployment.

Naturally, the industries in which our alumni were employed were adversely affected by the economic stagnation during the period. In all industries domestic demand was sluggish. Manufacturing industries were doubly hit by a strong yen that dampened exporting. Such industries as textiles, industrial machinery, and electric machinery accelerated overseas production. Other industries (including steel and petrochemicals), ill prepared for overseas production, resorted to restructuring, diversification, business alliances, and mergers.

General trading companies were in a "second winter." An increasing number of commodities came to be exported by manufacturers without the involvement of general trading companies. As a result, more emphasis was placed on importing, off-show trading, and overseas investment.

Banks fell victim to bad loans. Many survived only with the infusion of a huge amount of public funds, while a number of banks, including several major ones, went under. Those that survived went through restructuring, business alliances, and mergers. The air transport industry suffered, as the international price cartel of IATA ceased to function and the market came to be flooded with discount tickets.

The brewery industry, which had long enjoyed oligopolistic price practices, were suddenly faced with the increased bargaining power of large supermarkets and discount stores armed with inexpensive import beer. As a result, the manufacturers lost control of the retail prices that they had long been able to maintain at a high level.

Department stores, which had enjoyed a temporary boom during the bubble period, lost customers to supermarkets. The recent bankruptcy of a major and fast-growing department store was symbolic of the poor performance of the industry. Here again, the catchword is restructuring. Finally, wholesalers of building materials were hard hit by the burst of the bubble. New housing starts fell sharply and an increasing number of small distributors went bankrupt.

During this period of economic turmoil approximately half of the thirty alumni arrived at the top management position of *torishimariyaku* (or member of the board of directors) in various organizations, including original employers and their subsidiaries. Therefore, one of our concerns was decision making at the top management level, in particular the use of the *ringi* system.

Our findings suggest that although ringi was used in all but one case, it plays a rather limited role in making company-wide decisions at the top management level. Instead, various kinds of executive meetings were found to play a dominant role. In most cases agenda items were generated both from above (chairman and president) and from below (general manager). In those meetings not only consensus-style decision making but also consultative-style decision making were in actual use. Therefore, it is an oversimplification to say that Japanese corporations use consensus-style decision making.

In regard to the career patterns of our alumni, six of the thirty alumni stayed with their original employers until approximately their sixtieth birthday. A further eight alumni were transferred to subsidiaries where they served as top managers until approximately their sixtieth birthday. No alumnus suffered involuntary termination of his employment. These findings suggest that the employers' commitment to permanent employment (providing employment security until mandatory retirement at the age of sixty) was very strong.

If we classify our thirty alumni in terms of Schein's career anchors, as of

1998 eighteen cases were found to be anchored in managerial competence, eight in technical/functional competence, and four in autonomy/independence. There was no case that was anchored in creativity. The security anchor was observed in those whose primary anchors were managerial competence and who were transferred out to subsidiaries. Also, several cases were observed in which career anchors changed. These findings are somewhat at variance with Schein's hypothesis that people will develop a single career anchor that remains stable throughout their careers.

Finally, although Schein is silent about career anchors of women, our study suggests that for our alumnae a job career was an important part of their total lives. Of the five alumnae who held a job, at least four were found to be anchored in technical/functional competence. It appears that their talents, needs, and values played an even greater role in shaping their career anchors than those of their male counterparts.

Part VI

Contemporary Views on
Japanese Society and Management

23
Continuity and Change
in Japanese Values and Society

In Chapter 1 we introduced the view of James Abegglen (1958, 1973) in the context of the convergence-divergence debate. Simply put, his view, which represents the divergence school of thought, is that Japanese management practices are unique, because Japanese culture is unique. In this chapter and the next we will introduce the views of our participants in this study on these two questions: the uniqueness of Japanese culture and the uniqueness of Japanese management.

This chapter summarizes the answers of thirty-six participants (thirty alumni and six alumnae) on the following seven questions:

(1) Do you think that the Japanese people's way of thinking, their values, and temperament are unique among many foreigners you have encountered? Or are they fundamentally common to the rest of the world?

(2) If unique (or common), in what respects are they unique (or common)?

(3) Do you think that Japanese people are more homogeneous than foreigners? Or is there much difference among individuals?

(4) It is said that gender-based role differentiation is stressed in Japan. To what extent do you agree with this?

(5) To what extent do you think gender-based role differentiation has changed over the years?

(6) Do you think that in the future gender-based role differentiation will be completely rejected in Japan as it is in the United States today?

(7) There is a view that Japanese economic growth has been achieved at the sacrifice of family life and family members. To what extent do you agree with this view?

First, in response to the question on the uniqueness of the Japanese people, six of the thirty alumni answered that the Japanese people's attitudes are unique, while seven answered that they are essentially common to other peoples of the world. The remaining seventeen answered that Japanese people possess both common and unique elements. Of the six alumnae, five answered that Japanese people share fundamentally common values with other peoples of the world, although they admitted some differences as well. One alumna stressed the uniqueness of shortcomings of the Japanese people. She says:

> The most unique feature of Japanese society is that, in politics and business, Japan is a male-dominated country, in sharp contrast to Western countries, where there are many female business executives. Second, the behavior of Japanese abroad is deplorable. Young women going on shopping trips overseas hunting for brand-name products and young men dressed in shabby clothes walking on main streets of foreign cities are indicative of their loss of the national pride. Finally, the lack of the spirit of fairness is another shortcoming of the Japanese people. (business executive)

The following remarks are from the alumni who hold views about the uniqueness of the Japanese people. We observe in some remarks a tone of self-criticism, although perhaps not as strong as the statement of the above alumna.

> The Japanese are unique in that they lack religious beliefs, the spirit of service, and consideration for the handicapped. These qualities of Japanese people need to be taken into consideration in management. (senior manager, airline company)

> I agree that the Japanese are unique. For example, while the European/U.S. way of thinking is that of a hunter, the Japanese way of thinking is that of a farmer. We believe in incrementalism, while they are more dynamic. Therefore, if a Western company fails in a business, all they do is fire the top executive in charge of the business and retreat from the business. In dismissing employees, Western managers do not worry about the employees as we do. Japan is different from Malaysia, where religious influence is strong. Japan is different from Hong Kong, where people's way of thinking has become British after a long period of colonial rule. It must be pointed out, however, that certain aspects of the way of thinking of Japanese business people have been formulated under a particular political system after 1955 rather than [as] the result of historical influence; therefore, it may change in the future when the system has changed. Besides, "overseas returnee children" are a new type of Japanese. (managing director, synthetic fiber company)

> I think that the Japanese are considerably unique. However, the young gen-

eration in their thirties and younger are becoming rapidly Westernized, with the result that they possess a way of thinking and values different from those of old Japanese. Areas in which old Japanese are unique include: (1) putting the group before oneself (or the spirit of sacrificing oneself for the benefit of the master); (2) following the crowd (or doing as your neighbors do); and (3) being particular about the group of which one is a member. (self-employed in the Philippines)

Yes, I think that Japanese people are unique. They lack originality. Also, the quality of kindness is different. Japanese people's kindness is in form only; it does not come out of inner friendliness. This can be seen from the way Japanese people offer help to the handicapped. (senior manager, general trading company)

Japanese people's way of thinking, values, and temperament are considerably unique relative to Americans and Indonesians, although there are certain elements of commonality. The most distinct trait of temperament of the Japanese people is the "external locus of control," in which personal behavioral criteria depend on other people's behaviors. Perhaps this temperament was formed as a result of the 300 years of national isolation policy in the Tokugawa era. (educational consultant, nonprofit organization [NPO] in Indonesia)

I think that Japanese people are unique, although by thorough discussion reaching an understanding between Japanese and other people is possible, and in this sense we may be able to say that Japanese people are the same as any other people. The Japanese people are most unique in that essentially the same language has been used (in the same place) for the past 2,000 years, while in Europe national borders have always changed due to wars and the like. I think that this difference (between Japan and Europe) is the source of Japan's uniqueness in various aspects. (senior manager, casualty insurance company)

As the above statements illustrate, some of those who say that the Japanese people are unique qualify their statements by admitting that there are elements of commonality as well. We can observe the same tendency among those who reply that the Japanese people are not unique. Here are their remarks:

Using my American friends as a reference group, I think that Japanese and Americans are essentially the same, except that the ways of expression are different. In both countries workaholics are workaholics, and family men are family men. In either case these people are self-centered. Although the cultures are different, the two peoples are the same as human beings, and in both countries there are groups of people who share the same values. (managing director, trading company)

I think we share fundamentally common ways of thinking, values, and temperament with the rest of the world. We simply express ourselves differently because of a difference in culture and history. In personal relations I have much in common with foreigners. However, in business dealings I have encountered reactions from foreigners that would not be expected from Japanese due in large part to differences in political and economic systems rather than culture. For example, in negotiating with Russians, [the] negotiating official(s) never made any compromise; therefore, no agreement was reached until the matter was brought up to the ministerial level. I do not think that this rigidity was a reflection of the temperament of Russian people; rather it was a reflection of the centralized decision-making system under the old communist regime. (senior manager, fishery company)

I have found Jewish American lawyers, with whom I have had close business dealings, basically similar to Japanese counterparts in many respects. Both groups are hard working (working on weekends), put work before family, have a strong sense of loyalty, and possess strong endurance. The main difference was that Japanese lawyers emphasized harmony and mutual compromise more than [did their] American counterparts. (senior managing director, airline ground service company)

I think the perceived uniqueness is a reflection of one's preconceived ideas. Basically, we are on the same footing if we put mutual trust first. One shortcoming of Japanese people, however, is that communication skills on the part of many Japanese are not as good as those of people from other countries. (auditor, department store)

Basically, there are many common elements between the Japanese people and peoples of other countries. Within each country individual differences exist due to differences in generations and environments in which people work. Besides, differences in value judgments are of less importance than the policies of an organization or an individual. (public relations consultant)

I think the way of thinking of the Japanese people is basically the same as that of other peoples. As for value judgments there seems to be wide variation among individuals. If there is a value (or virtue) that looks unique to Japan, we should not blindly take it for granted; rather it must meet the test of global acceptance. (managing director, plant construction company)

I do not think that the Japanese people are especially unique. The basics are common. (self-employed)

The majority view is eclectic to a significant extent, as exemplified in the following statements:

Compared with Americans, British, Dutch, Koreans, Taiwanese, and Aus-

tralian business associates and friends, 80 percent of Japanese characteristics are common, while the remaining 20 percent are uniquely Japanese. Common elements include diligence and humanity, while elements unique to Japanese friends and business associates include less concern for family, prudence, and samurai-like pride. (president of Japanese subsidiary of foreign company)

In the past, Japanese people and business practices were considered unique. Now about 60 to 70 percent of Japanese characteristics are common, while the remaining 30 to 40 percent are uniquely Japanese. What is unique to Japanese people is a group mentality that precludes standing out. Because of this nature, Japanese companies in adversity tend to lose control and run into further difficulties. On the other hand, logical communication is effective in all cultures. Through logical communication peoples of different cultures can understand each other to a large extent. (senior consultant, human resource management)

Five of the six alumnae answered in support of the universalist view. However, on closer examination their views are more eclectic than definitive. Here are some examples:

I think how Japanese think or what their values are is basically a matter of individual differences rather than a general value orientation or quality of being Japanese. (art gallery co-owner)

But she quickly adds:

People of foreign countries are proud of their countries. Every Japanese should have confidence and pride in his/her country. If we have confidence and pride in ourselves, then we can also accept others. Because we are not making an effort to be understood by others, our views and understanding become narrow and limited.

In general, I don't think the Japanese people are unique. Human nature remains the same, but the culture and self-expression differ. (self-employed)

Then she adds:

Establishing oneself relative to others within a group rather than absolute self-identity is a characteristic of Japanese people. Besides, setting a high value on being the same with others may show a lack of confidence and pride.

I think that it is basically a matter of individual differences. (English-language instructor)

However, she adds:

> What is unique to Japanese is that they seek sameness by blending within the group. People from Western countries value individuality. For them, it is important to be different from others even within the group.

> I don't regard Japanese values or their way of thinking as unique. I have a suspicion people from other countries think the same things are unique to them as the Japanese think are unique [to Japanese]. (Japanese branch, foreign educational/cultural organization)

Then she goes on to talk about the difference:

> Japanese people try not to show their confidence, while foreigners try to show theirs. Foreigners need to express themselves in order to live in a culture where silence is *not* golden. Is this kind of behavior required in Japanese society?

It seems that various statements about the uniqueness of the Japanese people may be aptly epitomized in the following two statements:

> Japan alone is not unique. The mentality of people of any nation is unique on account of its own geography, history, religion, and society. (managing director, plant construction company)

> It is fair to say that in the past Japanese were unique people. However, I think that the unique values Japanese people possessed were largely a reflection of the specific environmental conditions under which they lived. In a broader perspective we could say that Japanese people had a common temperament with Europeans in readily accepting capitalism. (managing director, petrochemical engineering company)

In summary, then, the way of thinking, values, and the temperament of the peoples of the world are different from one another; it is not correct to say that Japan alone is uniquely different from the rest of the world. Second, the way of thinking, values, and the temperament of the Japanese people are not immutable; they have changed and will continue to change according to changing environmental factors. In reviewing the statements of our participants, we found that the following characteristics were often referred to as "uniquely" Japanese: a group mentality, harmony with others, lack of individuality, and lack of originality. These traits may be grouped together under "homogeneity." Therefore, a question was asked about the extent of homogeneity among the Japanese people. Twenty-five of the thirty alumni answered that homogeneity is high among the Japanese people, while the remaining five answered that it is not. Of the six alumnae, four answered in favor, while the remaining two did not.

The following statements represent the minority view that homogeneity is not as high as is generally believed:

In prewar Japan homogeneity among Japanese people was high, based on common religious beliefs. Since the war Japan has been in confusion; there is no common value system unifying the Japanese people. (president, joint venture with foreign company)

Individual differences among Japanese people are much bigger than generally believed. However, since Japanese people rarely express their ideas openly, they are misinterpreted (by foreigners) to be homogeneous. On the other hand, Americans tend to express their ideas openly and directly. (managing director, trading company)

I think there is considerable difference among individuals. Superficially viewed, Japanese may look as if they behave in similar ways. For example, in meetings Japanese tend to nod in response to other people's statements; however, this behavior does not mean agreement, it simply means polite indications that they are listening attentively. (senior managing director, airline ground service company)

I think that there are individual differences. This applies to all nations (including Japan). (public relations consultant)

I think it's the same for foreign countries as well. There is no fundamental difference. (adviser to Japanese subsidiary of foreign bank)

Two alumnae make the following comments:

I do not think that Japanese people or any other people possess uniform values or traits. There are individual differences among any racial group. The same applies to the issue of homogeneity. (married to university professor of medicine)

I think that, at present, there is a great deal of difference among individuals. Young people, in particular, openly express their different opinions. However, on closer examination, they may be conforming to the general trend among young people to express themselves openly. (co-owner of art gallery)

However, by far the majority of the alumni answered that the Japanese people are homogeneous, and some backed up their opinions with reasons. Here are some typical statements:

I think that up to now homogeneity among Japanese people has been high. However, from now on we need to diversify; otherwise, we will be left behind in the world." (managing director, synthetic fiber company)

Generally speaking, homogeneity among Japanese people is high. Japanese people are not individualistic. (managing director, chemical engineering company)

I agree that homogeneity among Japanese people is high. In a sense, foreigners are homogeneous in terms of ethnic identity and religion, but Japanese are homogeneous in other areas. (president, subsidiary of construction machine company)

I think it is high, because Japanese people have a strong inclination toward *yokonarabi* (or pattern following). (managing director, plant construction company)

I think homogeneity is high. Perhaps this is because Japanese people place more value on the organization or group than on individuals. (business consultant)

I think homogeneity is high and heretics are excluded. At the corporate level Japanese companies have strong corporate culture. Among the disadvantages of strong homogeneity is that it discourages new ideas and fosters repeated mistakes. (senior manager, brewery company and registered professional consultant)

Although there are differences among Japanese, overall, Japanese people are more homogeneous than foreigners as a result of historical and cultural background. What Japanese people are lacking is the establishment of individual identity and the willingness to accept others as they are. (senior manager, fishery company)

A high degree of homogeneity is the result of "bureaucratic leadership" supplemented by "industrial cooperation." However, young people are becoming more individualistic. (auditor, department store)

I think homogeneity is high as a result of education from childhood (senior manager, Japanese subsidiary of U.S. electric machine company)

Highly homogeneous. There is a tendency to exclude those with distinctive personalities. For example, overseas returnee children from English-speaking countries have to "learn" the Japanese way of pronouncing English words in order to avoid ostracism from classmates. (educational consultant with NPO in Indonesia)

Japanese people are highly homogeneous to the extent of being able to understand other Japanese without things being put into words. The United States has systems that assume the diversity of people. In Europe, managers and blue-collar workers are like people belonging to different racial groups. (director, chemical company)

Generally speaking, the degree of homogeneity is high in the sense that we tend to blindly follow the trend—the hula hoop phenomenon, the *dakko-chan* doll boom, and panic buying at the time of the oil crisis—to mention a few. But all of these are transient phenomena. In terms of having an esprit de corps born of being a singular nation, I think we compare unfavorably with other nations. (managing director, travel agent)

To me it seems that Japanese people are alike and therefore homogeneous. What I cannot understand is that, although people criticize the bureaucracy for forcing us to conform, they go along with that. Perhaps this is the underlying reason for demand for deregulation. (retired, former president of subsidiary of a general trading company)

Several other alumni simply answered that homogeneity among Japanese people is high, without giving any reasons for their opinion. Alumnae who share the same view make the following statements:

The degree of homogeneity is high. It is expected that individuals are to be buried within the organization and that people are to suppress themselves in order to meet that expectation as much as possible. That the clothes worn by the young women are all the same is indicative of this idea. (English-language instructor)

Compared to peoples of foreign countries, the degree of homogeneity among Japanese people is strong. This comes from their having a singular ethnicity and a single language. Of course, this does not preclude differences among individuals. (business executive)

A high degree of homogeneity among Japanese people may be due to the fact that they have historically had little experience dealing with foreigners. (Japanese branch of foreign educational/cultural organization)

An interesting observation is made by one alumna (self-employed, language school and translation) who says that "the degree of homogeneity within the group is quite high, but it is low between groups." Indeed, this view is shared by several alumni who pointed out the existence of acute rivalry among corporations with distinctively different organizational cultures.

Overall, then, our participants tend to support the popular view that the degree of homogeneity is high among Japanese people. As for the causes of such high uniformity, they often refer to Japanese history and education. That is, historically, Japan has had little contact with foreign countries, as highlighted by the national isolation policy of the Tokugawa era (1600–1868). After the Meiji era (1868–1911) homogeneity was even strengthened by the unified education that placed high values on a conformist way of thinking and on conformist behavior.

As stated in Chapter 3, Geet Hofstede (1983) identified "masculinity versus femininity" as an important dimension of national culture. It relates to the division of roles between the sexes in society. Masculine societies make a sharp division between what men should do and what women should do, while feminine societies allow both men and women to take many different roles with a relatively small social division in sex roles. In the Hofstede study of 1983, in which forty nations were surveyed, Japan was highest of all nations in terms of the masculinity index. Questions 4 through 7 were asked in order to address this issue of gender-based role differentiation in society and in the workplace.

To what extent do our participants subscribe to gender-based role differentiation? The answers obtained from the thirty alumni varied, but they can be grouped more or less evenly into three broad categories: those who were opposed (11), those who were in favor (9), and those who did not take a position (10). Of the six alumnae only two took clear-cut positions (one in favor, the other against), while the remaining four provided mixed answers.

Here are some of the statements of those who were opposed:

> I do not subscribe to gender-based role differentiation. However, I do not advocate that everyone should be treated in the same way. The treatment should depend on an individual's motivation and ability. (managing director, trading company)

> As a matter of principle I am opposed to gender-based role differentiation. In reality, however, a differential treatment may be more beneficial and therefore appealing to women. (president, subsidiary of construction machine company)

> My opinion is that, as a general rule, men and women should be treated equally. However, special protection is needed for women in childbirth and related matters. Apart from my own opinion, I think that Japanese society as a whole still supports gender-based role differentiation. (business consultant)

> My basic value judgment is to reject the idea one hundred percent. (owner of travel agency in the Philippines)

> I do not attach great importance to the idea. To me the ideal society is one in which everyone can play an active part regardless of gender and other differences. (advisor, Japanese subsidiary of foreign bank)

> There are too many people (both male and female) who believe that serving tea in the office is a female job. Discarding such an idea is a precondition for efficient business performance. (educational consultant, NPO in Indonesia)

> Japanese men are foolish in blocking female employment, thereby failing to make use of female abilities. There are many countries that are economically less advanced than Japan but that are more advanced socially. (executive councilor, economic association)

Finally, an alumna has this to say:

> Japan is less advanced socially. Although 50 percent of the Japanese population is female, female advancement in society is sabotaged. Japanese society will change for the better when more women play active roles in more areas. The present male-dominated society looks very unnatural to me. At home, however, total elimination of role differentiation will never be achieved. (co-owner of specialty store)

On the other hand, there are those who were more or less in favor of gender-based role differentiation, as the following statements suggest:

> Under the family system established during the Tokugawa era, there was the idea that "men run the world and women run men." I am basically in favor of gender-based role differentiation, although I am not opposed to women working in offices. (managing director, synthetic fiber company)

> I am in favor of the differentiation because women have become too strong, although I realize that no one can stop the current trend for equal employment for women. (managing director, chemical engineering company)

> These days women seem to fulfill less responsibility in raising children at home than before, while they have come to occupy jobs that were considered to be male jobs before, such as sales. (senior managing director, family business)

> The most important thing for human beings is to leave good descendants, and in this respect the role of women in childbirth, rearing, and training is crucial. After that period is over, the barrier of role differentiation may be overcome by women with sufficient abilities. (senior managing director, airline ground service company)

> If women have elected to have children, it's their responsibility to raise children as full-time housewives until children reach a certain age. I think that women should share 70 percent of the responsibility in raising children. After the period of child rearing, a woman may choose her own way of life. Women these days have too strong a sense of equality, despite their low job abilities. (former senior manager, general training company)

> It depends on the issue. As an individual (before marriage) there is no need for role differentiation. But in a family (after marriage) there has to be division of labor between husband and wife. (managing director, plant construction company)

> Male and female are fundamentally different; therefore, their roles are different. Motherhood is important and women have an important role in raising a child until he/she grows up. (director, chemical company)

> In our company's experience, the resignation rates of female employees who opted for *sogoshoku* [the major career path] created for female university graduates under the Equal Employment Opportunity Law (EEOL) of 1985 have been high simply because they could not work as hard as men. Since that is the case, it's better to assign women to different jobs from jobs held by men. (managing director, plant construction company)

One alumna (married to university professor of medicine) supported the idea by saying, "Gender-based role differentiation has worked well for me."

Next, statements from some of those who did not take a position either for or against gender-based role differentiation are in order here:

> Between me and my wife, role differentiation has worked well and both of us have been happy. However, complete role differentiation has become difficult for our children's generation. To maintain a high level of consumption a wife's income is necessary. (senior manager, brewery company and registered consultant)

> Gender-based role differentiation is a thing of the past. At present we should not be misled by a few isolated cases. (auditor, department store)

> In the workplace, gender-based work assignment has been decreasing. In personal life, it is regrettable for men and women to lose their distinctive manliness and womanliness. (public relations consultant)

> It existed while we were growing up. (senior manager, general trading company)

> I believe I have always respected women and for that reason I do not have any prejudice against women. In the workplace, I have always demanded that women should upgrade themselves. (president, joint venture with foreign medical company)

Four female alumni provided the following answers:

> I do not have a strong position on this issue. My husband and son readily clean up the table and wash dishes after meals. I do grocery shopping and laundry. (co-owner of art gallery)

> Since physical structure is different, perhaps the way of thinking is different. As a result, gender-based role differentiation seems natural to me. However, we need not restrict women who want to play the traditionally male role. (self-employed, language school and translation)

> There should be equal employment opportunity for men and women. However, since there is a physiological difference, complete enforcement of the law without any exception will be difficult. Some women may feel robbed of the pleasure of rearing children, yet participation by the husband in

child-rearing out of consideration for the wife is necessary. (English-language instructor)

Serving tea in an office should be done in turn by all members of the office, not just by the female workers. However, some Western men who are transferred to Japan seem to think that Asian women are glad to do such a thing. (Japanese branch of foreign educational/cultural organization)

Follow-up questions were asked on whether gender-based role differentiation had changed over the years and if the idea as well as the practices based on the idea would be rejected in the future the way they are in the United States today. Virtually all members answered that they had become less popular and that such a tendency would continue in the future. However, the answers differed somewhat in terms of the pace of change. Generally speaking, those who were opposed to gender-based role differentiation took the position that the changes so far had been too minor and the changes from now would be slow, while those who favored it answered the opposite. Here are some remarks by those who were opposed to gender-based role differentiation.

The alumnus (self-employed in the Philippines) who was "one hundred percent" against differentiation says:

The idea and practices have changed for the better somewhat but compared with other countries Japan is still backward. In this regard, the Philippines is much advanced. And in the future, such ideas and practices should be totally prohibited.

An alumnus with a foreign bank who maintained that there should be no differential treatment on the basis of gender and other factors says:

Changes so far are so insignificant, we have just moved in the right direction; therefore, it will take a long time for Japan to become like the United States today. Perhaps total elimination of the discriminatory ideas and practices will never be achieved.

An alumnus staying overseas as a consultant with an NPO who was very critical of the differential treatment of women in the workplace says that the change has been "little." As for future prospects he has this to say:

Elimination of the ideas and practices is possible depending on the will and efforts of women themselves. So long as they feel comfortable with gender-based differential treatment and find it painful to work on equal terms with men, complete equality such as exists in the United States will never be achieved.

An alumnus with an economic association who said that the thinking of Japanese men was backward in not making use of female abilities admits that the situation has improved somewhat. He feels, however, that a majority of Japanese males still hold the old idea, so that change will be very slow.

The alumna who was critical of male-dominated Japanese society has this to say:

> Since our parents' generation the change has been negligible. In the future, male-female role divisions will never disappear, because there will be many young people who follow their parents' practices.

On the other hand, those who were in favor of gender-based role differentiation generally said that substantial change has taken place. Their answers in regard to future prospects varied.

An alumnus with a general trading company who was most critical of working women neglecting household duties has this to say:

> In those U.S. families where men and women share an equal responsibility, their children suffer and cause problems. In wise families, where women share 70 percent of the household responsibility, their children are raised well without problems. Japanese women (wrongly) look too much toward the United States. I am very much worried about the future of Japan.

An alumnus with a synthetic fiber company who essentially agreed with gender-based role differentiation says:

> Japan has changed in such a way that role differentiation is less clear-cut now. In Japan, like Europe and the United States, some women have taken traditionally male jobs, while some men have come to be engaged in domestic jobs.

As for the future, he predicts some backlash will take place in Europe and the United States as a result of religious values, and he says, "In the end (both in Japan and the West) role differentiation will disappear in the workplace but it will remain in personal (or family) life."

An alumnus with a chemical company who emphasized the female role of motherhood sees that role differentiation has changed. He says:

> It's lamentable that university-educated women cannot cook. It will be fine if in the future capable women are promoted to higher positions in the workplace, provided that no special treatment is given them because they are women.

An alumnus with an electric machine company who advocated differential treatment of men and women in the workplace has this to say:

> Japanese companies have invested heavily in male employees because under permanent employment they could recoup the benefit of that investment. As female employees tend to quit prematurely, companies hesitate to invest in them. In the future, differential employment practices will con-

tinue, based on the principle of the right person in the right place. Women should not pursue the general management career path but a specialist path that requires special skills or abilities.

The above statements show that those alumni who favor gender-based role differentiation have strong reservations about its elimination in the future. However, some foresee that, whether they like it or not, the current practice of role differentiation will largely disappear.

For example, an alumnus with a chemical engineering company who favors role differentiation because, in his view, female power is already too strong, predicts that if things continue like this, current practices will be completely abandoned. Another alumnus with a Japanese subsidiary of a foreign electric machine company who emphasized the division of labor in a family says, "In the future, unless justified on some grounds, all differential treatment will be judged acts of discrimination." An alumna who is completely satisfied being a full-time housewife and assistant to her scholar husband also foresees that:

> In the future gender-based role differentiation will be diminished, although women will not be able to work exactly in the same way as men do, because of physical differences.

The third group of alumni, those who did not take a clear position, generally answered that the ideas and practices of role differentiation have changed and will continue to change. Two of them referred to the EEOL of 1985 (revised in 1999) as a major cause for more equal treatment of women in the workplace.

One of them with an airline ground service company says:

> Gender-based role differentiation has been rapidly disappearing in the workplace as a result of the enactment in April 1999 of the revised EEOL and of the Labor Standards Law.

The other, an alumnus with a department store, referred to specific stipulations as particularly responsible for the change: (1) prohibition of discrimination in hiring, job assignment, promotion, and so forth; (2) prohibition of gender-based recruitment terms such as "stewardess" or "salesman"; and (3) guidelines against sexual harassment.

Here are additional comments from some other alumni in the third category.

> For younger generation women it has become commonplace to work for a company. The company has come to provide female employees with various assistance programs (especially in regard to childbirth and rearing). As a result, female employees no longer quit at an early age, and the average age of female employees has risen. I think that the reason female employ-

> ees keep working is largely economic; the intrinsic value of work to live
> for is of secondary importance. (senior manager, brewery company)

As for the future, he feels that, although role differentiation will weaken, it
will not totally disappear, because the roles of men and women remain different in regard to childbirth and rearing.

> As a general trend, Japan will become much like the United States. Al-
> though certain differential practices will remain, most will disappear. I am
> of the opinion that both men and women should keep their respective strong
> points. (senior consultant, human resource management)

> Women's superior academic performance is conspicuous these days. As a
> result, an increasing number of women are entering the world of work and
> their status will continue to rise after marriage. First, the equality of men
> and women as an ideology will move forward and then an increasing num-
> ber of women will enter sectors where female sense and sensibility play an
> important role, such as fashion-oriented industries and the tourist industry.
> Thus, in reality and in ideology, gender-based role differentiation will be
> completely eliminated. (travel agent)

The four alumnae commented as follows:

> It appears that many Japanese young husbands enjoy helping their wives in
> family chores. On the other hand, from my personal experience, U.S. hus-
> bands made conscious efforts to entertain their guests. Also, American work-
> ing women looked rather uptight in keeping up with male co-workers in
> being fully responsible in what they said and did. (co-owner, art gallery)

> It seems that, since the EEOL, female employment has been changing on the
> surface. However, women in the so-called *sogoshoku* (or major career track)
> seem to be overstretching themselves, as there are so many hurdles to clear as
> an "organization woman." Perhaps freelance occupations such as interior de-
> signer or architect are more suited to women. As for the future I don't know if
> Japan will become like the United States today. It is true that fewer and fewer
> women marry at a young age these days. To me, that is a reflection of their lack
> of confidence in marriage and child rearing rather than their strong career ori-
> entation. (self-employed, language school and translation company)

> Not only are more wives working but also more husbands are helping their
> wives at home. Due to recent changes in legislation more equality has been
> achieved, but at the same time some degree of protection for women, such
> as the prohibition of night-shift work, has been removed. This means that
> in the future more opportunities will be available for women, but they will
> have to compete with men on an equal footing. (Japanese branch, foreign
> educational/cultural organization)

> In the future women will be able to test their possibilities, but at the same time they will be held responsible for their choices. (English-language instructor)

It is interesting to observe certain common tendencies among each of the two groups of people, namely those who are opposed to gender-based role differentiation and those who support it. First of all, in regard to the pattern of answers to the three questions, we can say that those who are opposed to role differentiation feel that the change has been slow so far and that it will take a long time before the idea as well as the practices will be completely eliminated, as in the United States. To them today's United States is the model for Japan to follow. On the other hand, those who are in favor of role differentiation see the change as being so rapid and widespread that the trend cannot be stopped. They have strong reservations about today's U.S. society and family and feel that Japan should not follow the footsteps of the United States.

Second, we find that the profiles of the two groups of people are different. Of the eleven people who were against, five were anchored in management competence, three in autonomy, and two in technical/functional competence. Furthermore, with the exception of one alumnus, all changed their jobs, many at relatively early stages of their careers. Two of them were staying abroad when they responded to the questionnaire. Three were working for NPOs. On the other hand, of the nine people who were for it, eight were anchored in management competence, with only one anchored in technical/functional competence. Only one changed his job at an early stage. At the time of the interviews, two were working for the original employers, another three with the subsidiaries, and another three were working for different companies after more than thirty years of service with the original employers.

Thus, we may be able to call the first group of people "movers" and the second group of people "stayers." So it is only natural that movers are more progressive and are thus against gender-based role differentiation, while the stayers are more conservative. The third group of people is similar to the second group in terms of their career make-up. However, their positions are not as clear-cut as those of the first group. Perhaps factors such as their family background and their relations with their own family members might account for the difference.

The final question asked if the Japanese economic growth had been achieved at the expense of our participants' family lives and family members. Of the thirty alumni, only five answered "no." The remaining twenty-five agreed with the statement to varying degrees. In addition, we could not observe clear-cut relations between the answers to this question and the answers to the earlier questions on gender-based role differentiation, as most alumni answered "yes" to this question.

The five alumni who answered "no" to this question offer the following reasons:

I believe that Japanese economic prosperity would have been possible without the sacrifice of family life. It is true that Japanese men have worked long hours and in this sense their family lives were sacrificed. I do not think, however, that the intensity of work of Japanese people is by any means high. Therefore, high economic growth would have been possible if Japanese men had worked rationally and gone home at 5 P.M. every day. Working long hours is a course of behavior peculiar to Japanese men on the value premise that one has to sacrifice one's personal life for the benefit of one's master to win in the race for promotion. (business consultant)

Japanese economic growth was a result of Japan's successful production system. Sacrifice of family life is a secondary and less significant factor. In fact, workaholics exist in other countries as well. Rather, working while separated far from one's family was a factor contributing to a bad image about the quality of life in Japan. (auditor, department store)

I think the evaluation is relative in that, if a majority of people in society put a higher priority on work, then family members tend to accept it. However, when the proportion of people who put a higher priority on personal life is greater, then the evaluation will change. My own opinion is that to the extent that Japanese economic growth has brought about prosperity in individual lives, we cannot say that family life was sacrificed. (business consultant)

If there were positive returns to the family, then we cannot say that the family was sacrificed. If the husband's promotion results in a higher income for the family, then it's natural for family members to accept [the long hours of work of] the husband (father). In retrospect, however, I feel that I should have had more opportunities to go out with my family. (president, medical machine company)

Although our family suffered a bit in the education of our children, I think that, overall, our family was not sacrificed by my work career, rather they are happy in many respects. (managing director, dept. store)

It seems that this alumnus is referring to their lives in foreign countries—London and New York. In fact, two of the twenty-five male alumni who agreed to the question qualified their statements to the effect that although their family lives were sacrificed in Japan, on their overseas assignments their family members enjoyed living abroad. As we have seen in Chapters 8, 12, and 17 with a few exceptions, our alumni stated that they very much enjoyed their family lives abroad, especially when their children were small.

Of the twenty-five alumni who agreed with the statement, some referred specifically to their own cases, while others provided more general observations. In the following we will first look at the former type of response:

I agree with the statement to a large extent and I think my wife agrees, too, because she often complains that we have had little conversation. I think that Japanese men in our generation have a tendency not to talk about work at home. Perhaps the younger generation has changed so that they have more work-related conversation at home. I also have to admit that I have not had enough conversation with my children either. (managing director, synthetic fiber company)

Overall, I have to say yes. Although I have tried not to sacrifice my family life, it's up to my wife to decide to what extent I succeeded in it. (managing director, petrochemical engineering company)

I have to agree to a certain extent. In particular, even though my wife and I are both from Tokyo, I was transferred to different locations many times, so my family experienced some difficulties in adjusting to new environments—schools, communities, and especially neighborhoods where the families of co-workers lived in the company-owned houses. (senior manager, brewery company and registered consultant)

When I look back on my life so far, I have to admit that I have sacrificed my family. Now, when my children are married and about to have their own children, their lifestyles are considerably different from what lifestyles were when I was their age. (senior managing director, family-owned lumber wholesaling company)

I was a secretary to the president, so that there was no time for our own family life when my wife was busy raising children. When I had time I played tennis. I never went to my children's school athletic meets or PTA meetings. In those days I never thought that I was sacrificing my family; rather, I thought that was the normal life for men. But my wife still complains about the hardships in those days. (senior manager, fishery company)

I had to leave the responsibility of raising my children entirely to my wife while I was away from home for six long years on my work assignment in Seoul. (former senior manager, general trading company)

The statement applies to my case to a certain extent. In my thirties and early forties I was so busy with work that I had to bring work back home. As a result, I did not spend much time with my family. It seems that the nature of family sacrifice changes over time. (senior consultant, human resource management)

I have tried not to sacrifice my family. But I think Japanese families in general were sacrificed. I am afraid that Japanese men are paying the price now. (senior manager, Japanese branch of a foreign electric machine company)

I think this statement is largely true. Although I don't think that I've been a "company man," I have had a stronger work orientation than foreign people in my capacity. (executive councilor, economic association)

Those alumni who made general observations state the following:

What contributed to the growth and prosperity of "Japan Incorporated" were hard-working Japanese men under "Japanese-style" management. They sacrificed their personal time and family life in order to work for the company for twenty-four hours with utmost loyalty and endurance. (former senior manager, general trading company)

I agree with the statement. In my view, Japanese companies have deliberately adopted a slow promotion policy with the objective of letting employees participate in the promotion race for a long time. The most visible way to compete is to work long hours. As a result, Japanese men work long hours for a long period of time in the hope of getting a promotion. I am sure that such actions on the part of Japanese men have been a source of corporations' growth and prosperity. (educational consultant, NPO in Indonesia)

The above views are shared by many alumni, although they did not state them as explicitly as the above alumnus. There are also alumni who feel that long hours of hard work were the only way for postwar Japan to recover and catch up with the then more advanced economies. As for the future, then, one alumnus states:

In the past, Japanese men were very naive in that they worked very hard and found pleasure in doing that. From now on, when the chances of promotion become even slimmer, many people will feel it's absurd to sacrifice their family lives for the sake of the company. (former president, subsidiary of general trading company)

On the other hand, there is a minority view rejecting the idea that Japanese men are the only workaholics, as we see in the following statements:

I agree with the statement only 50 percent, because there are workaholics in the United States, too. (managing director, trading company)

In any growing economy people tend to work hard and for long hours. (adviser, Japanese subsidiary of foreign bank)

As for alumnae, opinions were split—three in favor, two against, and one no response. Those who were in favor have these remarks to make:

To a certain extent we can say that families were sacrificed. Transfer to a new post without taking the family along is a good example. However, when I see male office staff working overtime I wonder if they really need to work overtime. It looks like there is much room for improvement in their work methods. (Japanese branch, foreign educational/cultural organization)

In a sense, Japanese economic prosperity was achieved at the cost of sacrifices of families. It is unnatural for the father to be always away from the home. Isn't work intensity more important than hours of work? (English-language instructor)

I agree with the statement. When looking back, I think there was a long period of being a "fatherless family," although I did not always feel that we were a victim of the system. (co-owner, specialty store)

Those who were against say:

I do not think that I was a victim. It depends on which of the two alternatives a wife chooses: to do everything together with the husband or to enjoy her own activities alone. (self-employed, language school and translation)

Since both my husband and I worked at our own art gallery, our son was a latchkey child. But now he says that he wants to marry a woman with a full-time job, so I don't think he feels that he was a victim of working parents. Of course, I have never thought that I was sacrificed by our busy work. (co-owner, art gallery)

Overall, our participants, both men and women, agree that Japanese men worked hard and for long hours for their companies, to the neglect of their families. While many think that this was the major cause of the success of Japanese businesses, some deny the connection. Furthermore, many admit that the above-mentioned traditional lifestyle is changing: younger-generation Japanese men place more values on their family lives than their parents' generation did, while an increasing number of married women continue to work after marriage.

The views of our participants introduced in this chapter may be summarized as follows: first, at the basic (emotional) level, Japanese people are not different from people in the rest of the world, and only the method of expression is different. Second, the way of thinking, values, and temperament of the peoples of the world are somewhat different from one another, and it is not true that Japan alone is different from the rest of the world. Third, the traits of the Japanese people have changed and will continue to change according to changing environmental factors. Fourth, the degree of homogeneity is high among Japanese people because of Japan's history and education. Fifth, although opinions were divided about gender-based role differentiation, there was an agreement that employment discrimination against women will sooner or later disappear. Finally, although Japanese men worked hard and for long hours for their employers to the neglect of family life, younger-generation Japanese will prefer more diversified lifestyles.

24
Change of
Japanese-Style Management

This chapter introduces the views of twenty-six alumni on Japanese-style management. Information was not available from four alumni. Furthermore, no attempt was made to obtain information from the six alumnae, because none of them worked for a typical Japanese corporation.

The following four questions were asked:

(1) During your work career extending over thirty-five years, to what extent did you practice the so-called Japanese-style management? Has the practice changed over the years?

(2) In what situations were Japanese management practices a success (or a failure)?

(3) Do you think Japanese-style management practices are based on spiritual attributes such as perseverance, diligence, loyalty, and modesty? Or, were the practices adopted in an attempt to deal with a specific set of environmental conditions?

(4) In the future, when globalization is expected to accelerate, what will happen to each element of Japanese-style management?

In asking the above questions we did not provide a uniform definition of "Japanese-style management," because we were interested in soliciting diverse views from our alumni. As expected, many different answers were given, especially to the first question. A few alumni doubted, or even rejected, the existence of "Japanese-style" management, while a majority accepted its existence. Some provided their own definitions, while others answered the question without defining it. Some made specific reference to their overseas experiences, while others gave answers in reference to their entire work career.

Those alumni who rejected or doubted the existence of Japanese-style management provided the following statements:

> After graduation I was employed by a large corporation for only seven years, so I cannot tell from my own experience what Japanese-style management is, exactly. After I started my own business, I have muddled through; I have never given thought to corporate philosophy. (self-employed, employment agency)

Apart from his own experience, he has the following observation to make:

> I have strong reservations about the view that a Japanese management system was consciously created by Japanese managers with permanent employment, a length-of-service wage and promotion system, and enterprise unionism as its components; rather, it evolved naturally out of the employers' need for workforce maintenance and employees' need for job security. I do not think that the top management of large Japanese corporations are that far-seeing; they can take into consideration only two to three years ahead, as exemplified by their behavior during the bubble economy period.

> Throughout my career with my original employer (general trading company), I gave no thought to whether business and management practices adopted by the company were uniquely Japanese. Even today I wonder if there has been a uniform management system that is uniquely Japanese and that applies to all Japanese companies. (managing director, trading company)

> I have given little thought to whether I have personally practiced Japanese-style management. In my experience, it was difficult to solicit good ideas and suggestions from the bottom of the management hierarchy. Important issues were discussed and decided at the top management level and directions were given to the lower level. (managing director, department store; formerly senior manager, bank)

> I disagree with the notion that the so-called Japanese-style management is uniquely Japanese. It largely reflects a specific set of circumstances of postwar Japan. American management prior to the Great Depression had elements similar to those of the so-called Japanese-style management. (adviser, Japanese branch of foreign bank; formerly senior manager, trust bank)

However, by far a majority of alumni accepted the existence of Japanese-style management either explicitly or implicitly. Those who provided their own specifications did so in terms of underlying values, practices, or both. Those who stressed the underlying values gave the following answers:

> Japanese-style management has been supported by formal education since the Meiji era that has emphasized such ethical values as the disavowal of

betrayal, a sense of responsibility, and the concept of shame. These Japanese attitudes are weakening, but I think they will continue to a certain extent. If they no longer serve as the guiding principles for business people, then Western methods of management will become necessary. (president, joint venture with foreign company)

I think that the underlying value premise of Japanese-style management is sincerity, or the idea of treating people with respect. This is not only a Japanese but also a universal value premise. Permanent employment and length-of-service-based practices originate from this concept, and, as such, I highly value these practices. I do not think that it will change with time. (co-owner and former senior managing director, family-owned bedding company)

I think that loyalty to the company is the most distinct feature of Japanese business people. I am often asked by my foreign business associates what Japanese are working for and why Japanese managers sometimes violate laws (e.g., making illegal payments to *sokaiya,* or professional trouble-makers at shareholders meetings). My answer of "for the sake of the company" is quickly countered by a follow-up question: "Is the company a god or religion?" It is difficult to answer this question. In reality, on the part of the company (including my former employer) the length-of-service-based pay system is being replaced by a performance-based pay system, and permanent employment is being eroded by workforce reduction. (senior manager, Japanese subsidiary of U.S. electric machine company)

The last statement refers both to values (loyalty) and to practices (permanent employment and length-of-service-based payment and promotion). In fact, these two practices were most frequently referred to by those alumni who answered that Japanese-style management was indeed practiced in their companies. Here are some examples:

Although there is no consensus as to exactly what is the Japanese management system, permanent employment and length-of-service principles clearly existed at my original employer. In addition, consensus decision making and group-based performance may also be mentioned as elements of the so-called Japanese-style management. All these elements are disappearing now, and employees have come to accept the changes. (former senior manager, general trading company)

My employer is a nonprofit federation of large business corporations; however, since it is a Japanese organization, it shares with business corporations common characteristics, including permanent employment, length-of-service principles, and intra-organizational unionism (I served as union president). The only difference with business corporations is that performance evaluation of individual employees is more difficult. Another key feature involving our organization (that may be unique to Japan) is the close collaboration with government ministries, with which we often work together. (executive counselor, economic association)

One alumnus identifies the length-of-service principle, permanent employment, and delegation of authority as the key elements of Japanese-style management and provides the following analysis:

These practices were born out of the specific environmental conditions of the postwar high economic growth period. As an example, as far as I know, permanent employment was not widely practiced in prewar Japan. In the postwar high economic growth period, companies provided high wages and welfare facilities to recruit and maintain a large number of employees. Also, since experienced senior managers from the prewar period were "purged" by the Allied Occupation forces, management authority was given to younger managers. (managing director, petrochemical engineering company)

Naturally, this alumnus sees that a lot of change has taken place since the collapse of the bubble economy. He says:

With the end of high economic growth, the collapse of the postwar politics–bureaucracy–business triad, and the decrease of the young-generation population, Japanese business is experiencing agonizing pain over structural change and the creation of a new system. Companies are forced to sell off welfare/recreation facilities, to adopt an early retirement system, and to scrap excess production facilities. The practices that were so praised in the 1980s are now totally rejected and nowhere to be found. Japanese people have lost confidence in Japanese business methods and are beginning to wonder if, after all, the American way isn't the best.

There is an alumnus who provides a penetrating analysis of permanent employment and the length-of-service principle. He notes:

These two practices are not uniquely Japanese, because they exist in certain companies in the United States or in European countries." (educational consultant, NPO in Indonesia)

According to him:

The length-of-service-based promotion practice is a reflection of a slow promotion system, which makes a sharp contrast with a fast-track system adopted in many U.S. and European companies. Under the slow promotion policy, Japanese employees work hard for a long period of time to stay in and win a promotion race.

Thus, he argues that, although permanent employment may look paternalistic, its essence, namely, slow promotion practices, are a rational management policy to extract a high level of efforts from a large number of employees for a long period of time.

According to this alumnus, slow promotion is also an egalitarian system, as it does not sharply distinguish between "winners" and "losers" at an early stage of the game. Egalitarianism is also apparent in Japanese companies in that there is no differential treatment associated with status between white-collar and blue-collar employees. He recognizes that Japanese-style management, thus defined, was in full operation in the original company who employed him for more than twenty-five years. He also observes that, since the collapse of the bubble economy, permanent employment has been substantially eroded, while the length-of-service principle has remained in most large companies.

There are alumni who identified other practices as important elements of the Japanese business/management system. One alumnus in the airline industry points out that a distinct characteristic of Japanese-style management is found in the method of decision making. He says:

> The process of decision making in Japan is not "top-down" but "bottom-up," and consensus building through behind-the-scenes maneuvers is characteristic of the Japanese system. Although it has been alleged that in this system the approval cycle is too long and slow, from my experience it has never been the cause of lost business opportunities; rather, it has worked well in ensuring reliable work execution. (senior managing director, airport ground service company)

Another alumnus (auditor, department store) shares with many others the view that "employment stability" is a distinct characteristic of Japanese-style management. He also adds that "guidance of private industry by the bureaucracy" is an important feature of the Japanese business system at the macro level. However, another alumnus points out that in his industry (fishery) government-industry collaboration is weaker in Japan than in other countries with major fishery industries. Instead, he identifies the "manufacturers' control of the distribution channels" as a distinct feature, although it has been considerably weakened lately.

In regard to marketing, another alumnus, senior marketing manager with a major brewery company, talks about his company:

> After decades of successful experience following World War II, the top management became complacent and did not come up with new products or strategies. Instead, they counted on the hard work of salespeople motivated by their perseverance and loyalty to the company. However, their efforts did not produce the desired results and the company's market share declined. This caused the salespeople's motivation to decline, too. Only when a new product line was introduced to the market through new distribution channels could the company reverse the trend of a declining market share.

His story suggests two key features of Japanese-style management: the hard work of lower-level employees out of a sense of perseverance and loyalty to the company, and neglect of a strategic approach on the part of top management.

A most comprehensive characterization of Japanese-style management is given by an alumnus who has taken part in the management of his uncle's company since a young age. His statement serves as a good summary of the various statements introduced so far. He says:

> The foundation of Japanese-style management is people, or placing a high value on the employees. By emphasizing the unity of interests of the employees and the employer, the employer attempts to strengthen the employees' sense of belonging to the company. The length-of-service-based pay and promotion practices, as well as permanent employment, have been effective devices for that purpose. The company has extracted devoted service from the employees by making them believe that working for the sake of the company is, after all, working for themselves. In a sense, this method of relying on employees' high work motivation was an easy way for the employer to manage the company. And the president and I ran the company this way for a long time. (senior managing director, construction materials wholesaler)

He continues:

> However, the sense of belonging to the company has recently been declining among employees, especially young employees. In particular, they are not happy with our practice of paying long-serving employees, who contributed to the company in the past, high wages. Therefore, we have substantially modified the length-of-service pay system. However, it is difficult to abolish the permanent employment practice.

Finally, we will introduce the views of two alumni who worked for U.S. firms in Japan for most of their careers. They provide insightful views on Japanese-style management, although they themselves did not work under it. Here are their comments:

> Between Japanese and Americans I notice a big difference in the thought process and the style of communication. While the American thought process is rational and logical, the Japanese thought process is influenced by emotional concern for the other party. As a result, the Japanese prefer indirect expressions, while the Americans prefer straight talk. In business settings, direct U.S. expressions cause friction with the Japanese, and indirect Japanese expressions cause frustration on the part of the Americans. So, for U.S. business people operating in Japan, fluency in the Japanese language is not sufficient; they must change their thought process and ways of

expression to the Japanese style. The same applies to the Japanese business people who are fluent in English. (public relations consultant; former senior manager, Japanese subsidiary of U.S. oil company)

I have never worked for a large Japanese company, and, therefore, I have no clue as to what the so-called three sacred treasures are like. However, from my experience as a consultant and a practitioner in human resource management, I can point out one big difference in the pay system between the Japanese companies and foreign companies operating in Japan. While in Japanese companies wages are paid to people according to their job ability (often measured by the employee's length of service), in foreign companies wages are paid to the jobs according to their values. It is difficult to apply the latter type of "pay for job" to Japanese employees in Japan, where the concept of job is not well established and job descriptions rarely exist. (senior consultant in human resource management)

Based on the above two statements, we can add "indirect communication" and "a lack of the concept of the job" to the list of the characteristics of Japanese business and management. As our alumni suggest, we can safely say that these two features are observed in virtually all Japanese corporations.

After reviewing a number of statements of our alumni on Japanese-style management, we are now in a position to answer the two-part question raised at the beginning of this chapter: (1) to what extent was Japanese-style management actually practiced? and (2) have those practices changed over the years?

Regarding the first part of the question, a majority view seems to be that the so-called Japanese-style management with permanent employment and the length-of-service principle as the key components were indeed practiced in the companies that employed our alumni. As for the second part of the question, virtually all alumni concur that the characteristics of Japanese management have been weakened, especially since the burst of the bubble economy almost a decade ago. Only a very few defend the position that the underlying values of Japanese management—concern for people—have remained essentially unchanged.

Before leaving this topic we will introduce the comments of alumni regarding their experiences overseas. While some alumni practiced, or at least attempted to practice, Japanese methods of management, others did not. We begin with the statements of those who did.

Of the elements of Japanese-style management, those related to production and technology were quickly and fully adopted in overseas factories, while those related to sales and accounting took much longer. This tendency has not changed over time; rather, the time required for introduction differed according to the culture of the countries to which I was assigned (the United States, Malaysia, Hong Kong, and the United Kingdom). (managing director, synthetic fiber company)

In all overseas offices to which I was assigned (Melbourne, Portland, San Francisco, and Seattle) the business and management practices of the main office were followed. The only exception was the management of local employees. Neither permanent employment nor the length-of-service-based pay was adopted because the turnover rate of local employees was high. (senior manager, general trading company)

I introduced certain elements of the company's standard office procedures (in Honolulu and Saipan). They included greeting customers without fail and answering the telephone before the fourth ring as concrete expressions of the "customers come first" policy. I had group leaders be the first to follow these procedures, thereby demonstrating to the rank-and-file employees desirable behaviors. I also set up suggestion boxes in an attempt to solicit and reflect employees' ideas on office management. In the beginning, I encountered some resistance, but, in the end, the employees understood the importance of customer service and accepted these practices as part of standard office procedures. (senior manager, airline company)

On the other hand, there are alumni who did not introduce Japanese methods overseas. They were rather critical of the Japanese practices, as the following statements suggest:

I have always rejected many aspects of the so-called Japanese-style management, as they were personally unacceptable to me. Therefore, I have made every effort not to follow them throughout my career. (owner and general manager, travel agent in the Philippines)

It may be worth noting that, after early "retirement" from a major airline company, he opted to start his business overseas, not in Japan.

In Japanese-style management, it is not clear where responsibility lies, because Japanese prefer collective responsibility; the presidents of Japanese companies usually do not express their own opinions in public. However, collective responsibility tends to degenerate into irresponsibility. This is where foreign business people feel uneasy with Japanese companies. (senior manager, general trading company)

Looking back on his days in Seattle, where he was general manager of the branch office, he continues:

I told them in my own words where I stood and where responsibility lay. For example, I took the initiative in involving local employees in discussing lawsuit cases. I took charge in sales promotion, writing job descriptions, and setting up procedures for job assignments.

In my opinion Japanese people are highly observant of what others do. As a result, many Japanese top managers lack their own management philosophies. Although there may be company rules and codes of ethics, they often are not observed; instead, they may easily be swept aside by the current of the times. Within the organization unique opinions tend to be neglected because of the strong pressure to conform. (senior manager, construction machine company)

Therefore, this alumnus did not force the use of Japanese methods in overseas offices; instead he followed local practices—managing in accord with the rule of the company (Germany), managing with flexibility (United Kingdom), and managing in line with company policies, including no bribery, no employment discrimination, and active support to charities (Canada). At a more concrete level he assigned jobs according to job descriptions in these countries.

The above six cases are evenly split between those in which Japanese methods were used and those in which they were not. On closer examination, however, the three positive cases provide much weaker evidence than the three negative cases. The first case refers mainly to production management in factories rather than to management practice in offices, which is the main focus of this study. In the second case, the core elements of Japanese-style management—permanent employment and the length-of-service principle—were not applied to the local employees. In the third case, although certain home office practices, such as greeting the customers and answering the telephone promptly, were successfully transplanted, they could hardly be called the main characteristics of Japanese-style management.

On the other hand, the three negative cases are indisputable. In all three cases, our alumni opted not to use Japanese methods at all, either because of their own Westernized value premises, or because of circumstances in which Japanese methods simply would not have worked, or because of both. Whichever may be the case, Japanese methods were intentionally and totally avoided in those three cases. Overall, then, we can safely say that in the overseas offices Japanese-style management was not widely practiced throughout the period under study.

In the second question, it was asked in what situations our alumni considered Japanese-style management practices to be a success or a failure. Apparently, this was a difficult question, because one-third did not answer, and those who answered provided rather indirect answers. The answers we were given were categorized into two groups according to the level of practices to which our alumni were referring: the company (or office) level, and the national (or general) level.

We will begin with the statements at the company level. An alumnus with a synthetic fiber company that transplanted a Japanese-style production system to overseas factories has this to say:

> From my personal experience of overseas operations, I have come to the conclusion that it is possible to change the "practice" but not the "culture." The problem is where to draw a line between the practice and the culture. (managing director, synthetic fiber company)

He gives an example:

> In our factory in the United Kingdom, supervisors working in shifts used to go home on time when the shift was over, even though there was a problem, if it occurred in a process for which a particular supervisor was not directly responsible. By asking the supervisors in the process where a problem occurred and [the supervisors] in the next process that would be affected by the problem to stay for thirty minutes to discuss and solve the problem, the work flow resumed smoothly. In this case, thirty minutes were the limit, in that a request to stay up to thirty minutes longer was accepted as a change in practice. Beyond thirty minutes would have resulted in a change in lifestyle (or culture), and therefore would have been unacceptable.

Another alumnus with a general trading company recalls his experience as general manager of a Seattle branch office:

> Our office ran into many lawsuits involving employment discrimination. Such matters as the ratio of Japanese employees to local employees became a focal point. As a company operating in the United States, we had to do a number of things to rectify the situation. (president, subsidiary of general trading company; formerly senior manager, general trading company)

His statement is not specific about what practices were alleged to be discriminatory, and therefore it begs analysis and interpretation. A statement from another alumnus, who was also working for a general trading company, illustrates the point. He says:

> In the case of management of overseas offices of general trading companies, head office personnel and employees hired overseas are dealt with under different systems. The kind of general trading work or line jobs in general trading companies requires knowledge and experience built up over a long period of time, while local employees are hired on the premise that they would not be working for a long time. As a result, personnel hired by overseas offices are assigned not to line jobs but to staff and support jobs. (senior manager, general trading company)

This kind of logic would have been perfectly acceptable in Japan. But in the United States, it borders on employment discrimination. "Differential treatment" on the basis of nationality, gender, age, and so forth may be called a shortcoming of Japanese-style management when practiced in countries with strong anti-discrimination legislation. The experience of our alumnus in Seattle was ironic, because he always had doubts over Japanese methods of management and made every effort to introduce American-style management.

Referring primarily to the domestic operations of their companies, two alumni made the following comments:

> In regard to bottom-up management, unless there is, in daily work, an organizational climate in which employees are encouraged to come up with new ideas, and unless higher-level managers are willing to listen to the opinions of their subordinates, bottom-up management would not work. (managing director, department store; formerly senior manager, bank)

Thus, this alumnus stresses the importance of congruity with the organizational climate.

> The plant profit center system adopted in our company, whereby the manufacturing plant is responsible for devising measures for preventing losses, bore success up to a point. However, that system caused delays in properly dealing with sudden changes in market prices, resulting in the decreased competitiveness of the company. (managing director, plant construction company; formerly senior manager, electric machine company)

It seems that making light of the market discipline was not limited to this company alone.

In regard to business and management practices at the national or general level, several alumni have already stated in their answers to the first question that, in effect, the Japanese style was suitable under a high growth economy, but not so under a low growth economy. A large number of alumni echo this sentiment. Here are some of their comments.

> The so-called Japanese-style management was born naturally, out of necessity in the postwar conditions. It was considered successful because of Japan's postwar economic success. Since the environment is changing, there is no point sticking to the old practices; top-level managers have to come up with new ideas. (advisor, Japanese subsidiary of U.S. bank; formerly senior manager, trust bank)

> Japanese-style management was very successful when the economy was growing rapidly. It serves as a constraining factor when companies have to downsize. (business consultant; formerly senior managing director, family-owned bedding manufacturer)

Since the collapse of the bubble economy, permanent employment is being eroded by restructuring under pressures for improvement in profitability, globalization, computerization, and quick decision making. (educational consultant, NPO in Indonesia)

The length-of-service system functioned well under consensus management or the system of group decision making. However, when environmental change forces the company to seek individual ability and performance, then it becomes necessary to promote talented young people over those with long service but without much ability, thus eroding the length-of-service promotion system. (managing director, travel agent; formerly senior manager, general trading company)

In the past, such spiritual attributes as loyalty on the part of employees contributed to the growth of corporations, especially those in manufacturing. However, as we are witnessing now, when this goes too far, employees violate laws for the sake of their company. (senior manager, Japanese subsidiary of U.S. electric machine company; formerly senior manager, electric machine company)

With the transition to a low-growth economy, intensification of global competition, deregulation, and commitment to the market mechanism, changes are taking place at the microeconomic level. Under increased pressure for restructuring, companies are rapidly changing various management practices. In a word, the foundation that has supported Japanese-style management has collapsed and the time has come to search for new management methods suitable for a new set of environmental factors. (executive counselor, economic association)

Finally, an alumnus who worked for a Japanese subsidiary of a major U.S. oil company throughout most of his career comments:

Japanese companies have incorporated European and American business concepts and institutions as useful tools. However, Japanese business people still fare poorly in skills of straight talk and direct debate when it comes to communicating in the international setting. . . . Further, in Japanese corporations, individual responsibility has not yet been established. In particular, top management tends to be complacent and to rely on government regulations in conducting business. These behaviors result in higher costs in Japan, which reduces international competitiveness. (public relations consultant; formerly senior manager, Japanese subsidiary of U.S. oil company)

The statements of our alumni on the second question may be summarized as follows:

(1) Japanese methods of production management can be transplanted to overseas factories with minor adjustment to local cultures;

(2) Japanese methods of personnel management are difficult to transplant to overseas offices because of differences in labor market institutions and legislation (including laws on equal employment);

(3) Japanese-style management was born out of the postwar high growth economy, and, as such, it functions well under a high growth economy but not under a low growth economy; and

(4) there is a lot of room for improvement in Japanese-style management to stand the test of rigorous global market competition.

The third question asked whether Japanese-style management practices are based on spiritual attributes such as perseverance, diligence, loyalty, and modesty, or shaped by a specific set of environmental conditions. Eight alumni were in favor of spiritual attributes, seven were in favor of environments, ten did not take a position, and information was not available from the remaining five alumni.

The following are the statements from those who were in favor of spiritual attributes:

> I think that spiritual attributes are more important in shaping Japanese-style management practices. In this sense, the role of education is important. I advocate education on the basis of Confucian values. (president, joint venture with foreign medical company)

> I think that perseverance, loyalty, modesty, and the like, are imprinted in the spiritual nature of the Japanese people. These attributes play important roles in business management not only in certain specific conditions but also in all conditions. (president, Japanese subsidiary of foreign manufacturing company)

> These spiritual attributes may be summarized by "sincerity," as I said before. It means to be honest with oneself and to be comfortable with what one does. If one can do this, one is happy. I think this concept is universal; its applicability is not limited to a certain specific situation. (business consultant; formerly senior managing director, family-owned bedding company)

> Spiritual attributes always exist within oneself. In case of a failure they are used as an excuse, and, in case of a success, they work as a driving force. (registered professional consultant; formerly senior manager, brewery company)

> I completely agree with the spiritual theory. They are uniquely Japanese spiritual attributes. They have to be taught since childhood. (senior manager, real estate company; formerly senior manager general trading company)

> I support the spiritual theory. As for the situational explanation, it's difficult to decide to what extent a certain practice is Japanese. For example,

the U.S. auto industry introduced certain Japanese methods. Those adopted methods may no longer be called uniquely Japanese. (senior manager, Japanese subsidiary of U.S. electric machine company; formerly senior manager, electric machine manufacturer)

I think the so-called Japanese-style management is a carryover of practices from the Edo era. They solely depended on the employees' perseverance, diligence, loyalty, and modesty. As the twenty-first century approaches, they are totally outdated. (owner and general manager, travel agent in the Philippines; formerly senior manager, airline company)

A management style that emphasized those spiritual attributes was a most appropriate method in postwar conditions, where we had to start from nothing. Many of my business associates in Southeast Asia recognize that Japanese people's spiritual attributes were the driving force for Japan's postwar economic reconstruction. (senior managing director, family-owned construction materials wholesaler)

In addition to emphasis on the importance of the spiritual foundation of Japanese-style management, there are other common threads running through the above statements. First, with the exception of one case, perseverance, diligence, loyalty, and modesty are considered to be characteristic, if not unique, to Japanese people. Second, these spiritual attributes are considered to be more or less stable over the years. In this connection, it may be added that in two cases the role of education is stressed as a means to retain and reinforce these attributes.

We will now introduce the statements that placed more emphasis on the influence of the environmental factors.

As mentioned before, many practices that constitute Japanese-style management were born out of the specific environment of postwar Japan, although I do not completely deny the influence of unique cultural values stemming from Buddhism and Confucianism. I think the fact that Japanese people adopted polytheism has greatly contributed to the shaping of the realistic and flexible ways of thinking of Japanese people. For this reason Japan has been able to achieve structural alteration through abandonment of past practices on a regular basis. So, postwar Japanese-style management is a reflection of the realistic and flexible nature of Japanese people. (managing director, chemical engineering company)

The so-called Japanese-style management has been nurtured in the political, geographic, and cultural environment and history specific to Japan. However, when compared to other non-Western countries, Japanese management practices are not so unique. Through business dealings and negotiations with non-Western countries, I strongly feel that our ways of thinking and behavior have been considerably Westernized. For example, in negotiating a joint venture with the former Soviet Union, we had great difficulty explaining to them the concept of interest and the fact that in Japan fish prices change from day to day according to supply and demand in the wholesale market; in the Soviet Union fish prices used to be determined by the Ministry of Fisheries and announced daily. (senior manager, fishery company)

I do not subscribe to the spiritual attributes theory. Business and management methods arise and are passed down in accordance with the economic, social, and international circumstances in which we find ourselves. Therefore, management practices change when circumstances change. There is no universal and immutable management system. (managing director, department store; formerly senior manager, bank)

I think environmental factors were more important than spiritual attributes. I admit, however, groupism, an important element of Japanese-style management, stems from the old concept of family, which places more value on the family than on the individual. (adviser, Japanese subsidiary of U.S. bank; formerly senior manager, trust bank)

Elements of Japanese-style management such as permanent employment and the length-of-service system were created out of the needs of both employers and employees; they were not born out of uniquely Japanese spiritual attributes. Bottom-up decision making may be unique to Japan; however, real decisions are made by top management, and the bottom-up process is a method of creating formal consensus. (owner and general manager, employment service company)

I cannot support the spiritual theory, because it will not stand the test of time. During the "catch up and pass" period, a group mentality founded on the spirit of harmony was good, but from now on, establishment of individuality and specialization will be increasingly sought after. (executive counselor, economic association)

As can be seen from the above statements, those who support the environmental interpretation do not view Japanese-style management to be immutable; rather, it changes with the changing environment. Some of them concede, however, that spiritual attributes cannot be totally disregarded.

A variety of answers were provided from those who did not take a position. Some incline more toward the spiritual theory, as the following remarks suggest.

The religious background of spiritual attributes is being lost, and, therefore, they are no longer characteristic of Japanese management. However, the spiritual theory may have been true to some degree up to the first half of the 1980s, when top-level managers possessed their firms' philosophies. (president, subsidiary of construction machine company; formerly senior manager, construction machine company)

It seems that loyalty was nurtured by helping each other in times of difficulty with family-like unity, by sacrificing oneself to some degree to achieve success, and by sharing the pleasure of success. (managing director, plant construction company; formerly senior manager, electric machine company)

One alumnus comments on the relationship between management practices and certain spiritual attributes.

Given the system of permanent employment and length-of-service wages and promotion in which one is automatically promoted if one works diligently, many people must have worked with perseverance and loyalty to the company. (managing director, travel agent; formerly senior manager, general trading company)

In a sense, his statement reverses the relationship between management practices and certain spiritual attributes in that he thinks Japanese management institutions induced desirable employee attitudes and behaviors.

Another alumnus comments on transplanting certain values overseas.

In regard to spiritual attributes, it is not possible to force certain value judgments on foreign peoples. However, one can convey a message to a certain extent if one uses expressions familiar to them, such as "never give up" or "for the team." The point is that one must appreciate the culture of the country to which one is assigned and find expressions congruent with the local culture. (managing director, synthetic fiber company)

Others simply identified some management practices or spiritual attributes they considered characteristic of Japanese business or Japanese people in general.

I think some spiritual attributes derive from the world of Japanese martial arts. (senior manager, airline company)

Basic to Japanese management is "prudentialism" born of the perception that Japanese are a homogeneous race and the belief in the concept of "one race, one mind," held by Japanese people. (managing director, trading company; formerly senior manager, general trading company)

The Oriental side of Japan has not changed much. While there are many good facets in this, it poses a problem in regard to interaction with societies with different cultures. (public relations consultant; formerly senior manager, Japanese subsidiary of U.S. oil company)

> Key features of Japanese management include groupism, organizational power, and people-oriented management, often resulting in a system in which the locus of responsibility is unclear. On the other hand, in foreign firms, both in Japan and abroad, as one moves up the corporate hierarchy, one is required to make a decision òn one's own. (senior consultant in human resource management; formerly senior manager with several foreign companies in Japan)

> Looking at Japan internationally, instead of permanent employment or the length-of-service promotion system, I consider "egalitarianism" or disavowal of elitism to be the most distinct feature of Japanese management. (educational consultant, NPO in Indonesia)

As we have seen so far, the answers to the third question are not conclusive. It may mean that many alumni feel that both spiritual attributes and environmental factors contributed to the shaping of Japanese-style management and that many alumni found it difficult to choose one side over the other. This observation can be supported by the fact that, of those who took a position, some qualified their answers.

Our final question asked what will become of individual elements of Japanese-style management as internationalization and globalization evolve. Of the twenty-six alumni who answered this question, all except one alumnus predicted that, overall, Japanese-style management will change sooner or later, although some qualified their answers by stating that certain elements will remain unchanged.

One alumnus who predicted that there will be no change referred to his own employer (an airline company), while all others provided general observations. Essentially what this alumnus says is that the airline company will continue to use certain sales and personnel management methods in a few overseas offices; he does not talk about corporate-level business and management practices.

Some alumni commented on Japanese-style management as a whole, while others were more specific about what element(s) would remain unchanged and what element(s) would change. We will turn to the first type of (general) statements.

> In the face of internationalization and liberalization, Japanese-style management will become more Westernized. (president, Japanese subsidiary of foreign company)

> On average, Japanese management stresses the importance of people (or humanity), while American management stresses economic rationality. I think it's important for individual managers to maintain a balance between these two goals. Relative weights will vary according to the specific envi-

ronment in which a business exists as well as the value judgments of individual managers. Although it has become difficult to maintain a balance under a low growth economy, individual managers must deal with the situation with sincerity. (business consultant, formerly senior managing director, family-owned bedding company)

This statement could be interpreted to mean that Japanese-style management will shift more toward the American type of management that seeks economic rationality.

As the Japanese economy and society become more international, the management practices will also change or will have to change. (senior manager, fishery company)

Today, a faster-acting and transparent management style is greatly called for. Japanese management practices that do not lend themselves to this new trend will fade. (senior managing director, airport ground service company; formerly senior manager, airline company)

Japanese-style management will gradually decline or will have to change, because it is behind in many respects. We cannot expect that things will continue to go well simply because they have thus far. (president, subsidiary of general trading company; formerly senior manager, general trading company)

A couple of alumni say that not all companies will change the same way:

Japan's labor cost is the highest in the world, and many Japanese companies have already lost the ability to compete internationally; nevertheless, they keep losing money in the international market. Only those firms that have realized this fact will restructure themselves and survive global competition. Under a low growth economy, polarization of industries and companies is taking place. (managing director, chemical engineering company)

Polarization of industries and companies into the so-called Western-type and Japanese-type will evolve. In the traditional industries, current Japanese-style management in personnel and decision making will undergo no great change; while in new industries (primarily computer and information-related industries), Western-type management methods will be quickly adopted. (managing director, trading company; formerly senior manager, general trading company)

Not all alumni think that change will be in the right direction, as the following statement suggests:

The virtues of Japanese corporations are all gone. For example, the corporate philosophy of Sumitomo *zaibatsu*, "never go after easy money," has long gone. Without such corporate philosophies, Japanese companies will be half Americanized. Japanese business on the whole will change in the wrong direction. (president, subsidiary of construction machine company; formerly senior manager, construction machine company)

Virtually all of the above statements suggest that in the face of accelerating business globalization, Japanese-style management will undergo change, and that the direction of change is toward Western, or, more specifically, American-style, management with strong market orientation. This implies that, among other changes, both permanent employment and length-of-service-based pay and promotion practices will be replaced by increased labor mobility and pay for job.

Those alumni who refer to specific elements of Japanese-style management make the following statements:

I think that, although Japanese spirit will continue on to some extent, on the whole, Japanese-style management will decline, because Western-style management with top-down decision-making and a performance-based reward system has a competitive advantage. There will be more competition in the labor market. Also, bottom-up management would not work; I would advocate "middle-up" management through intensive education and training of middle managers. (president, joint venture with European medical company; formerly senior manager, synthetic fiber company)

Japanese companies will adjust to such external pressures as the financial big bang and deregulation and will manage to survive in the new environment. In the process, however, Japanese companies will continue to rely on spiritual attributes such as the perseverance and diligence of their employees. Globalization means adopting common standards, and, in this sense, we must do away with the narrow idea that everything is OK as long as Japan or our company is OK; instead we must develop a broader point of view. (registered professional consultant; formerly senior manager, brewery company)

In terms of the degree of globalization, Japan is most advanced in the production and trading of goods, followed by capital and financial markets, management, lifestyles, and values, in that order; it is least globalized in workforce migration. As for future prospects, there is no room for further globalization in production and trading. Globalization will proceed in each of capital and financial markets, management, and workforce migration. It is difficult to predict if Japan will globalize in people's lifestyles and values. (managing director, department store; formerly senior manager, bank)

Those practices that mesh with the natural sentiment of Japanese people will be maintained, as long as they do not conflict with economic rationality or efficient operation of business. It seems that many practices of the so-called Japanese style management rob Japanese people of their innate adventurous spirit. (adviser, Japanese subsidiary of U.S. bank; formerly senior manager, trust bank)

Japanese management practices will be increasingly Westernized. Spiritual attributes such as perseverance, diligence, loyalty, and modesty will be maintained as long as businesses remain healthy. These values are still useful in Southeast Asia. (senior manager, Japanese subsidiary of U.S. electric machine company; formerly senior manager, electric machine company)

While methods of dealing with products have become globalized, methods of personnel management and accounting have yet to globalize. A number of employment discrimination lawsuits against Japanese companies in the United States and slow adoption of international accounting standards attest to this. The Japanese people will change very little spiritually (mentally). Overall, it will take a long time before Japanese-style management practices will collapse. (senior manager, general trading company)

Japan excels in the areas of manufacturing technology, quality control, production management (for example, the just-in-time system), and safety control, including danger prediction methods. These elements of Japanese-style management will be preserved; otherwise, Japan will not be able to come out on top in international competition. The problem is research, especially basic research, in which Japan is far behind as a result of a uniform education that stresses conformity. To break the status quo and to encourage diversity, reform must begin in the field of education. In this sense, the role of overseas returnee children and women will increase. (managing director, synthetic fiber company)

The above half a dozen or so statements suggest what elements of Japanese management will not or must not change. First, spiritual attributes and those practices most deeply rooted in them are difficult to change, whether one likes it or not. Second, management practices involving production need not or must not change, not because they are uniquely Japanese but because they are universal and superior. It is interesting to note that, on the scale of globalization, Japanese spirit and production management are at opposite ends.

We will now look at the elements that will or must change and what the direction of change will be. We have already seen some of them in the statements introduced so far. They include permanent employment, the length-of-service system, and bottom-up decision making. The following are additional comments.

Japanese-style management is in the process of fading out. Both permanent employment and the length-of-service pay system are undergoing change, with the latter being replaced by ability-based pay. Besides, the ideas behind QC circles did not originate in Japan. (formerly senior manager, general trading company)

While permanent employment is on the way out, the length-of-service promotion system may not be easily replaced by the elitist or fast-track promotion system. I wonder if there is a third system of selectively employing excellent personnel, while at the same time being careful not to discourage the non-selected group of people. (educational consultant, NPO in Indonesia)

I think that Japanese-style management will be replaced by American-style management. The American system, as I understand it, includes the following features: employees and the employer are on an equal footing and connected by an employment contract; evaluation of employees is made on the basis of performance or results; and the company helps the employees to develop their abilities. If not completely Americanized, most Japanese companies will move in that direction. (senior managing director, family-owned construction materials wholesaler)

In regard to how rapidly the change can be achieved, one alumnus provides the following observation.

I don't think that the character of Japanese management will change unless labor mobility becomes higher. However, changing a job is difficult in today's Japan. In my estimate, less than 10 percent of people possess the ability to find a new job on their own. Besides, job change often changes the social lives of family members. On the other hand, our values are undeniably changing, and we are verging upon a society in which all lifestyles will be acceptable. All in all, I would think that changes will probably occur within a ten-year span. (executive counselor, economic association)

Another alumnus also comments on labor mobility as follows:

We find movement of people with specific skills between companies. This movement tends to weaken traditional values such as perseverance, diligence, and loyalty to the company one is employed by. . . . For the companies to grow and prosper from now on, top managers themselves have to work and lead the company. (managing director, travel agent; formerly senior manager, general trading company)

On the latter point, an alumnus with long service in a foreign-owned petroleum company comments:

In the Japanese petroleum industry, foreign-owned companies outperform Japanese counterparts in terms of profit ratio. This is so because the speed with which these foreign-owned companies pursue managerial efficiency is incomparable due to much stronger pressure from their stockholders. If Japanese companies are to change, they would do well to develop a system of external directors who continuously monitor management performance and maintain intensity. (public relations consultant; formerly senior manager, Japanese subsidiary of U.S. oil company)

Here is another diagnosis:

Virtually all big companies are suffering from the "big firm disease," and its cause is group mentality. Big businesses should be broken up into a number of independent companies that in turn should be composed of a number of small groups. (senior consultant in human resource management; formerly senior manager of several foreign-owned companies in Japan)

Finally, one alumnus provides a contingency view:

We cannot generalize as to which elements are good or bad. I think that it depends on each company and on each situation. Only the results will tell. Nevertheless, overall, I think that Japanese-style management will begin to disintegrate. In particular, bottom-up management is too time-consuming, and, therefore, would not work in the age of globalization. (owner and general manager, employment agent)

The above statements suggest that, with the exception of production management, all elements of Japanese-style management will change— personnel management, decision making, and corporate governance. Our alumni seem to agree that, with globalization, Japanese markets are no longer insulated from external pressures and that, in order to survive in the Japanese market, Japanese companies must win competition in the global market under uniform rules of the game—rules called "free market competition."

The objective of this chapter was to introduce the views of our male participants on Japanese-style management. The findings may be summarized below.

(1) So-called Japanese-style management with permanent employment and the length-of-service principle as the key components were indeed practiced in the companies where our alumni were employed.

(2) The characteristics of Japanese management have been weakened, especially since the burst of the bubble economy.

(3) In the overseas offices, Japanese-style management was not widely practiced, while in overseas factories, Japanese production-management practices were widely used.

(4) Japanese-style management functions well under a high growth economy but not so well under a low growth economy.

(5) Both certain spiritual attributes and environmental factors contributed to the shaping of Japanese-style management; it is difficult to determine which was more important.

(6) Japanese-style management will undergo change in the direction of American-style management, although Japanese-style production management will be maintained and transplanted to other countries.

Conclusions: From Developmental Capitalism to Globalism?

The central question addressed in this book was whether Japanese business and management practices as well as the work lives of women will converge toward the Western model or will remain "uniquely Japanese" (Chapter 1). As the first step to answer this central question a number of key questions were identified and developed into interview guidelines (Prologue):

• To what extent is Japanese management unique?

• To what extent do attitudinal attributes alleged to be unique to Japanese, such as harmony, hierarchy acceptance, benevolence, loyalty, and love for learning, affect Japanese management?

• To what extent have Japanese companies overseas practiced Japanese management?

• In what ways is the social life of employees and their families living abroad different from that at home?

• What are the strengths and weaknesses of Japanese management? Or, under what conditions was Japanese management a success (failure)?

• Is Japanese management immutable? Or has it changed over the years?

• In what ways have Japanese women participated in economic activities over the past thirty-five years?

• To what extent has sex-based role differentiation changed over the past thirty-five years?

Management practices take place in certain environmental settings. Therefore, secondary source information was obtained with a view to answering the following question:

• In what ways have environmental factors—international, political, economic, social, as well as industry-specific—affected Japanese management?

After studying the career histories of thirty-six alumni and alumnae as well as general and industry-specific environments over the past forty years, we were able to answer the above questions, some more thoroughly than others. The following is a summary of our findings.

Japanese Management and Society

Permanent Employment and Bottom-up Decision Making

The first question addresses the "uniqueness" of Japanese management. After identifying the six areas of business and management practices, namely, human resource management, interorganizational relations, management decision making, production management, international operations, and corporate governance, we dealt primarily with human resource management (of managerial employees), management decision making, and international operations. Here we will comment on the first two issues, while the third issue will be discussed later.

First of all, in regard to managerial careers, we drew heavily on the concept of Schein's "career anchor" (Schein 1978). The Japanese system of permanent employment seems to emphasize managerial and security anchors. The nature of our sample was such that, of thirty alumni, twenty-eight started their careers with business organizations in which permanent employment seemed to be in operation, while the remaining two obtained a job with nonprofit organizations.

As it turned out, six were still with their original employers as of 1998, when our alumni were about sixty years old. Another fourteen were with their original employers in 1990 when they were in their early fifties. The fact that nearly two-thirds of the male alumni worked for the original employers for thirty years or more suggests that the commitment to long-term employment was strong on both sides, the employers and the employees. At the same time, a total of twelve employees were transferred out of the company (mostly to subsidiaries) before they reached the normal retirement age of sixty. In view of this, it would be more accurate to call the Japanese employment system "long-term" employment rather than "permanent employment" or "life-time employment," as far as managerial employees are concerned.

In terms of Schein's career anchors, while eighteen of the thirty alumni were judged to be anchored in managerial competence, anchors other than managerial competence were observed in twelve cases: four were autonomy/independence anchors and eight were technical/functional anchors, and none were anchored in creativity. Also, security anchors were observed as secondary anchors for those whose primary anchor was managerial competence. Considering the high degree of homogeneity in our sample in terms of academic background and initial career orientation, we may say that this variation is rather high.

Although Schein hypothesizes that career anchors are formulated at relatively early stages and remain stable throughout a person's entire career, several cases were observed in our sample in which career anchors changed. Furthermore, as the age of retirement approached, the security anchor tended to affect career decisions more than it did when the employee was young.

Next, in regard to decision making, we made observations at three different levels of management: lower middle (*kacho*) level, upper middle (*bucho*) level, and top management (*torishimariyaku* and above) level, along the lines of the Vroom-Yetton model (Vroom and Yetton 1973).

At the lower middle management level, most of our alumni were engaged in sales; therefore, our observation was limited to this function. With regard to the determination of the sales goals of a section, section managers were consulted, usually in a meeting called by the general managers. The general manager played a crucial role because the sales goals of a section were usually determined as part of the sales goals of the department. Usually, input from rank-and-file members of a section was nil or at most minimal.

This type of decision making cannot be called consensus or bottom-up decision making, as far as rank-and-file members were concerned. Neither was it group decision making, because they were not directly involved. For section managers, it may be called a group style because they were usually consulted in groups.

At the upper middle management level, our analysis focused on the use of *ringi*, supposedly a bottom-up decision-making process. Our findings suggest that the role of the rank-and-file members of a department in the *ringi* decision-making process was minimal; rather, the role of the general manager was crucial. Often he would write a *ringi* proposal and it would be his responsibility to sell the proposal to all concerned.

The *ringi* methods did not represent genuine bottom-up decision making about significant issues as far as the rank-and-file members were concerned. On the other hand, from the standpoint of the general manager, the *ringi* system may be called a form of bottom-up decision making as long as the general manager possesses the power to start a proposal to go to higher-level management on those issues that are not completely within his authority. It may also be called a form of consensus-building decision making in that he has to "sell" the documents to relevant people, including his fellow general managers.

At the top management level, it was found that *ringi* played a limited role in making company-wide decisions; various kinds of executive meetings (or committees) played a dominant role. Two of the five decision-making styles suggested by Vroom and Yetton, which may be called the consultative style and the consensus style, were found to be in operation. It seemed that the consensus style was used in manufacturing and transportation industries, while the consultative style was used in trading and service industries—a reflection of the paces required for different kinds of decision making.

Our observations so far may be summarized as follows:

(1) Long-term employment was practiced by all the employers in that employment was guaranteed at least until employers were in their early fifties. About two-thirds of our alumni preferred long-term employment, while the remaining one-third did not.

(2) Bottom-up management was not widely practiced; rather, "middle-up" management was practiced in most organizations. Consensus or consultative decision making was indeed preferred to individual decision making at the top management level.

Our findings suggest that both permanent employment and bottom-up decision making were an exaggeration. It is our conviction that Japanese personnel management and decision making are not diametrically opposed to their Western counterparts, but the difference is a matter of degree. Abundant cases are reported in the U.S. literature where both long-term employment and participative management are encouraged and practiced (Ouchi 1981).

Japanese Culture and Management

The second question addressed the role of Japanese culture, based on certain Confucian values, including harmony, hierarchy acceptance, benevolence, loyalty, and love of learning, on Japanese management practices. To answer this question we obtained the views of thirty alumni on whether spiritual attributes or environmental conditions were more influential in shaping Japanese-style management (Chapter 24). Eight alumni were in favor of such spiritual attributes as perseverance, diligence, loyalty, and modesty; seven favored the environment; ten did not take a position, and information was not available from the remaining five alumni. Thus, answers to this question were not conclusive. This may mean that many alumni felt that both spiritual attributes and environmental factors contributed to the shaping of Japanese-style management and that many find it difficult to choose one side over the other.

In this respect, we probed into the question of the uniqueness of Japanese people's way of thinking, their values, and temperament (Chapter 24). Of the thirty alumni, six agreed with the concept of uniqueness, seven disagreed, and the remaining seventeen answered that Japanese people possessed both common and unique elements. Of the six alumnae, only one stressed uniqueness, while the remaining five acknowledged both uniqueness and commonality.

Thus, by far, the majority view was eclectic: the way of thinking, values, and the temperament of the peoples of the world are different from one another, and it is not correct to say that Japan is uniquely different from the rest of the world.

In the interviews the following characteristics were often referred to as "uniquely" Japanese: a group mentality, harmony with others, lack of individuality, and lack of originality. Naturally, there is much overlap between this list of attributes and that of the attributes forming the basis of Japanese-style management mentioned above, although it is interesting to observe a tone of self-criticism in this list. It is also apparent that the attributes in the two lists draw heavily upon Confucian teachings.

It is generally believed that one is born into a national culture. This does not mean, however, that people naturally acquire culture; they learn culture from parents at home, teachers at school, and people in general in society. The role of formal education is particularly important. In this sense, Confucian-based moral education as exemplified by the Imperial Prescript of Education was of particular importance in prewar Japan (Chapter 3). Although the Prescript was repealed by the U.S. occupation forces after World War II and replaced by the Fundamentals of Education Law emphasizing democratic values, Confucian values have long been ingrained in corporate managers. They form the basis for corporate culture to be acquired by newly hired employees through systematic introductory in-house education and the early socialization process.

In summary, it is our view that, until recently, Japanese management succeeded in making wise selection and use of those values from the list of Confucian virtues that would maximize employees' contribution to the prosperity of the company within a set of political, economic, and social environments. However, the mass displacement of employees under corporate "restructuring" these days suggests that some employers are discarding the important Confucian value of benevolence, thus leading to the collapse of Confucianism as a foundation of Japanese management.

Japanese Companies Abroad

In regard to the overseas operations of Japanese companies, a number of issues were addressed, including the degree of ethnocentrism, the reasons for low "failure rates," and the extent to which Japanese-style business and management are practiced overseas.

As for the question of ethnocentrism, differences were found between general trading companies and other companies. General trading companies were found to adopt a more ethnocentric policy than sales subsidiaries of manufacturing companies. Two reasons were identified. The job of general trading was affected by long-term relations with many organizations in Japan, including the manufacturers whose products they were selling, and these were factors considered beyond the comprehension of foreign employees in overseas offices. In addition, general trading companies had long accumulated market information on the various commodities with which they dealt, while manufacturing companies, which were relatively new, did not have much market information, and, therefore, they had to depend on local dealers and employees.

As to the reasons for low failure rates, both employees' aptitudes and systematic job rotation were found to be most important, while special training for the overseas assignment, special assistance while on the overseas assignment, and cultural factors were found not to be important. Of particular significance was the finding that overseas assignments were not a special type of assignment, but rather were closely related to assignments in Japan. It seemed that, under the system of lifetime employment, each company had well-defined routes of job rotation, such that an employee's current assignment would serve as a preparation for the next assignment, which could very well be an overseas assignment.

In regard to the extent to which Japanese-style business and management practices were followed in overseas offices, differences were again found between general trading companies and other companies. Simply put, in overseas offices of general trading companies, since a local equivalent did not exist (as they were a uniquely Japanese institution), they followed the company's standard methods and procedures subject to host country laws and regulations. To a certain extent, the same applied to establishments located in Asian countries. In terms of the management of local employees, local methods were followed almost without exception throughout the entire period.

In virtually all cases, cultural factors worked favorably for our alumni. They enjoyed their family lives overseas—in the United States, the United Kingdom, Australia, Germany, and most other countries to which they were assigned. Unlike in Japan, our alumni had more time to spend with their families and paid more attention to their family lives, to the delight of their wives. They enjoyed traveling to different places and developed friendships with their neighbors. The only problem they encountered was the education of their children when the latter became teenagers. While adjusting to local schools was difficult, adjusting back to the Japanese education system was even more difficult. Ironically, for them it was Japanese culture, not foreign cultures, that created a formidable challenge associated with overseas assignments.

Only in four cases did our alumni experience difficulties: in Seoul and in Moscow in the late 1960s, in Teheran in the late 1970s, and, again, in Seoul in the late 1980s. In all cases, cultural difference was not the main cause. In the first two cases, it was government policies, in the next case, it was political unrest followed by a war, and in the last case, it was a major strike plus the fact that our alumnus had to leave his family in Japan for the sake of his daughters' education that caused difficulties.

In summary, ethnocentrism of Japanese corporations in overseas operations has been largely overstated; it was more prevalent among general trading companies and banks than in other industries. Special training for overseas assignment was not as widespread as generally believed; rather, overseas assignments were conducted as part of regular job rotation. Overall, cultural differences did not create difficulties in family lives overseas.

Strengths and Weaknesses of Japanese Management

With regard to the strengths and weaknesses of Japanese management, we draw primarily on the subjective assessments of our alumni as reported in Chapter 24.

Elements of the strength of Japanese management include the following. Production management practices were a success not only in Japan but also in foreign countries when due consideration was given to the host country culture. Employees' loyalty to the company, drawing upon Confucian values and cemented by permanent employment, was another source of strength; however, when loyalty to the employer went too far, it tended to result in antisocial activities. Furthermore, it is feasible to maintain permanent employment only when the company grows rapidly.

A slow promotion system, one aspect of the length of service-based pay and promotion system, was another source of strength because such a practice extracted a high level of effort from a large number of employees for long periods of time. However, the length of service system is most suitable when environmental conditions are stable. Thus, the advantages of permanent employment and the length of service system are contingent upon certain environmental factors.

As for the weaknesses of Japanese management, the most serious one mentioned by several alumni was the self-perpetuation of top management that often led to complacency or a lack of corporate strategy. Perhaps this was due to weak pressure from the stockholders. In some industries it was further nurtured by reliance on government (protective) regulations and guidance. Group decision making often resulted in a lack of individual responsibility, which bordered on collective irresponsibility on the part of top management.

"Differential treatment" on the basis of nationality, gender, age, and so forth, was another shortcoming of Japanese management. When practiced in countries with strong anti-discrimination legislation, they led to a number of lawsuits. Besides being unfair and illegal, discrimination robs the company of opportunities to make use of talented human resources. The work experiences of our female participants (to be discussed later) attest to this point. Both group irresponsibility and discrimination stem from certain features of Japanese culture (collectivism and masculinity) when they are carried to the extreme.

The preceding discussion may be summarized as follows:

(1) Generally speaking Japanese management functions well under a stable and growing economy; it does not function well under a turbulent and low-growth economy. It must be added, however, that no management style functions well under a stagnant economy.

(2) Certain negative aspects (as well as positive aspects) of Japanese management stem from Japanese culture. Employment discrimination is an example.

Change of Japanese Management

In regard to the question of whether Japanese management is immutable or has changed over the years, the answer varies among different elements of Japanese management. As mentioned before, permanent employment was more or less maintained as long as our alumni were concerned, although they noted (in Chapter 24) that Japanese employers have recently become less strongly committed to it. The fact that the unemployment rate is still less than 5 percent suggests that a majority of employers are still committed to providing their employees with a high degree of job security.

Decision making has not changed very much either. It is still characterized by group, rather than individual, decision making. Group decision making at the top management level takes the form of not only the consensus type, as is generally believed, but also the consultative type, whereby the chairman or the president plays a more active role.

Overseas offices of Japanese corporations have adopted a less ethnocentric staffing policy over the years. This is closely related to the fact that an increasing number of Japanese manufacturers have come to export directly to overseas markets. As these offices are engaged in retailing, they need the help of local managers who are familiar with the behavior of local consumers. As for the management of local employees, Japanese offices have continued to follow local personnel practices.

With regard to production management, it appears that no change has taken place either at home or abroad, judging from the experience of an alumnus working for a worldwide synthetic fiber company. The manufacturer–retailer relationship has changed since the mid-1990s in favor of the latter, as our brewery company case exemplifies. In addition, from secondary source information, we know that both the subcontracting system and the main-bank system have been weakened. Today, the dissolution of mutual stock holdings by means of selling of the "group" companies' stocks on the market is considered a major cause of stock price declines. Although not apparent from our interviews, corporate governance has changed somewhat since the revision of the Commercial Code. Stockholders can now more readily sue individual directors for the mismanagement of the company (or breach of trust).

The foregoing observations may be summarized as follows.

(1) A majority of Japanese employers still seem committed to long-term, if not permanent, employment, while other employers have come to adopt a more market-oriented approach.

(2) There is no evidence to suggest that group decision making has changed, for example, to individual decision making. Bottom-up decision making did not exist in Japanese offices in the first place.

(3) As more manufacturing companies have become globalized, an ethnocentric staffing policy has been followed to a lesser extent in overseas offices. In the management of local employees Japanese offices have followed local personnel practices.

(4) The Japanese production system, symbolized by TQM, has not changed; rather, it has become more widespread worldwide.

(5) Interorganizational relations, or business groupings of all kinds, have loosened, and more corporations have begun to follow market principles.

(6) Stockholders are beginning to gain some power over corporate managers and ROE has come to be recognized as a key measure of performance of top management.

It is important to note that the changes taking place inside Japanese corporations are recent phenomena (after 1995 or so) and that such trends are expected to continue in the future.

Women and Work

Our final observation is about gender-based role differentiation and participation of women in economic activities. It is safe to say that in 1962, when our female participants graduated from the university, Japan was a society characterized by gender-based role differentiation. Not only employers but also most women including our alumnae endorsed the idea that married women should concentrate on family lives and raising children. This is exactly how our alumnae started out. One married even before graduation. Of the five who obtained typical "female jobs" upon graduation, four quit when, or soon after, they married. Only one held a career job and remained single.

Nevertheless, it is abundantly clear that the life histories of our six alumnae do not conform to the prewar values of "good wife and wise mother." Although their life histories were diverse, our alumnae were not satisfied with the roles of wife and mother alone (indeed, one remained single); at various stages of their lives, they were able to identify and achieve their own goals. Three alumnae identified with the work goals of their husbands, while the two who could not do so developed work goals of their own, despite their husbands' initial objections. For all six alumnae, their work lives clearly were an important element of their total lives.

During the past forty years, the legal framework for women's work has changed considerably, although our alumnae have not directly benefited from it. The major breakthrough was the enactment of the Equal Employment Opportunity Law (EEOL) in 1985, more than two decades after the enactment of similar and more comprehensive legislation in the United States (Civil Rights Act, Title 7). The EEOL was modified in 1999 to further eliminate employment discrimination against women, although it stopped short of stipulating penalties for violation of the law.

In the interviews reported in Chapter 24, all participants, both male and female, agreed that gender-based role differentiation had weakened over the past four decades. They also agreed that it would further weaken in the future, although some difference was observed in their views about the pace of change.

In summary, under unfavorable social and legal conditions, our alumnae have been successful in achieving their work goals. Furthermore, the legal framework has been modified over the years so that it is more difficult to carry out overt employment discrimination against women now than it was forty years ago.

* * *

The above findings based on the interviews of our alumni and alumnae suggest that the uniqueness of Japanese management has so far been overemphasized. It is true that Japanese culture and Western culture are different, but the difference in management practices between the two is a matter of degree.

We must also remember that business and management practices take place in a broad international, political, and economic environment. The next thing we must do, therefore, is comment on the dynamic change in that environment with a view to addressing our central concern, the convergence hypothesis.

Developmental Capitalism and Japanese Management

The importance of the international environment to Japanese corporations cannot be overemphasized. Japan, as a resource-poor, small nation for the size of its population, depends on international trade for its survival. The supply of food and raw materials from abroad and exports to abroad cannot be disrupted by wars or regional conflicts.

In this sense, Prime Minister Kishi's decision four decades ago to reaffirm Japan's position as a capitalist democracy within the U.S.-led free world has greatly contributed to Japan's economic success. Under the U.S. nuclear umbrella provided by the Japan–United States Security Treaty, Japanese people were able to concentrate on economic pursuits. Indeed, Japan enjoyed economic prosperity for the first three decades of the period under study (1960–2000).

For the past ten years, however, Japan has been suffering from a prolonged post-bubble recession. With it, the once acclaimed Japanese-style management has come under serious criticism. Here, we must not be confused about the cause-effect relationship. It is our view that Japanese management in general has not been responsible for the economic slump; instead, it is the outdated Japanese political and economic systems that are responsible for the prolonged recession. On the whole, Japanese corporations are victims of misguided government policies.

The Japanese economic model is usually labeled "developmental capitalism," as against the "market capitalism" of the United States. In the 1980s, developmental capitalism was hailed (especially among Asian countries) as being superior to market capitalism.

The theoretical basis of developmental capitalism is the age-old "infant industry" argument, which claims to provide the only avenue for a late-developing economy to achieve industrialization. More specifically, developmental capitalism consists of three elements. First, it places higher values on economic growth than on any other sociopolitical considerations, thereby achieving the highest possible economic growth. Second, the relationship between business and the government is one of close collaboration. The role of the government is to "guide" the business sector by rationing scarce resources and by providing protective measures. Third, as an extension of the second element, in order to protect infant domestic industries, imports are restricted and exports encouraged.

For a long time, it was believed that developmental capitalism was successful in achieving a high rate of economic growth for Japan. Put differently, Japan's postwar economic success was considered a result of "wise" administrative guidance by government ministries. However, the burst of the bubble and its resultant economic slump changed this view. More recent studies report on the negative effects of administrative guidance and/or its ineffectiveness (Katz 1998; Porter, Takeuchi, and Sakakibara 2000).

We, too, take the view that administrative guidance has become increasingly dysfunctional. As noted in Chapters 14 and 19, the bubble economy was initiated by the speculative behaviors of the banks and securities firms most closely "guided" by the Ministry of Finance. The burst of the bubble, which triggered the present prolonged recession, represents the mismanagement of the economy by the Ministry of Finance and the Bank of Japan.

Successful industries and companies have long outgrown government guidance in becoming global competitors, while unsuccessful industries have continued to rely on even stronger government protection. Thus, today developmental capitalism has degenerated into a protectionist trade and industrial policy. Extralegal administrative guidance falls short of bureaucratic favoritism and discrimination to the neglect of market forces.

Another example of close business-government collaboration is "amakudari," or "descent from heaven," by which retired senior bureaucrats are hired into top management positions in corporations that are regulated by the very ministries from which they retired. Thus, business-government collaboration is a form of collusion that tends to breed corruption and seriously distort the normal workings of a market economy. Recent scandals involving home mortgage companies and the Ministry of Finance, and involving blood serum manufacturing companies and the Ministry of Welfare, attest to this fact.

Japanese bureaucrats distort not only the market economy but also legislative processes. Today nine out of ten bills are drafted by the bureaucrats, and only one-tenth are drafted by the legislators, or the members of the National Diet. Each ministry has a large number of staff involved in the formulation of policies within its own jurisdiction. Also, each ministry has a number of advisory councils composed of academics, business leaders, journalists, and former senior bureaucrats.

The recommendations of these advisory councils are then passed on to the government. Eventually many of them will be passed into laws. Deliberations in the Diet, then, are nothing but a ceremony. During the deliberations in various Diet committees, most notably the Budget Committee, the bureaucrats who drafted the bill in the first place are invited to participate in the proceedings (recently, this practice has been somewhat modified as part of administrative reform measures advocated by Ozawa). It is their role to collaborate with the members of the governing party against attacks from opposition party members by answering all questions of substance and making sure that these bills become laws. Thus, it can safely be said that it is not Japanese legislators duly elected by the Japanese people who legislate, but bureaucrats.

This type of political system substantially deviates from democracy in its pure form. To the extent that there is consensus among the Japanese people that economic growth is the most important national goal and that bureaucrats rather than politicians are better able to formulate bills to achieve that goal, it may be argued that the bureaucrats are entrusted by the people to achieve that goal. This kind of Japanese system is a form of democracy that may be called "developmental democracy."

For some reason, the Japanese mass media have continued to portray politicians as corrupt, self-serving, and incompetent people. On the other hand, bureaucrats have until recently been portrayed as honest, public-minded, and very capable people. The fact of the matter is that politicians were the first to realize that Japan needs a fundamental change in its political, economic, and administrative systems. Political reform was attempted in 1993 by the anti-LDP coalition governments of Hosokawa and Hata, although their efforts have largely been sabotaged by the LDP coalition governments.

What has been left undone is sweeping administrative reform, so that bureaucracy will not interfere with business and political decision-making processes. A small step was taken in this direction under the leadership of Hashimoto, whereby government ministries were reorganized in January 2001 and more politicians were involved in the running of government ministries. It is unlikely, however, that bureaucrats will easily give up their power under the LDP government, which, after all, has formed a powerful alliance with bureaucracy for more than four decades.

When we look back at the courses of action that Japan has taken, it us our view that the legitimate role of developmental capitalism and developmental democracy ended in the mid-1960s, when Japan's trade balance registered a surplus on a continuing basis. It was an indication that Japan had to shift from developmental capitalism and developmental democracy to become an "ordinary nation." Unfortunately, however, the Japanese mind-set of GNP idolatry, combined with historical accidents (notably, two oil shocks in the 1970s), prevented the country from changing its basic policy.

Viewed in this way, the demand-deficit recession Japan is experiencing today is a natural consequence of a developmental capitalism that has distorted the Japanese economy into an export-dependent economy. Strong domestic consumption, which led Japan's economic growth in the 1960s, has since been forgotten (with the exception of a brief bubble period in the late 1980s). Today the "paradox of thrift" is in full operation and the government's plea to spend more falls on the deaf ears of consumers.

In regard to domestic consumption, the role of organized labor is important because it is largely the wages of employees that determine the level of domestic consumption. As mentioned in Chapters 9 and 14, in the latter half of the 1970s and throughout most of the 1980s, the Japanese labor movement adopted a wage restraint policy. The impact of the first oil crisis on the psyche of the Japanese people was so strong that even trade union leaders shared the pessimistic view that a resource-poor, fragile Japan would lose its international competitive power and its economic prosperity would come to an end, unless substantial efforts were made to increase productivity. Labor-management cooperation, including wage moderation, was one such effort. The second oil crisis and rapid appreciation of the yen thereafter reinforced their belief.

In a word, since the mid-1970s the Japanese labor movement has ceased to function as an effective countervailing force to maintain a balance between the supply and demand of the Japanese economy. Instead, a policy was adopted that resulted in reinforcing developmental capitalism.

* * *

Francis Fukuyama (1992), in his book *The End of History and the Last Man*, addressed the same issue (the convergence hypothesis) raised by the four authors of *Industrialism and Industrial Man* more than four decades ago (Chapter 1; Kerr et al. 1960). Unlike the four authors, who were somewhat hesitant to take a definitive position, Fukuyama argued that the American capitalist liberal democracy is superior to any other form of political system, and, therefore, it represents the end state of the historical process. This is an expression of the convergence hypothesis that the cross-national variations in political and economic systems that exist at the early stage of development, will be reduced in the industrialization process and will become largely indistinguishable from one another at the final stage of industrialization. At any given time, variation between two systems may be largely a reflection of a difference in the stages of industrialization. In this sense, then, the Japanese-style developmental capitalism and developmental democracy represent less-developed forms of capitalism and democracy.

It seems that capitalist liberal democracy represents two fundamental goals of an industrial society, namely, economic efficiency and social equity, which are basically in conflict. Business and industry are the major vehicles for attainment of the economic goal of efficiency, while various sociopolitical movements, including trade union movements, civil rights movements, consumer movements, and environmental movements, represent attempts to create a more equitable society.

The convergence hypothesis as fleshed out by Fukuyama in his book suggests that the final stage represents a sort of static equilibrium situation. However, while the basic framework of the society may remain unchanged, a number of forces are operating within the system so that the economic and social lives of people improve over the years.

To the extent that business and management are carried out in a broad political and economic environment, convergence of Japanese-style management toward a higher level of management system, which we would call the "global management model," is inevitable (Yip 1995). Here we are not interested in questions such as which style of management is superior: Japanese or American. The global management model may include many elements of the current Western, or, in particular, U.S., management practices, but it may also include elements of Japanese production management.

Two powerful forces for convergence are business globalization and information technology. Today business corporations have to compete in a global market. Global corporations need to hire workers and managers, including top-level managers, from a number of countries. Such corporations need to be owned by stockholders from a number of countries. In such corporations ethnocentrism based on the home country's national culture, as well as gender-based role differentiation, will be difficult to maintain. Instead, a uniform culture unique to each corporation and shared by all members of the corporation, male and female, needs to be created and reinforced.

Information technology is another force that enhances universality. Not only the physical settings of a workplace but also work procedures will become similar, regardless of the national culture of the country in which a particular workplace is located. We are not saying, however, that national cultures will disappear. National cultures as well as other environmental factors will remain different across nations.

In a sense, the global management model is similar to the classical school of Taylor and Fayol in its universal orientation, but it is different from the classical school due to its contingency or open system view. In the global context, "correct" management practices depend on a number of environmental factors.

The global management model has a set of core universal principles supplemented by local variation to suit a set of environmental factors. Due to the complexities of environmental conditions, the global management model is far from complete. In developing the model, we must be careful not to be trapped into academic ethnocentrism, or the "country of origins" effects of ideas, old and new. If the United States best represents capitalist liberal democracy, we all know that neither capitalism nor democracy originated in the United States.

We believe that many more non-Western cases need to be assembled before the global management model is complete. This study is one such effort.

Bibliography

Abegglen, James G. 1958. *The Japanese Factory*. Glencoe, IL: Free Press.

———. 1973. *Management and Worker: The Japanese Solution*. Tokyo: Sophia University in cooperation with Kodansha International Ltd.

Adler, Nancy J. 1997. *The International Dimensions of Organizational Behavior*. 3d ed. Cincinnati: South-Western College.

Andreski, Stanislav, ed. 1983. *Max Weber on Capitalism, Bureaucracy and Religion*. London: George Allen and Unwin.

Aoki, Masahiko, and Ronald Dore, eds. 1994. *The Japanese Firm: The Sources of Competitive Strength*. New York: Oxford University Press.

Asahi Newspaper Co. [Asahi shimbunsha]. Annual. *Asahi nenkan* [Asahi Yearbook]. Tokyo.

Asuka, Shigetaka. 1998. *Sogo shosha ron* [A Treatise on GTCs]. Tokyo: Chuo keizaisha.

Avineri, Shlomo. 1971. *The Social and Political Thought of Karl Marx*. London: Cambridge University Press.

Baird, Lloyd S.; James E. Post; and John F. Mahon. 1990. *Management: Functions and Responsibilities*. New York: Harper and Row.

Barbalet, J.M. 1983. *Marx's Construction of Social Theory*. London: Routledge and Kegan Paul.

Bartol, Kathryn M., and David C. Martin. 1994. *Management*. 2d ed. New York: McGraw-Hill.

Berle, Adolf A., Jr., and Gardiner C. Means. 1933. *The Modern Corporation and Private Property*. New York: Macmillan.

Chang, Chi-yun. 1980. *Confucianism: A Modern Interpretation*. Hong Kong: Hwa Kang Press.

Cole, R.E. 1971. *Japanese Blue Collar*. Berkeley: University of California Press.

Deresky, Helen. 1997. *International Management: Managing Across Borders and Cultures*. 2d ed. New York: Harper Collins.

Doeringer, P.B., and M.J. Piore. 1971. *Internal Labor Markets and Manpower Analysis*. Lexington, MA: D.C. Heath.

Economic Planning Agency [Keizai Kikaku-cho]. 1962–73. *Keizai yoran* [Summary Statistics on the Economy]. Annual. Tokyo: Okurasho insatsu-kyoku [Ministry of Finance, Printing Bureau].

———. Annual. *Keizai hakusho* [White Paper on the Economy]. Tokyo: Okurasho insatsu-kyoku [Ministry of Finance, Printing Bureau].

———. Annual. *Keizai yoran* [Summary Statistics on the Economy]. Tokyo: Okurasho insatsu-kyoku [Ministry of Finance, Printing Bureau].

Enkyo, Soichi. 1995. *Kin'yu jiyuka nyumon* [Introduction to Financial Liberalization]. Tokyo: Nihon keizai shimbunsha.

445

Environment Agency [Kankyo-cho]. 1972–73. *Kankyo hakusho* [White Paper on the Environment]. Annual. Tokyo: Okurasho insatsu-kyoku [Ministry of Finance, Printing Bureau].

Fair Trade Commission [Kosei Torihiki Iinkai]. Annual. *Kosei torihiki iinkai nenji hokoku* [Annual Report of the Fair Trade Commission]. Tokyo: Okurasho insatsu-kyoku [Ministry of Finance, Printing Bureau].

Fruin, W. Mark. 1992. *The Japanese Enterprise System: Competitive Strategies and Cooperative Structures*. Oxford: Clarendon Press.

Fukuda, John K., and Priscilla Chu. 1994. "Wrestling with Expatriate Family Problems: Japanese Experience in East Asia." *International Studies of Management and Organization* 24, no. 3: 36–47.

Fukuyama, Francis. 1992. *The End of History and the Last Man*. New York: Free Press.

Galbraith, John Kenneth. 1967. *The New Industrial State*. Boston: Houghton Mifflin.

Harbison, Frederick, and Charles A. Myers, eds. 1959. *Management in the Industrial World: An International Analysis*. New York: McGraw-Hill.

Hirschmeier, Johannes, and Tsunehiko Yui. 1981. *The Development of Japanese Business, 1600–1980*. 2d ed. London: George Allen and Unwin.

Hofstede, Geet. 1983. "The Cultural Reality of Organizational Practices and Theories." *Journal of International Business Studies* 14, no. 2: 75–89.

Hwang, Pyong Tai. 1979. "Confucianism in Modernization: Comparative Study of China, Japan and Korea." Ph.D. dissertation, University of California, Berkeley.

Iida, Tsunehiko. 1998. *Nihonteki keiei-no ronten* [Controversies on Japanese-Style Management]. Tokyo: PHP kenkyujo.

Imazu, Kenji. 1977. "Edojidai no chiteki suijun" [Intellectual Levels in the Edo Era]. In Mataji Miyamoto, ed., *Entrepreneurial Activities in the Edo Era*, 150.

Ito, Yasuko. 1990. "Sengo kaikaku-to fujin kaiho" [The Postwar Reform and Liberation of Women]. In *Nihon josei-shi 5 gendai* [A History of Japanese Women, vol. 5, Contemporary Period], ed. Josei-shi Sogokenkyu-kai. Tokyo: Tokyo daigaku shuppan-kai [University of Tokyo Press].

Iwao, Sumiko. 1993. *The Japanese Woman: Traditional Image and Changing Reality*. New York: Free Press.

JAL (Japan Airlines Co., Ltd. [Nihon koku kabushiki gaisha]). 1985. *Nihon koku shashi (1971–1981)* [History of Japan Airlines (1971 to 1981)]. Tokyo.

Japan Productivity Center [Nihon Seisansei Honbu]. 1966–74. *Katsuyo rodo tokei* [Practical Statistics on Labor]. Annual. Tokyo.

JDSA (Japan Department Stores Association). 1998. *Sales Statistics* (annual).

JFTC (Japan Foreign Trade Council, Inc.) [Nihon Boeki-Kai]. 1998. *Nihon boekikai 50-nen-shi* [Fifty Years' History of the Japan Foreign Trade Council]. Tokyo.

Jiyu Kokumin-sha. 1992. *Gendai yogo-no kiso-chishiki: bessatsu furoku* [Basic Knowledge About Contemporary Terms: Appendix]. Tokyo: Jiyu kokuminsha.

JPCA (Japan Petrochemical Industry Association [Sekiyu Kagaku Kogyo Kyokai]). 1998. *Sekiyu kagaku kogyo no genjo* [The Petrochemical Industry as It Is]. Tokyo.

JSIMM (Japan Society of Industrial Machinery Manufacturers [Nihon Sangyo Kikai Kogyo-kai]). 1998. *Sangyo kikai kogyo goju-nen-shi* [Fifty Years' History of Industrial Machinery Manufacturers]. Tokyo.

Kaizuka, Keimei, and Kazuo Ueda. 1994. *Henkaku-ki no kin'yu shisutemu* [The Financial System Under Reform]. Tokyo: University of Tokyo Press.

Kaizuka, Shigeki, ed. 1966. *Sekai-no meicho 3-kan koshi moshi* [Great Books of the World, vol. 3: Confucius and Mencius]. Tokyo: Chuo koronsha.

Karsh, Bernard, and Robert E. Cole. 1968. "Industrialization and the Convergence Hypothesis: Some Aspects of Contemporary Japan." *Journal of Social Issues* 24, no. 4: 45–64.

Katz, Richard. 1998. *Japan, the System That Soured: The Rise and Fall of the Japanese Economic Miracle.* Armonk, NY: M.E. Sharpe.

Kawahara, Mikio, and Masayoshi Hayashikawa. 1999. *Sogo shosha big bang* [A Big Bang for GTCs]. Tokyo: Toyo keizai shimposha.

Kerr, Clark; John T. Dunlop; Frederick H. Harbison; and Charles A. Myers. 1960. *Industrialism and Industrial Man.* Cambridge: Harvard University Press.

Kirin Brewery Company, Ltd. (Company History Compiling Committee) [Kirin biiru kabushiki gaisha, shashi hensan iinkai]. 1985. *Kirin biiru no rekishi, zoku-sengo-hen* [History of Kirin Brewery Company: Sequel to Postwar Edition]. Tokyo.

———. Company History Compiling Dept. 1999. [Kirin biiru kabushiki gaisha, shashi hensan iinkai]. 1985. *Kirin Biiru no rekishi, zoku-sengo-hen* [History of Kirin Brewery Company: Revised Postwar Edition]. Tokyo.

———. Public Relations Dept. [Kirin biiru kabushiki gaisha, Koho-shitsu]. 1969. *Kirin biiru no rekishi: Sengo-hen* [History of Kirin Brewery Company: Postwar Edition]. Tokyo.

Kobayashi, Masaaki. 1987. *Seisho no tanjo* [The Birth of Government-Favored Merchants]. Tokyo: Keizai shimposha.

Koike, Kazuo. 1988. *Understanding Industrial Relations in Modern Japan.* London: MacMillan.

Koyama, Shuzo. 1997. *Gendai no hyakkaten.* [Present-Day Department Stores]. Tokyo: Nihon keizai shimbunsha.

Kubo, Iwao. 1997. *Zukai shosha gyokai handbook* [Illustrated Handbook of the Trading Industry]. Tokyo: Toyo keizai shimposha.

Levine, Solomon B. 1958. *Industrial Relations in Postwar Japan.* Urbana: University of Illinois Press.

Maruoka, Hanako. 1982. *Fujin shiso-shi noto (Ge)* [A Note on the History of Thought on Women, vol. 2]. Tokyo: Domes shuppan.

Miner, John B. 1980. *Theories of Organizational Behavior.* Hinsdale, IL: Dryden Press.

Ministry of Foreign Affairs [Gaimusho]. 1963–74. *Waga gaiko-no kinkyo* [Recent Developments in Japan's Diplomacy]. Annual. Tokyo: Okurasho insatsu-kyoku [Ministry of Finance, Printing Bureau].

———. Annual. *Gaiko seisho* [Diplomatic Blue Book]. Tokyo: Okurasho insatsu-kyoku [Ministry of Finance, Printing Bureau].

Ministry of Labor [Rodosho]. 1962–73. *Rodo hakusho* [White Paper on Labor]. Annual. Tokyo: Okurasho insatsu-kyoku [Ministry of Finance, Printing Bureau].

———. Women's Bureau [Rodosyo, Fujinkyoku]. Annual. *Fujin rodo-no jitsujo* [Real Conditions of Female Work]. Tokyo: Okurasho insatsu-kyoku [Ministry of Finance, Printing Bureau].

Ministry of Transportation [Unyusho]. 1999. *Unyu hakusho, 1998* [White Paper on Transportation]. Tokyo: Ministry of Finance, Printing Bureau.

Ministry of Welfare [Koseisho]. 1969–71. *Kogai hakusho* [White Paper on Pollution]. Annual. Tokyo: Okurasho insatsu-kyoku [Ministry of Finance, Printing Bureau].

MITI (Ministry of International Trade and Industry) [Tsusan-sho]. 1995. *Kogyo tokei-hyo* [Census of Manufacturers]. Tokyo: Okurasho Insatsu-kyoku [Ministry of Finance, Printing Bureau].

Miwa, Ryouichi. 1993. *Gaisetsu Nihon keizai-shi, kin/gen-dai* [A Short History of Japan's Economy: The Modern Age]. Tokyo: University of Tokyo Press.

Miyamoto, Mataji, ed. 1997. *Edojidai no kigyosha katsudo* [Entrepreneurial Activities in the Edo Era]. Tokyo: Nippon keizai shimbunsha.

Miyashita, Masafusa. 1997. *Ryutsu no tenkan—21 seiki no senryaku shishin* [Changeover in Distribution: Strategic Suggestions for the Twenty-First Century]. Tokyo: Hakuto shobo.

Mosley, Donald C.; Paul H. Pietri; and Leon C. Megginson. 1996. *Management: Leadership in Action.* 5th ed. New York: Harper Collins.

Nagano, Hitoshi. 1997. "External Transfer System of Japanese Corporations: *Shukkoh.*" In *Frontiers of Japanese Human Resource Practices*, ed. Yoko Sano, Motohiro Morishima, and Atsushi Seike. Tokyo: Japan Institute of Labor.

Nihon keizai shimbun, Inc. 1999 (January). *Japan Economic Almanac 1999.* Tokyo.

Nihon kogyo nenkan. 1993. [Japan Industrial Annual]. Tokyo: Nihon kogyo shimbunsha.

Nihon Kogyo Shimbunsha. 1993. *Nihon kogyo nenkan, 1993 nen ban* [Japan Industrial Yearbook, 1993]. Toyko: Nihon kogyo shimbunsha shuppan-kyoku.

Ohtsu, Makoto. 1991. *Roshi kankei-ron: Nihonteki keiei-to rodo* [Industrial Relations: Japanese-Style Management and Labor]. Tokyo: Hakuto shobo.

Okochi, K.; B. Karsh; and S.B. Levine, eds. 1974. *Workers and Employers in Japan: The Japanese Employment Relations System.* Princeton: Princeton University Press.

Ouchi, William G. 1981. *Theory Z: How American Business Can Meet the Japanese Challenge.* Reading, MA: Addison-Wesley.

Patrick, Hugh, and Henry Rosovsky, eds. 1976. *Asia's New Giant: How the Japanese Economy Works.* Washington, DC: Brookings Institution.

Porter, Michael E. 1985. *Competitive Advantage.* New York: Free Press.

Porter, Michael E.; Hirotaka Takeuchi; and Mariko Sakakibara. 2000. *Can Japan Compete?* London: MacMillan.

Rostow, W.W. 1960. *The Stages of Economic Growth: A Non-Communist Manifesto.* London: Cambridge University Press.

Schein, Edgar H. 1978. *Career Dynamics: Matching Individual and Organizational Needs.* Reading, MA: Addison-Wesley.

Schmidt, Alfred (trans. Jeffrey Herf). 1982. *History and Structure: An Essay on Hegelian-Marxist and Structuralist Theories of History.* Cambridge: MIT Press.

Shimada, Katsumi. 1991. *Shosha—Sangyo no Showa shakai-shi* [Trading Companies—Social History of the Showa Era's Industry]. Tokyo: Nihon keizai hyoronsha.

Shirai, Taishiro, ed. 1983. *Contemporary Industrial Relations in Japan.* Madison: University of Wisconsin Press.

Sumiya, Mikio. 1966. *Nihon rodo undo-shi* [A History of the Japanese Labor Movement]. Tokyo: Yushindo, 80–81.

Taira, Koji. 1962. "The Characteristics of Japanese Labor Markets." *Economic Development and Cultural Change* 10: 150–68.

Takamura, Juichi, and Hiroyuki Koyama. 1994. *Nihon sangyo-shi [2-4]* [History of Japanese Industries. vols. 2–4]. Tokyo: Nihon keizai shimbunsha.

Taoka, George M., and Don R. Beeman. 1991. *International Business: Environments, Institutions, and Operations.* New York: Harper Collins.

Tomita, Nobuo; Masayuki Fukuoka; Etsushi Tanifuji; and Seiichiro Kusunoki. 1983. *Nihon seiji-no hensen: Shiryo-to kiso-chishiki* [Changes in Japanese Politics: Data and Basic Knowledge]. Tokyo: Gakubun-sha.

Tung, Rosalie. 1984. "Human Resource Planning in Japanese Multinationals: A Model for U.S. Firms?" *Journal of International Business Studies* 15, no. 1: 139–49.

Veblen, Thorstein (ed. Leon Ardzrooni). 1964. *Essays in Our Changing Order.* New York: Viking Press.

Vroom, Victor, and Philip Yetton. 1973. *Leadership and Decision Making.* Pittsburgh: University of Pittsburgh Press.

Walton, Richard E., and Robert B. McKersie. 1965. *A Behavioral Theory of Labor Negotiations.* New York: McGraw-Hill.

Weber, Max (trans. Talcott Parsons). 1958. *The Protestant Ethic and the Spirit of Capitalism.* New York: Charles Scribner's Sons.

Yip, George S. 1995. *Total Global Strategy: Managing for Worldwide Competitive Advantage.* Englewood Cliffs, NJ: Prentice Hall.

Yoshimura, Noboru, and Philip Anderson. 1997. *Inside the Kaisha: Demystifying Japanese Business Behavior.* Boston: Harvard Business School Press.

Yui, Tsunehiko. 1977. "Edojidai no kachitaikei to kanryosei" [The Value System and Bureaucracy in the Edo Era]. In Miyamoto, *Entrepreneurial Activities in the Edo Era,* 179–81.

Index